FAIRY TAIL

41

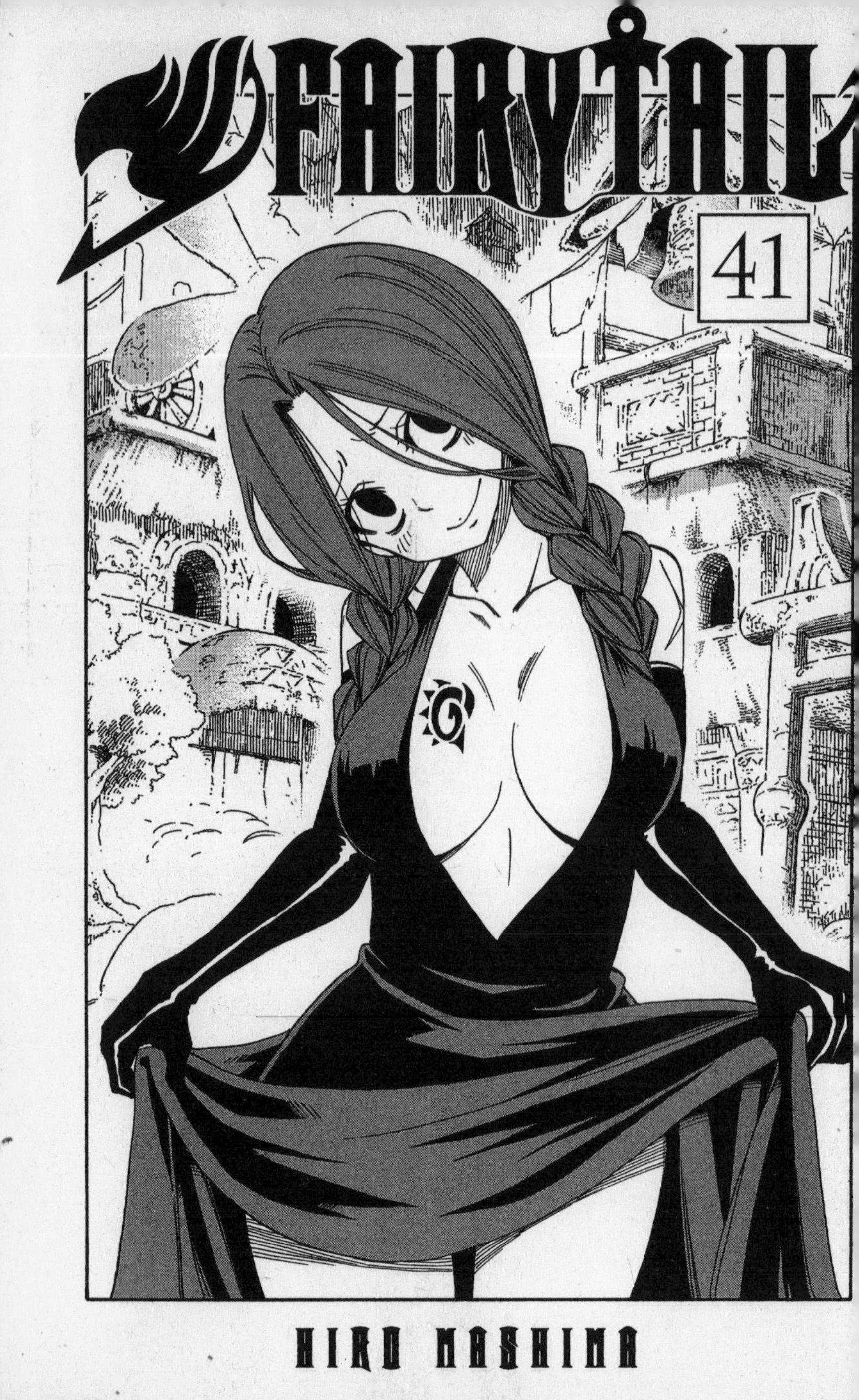

HIRO MASHIMA

FAIRY TAIL 41 CONTENTS

FAIRY TAIL

SABER TOOTH

Name: Rogue Cheney   **Age:** 19 yrs.

Magic:
Shadow Dragon Slayer Magic

Likes: **Dislikes:**
Frosch   Noon time

Remarks

One of the Twin Dragons of Saber Tooth.
When he was young, he looked up to Gajeel
of Phantom Lord, and he hoped to become a
member of Phantom Lord himself. During that
same period, hating the meaning of the name
Rogue, he started calling himself Lios. It is
not known when or where he first met his
partner Frosch, but he had not yet met him
seven years ago when he was a fan of Gajeel.
After the Grand Magic Games, Rogue was
shocked to learn that it was a future version
of himself who was behind the dragons'
attack, and he has made a solemn vow never
to fall into darkness.

Chapter 345: Somebody's Voice

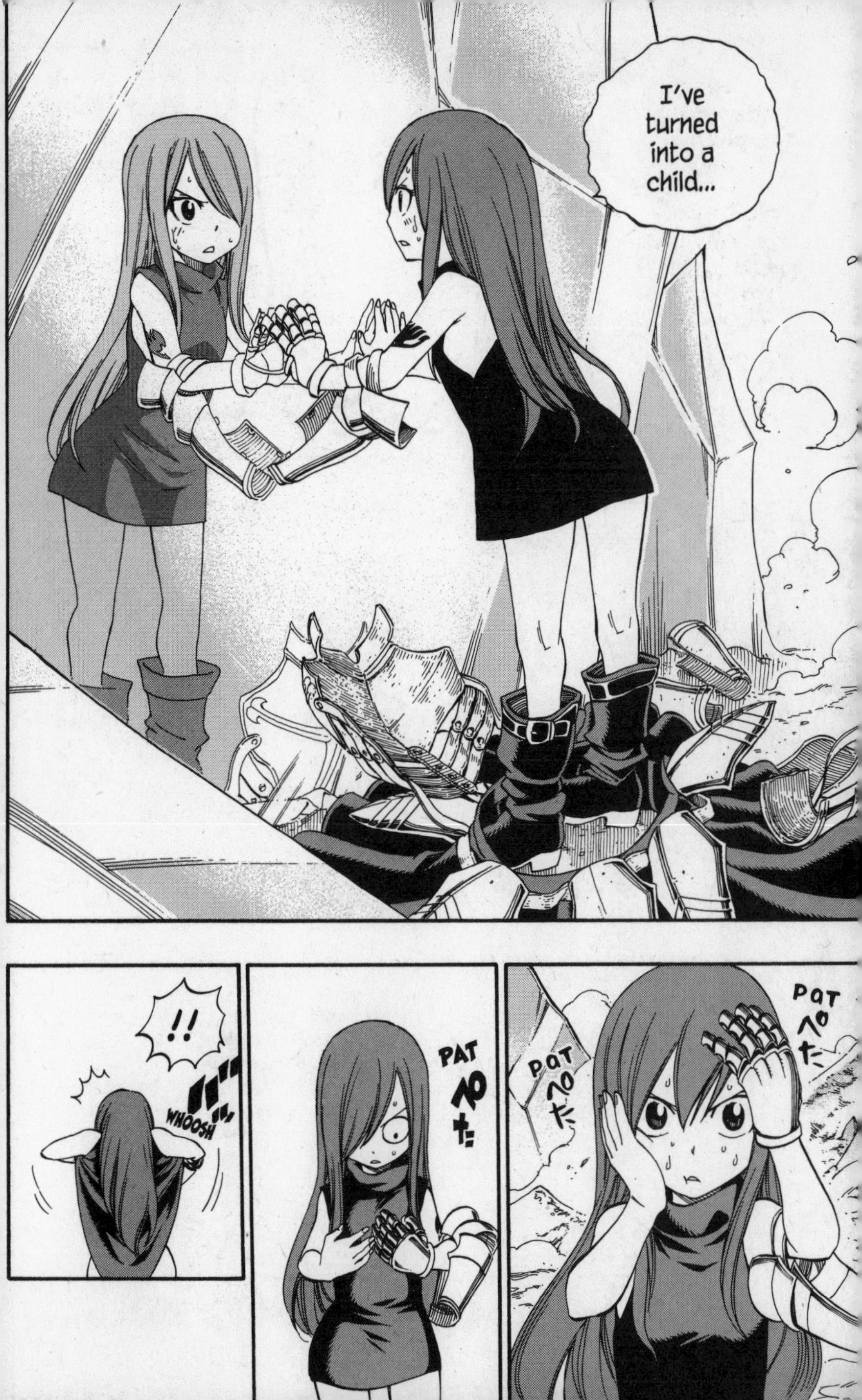

I've turned into a child...
PAT
PAT
PAT
!!
WHOOSH

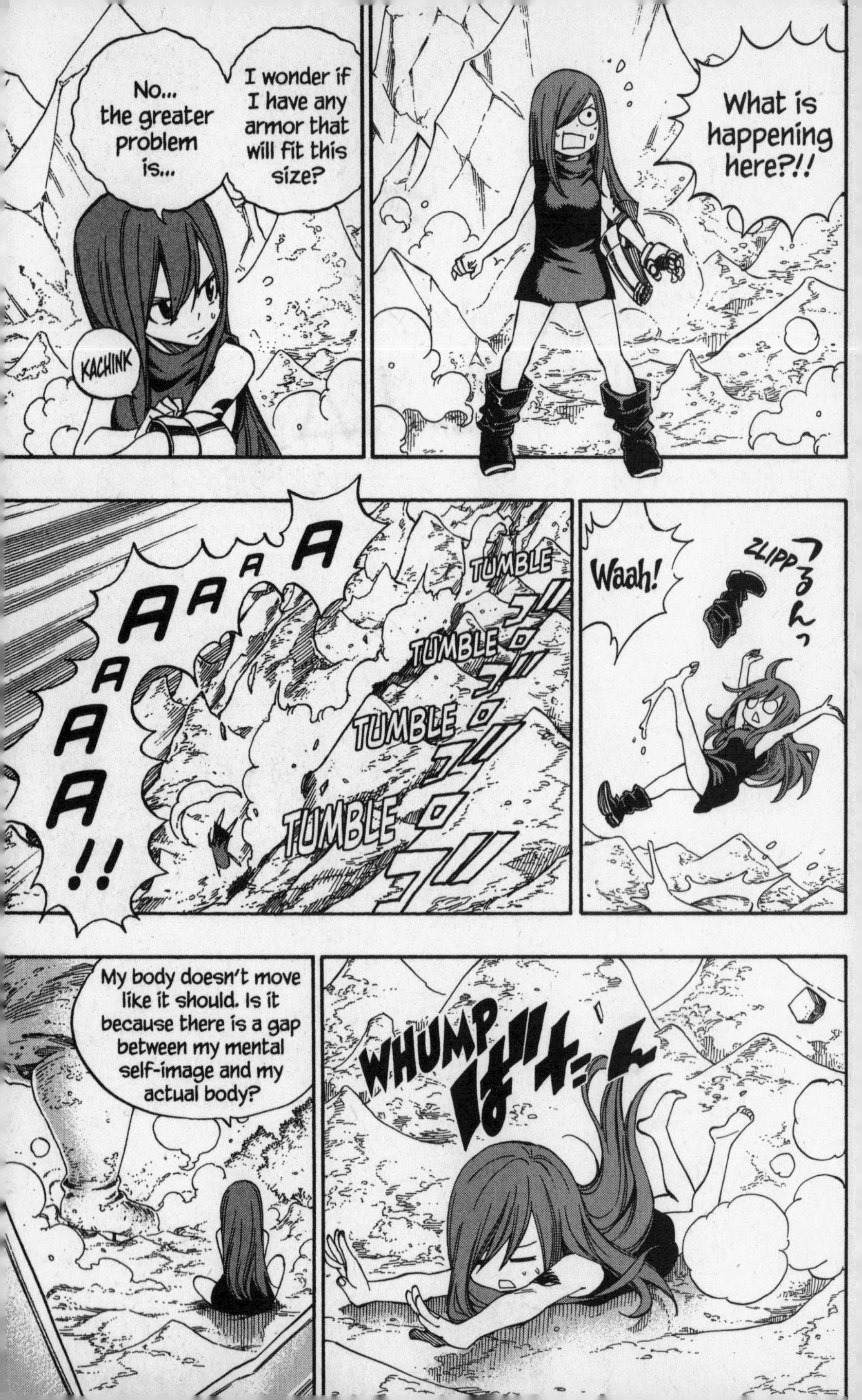

What is happening here?!!
I wonder if I have any armor that will fit this size?
No... the greater problem is...
KACHINK
ZLIPP
Waah!
TUMBLE
TUMBLE
TUMBLE
TUMBLE
AAAAAAAAA!!
WHUMP
My body doesn't move like it should. Is it because there is a gap between my mental self-image and my actual body?

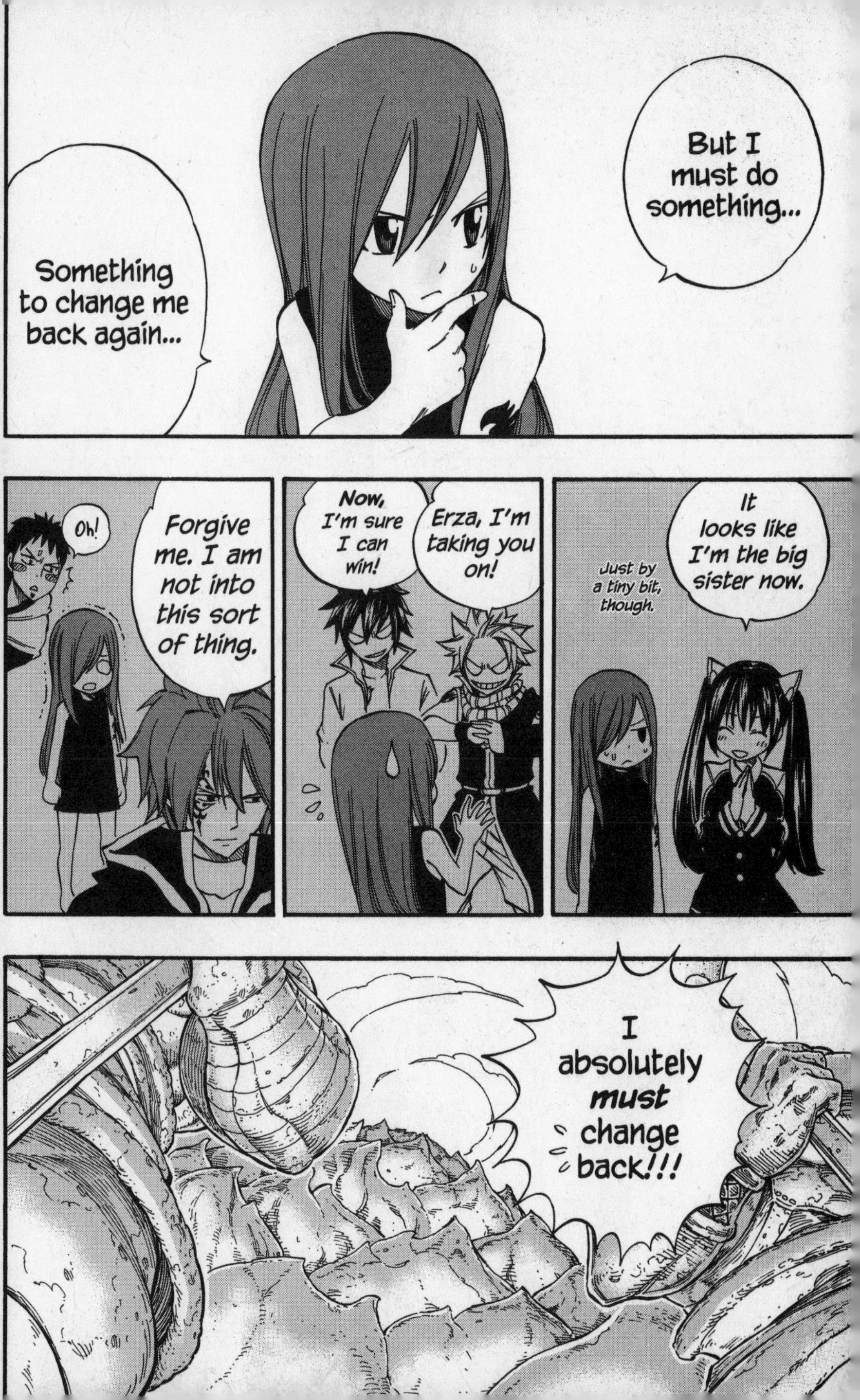
But I must do something...
Something to change me back again...
It looks like I'm the big sister now.
Just by a tiny bit, though.
Erza, I'm taking you on!
Now, I'm sure I can win!
Forgive me. I am not into this sort of thing.
Oh!
I absolutely *must* change back!!!

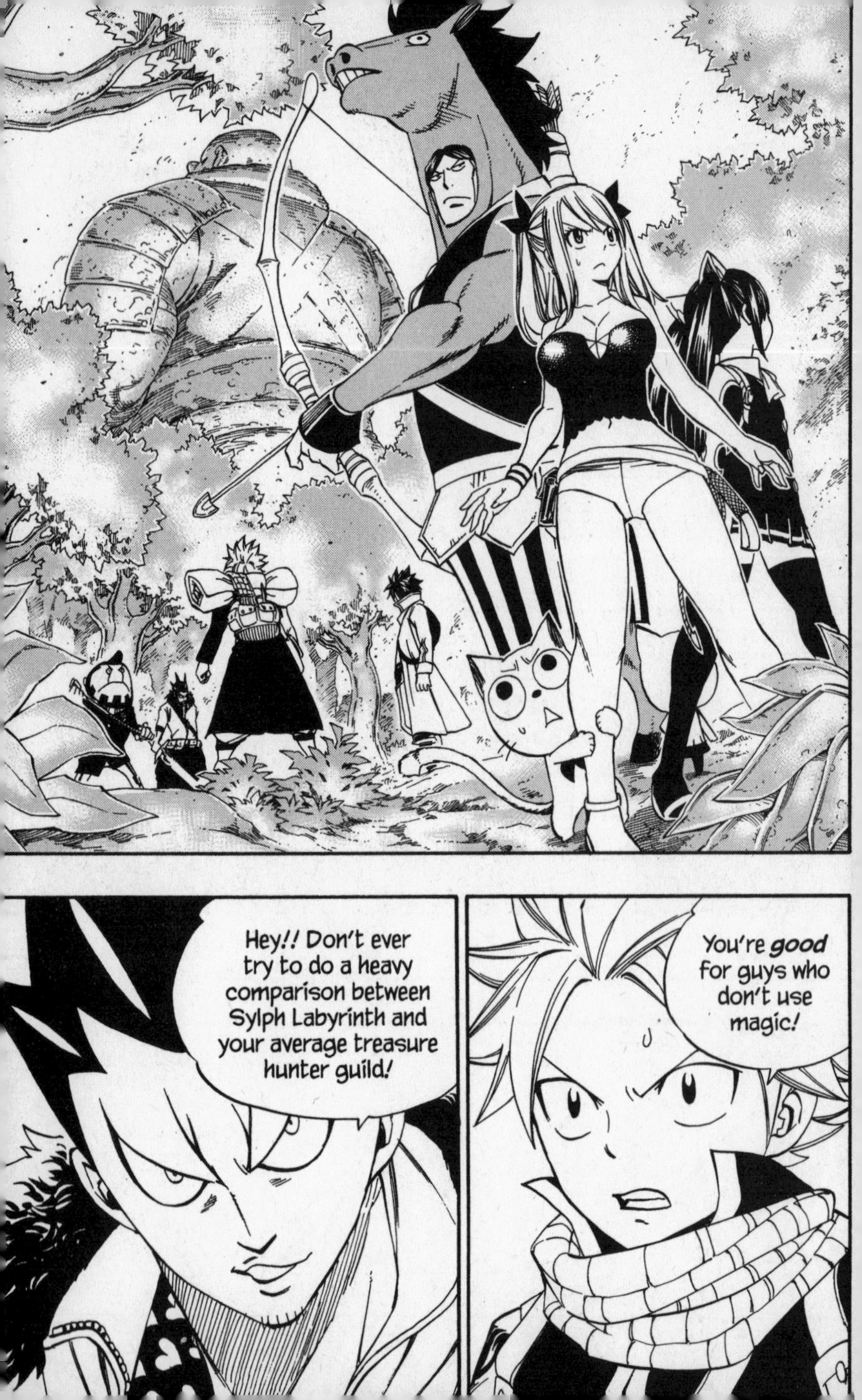
You're **good** for guys who don't use magic!
Hey!! Don't ever try to do a heavy comparison between Sylph Labyrinth and your average treasure hunter guild!

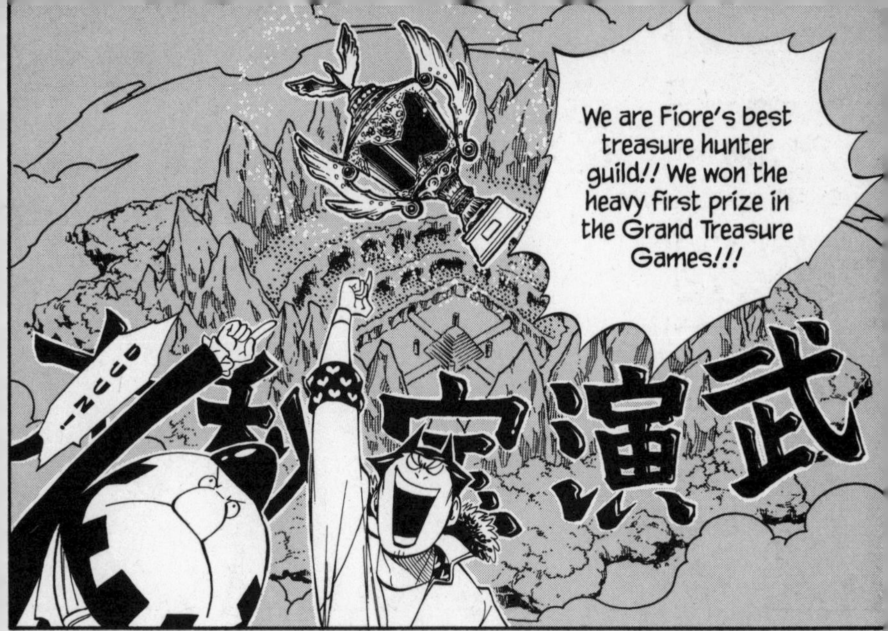
We are Fiore's best treasure hunter guild!! We won the heavy first prize in the Grand Treasure Games!!!

*Background Title: Grand Treasure Games

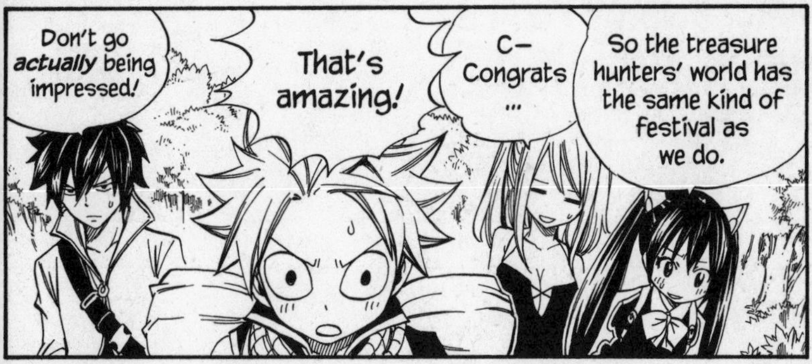
So the treasure hunters' world has the same kind of festival as we do.
C— Congrats...
That's amazing!
Don't go *actually* being impressed!

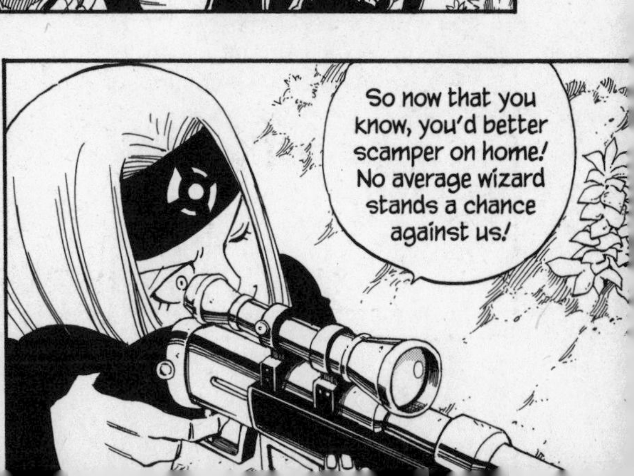
So now that you know, you'd better scamper on home! No average wizard stands a chance against us!

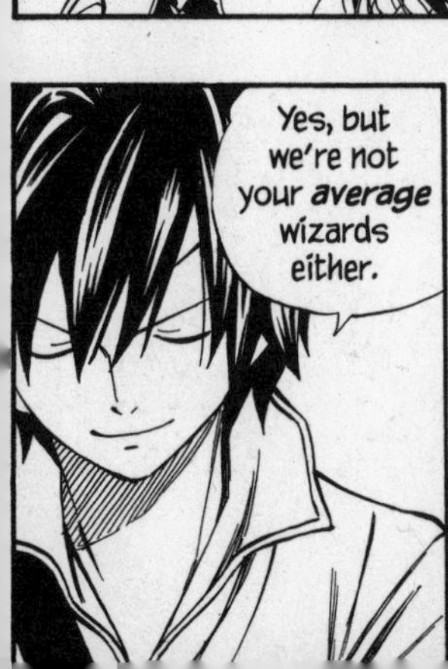
Yes, but we're not your *average* wizards either.

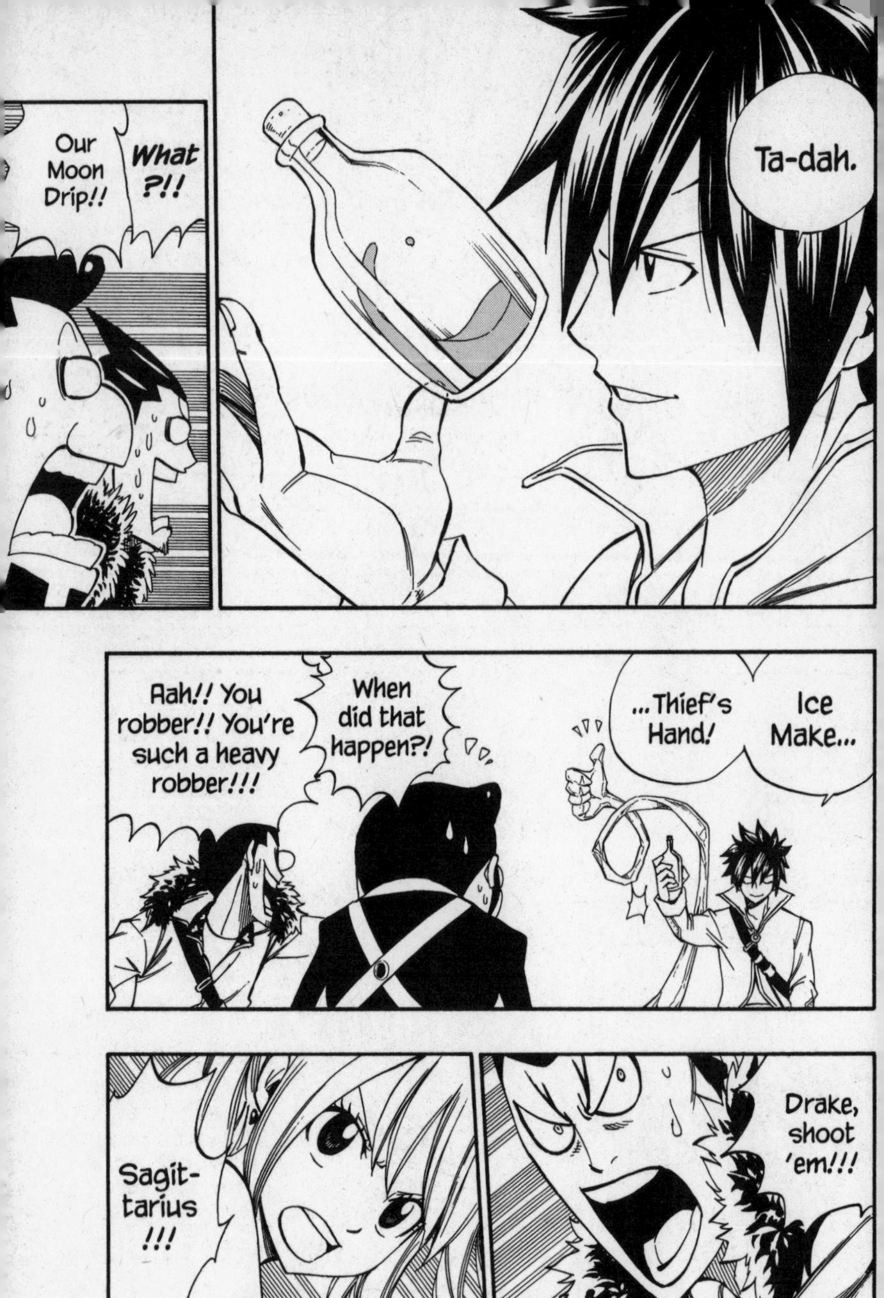
Ta-dah.
What?!!
Our Moon Drip!!
Ice Make...
...Thief's Hand!
When did that happen?!
Aah!! You robber!! You're such a heavy robber!!!
Drake, shoot 'em!!!
Sagit-tarius!!!

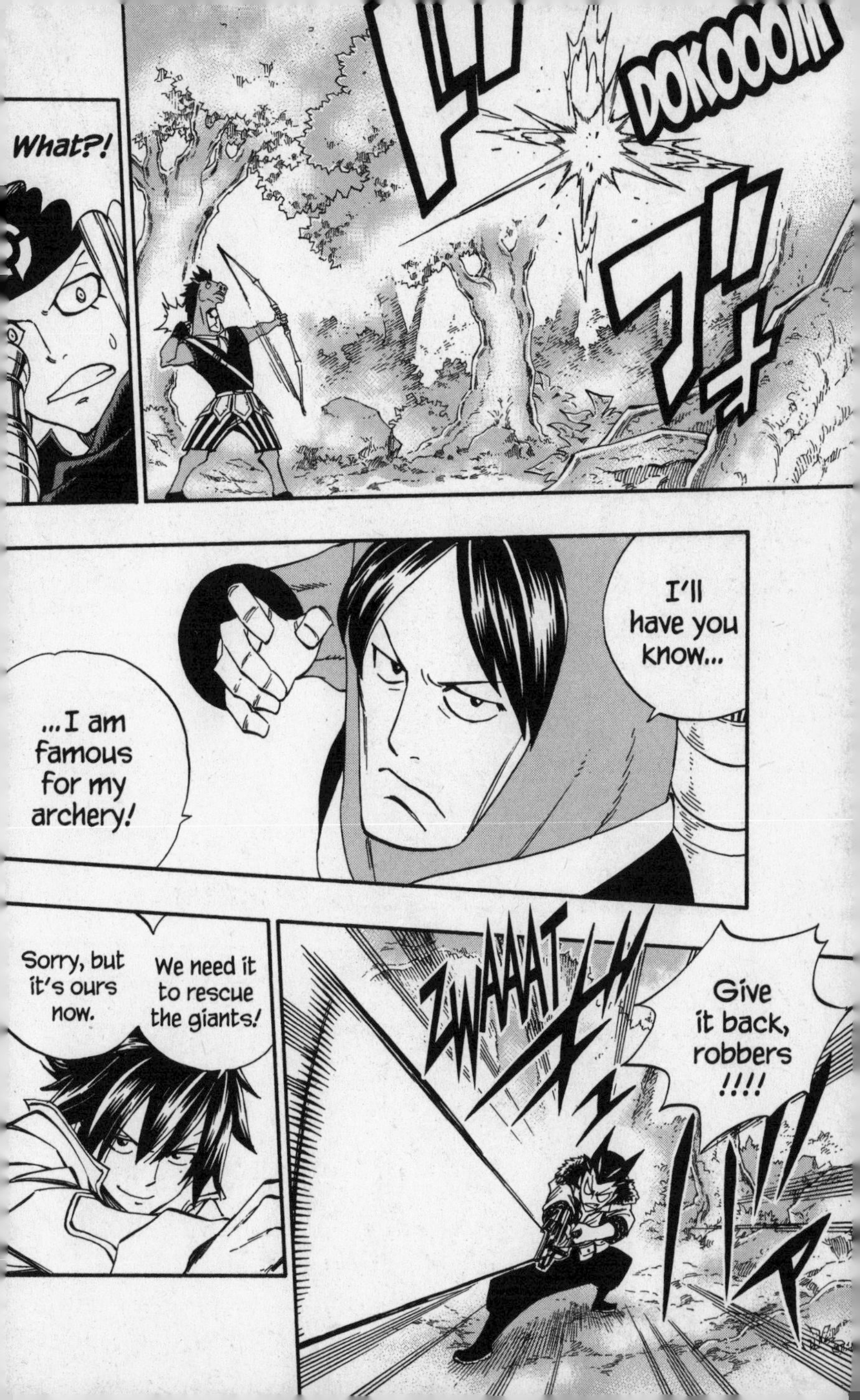
DOKOOOM
What?!
I'll have you know...
...I am famous for my archery!
Give it back, robbers!!!!
ZWAAATCH
We need it to rescue the giants!
Sorry, but it's ours now.

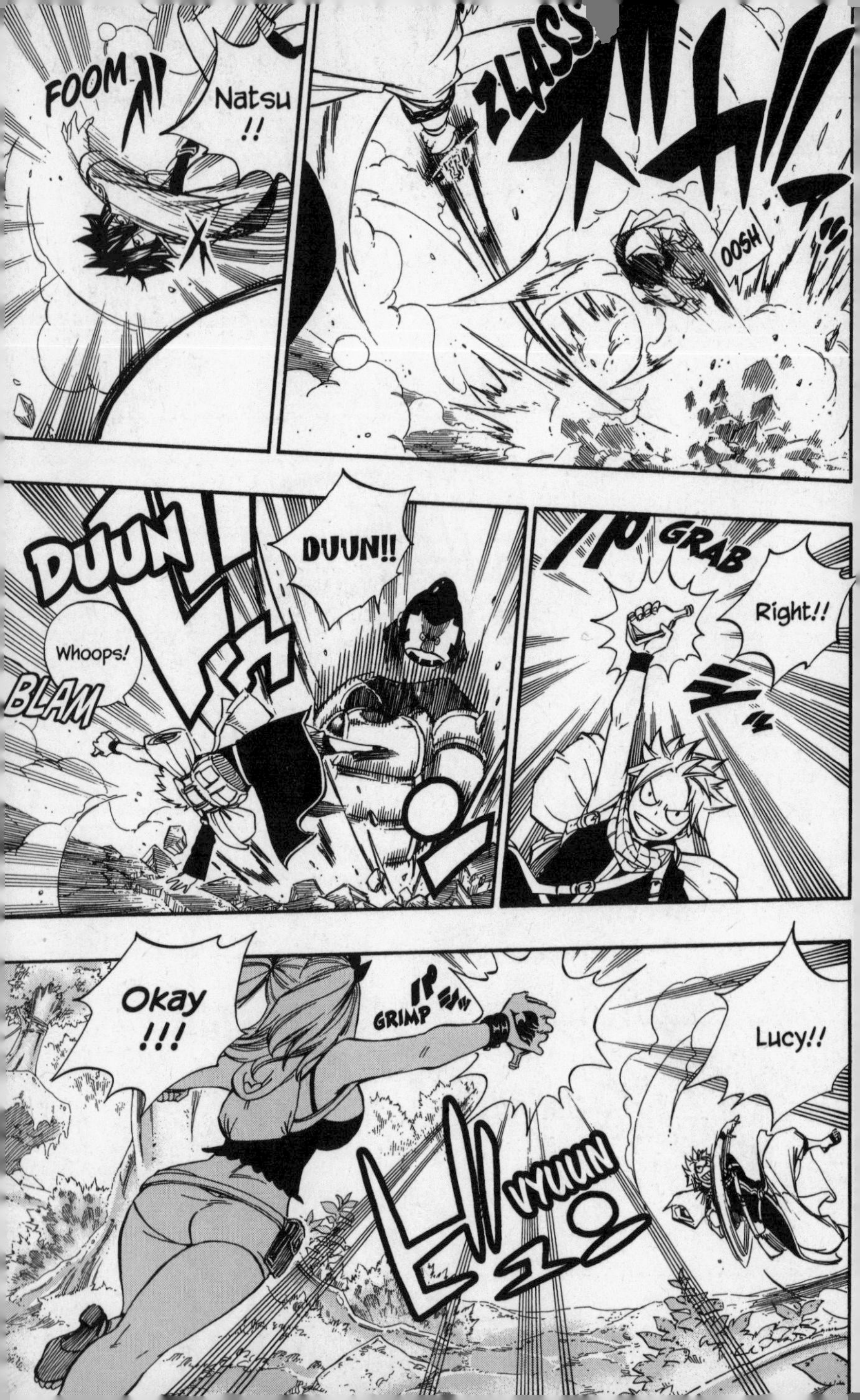
ZLASS
OOSH
Natsu!!
FOOM
GRAB
Right!!
DUUN!!
DUUN
Whoops!
BLAM
Lucy!!
VYUUN
GRIMP
Okay!!!

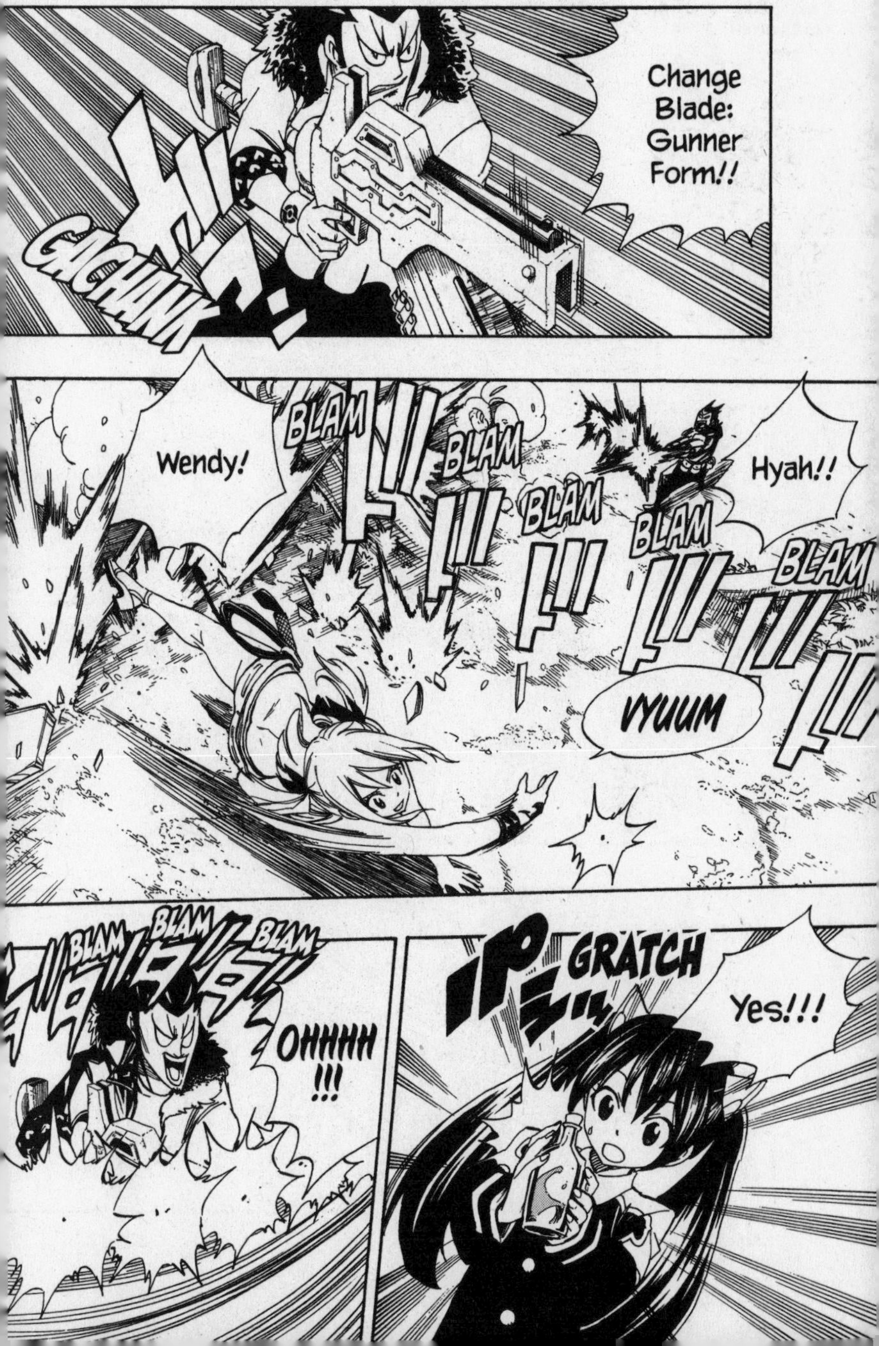
Change Blade: Gunner Form!!
GACHANK
Hyah!!
BLAM
BLAM
BLAM
BLAM
BLAM
VYUUM
Wendy!
Yes!!!
GRATCH
OHHHHH!!!
BLAM
BLAM
BLAM

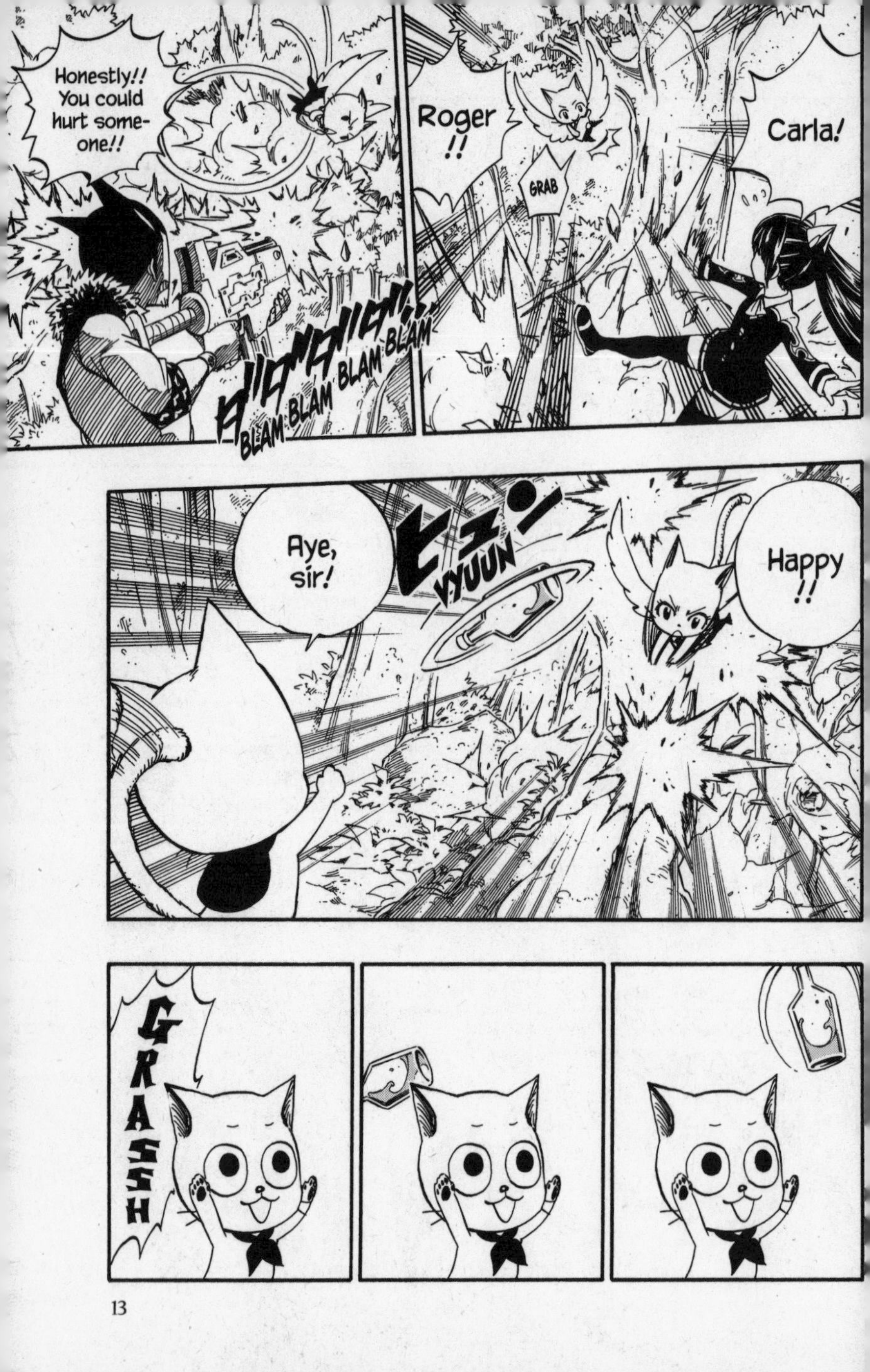
Carla!
Roger !!
GRAB
Honestly!! You could hurt some-one!!
BLAM BLAM BLAM BLAM
Happy !!
VYUUN
Aye, sir!
GRASH

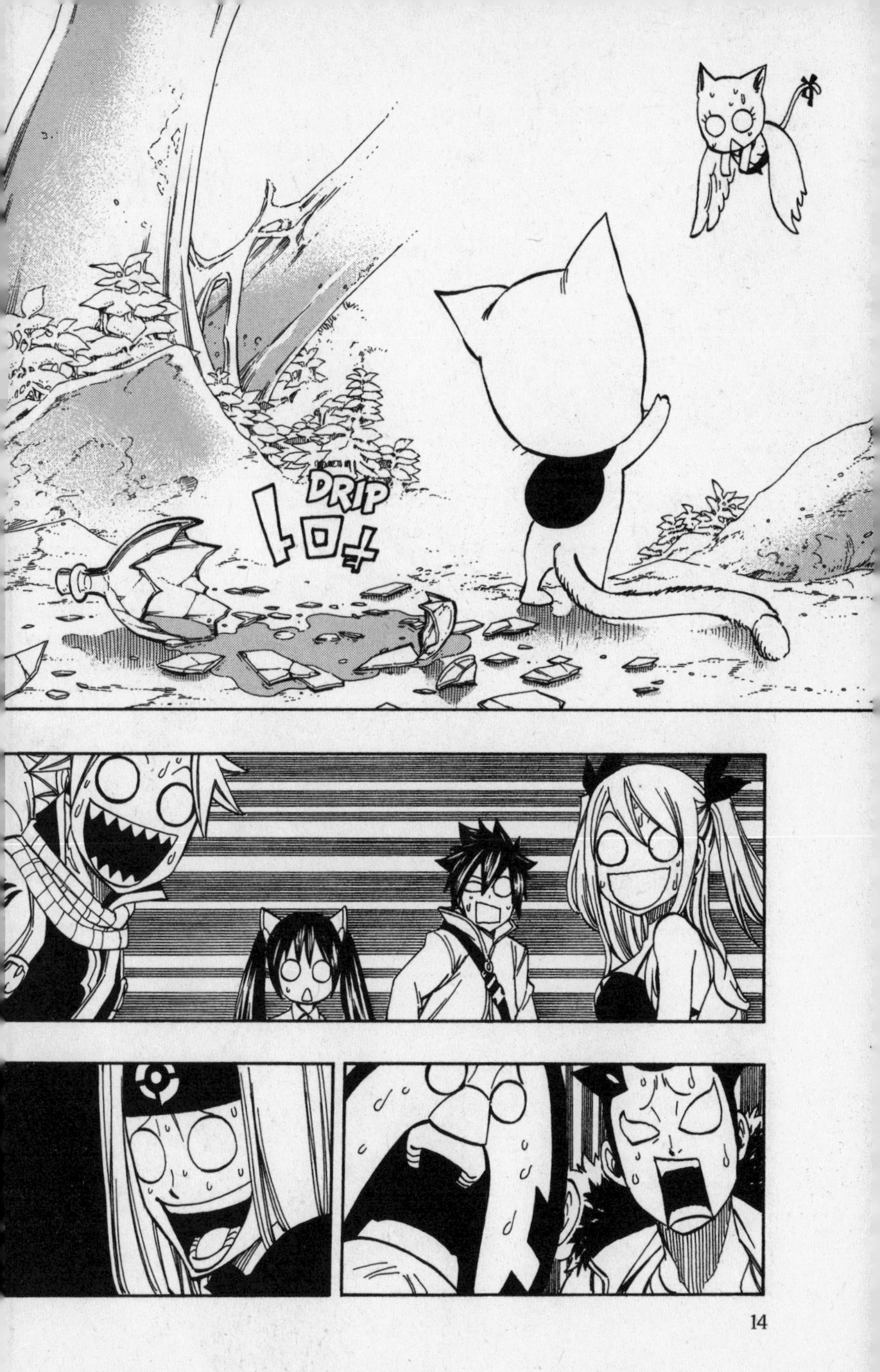
DRIP

It's broken !!!!

I'm sorry!

You *broke* what you stole... DUUN! DUUN!! DUUN!!!

What have you done?!!! You guys are heavy bad guys, you know!!!!

Ah!

But... look at that!

15

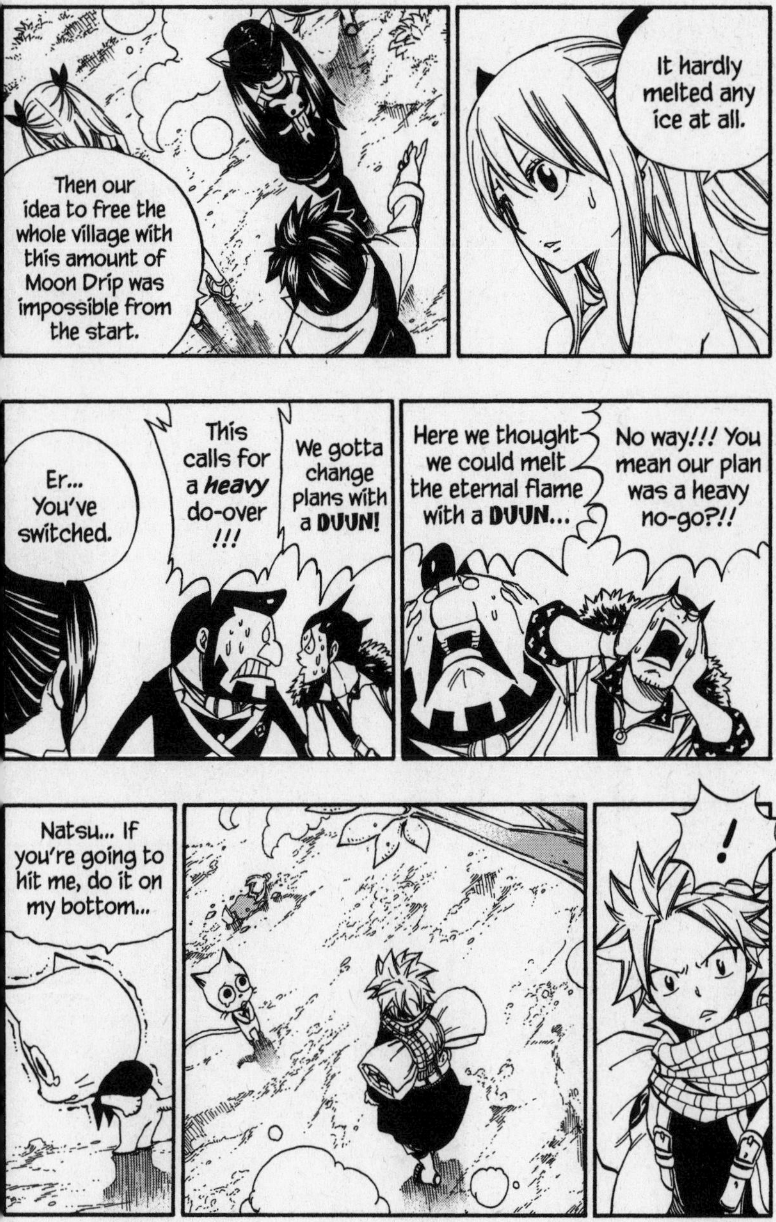
It hardly melted any ice at all.
Then our idea to free the whole village with this amount of Moon Drip was impossible from the start.
No way!!! You mean our plan was a heavy no-go?!!
Here we thought we could melt the eternal flame with a DUUN...
We gotta change plans with a DUUN!
This calls for a heavy do-over!!!
Er... You've switched.
!
Natsu... If you're going to hit me, do it on my bottom...

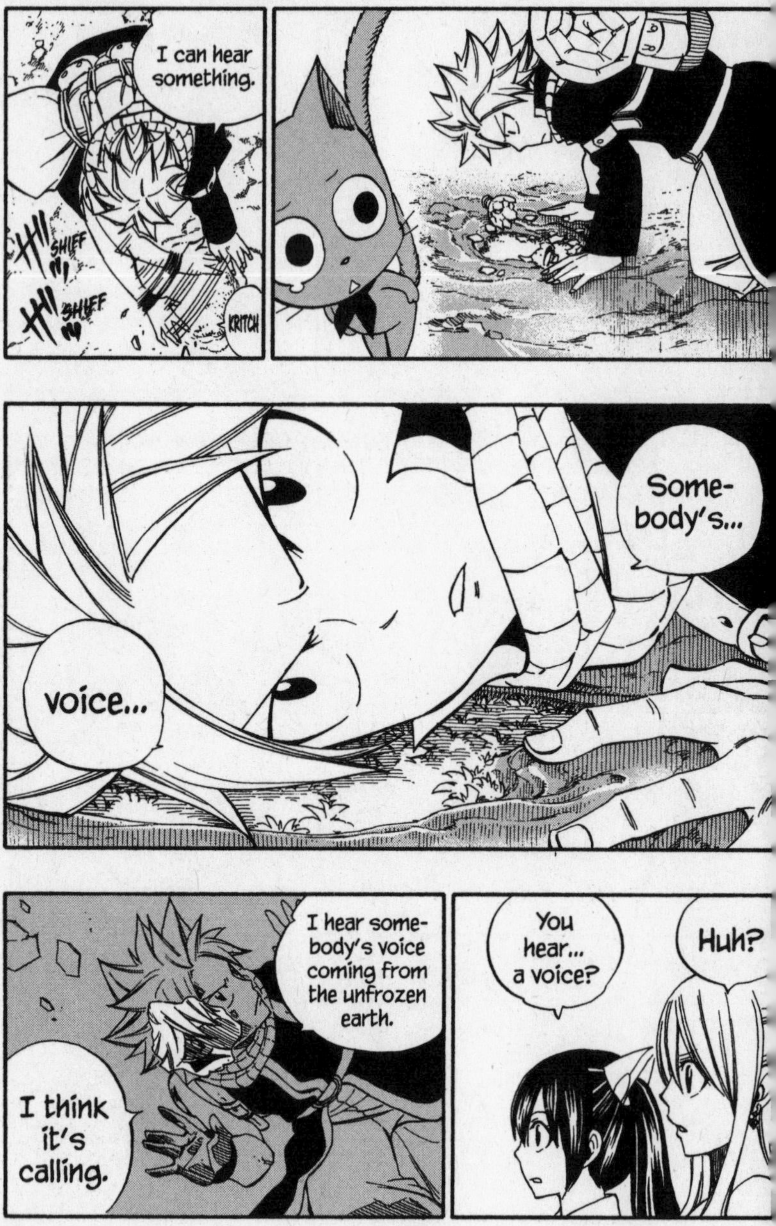
I can hear something.
SHIFF
SHIFF
KRITCH
Some-body's...
voice...
Huh?
You hear... a voice?
I hear some-body's voice coming from the unfrozen earth.
I think it's calling.

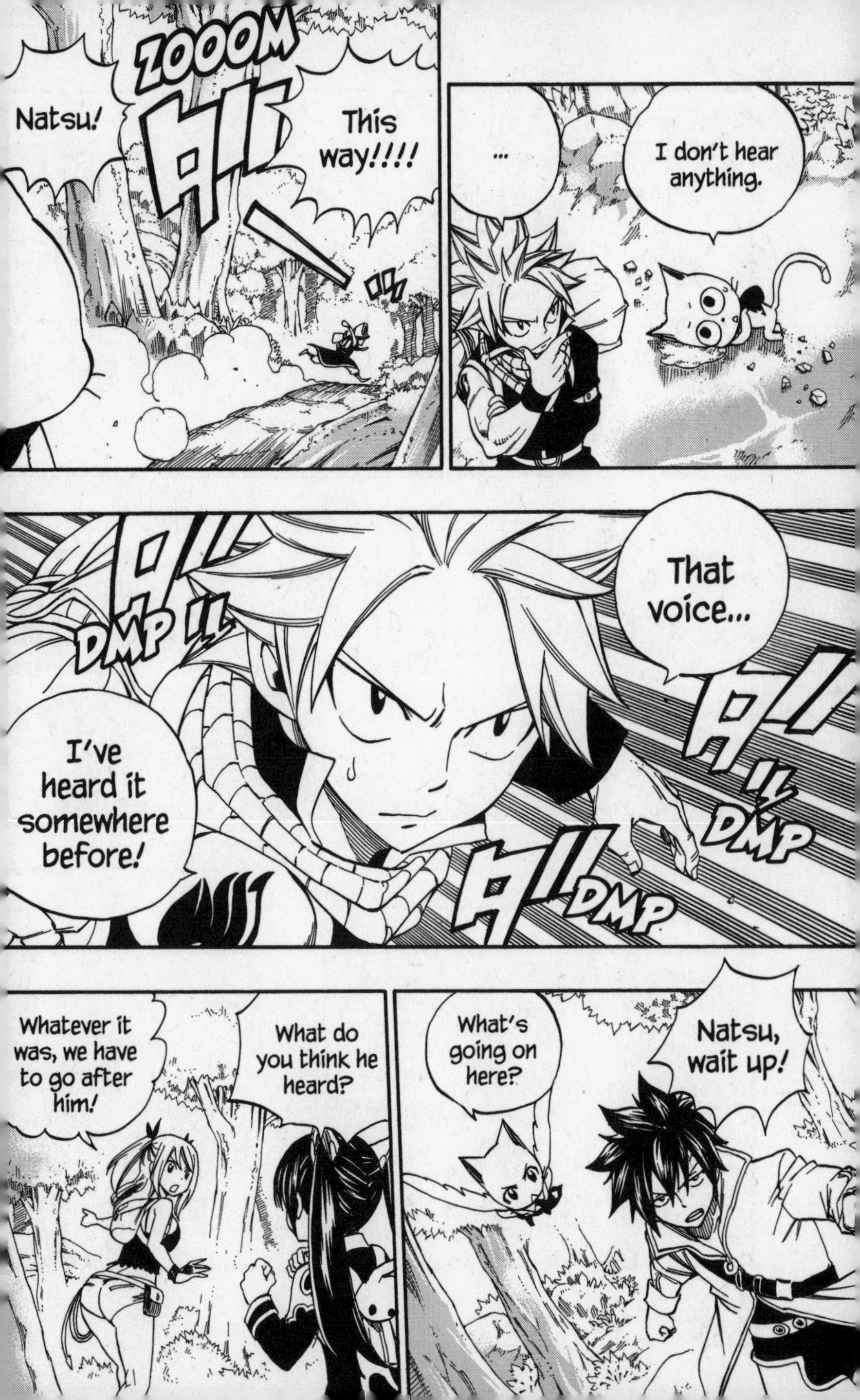
I don't hear anything.
...
This way!!!!
ZOOOM
Natsu!
That voice...
DMP
DMP
DMP
I've heard it somewhere before!
Natsu, wait up!
What's going on here?
What do you think he heard?
Whatever it was, we have to go after him!

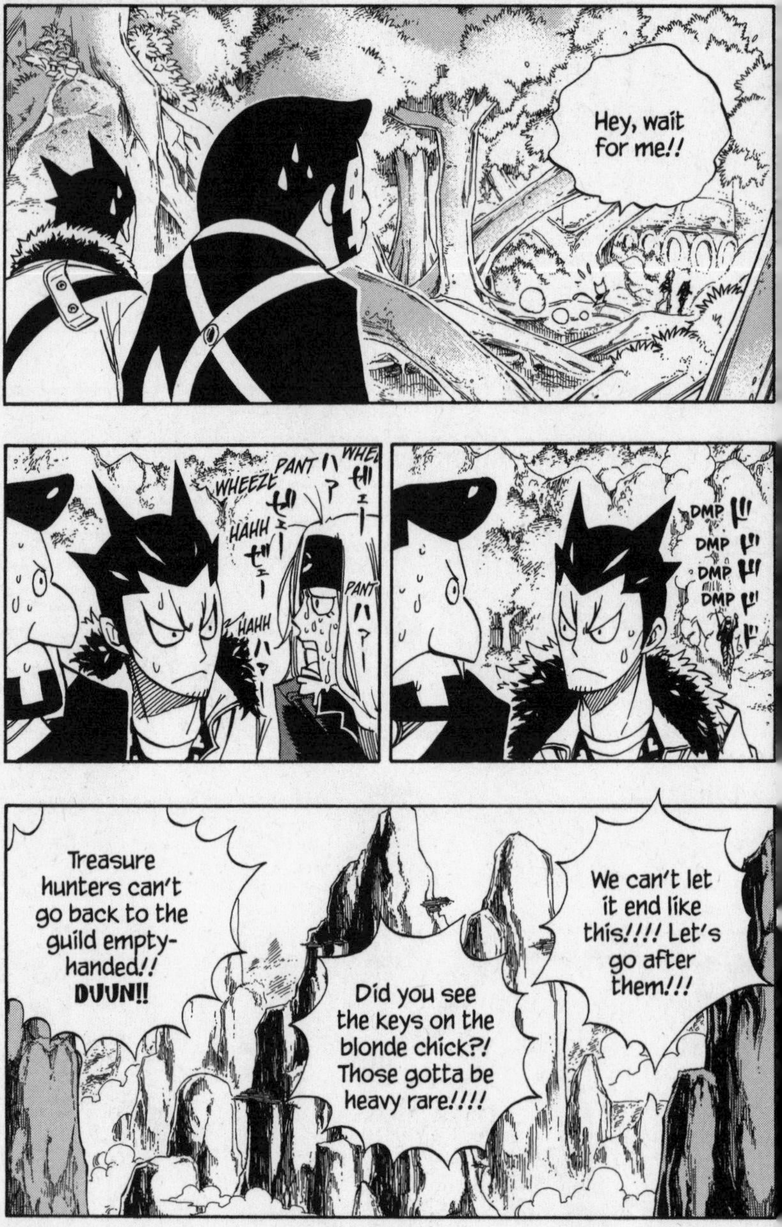
Hey, wait for me!!
DMP
DMP
DMP
DMP
WHEEZE
PANT
HAHH
HAHH
PANT
WHE
We can't let it end like this!!!! Let's go after them!!!
Treasure hunters can't go back to the guild empty-handed!! DUUN!!
Did you see the keys on the blonde chick?! Those gotta be heavy rare!!!!

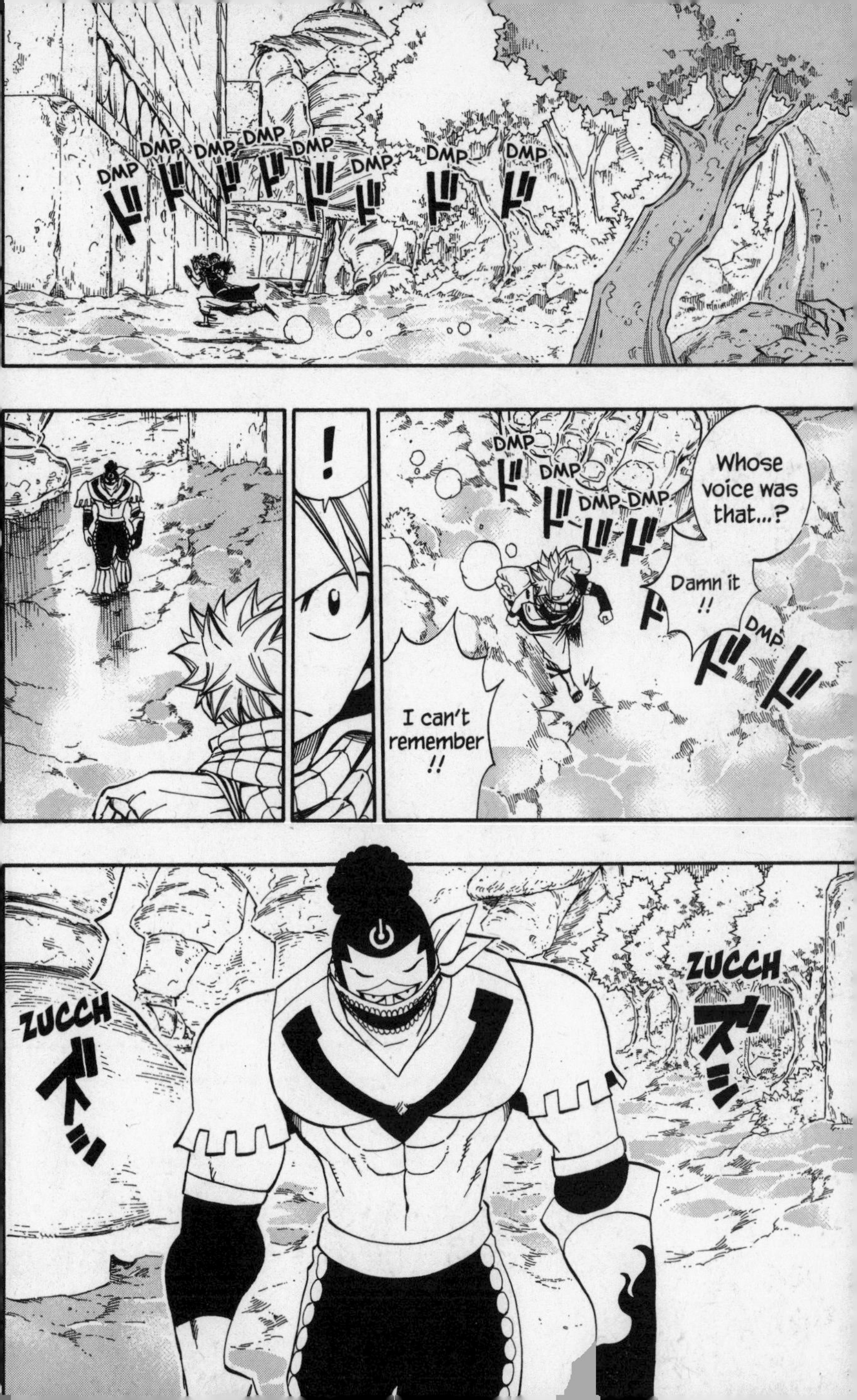
DMP DMP DMP DMP DMP DMP DMP DMP
Whose voice was that...?
DMP DMP DMP DMP
Damn it !!
DMP
I can't remember !!
!
ZUCCH
ZUCCH

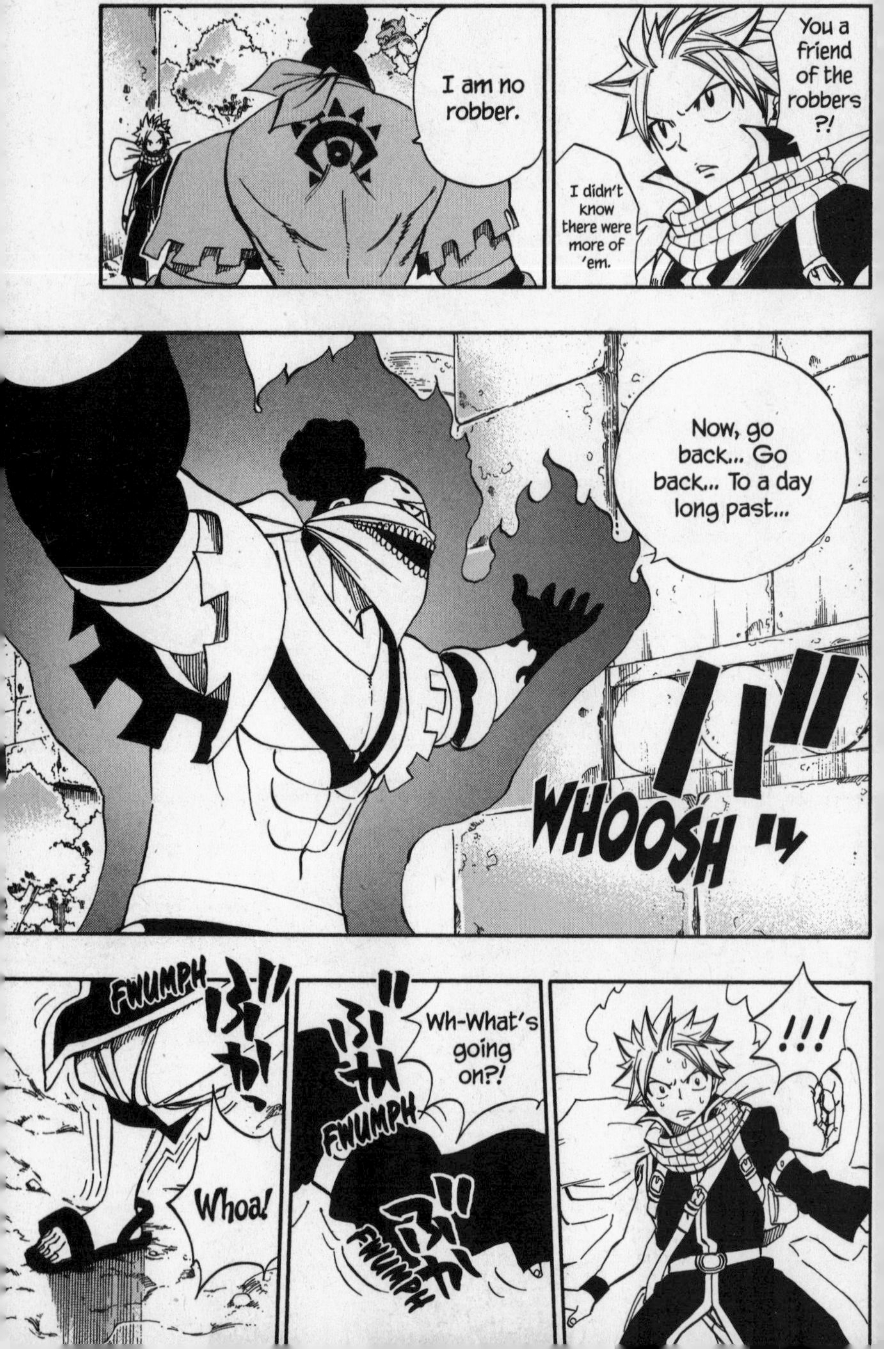

You a friend of the robbers?!
I didn't know there were more of 'em.
I am no robber.
Now, go back... Go back... To a day long past...
WHOOSH
!!!
Wh-What's going on?!
FWUMPH
FWUMPH
FWUMPH
Whoa!

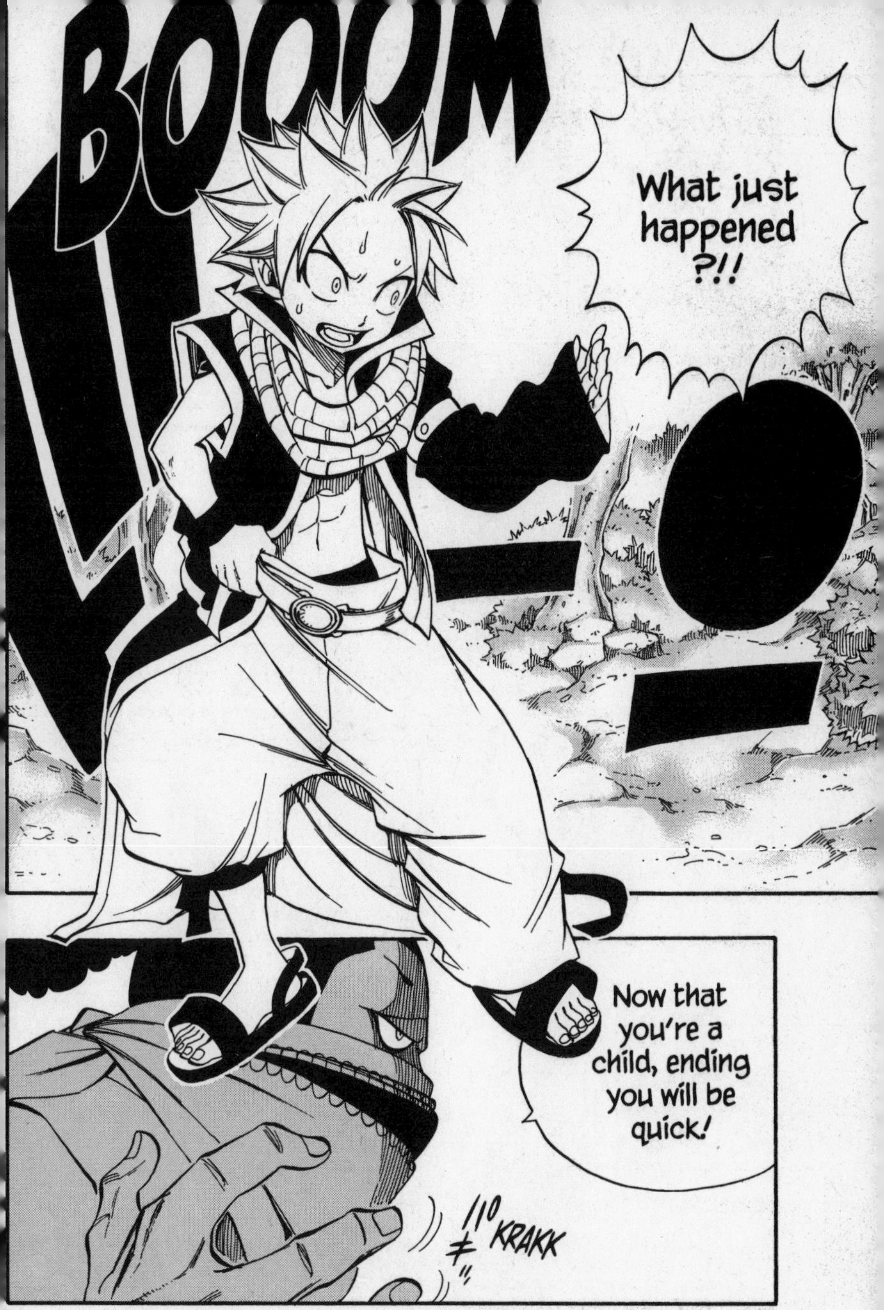
BOOOM
What just happened ?!!
Now that you're a child, ending you will be quick!
KRAKK

FAIRY TAIL

Chapter 346: The Way of Devolution

SABER TOOTH

Name: Lecter   **Age:** 13 yrs.

Magic:
Aera

Likes: **Dislikes:**
Sting-kun   Bullies

Remarks

Lecter is thought to be an Exceed who came from Edolas. He met Sting as a young child, and was drawn to him by his strength, then grew to like him to the point of worship. During the Grand Magic Games, he was nearly eliminated by Master Ziemma, but Minerva used her space-manipulation magic to keep him alive. He then attached himself to Millianna, who was also caught up in Minerva's magic, to escape.

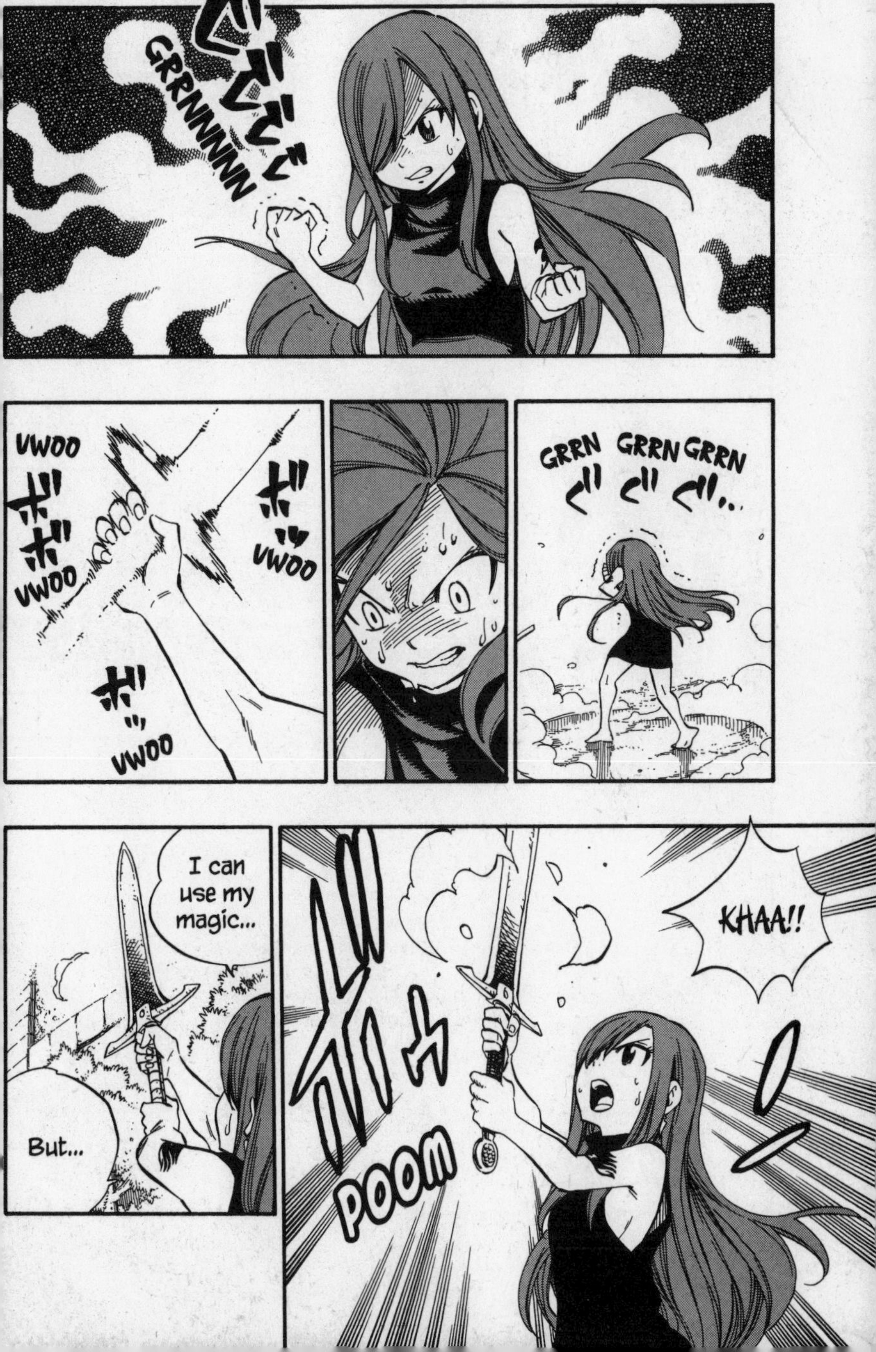
GRRNNNNNNN
GRRN GRRN GRRN
VWOO
VWOO
VWOO
VWOO
KHAA!!
POOM
I can use my magic...
But...

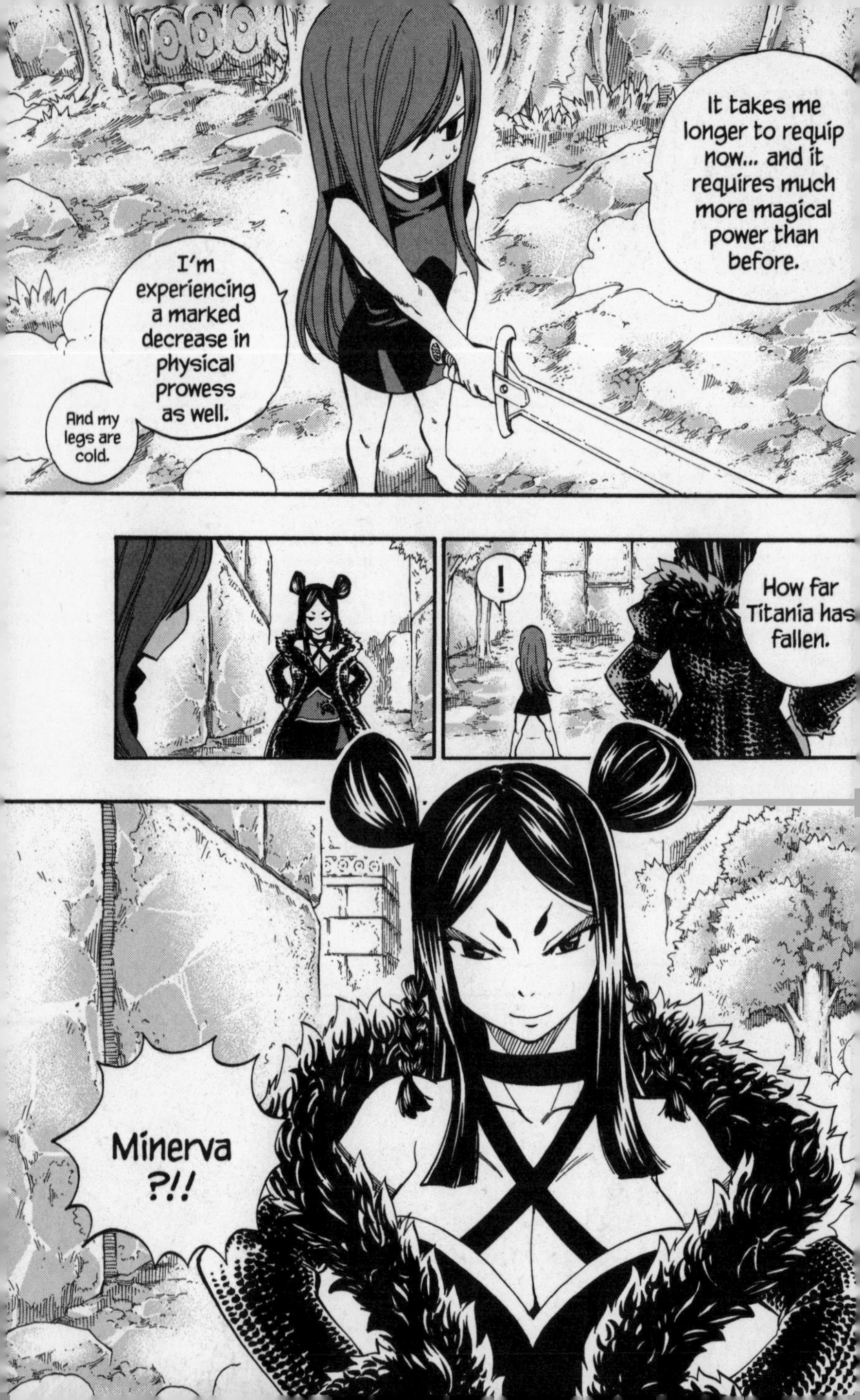

It takes me longer to requip now... and it requires much more magical power than before.
I'm experiencing a marked decrease in physical prowess as well.
And my legs are cold.
How far Titania has fallen.
!
Minerva ?!!

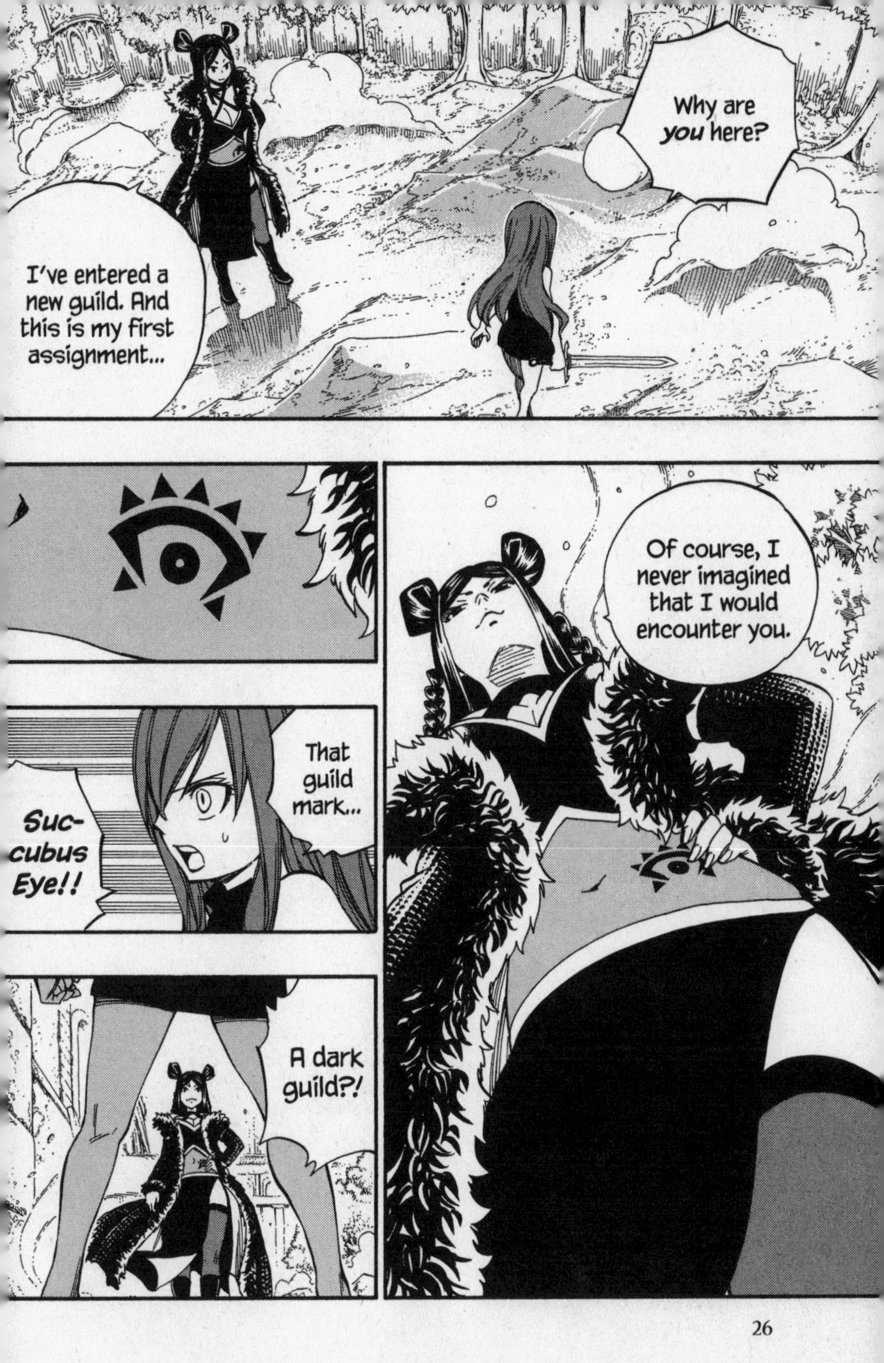
Why are you here?
I've entered a new guild. And this is my first assignment...
Of course, I never imagined that I would encounter you.
That guild mark...
Succubus Eye!!
A dark guild?!

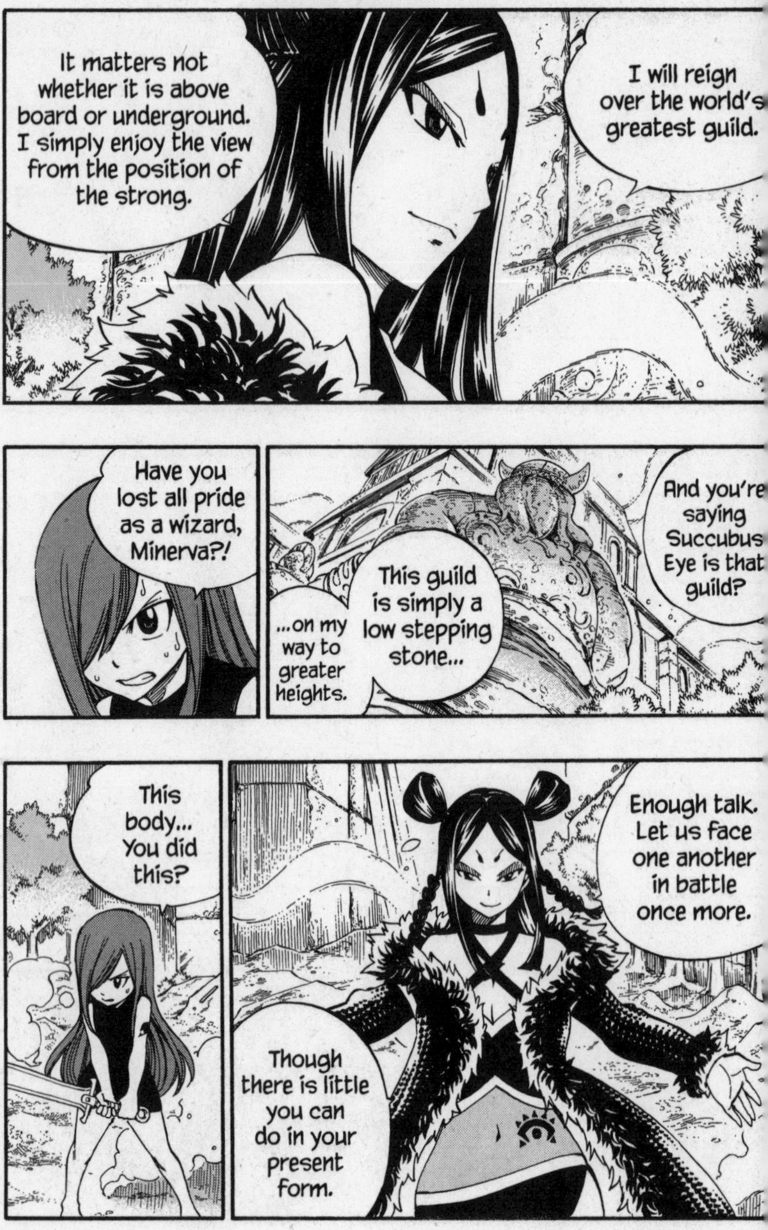
I will reign over the world's greatest guild.
It matters not whether it is above board or underground. I simply enjoy the view from the position of the strong.
And you're saying Succubus Eye is that guild?
This guild is simply a low stepping stone...
...on my way to greater heights.
Have you lost all pride as a wizard, Minerva?!
Enough talk. Let us face one another in battle once more.
Though there is little you can do in your present form.
This body... You did this?

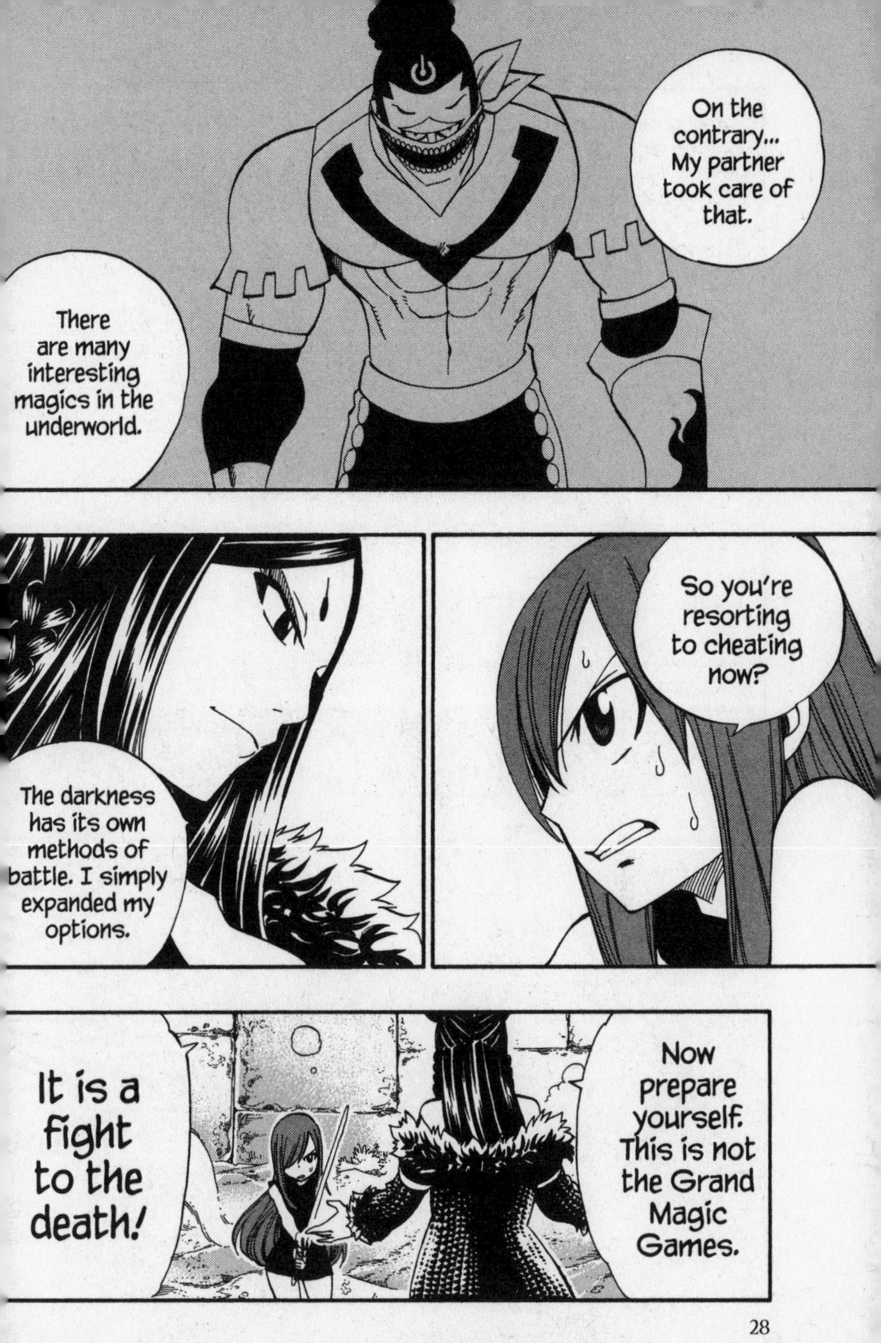
On the contrary... My partner took care of that.
There are many interesting magics in the underworld.
So you're resorting to cheating now?
The darkness has its own methods of battle. I simply expanded my options.
Now prepare yourself. This is not the Grand Magic Games.
It is a fight to the death!

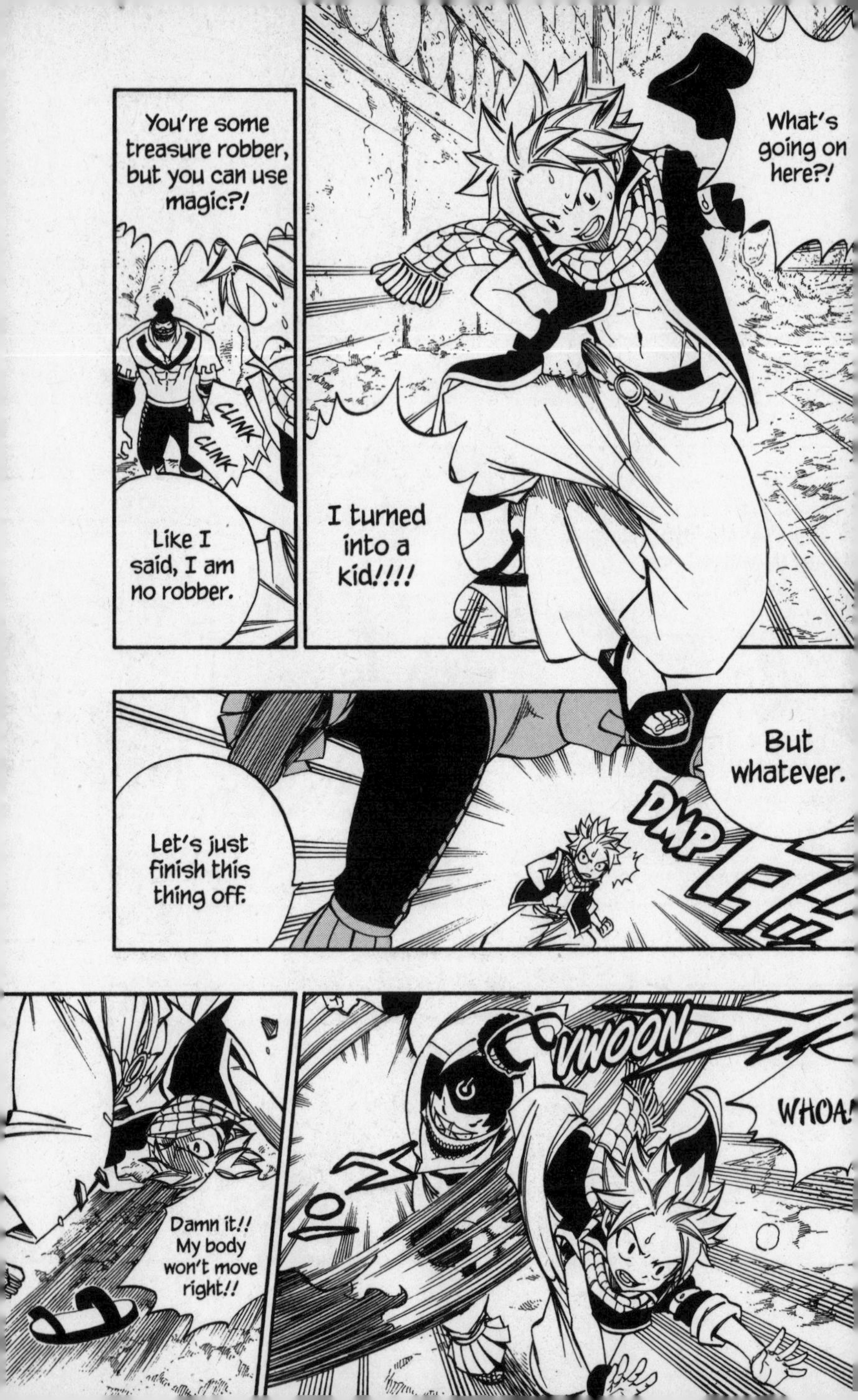
What's going on here?!
I turned into a kid!!!!
You're some treasure robber, but you can use magic?!
CLINK
CLINK
Like I said, I am no robber.
But whatever.
DMP
Let's just finish this thing off.
VWOON
WHOA!
Damn it!! My body won't move right!!

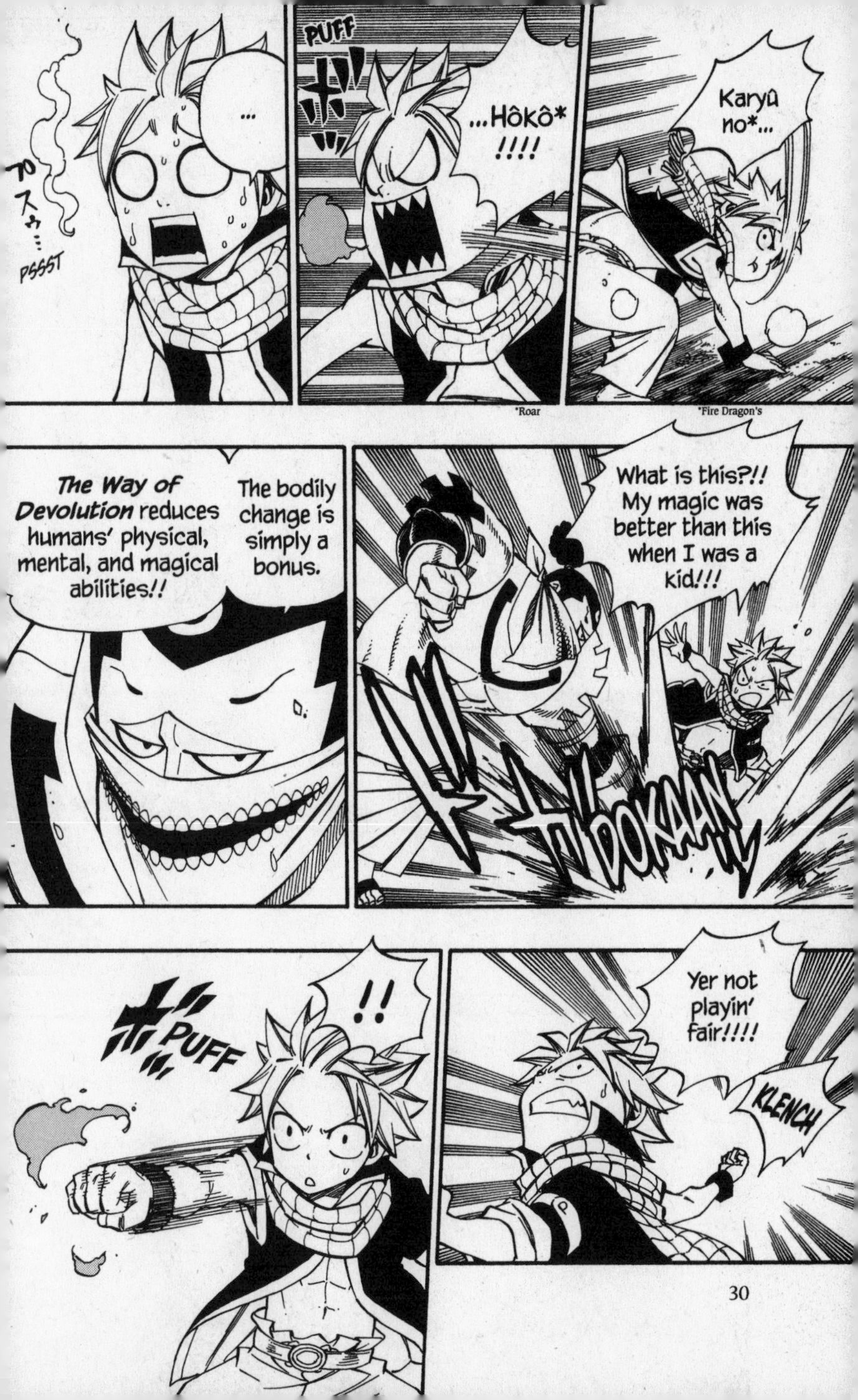
Karyû no*...
*Fire Dragon's
PUFF
...Hôkô* !!!!
*Roar
...
PSSST
What is this?!! My magic was better than this when I was a kid!!!
DOKAAN
The bodily change is simply a bonus.
The Way of Devolution reduces humans' physical, mental, and magical abilities!!
Yer not playin' fair!!!!
KLENCH
!!
PUFF

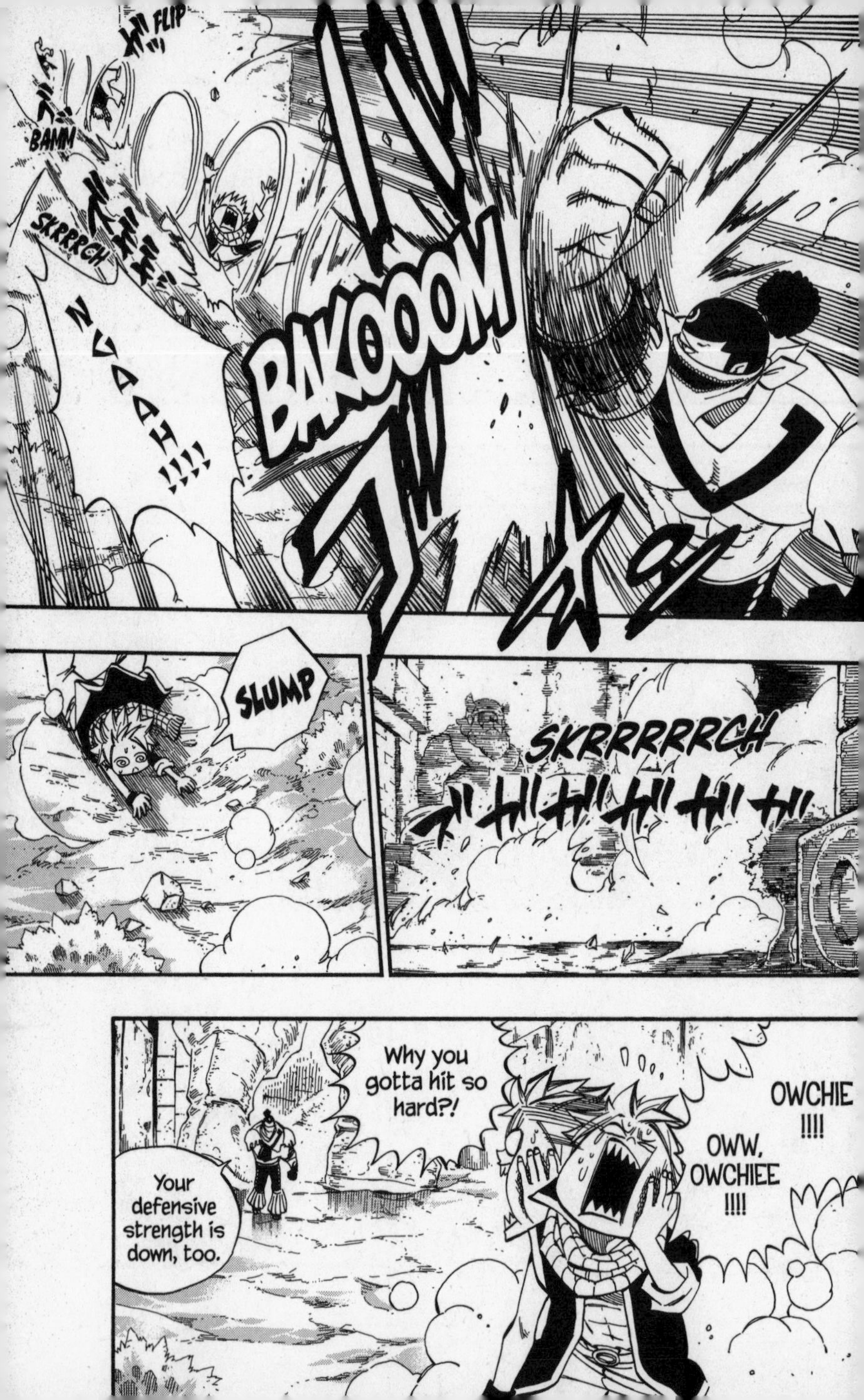
BAKOOOM
FLIP
BAMM
SKRRRCH
NUAAAH!!!!
SKRRRRRCH
SLUMP
OWCHIE!!!!
OWW, OWCHIEE!!!!
Why you gotta hit so hard?!
Your defensive strength is down, too.

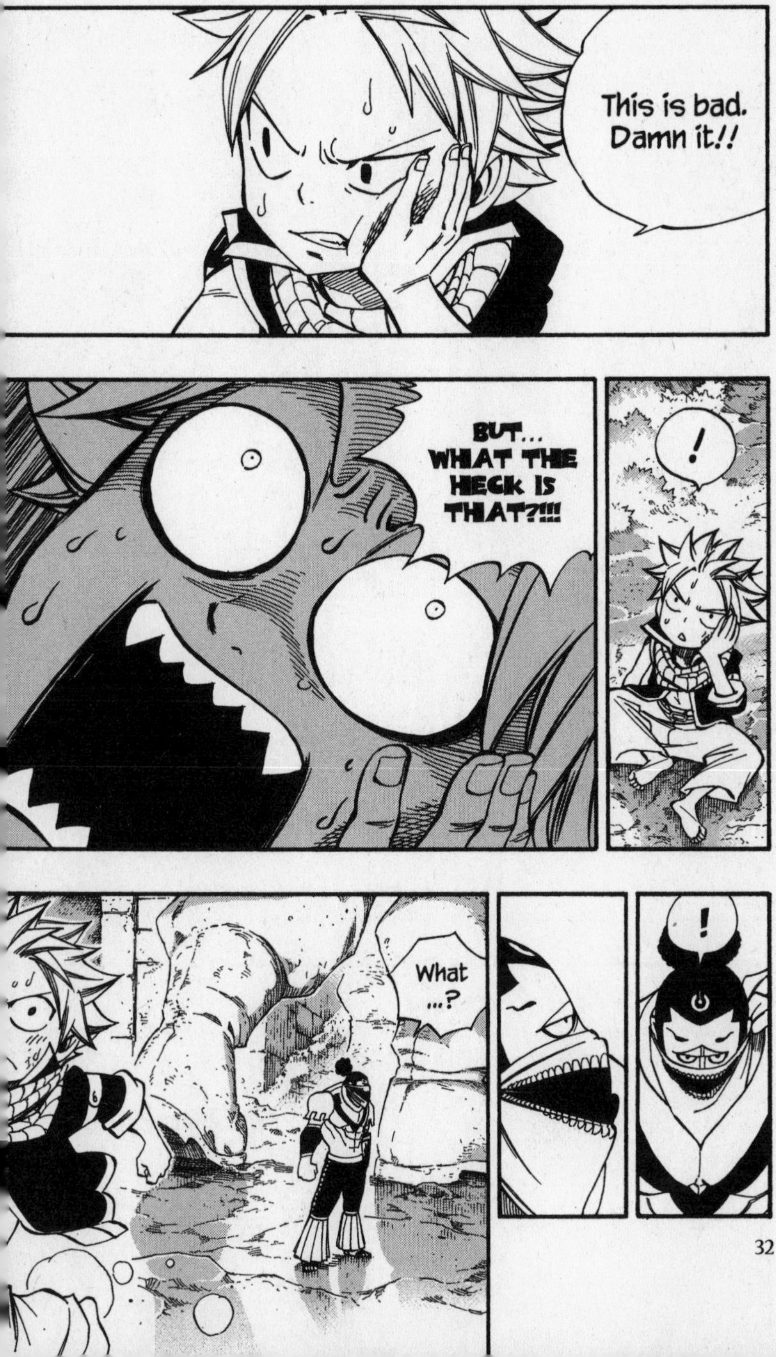
This is bad.
Damn it!!
!
BUT... WHAT THE HECK IS THAT?!!!
!
What ...?

Damn!!! He ran off!!!

Sorry, but I'm looking for a voice right now! See ya!!

Ha ha ha ha ha!!! Kids have their own ways of fighting!!!!

Gildarts fell for that tactic every time!! Brings back memories!

DMP DMP DMP DMP

That little brat thinks he can make a fool of me...

GWIP

He'll learn to fear the might of the Inhumans!

I'm sorry! The ground's frozen...

Are you all right, Wendy?

KYAA!!

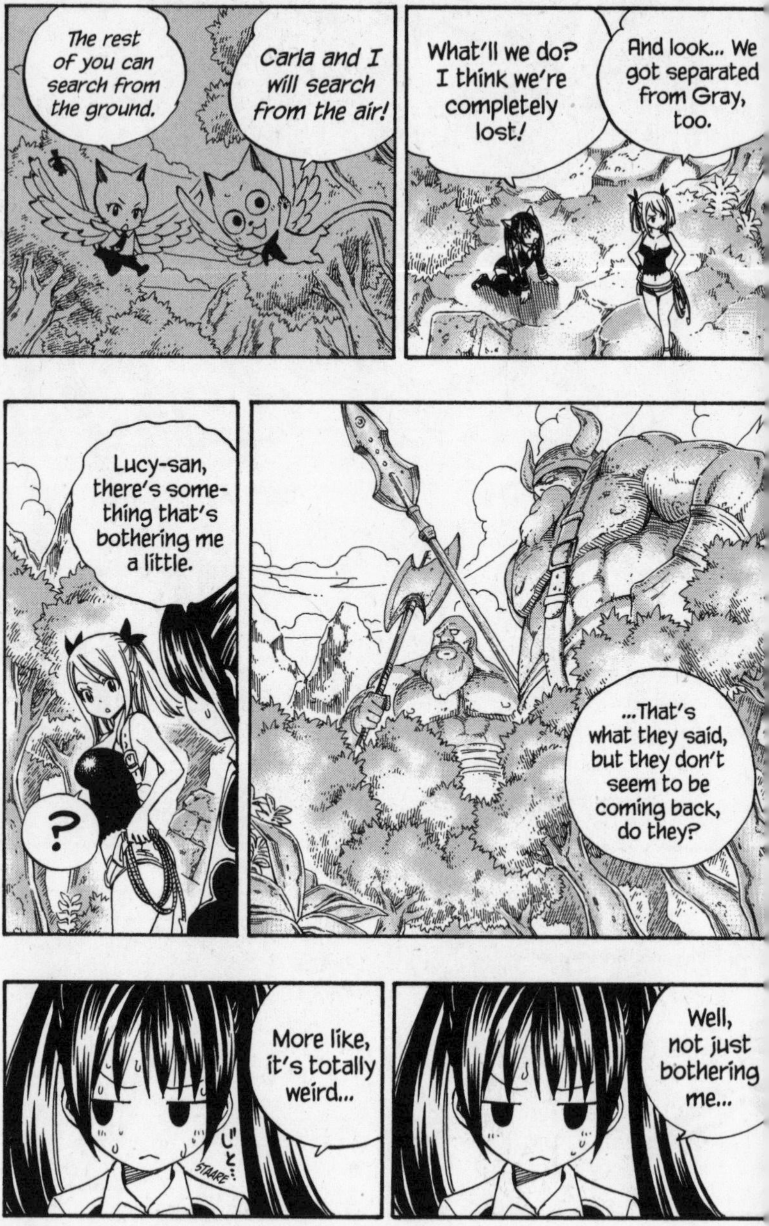
And look... We got separated from Gray, too.
What'll we do? I think we're completely lost!
Carla and I will search from the air!
The rest of you can search from the ground.
...That's what they said, but they don't seem to be coming back, do they?
Lucy-san, there's some-thing that's bothering me a little.
?
Well, not just bothering me...
More like, it's totally weird...
じと…
STARE

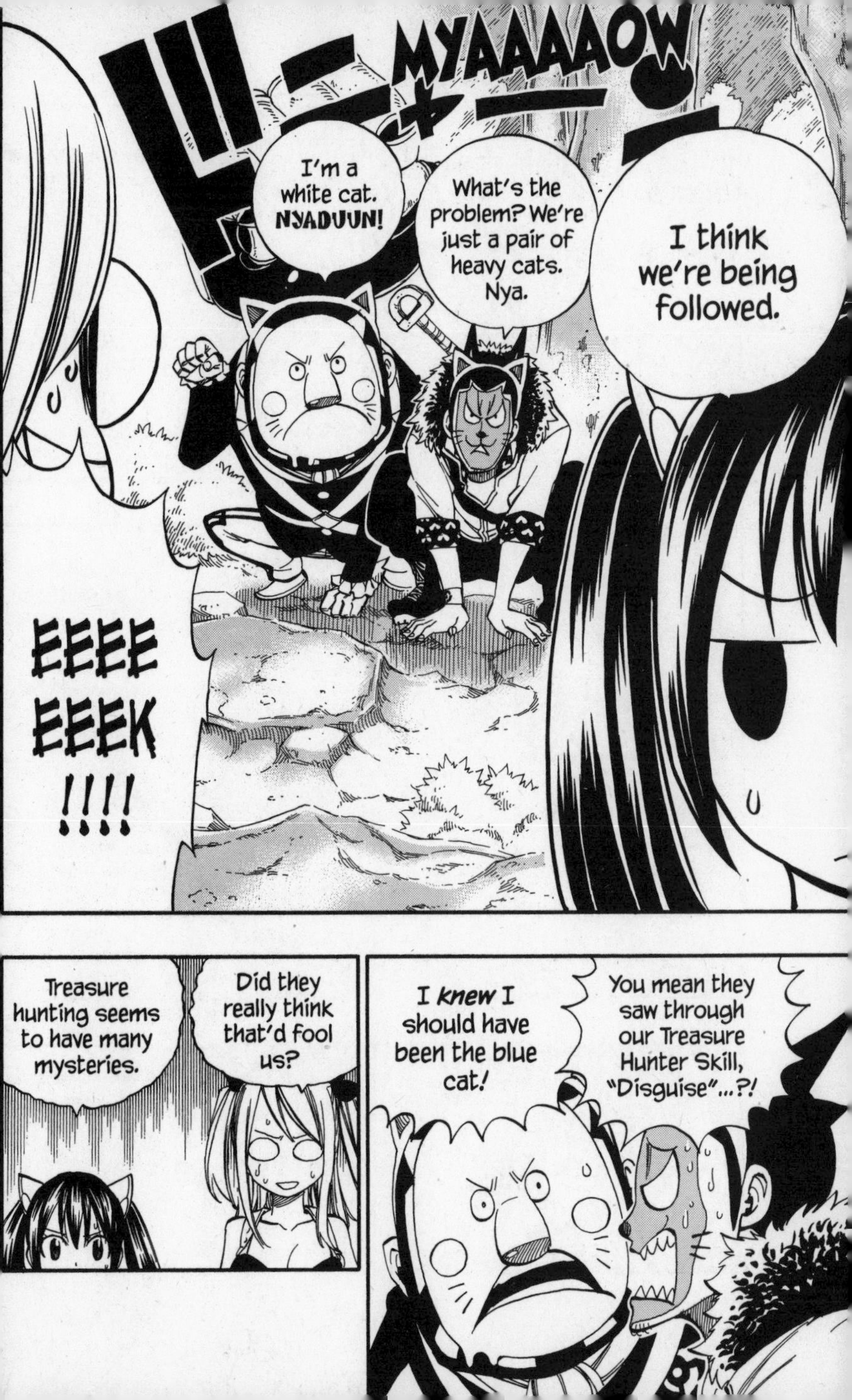
MYAAAAOW
I think we're being followed.
What's the problem? We're just a pair of heavy cats. Nya.
I'm a white cat. **NYADUUN!**
EEEE EEEK !!!!
You mean they saw through our Treasure Hunter Skill, "Disguise"...?!
I *knew* I should have been the blue cat!
Did they really think that'd fool us?
Treasure hunting seems to have many mysteries.

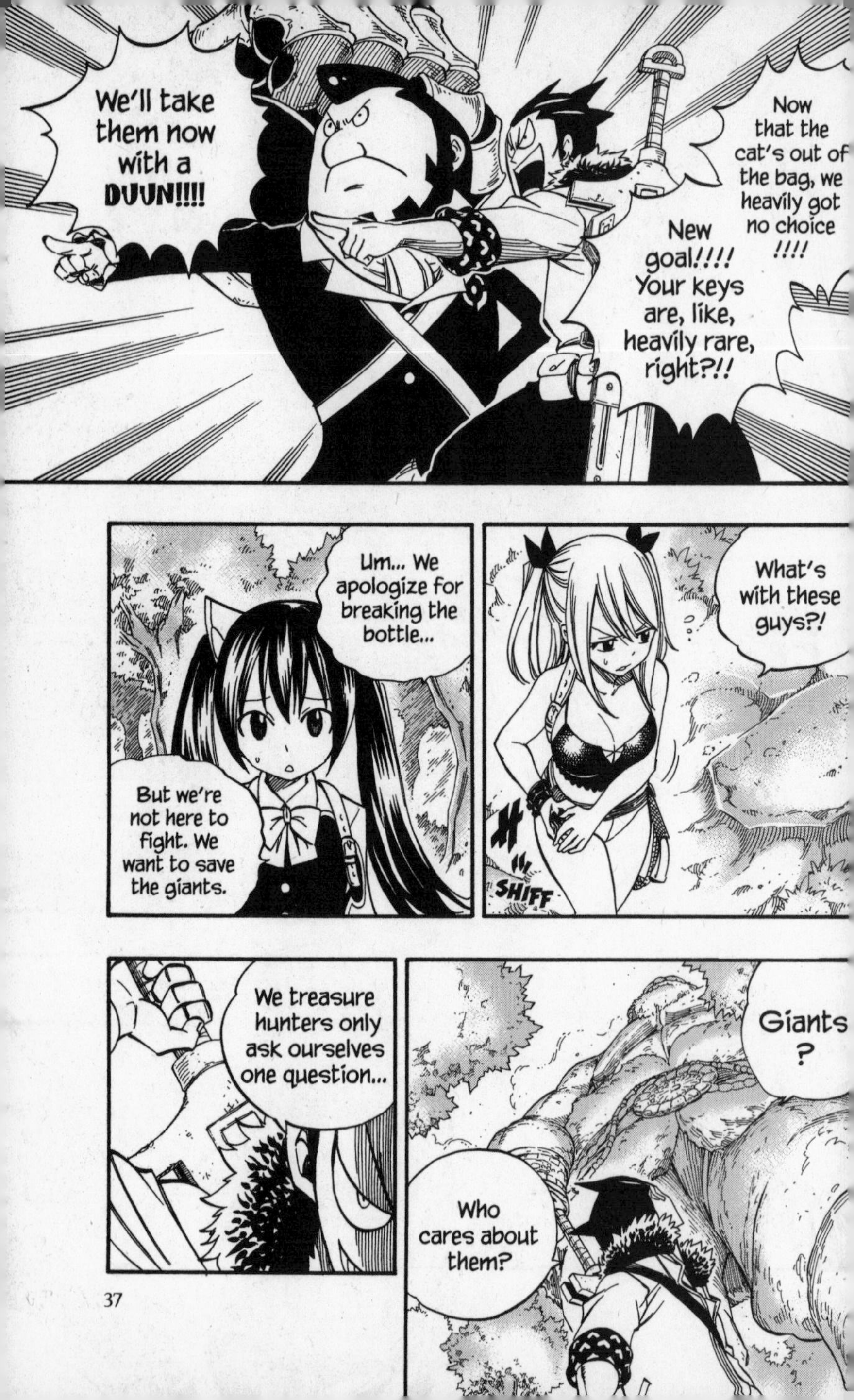
Now that the cat's out of the bag, we heavily got no choice!!!!
New goal!!!! Your keys are, like, heavily rare, right?!!
We'll take them now with a DUUN!!!!
What's with these guys?!
SHIFF
Um... We apologize for breaking the bottle...
But we're not here to fight. We want to save the giants.
Giants?
Who cares about them?
We treasure hunters only ask ourselves one question...

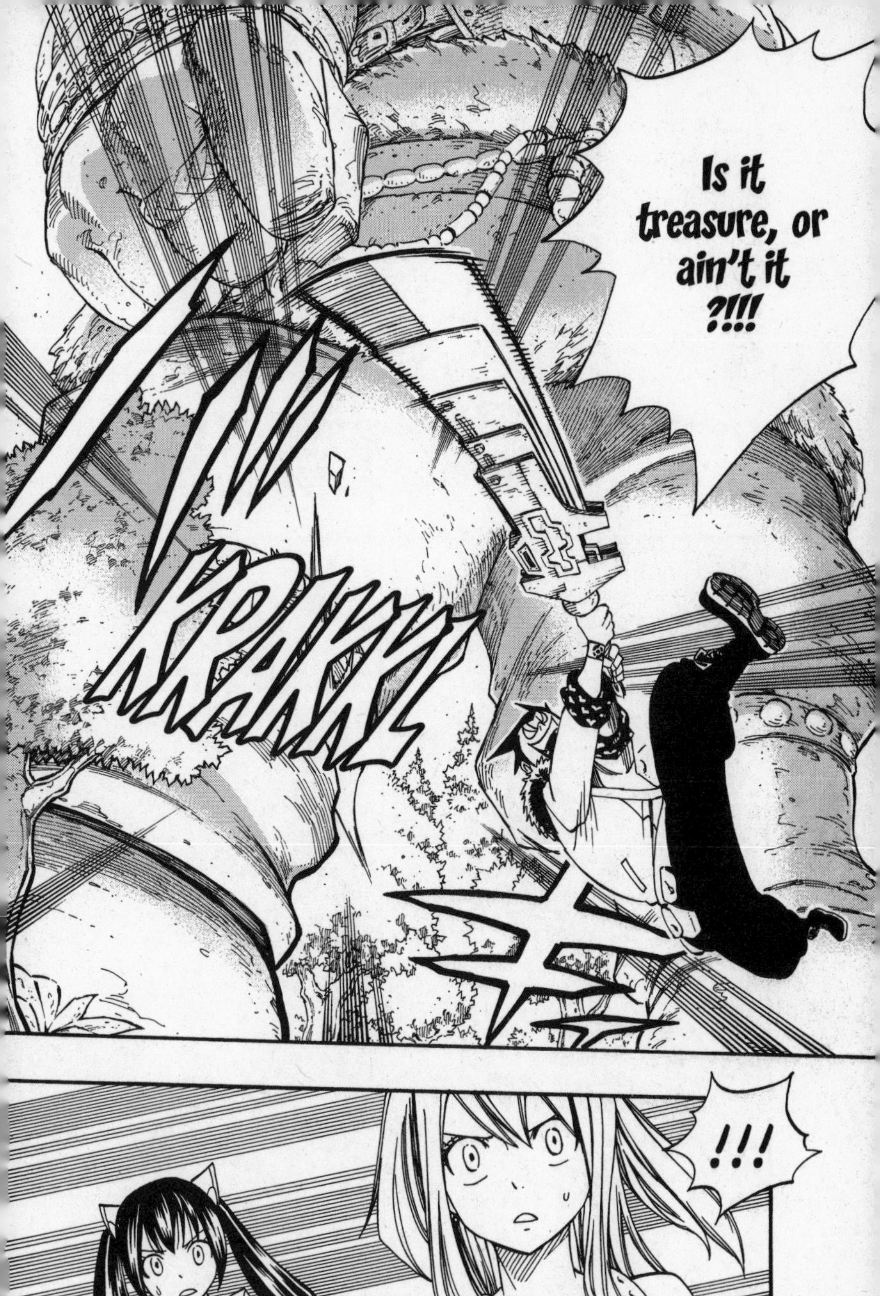
Is it treasure, or ain't it ?!!!
!!!

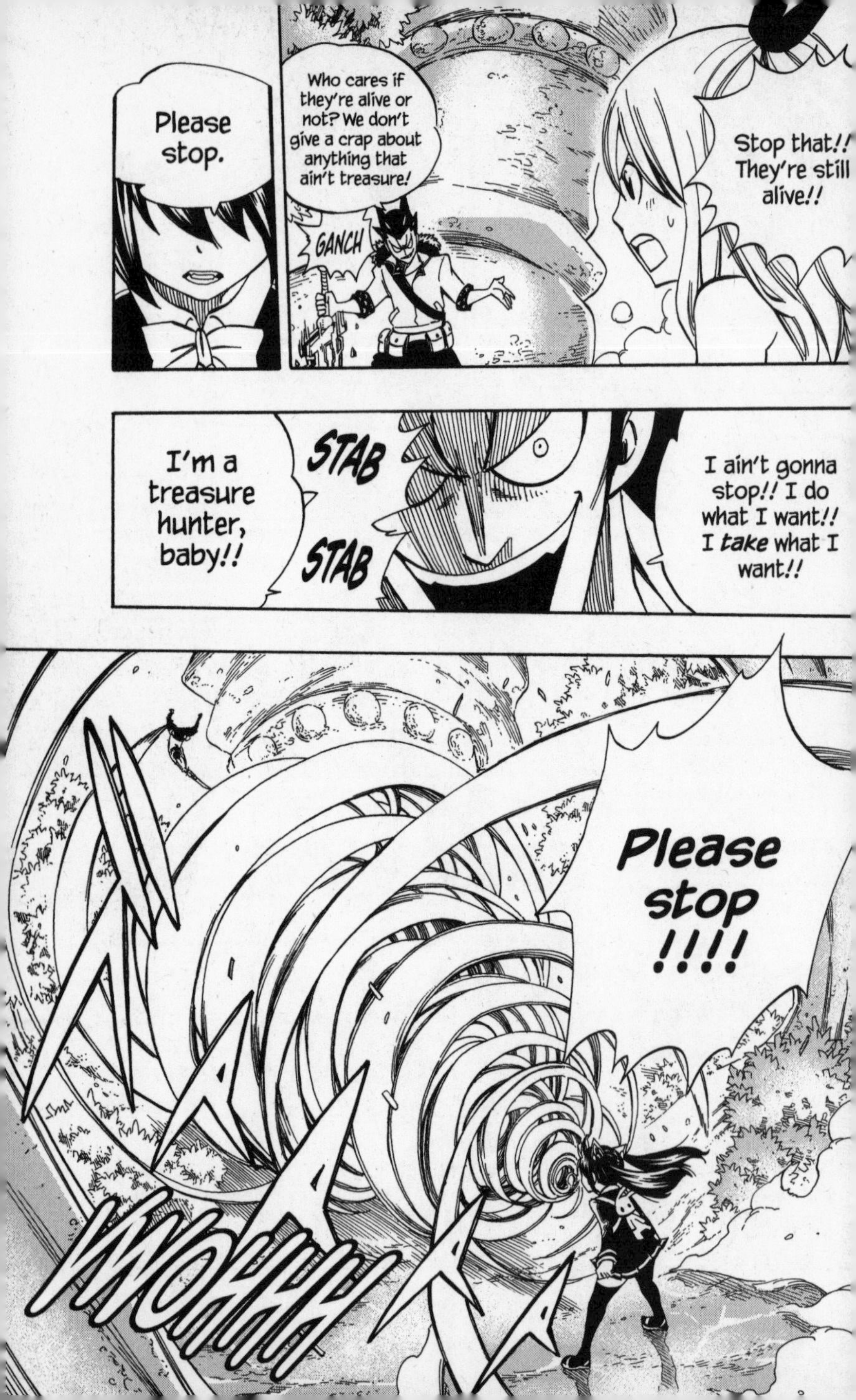

Stop that!! They're still alive!!
Who cares if they're alive or not? We don't give a crap about anything that ain't treasure!
GANCH
Please stop.
I ain't gonna stop!! I do what I want!! I *take* what I want!!
STAB
STAB
I'm a treasure hunter, baby!!
Please stop!!!!
WOHHH

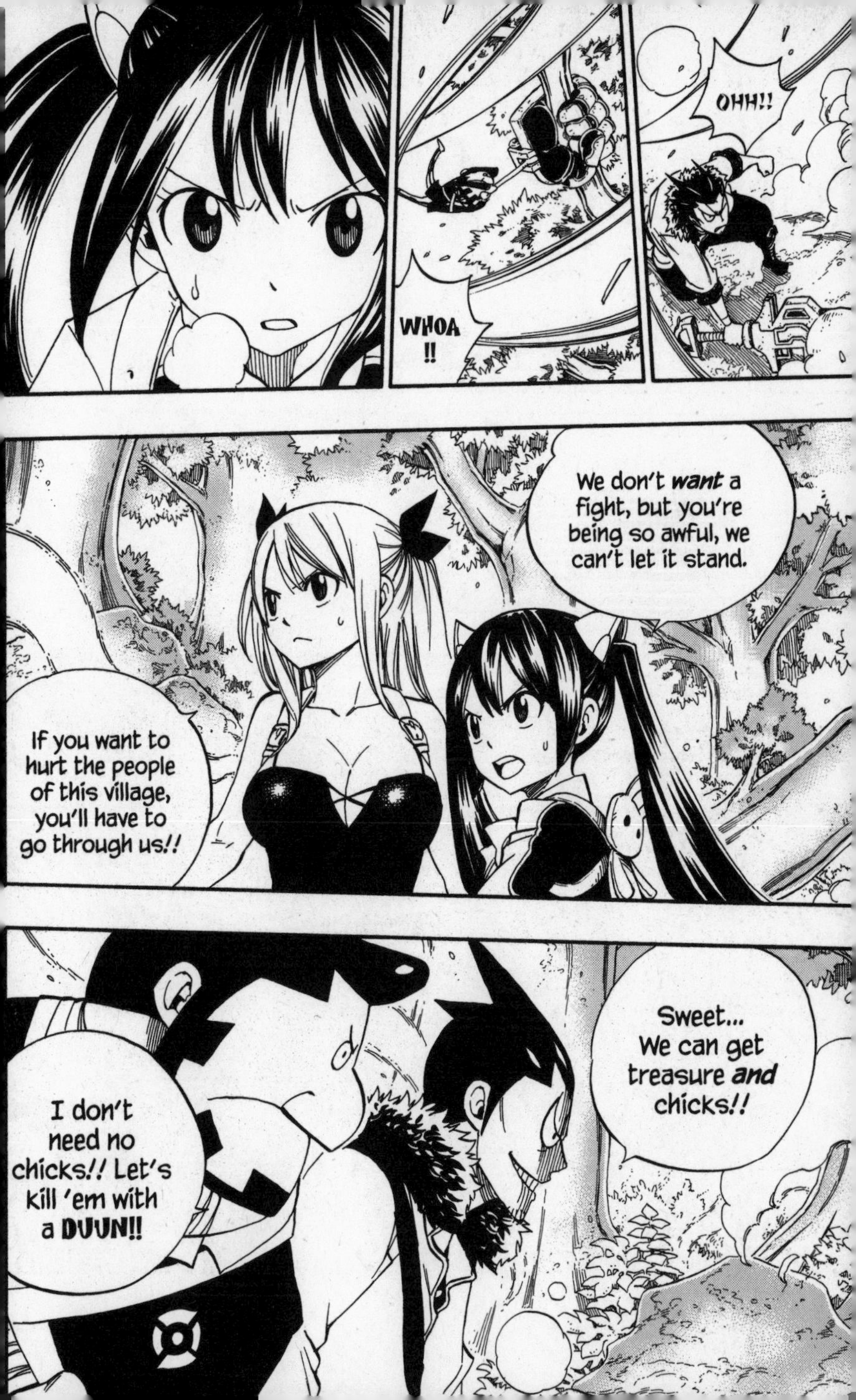
OHH!!
WHOA !!
We don't *want* a fight, but you're being so awful, we can't let it stand.
If you want to hurt the people of this village, you'll have to go through us!!
Sweet... We can get treasure *and* chicks!!
I don't need no chicks!! Let's kill 'em with a **DUUN**!!

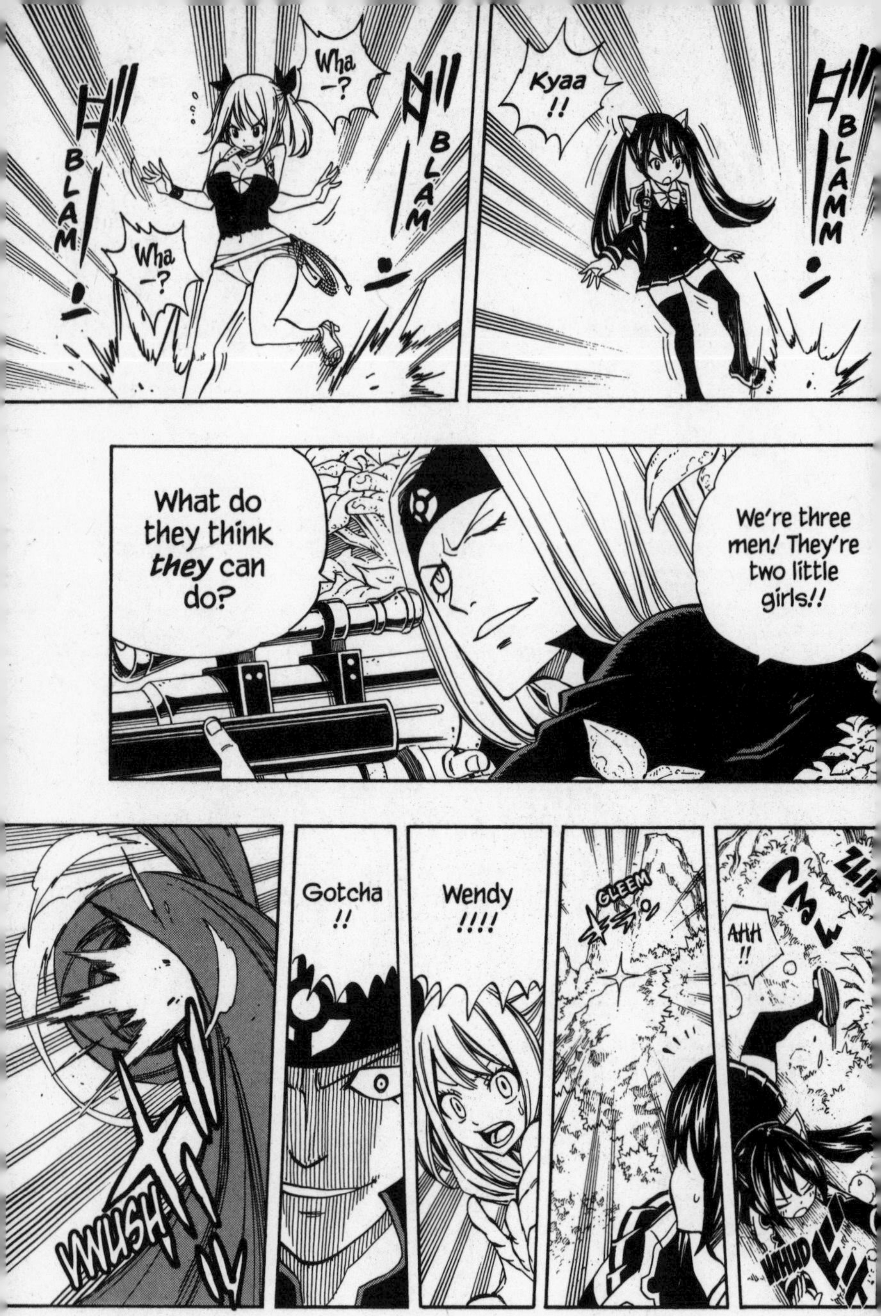

Kyaa!!
BLAMM
Wha—?
BLAM
BLAM
Wha—?
We're three men! They're two little girls!!
What do they think *they* can do?
ZLIP
AHH!!
WHUD
CLIK
GLEEM
Wendy!!!!
Gotcha!!
VWUSH

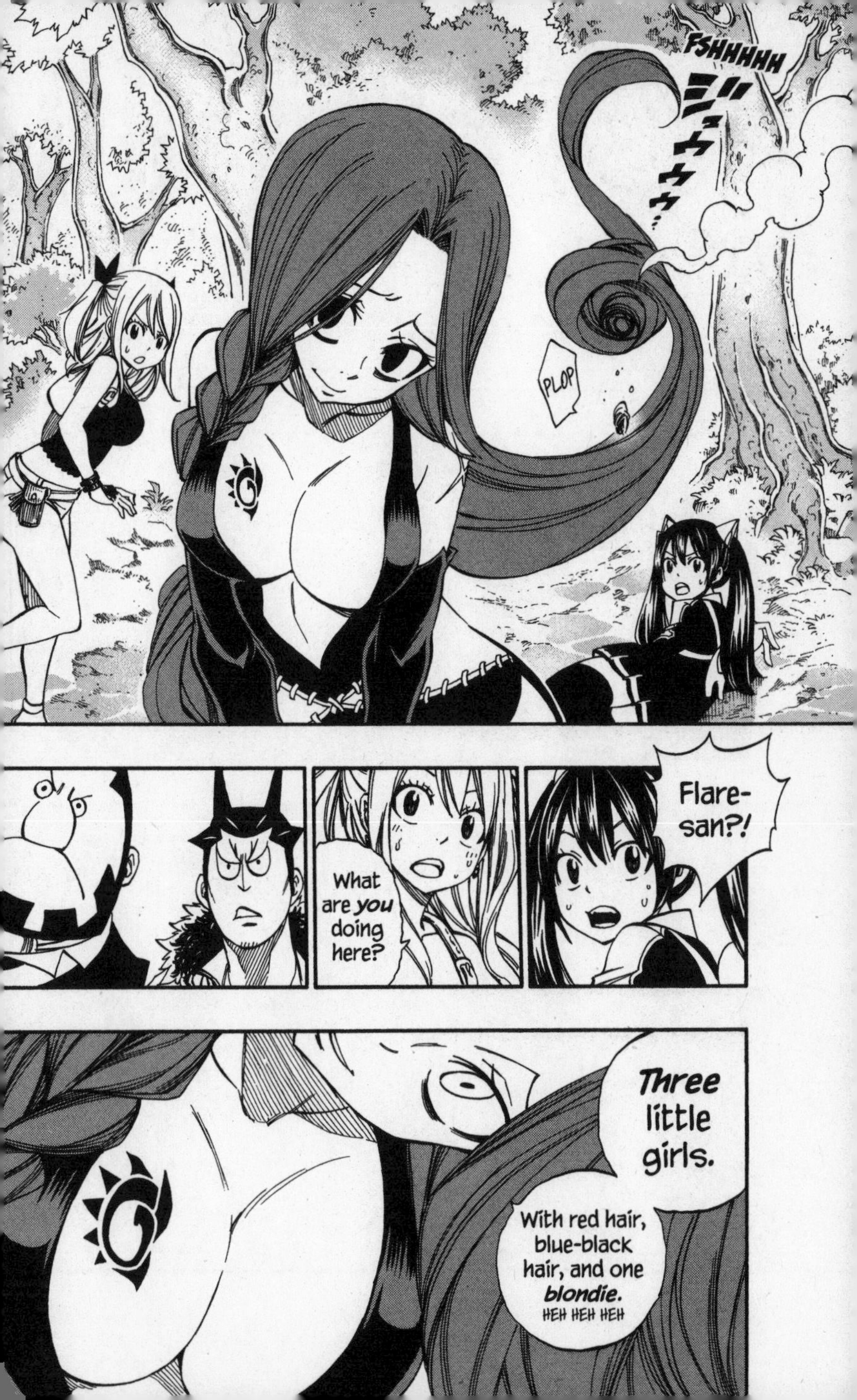
FSHHHHH
ジュウウウ…
PLOP
Flare-san?!
What are *you* doing here?
Three little girls.
With red hair, blue-black hair, and one ***blondie.***
HEH HEH HEH

FAIRY TAIL

Chapter 347: The Great Charge of the Red, the Blue, and the Blondie

↑
By the way, the costume is pink.

SABER TOOTH

Name: **Frosch**   Age: **?**

Magic:
Aera

Likes: Dislikes:
Frogs   **Worms**

Remarks

When Frosch was little, the cat believed it was a frog. Discovery of the truth brought on three days of tears.
Afterwards, the young Exceed received a frog costume, and has worn this beloved costume every day since.
From the day Frosch met Rogue, they've been inseparable. Lecter is another good friend.
Though a bit dim-witted, Frosch could beat Lecter in a footrace, believe it or not!
Frosch is destined to be killed in one year, but is not aware of this fate yet.

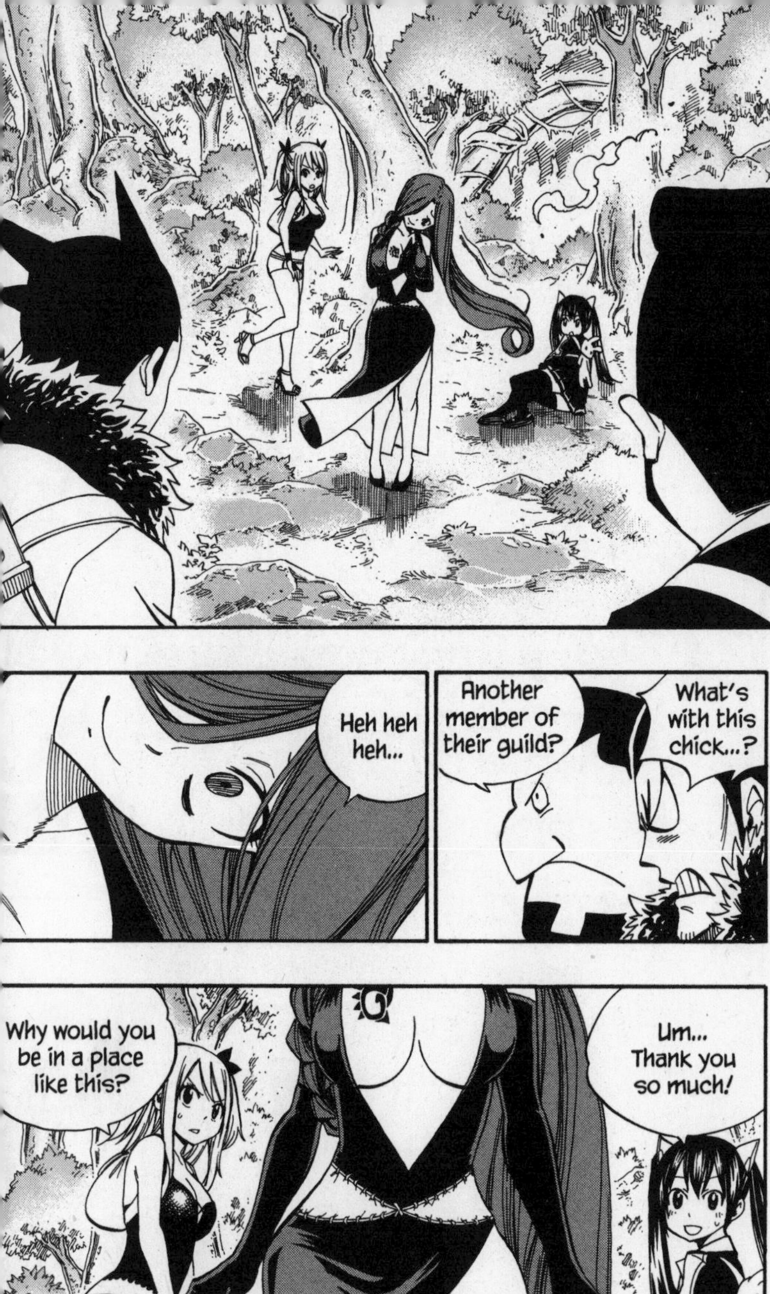

What's with this chick...?
Another member of their guild?
Heh heh heh...
Um... Thank you so much!
Why would you be in a place like this?

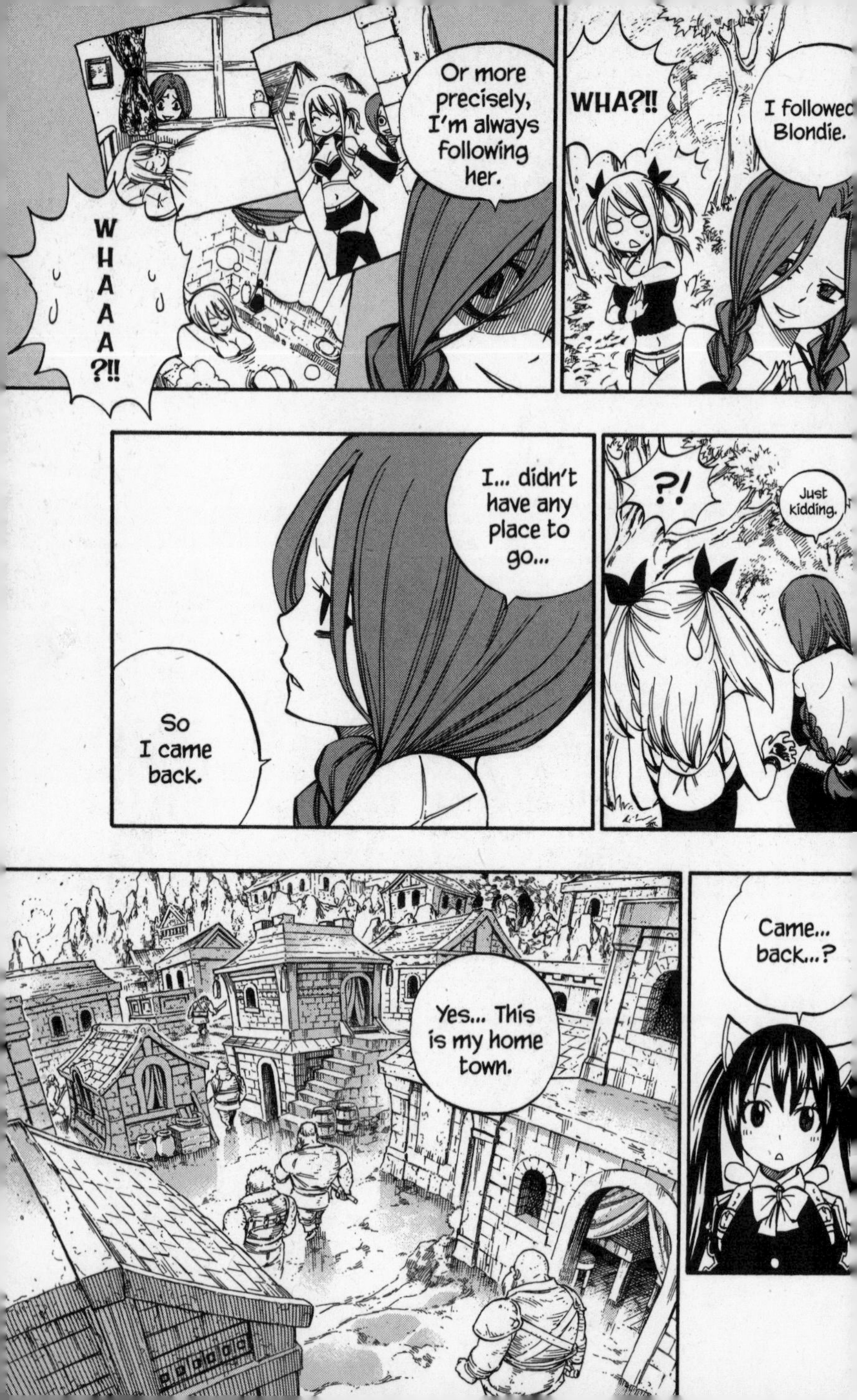
I followed Blondie.
WHA?!!
Or more precisely, I'm always following her.
WHAAAA?!!
?!
Just kidding.
I... didn't have any place to go...
So I came back.
Came... back...?
Yes... This is my home town.

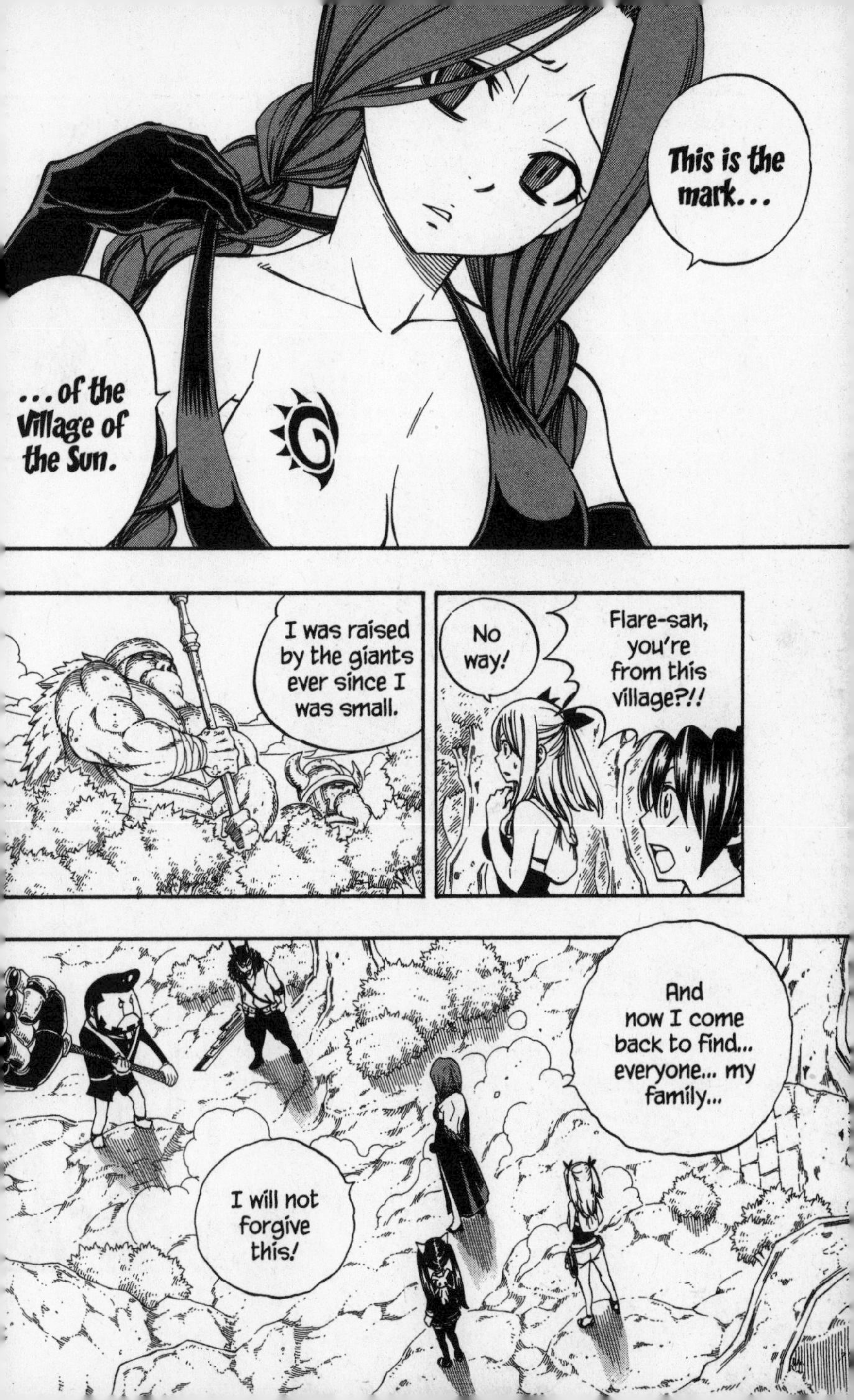
This is the mark...
...of the Village of the Sun.
Flare-san, you're from this village?!!
No way!
I was raised by the giants ever since I was small.
And now I come back to find... everyone... my family...
I will not forgive this!

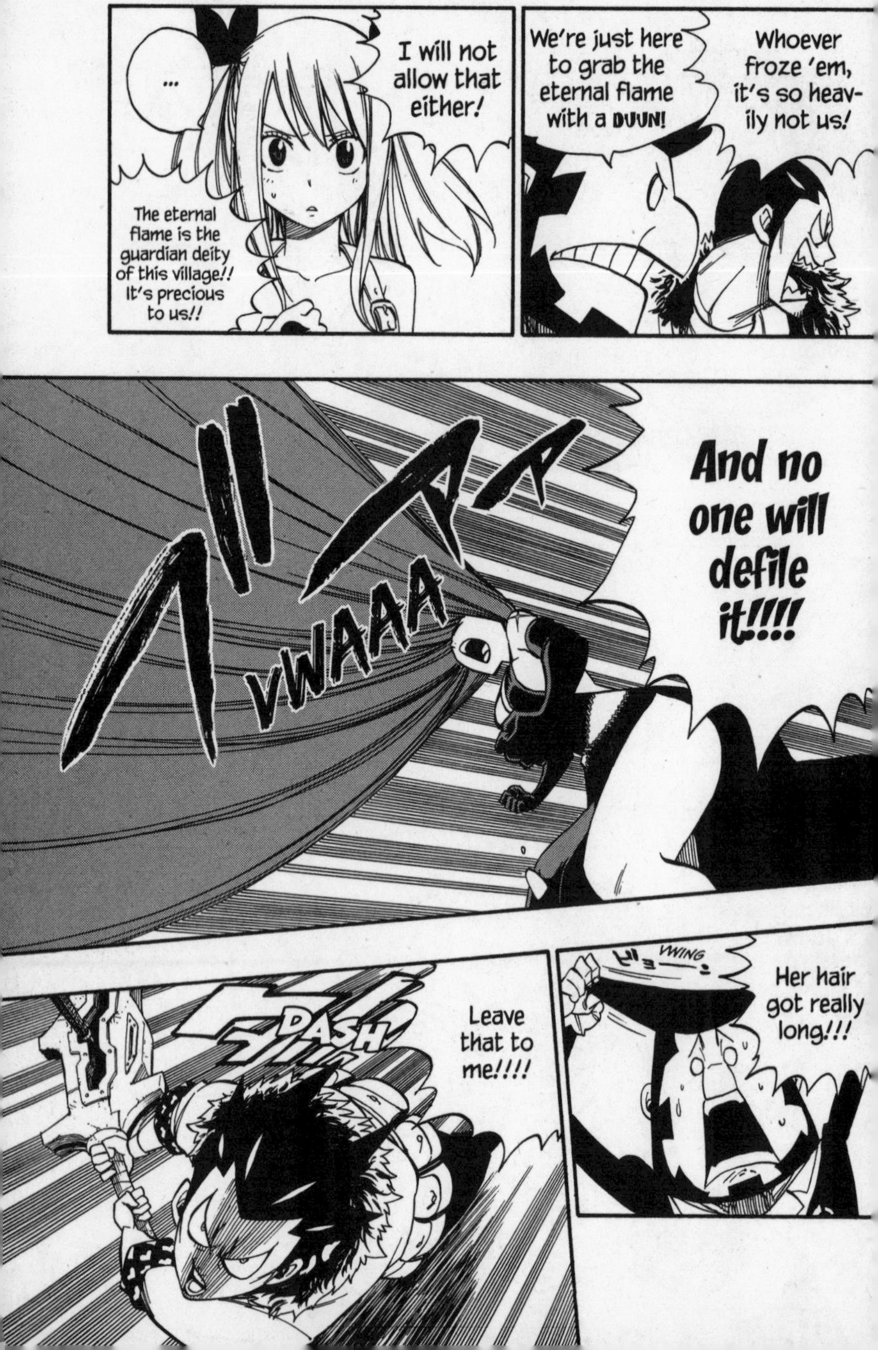
Whoever froze 'em, it's so heavily not us!
We're just here to grab the eternal flame with a DUUN!
I will not allow that either!
...
The eternal flame is the guardian deity of this village!! It's precious to us!!
And no one will defile it!!!!
VWAAA
VWING
Her hair got really long!!!
Leave that to me!!!!
DASH

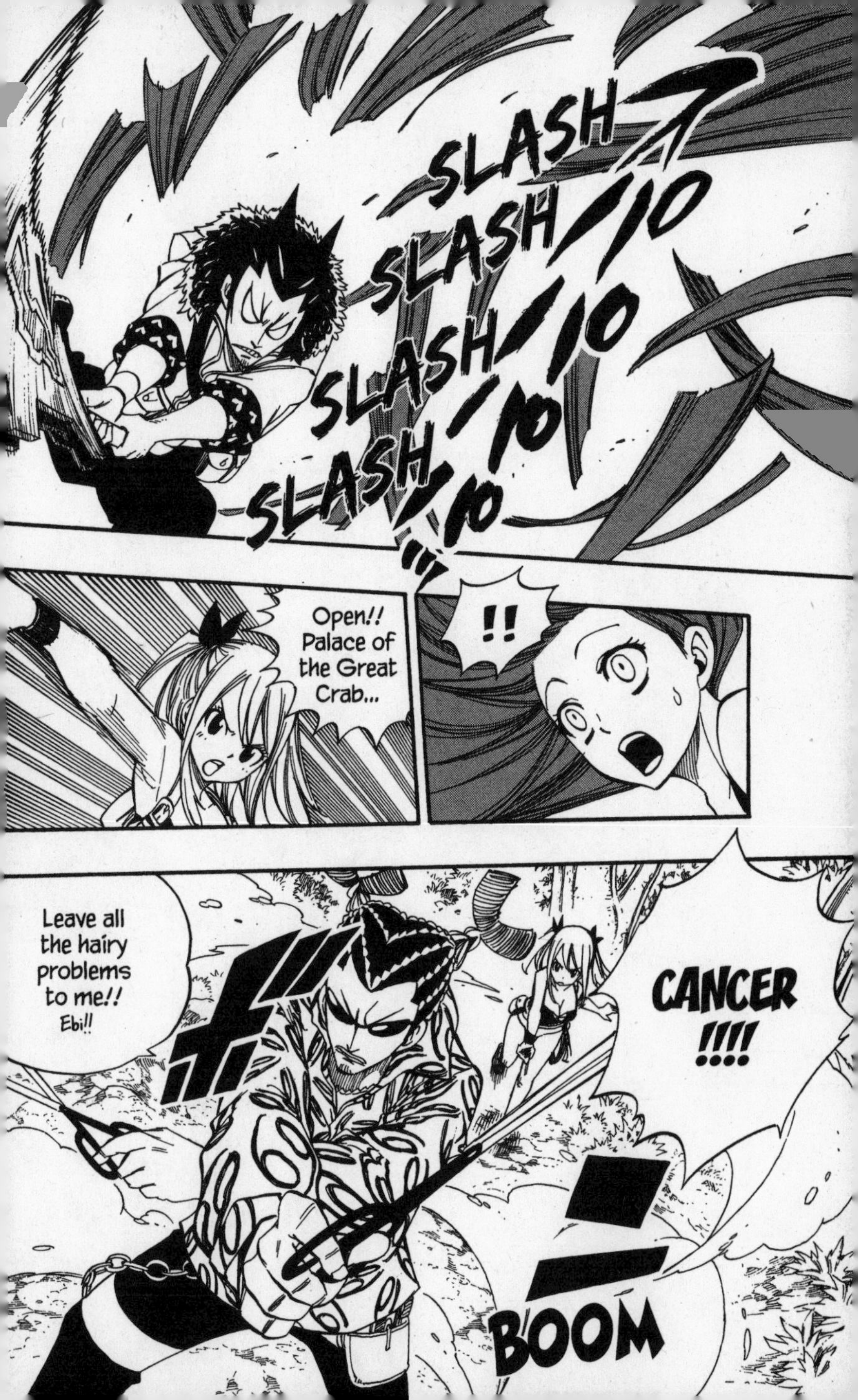
SLASH
SLASH
SLASH
SLASH
!!
Open!! Palace of the Great Crab...
CANCER!!!!
Leave all the hairy problems to me!! Ebi!!
BOOM

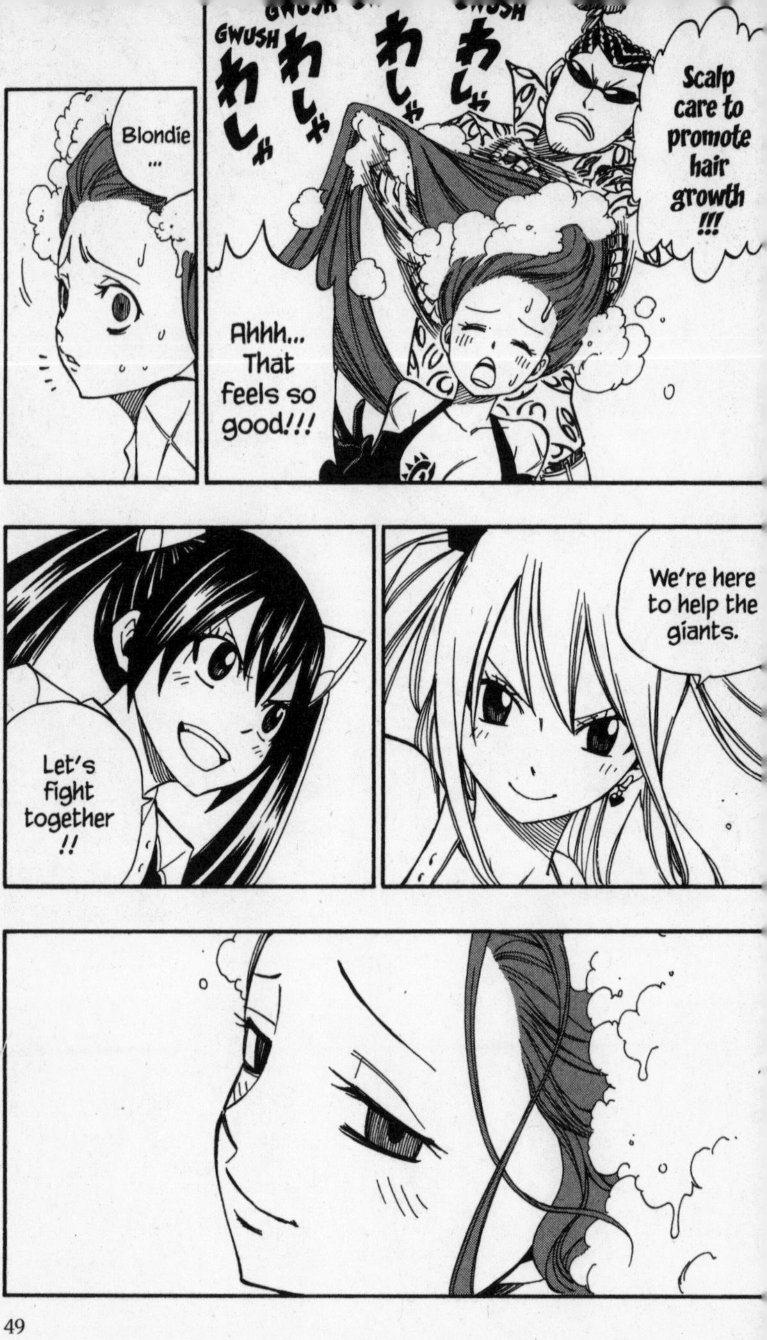
Scalp care to promote hair growth!!!
GWUSH
わしゃ
わしゃ
GWUSH
わしゃ
GWUSH
わしゃ
Ahhh... That feels so good!!!
Blondie ...
We're here to help the giants.
Let's fight together!!

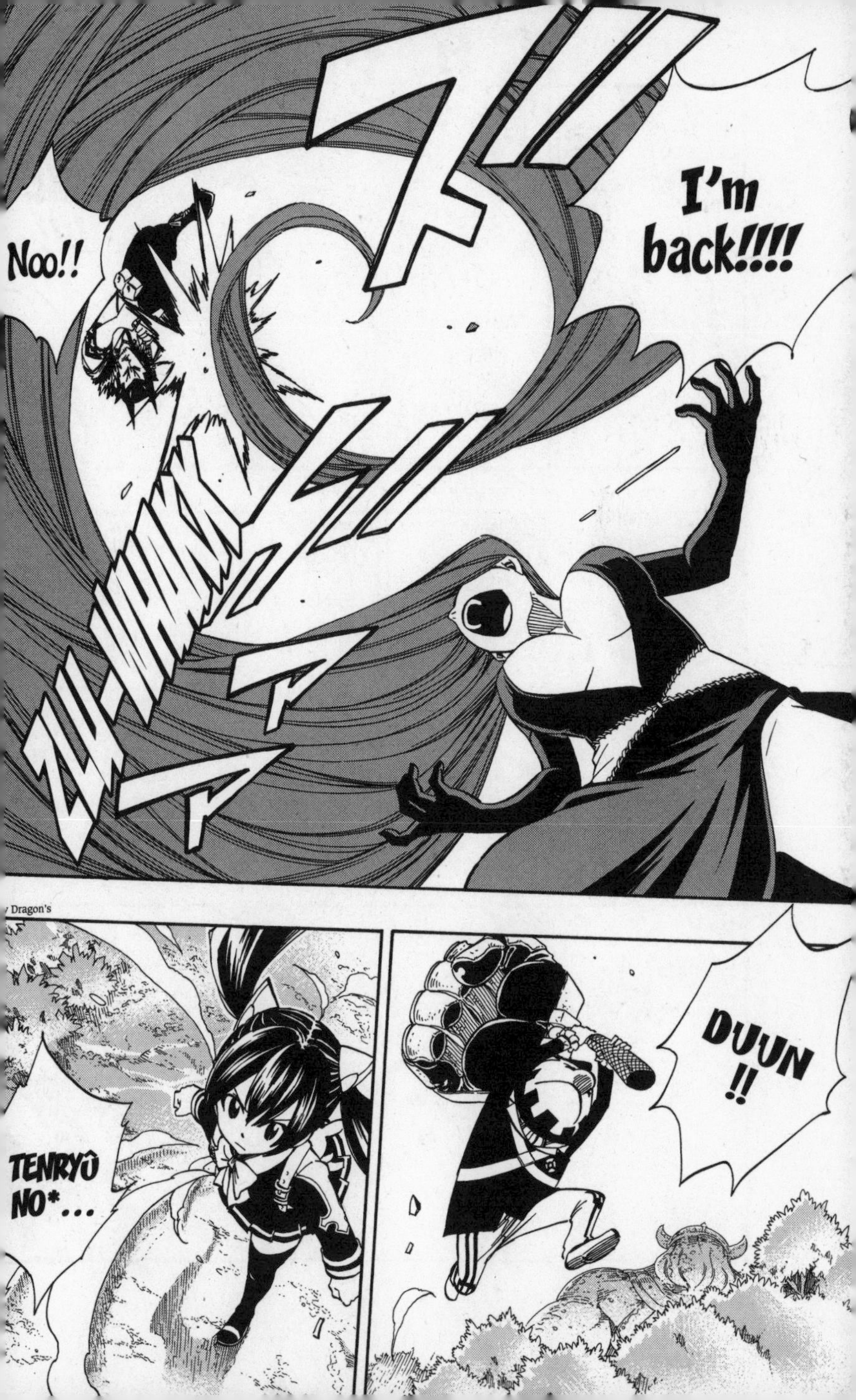
I'm back!!!!
ZU-WHAM
Noo!!
DUUN !!
TENRYÛ NO*...

y Dragon's

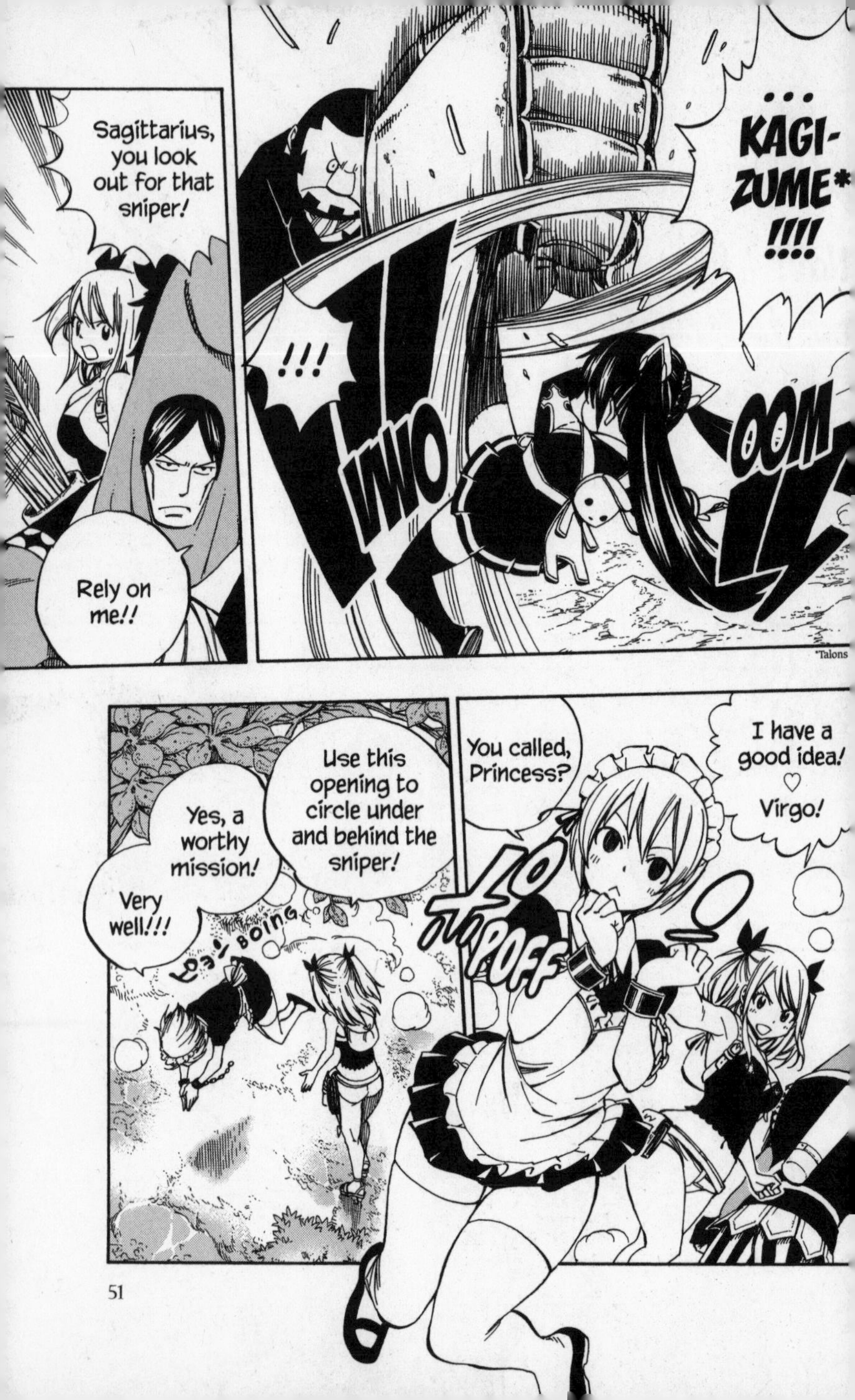
...KAGI-ZUME*!!!!
!!!
VWO OOM
Sagittarius, you look out for that sniper!
Rely on me!!
I have a good idea! ♡ Virgo!
POFF
You called, Princess?
Use this opening to circle under and behind the sniper!
Yes, a worthy mission!
Very well!!!
BOING BOING

*Talons

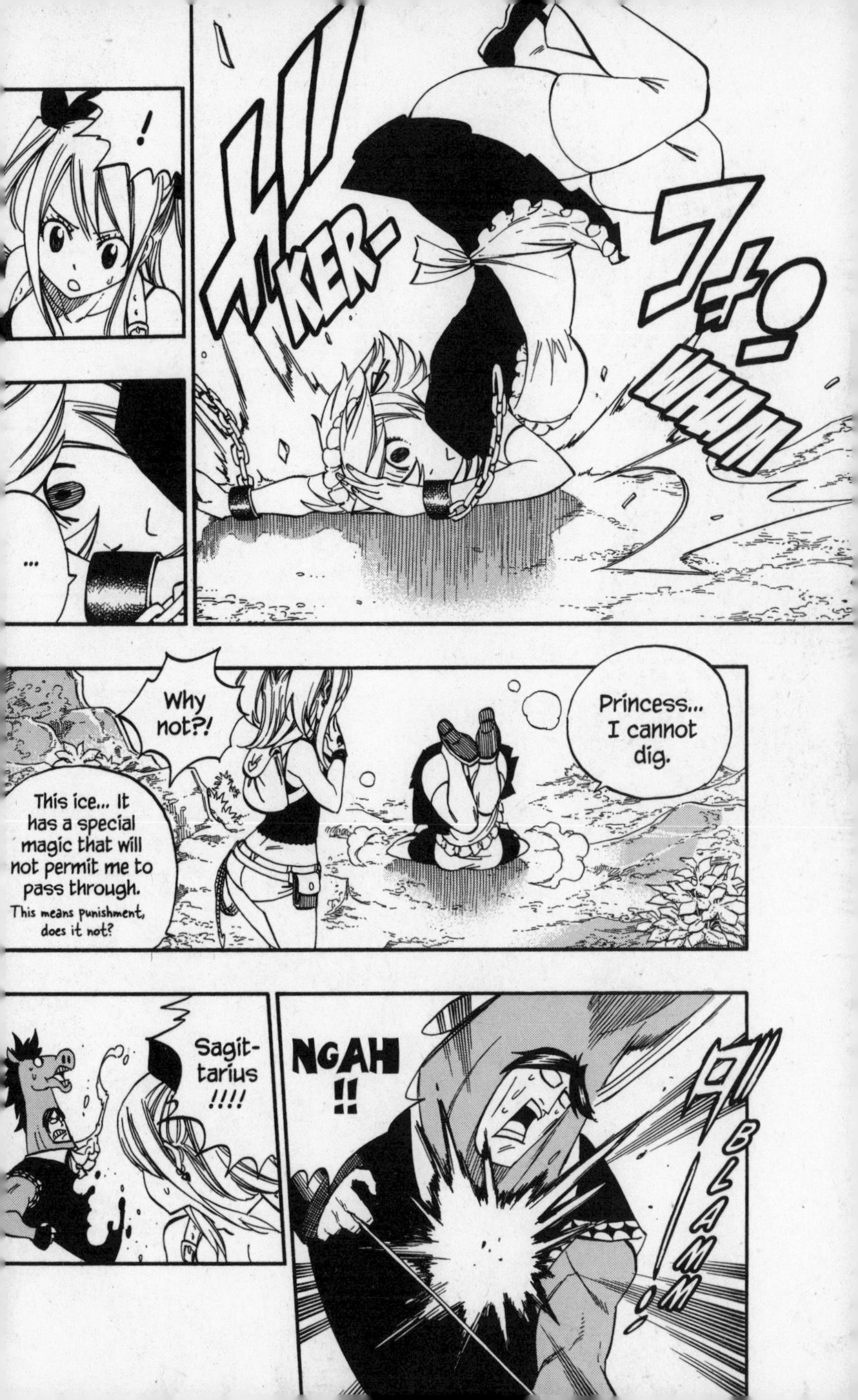
KER-
WHAM
!
...
Princess... I cannot dig.
Why not?!
This ice... It has a special magic that will not permit me to pass through.
This means punishment, does it not?
NGAH!!
BLAM!
Sagit-tarius!!!!

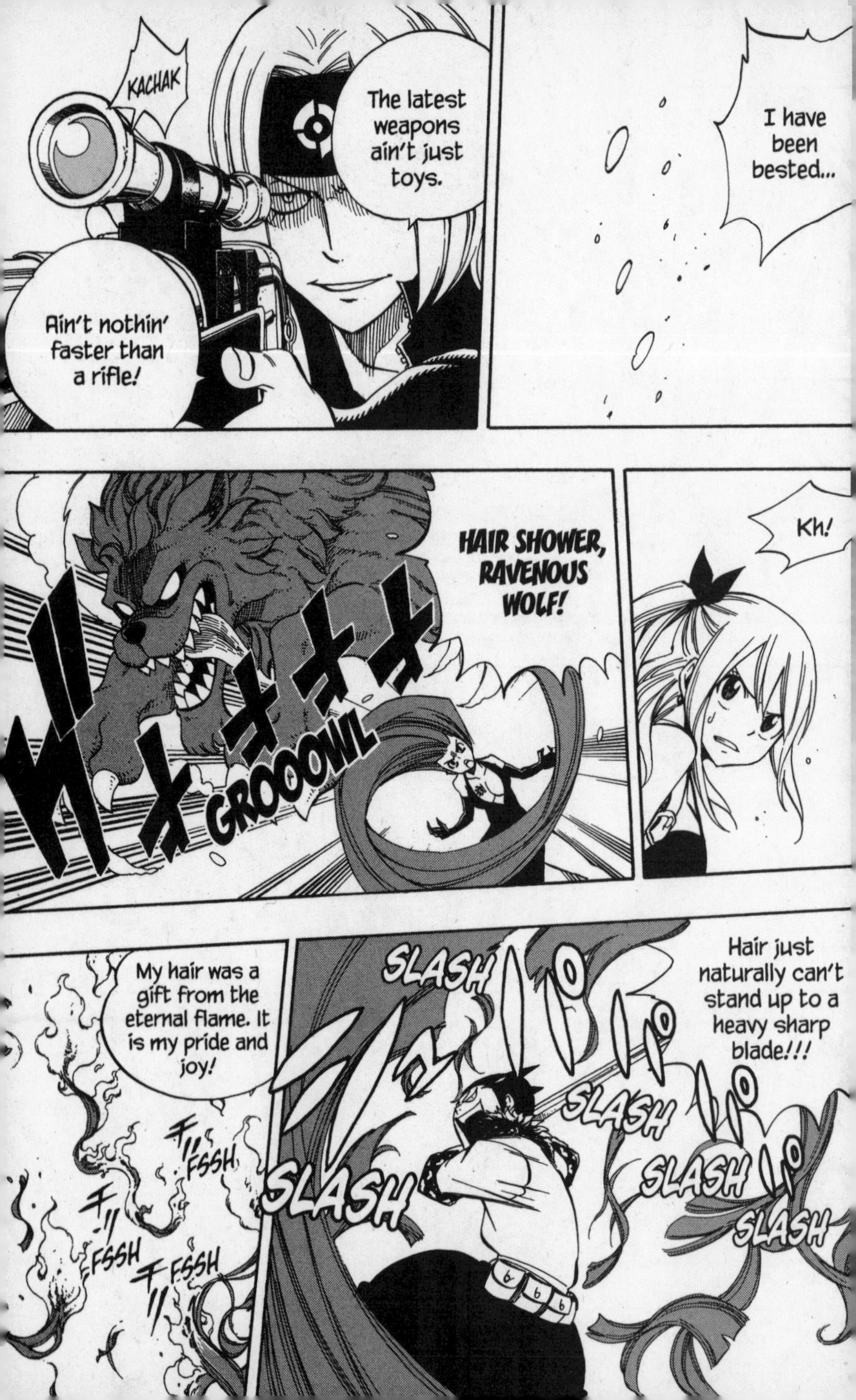
I have been bested...
KACHAK
The latest weapons ain't just toys.
Ain't nothin' faster than a rifle!
Kh!
HAIR SHOWER, RAVENOUS WOLF!
GROOOWL
Hair just naturally can't stand up to a heavy sharp blade!!!
SLASH
SLASH
SLASH
SLASH
SLASH
My hair was a gift from the eternal flame. It is my pride and joy!
FSSH
FSSH
FSSH

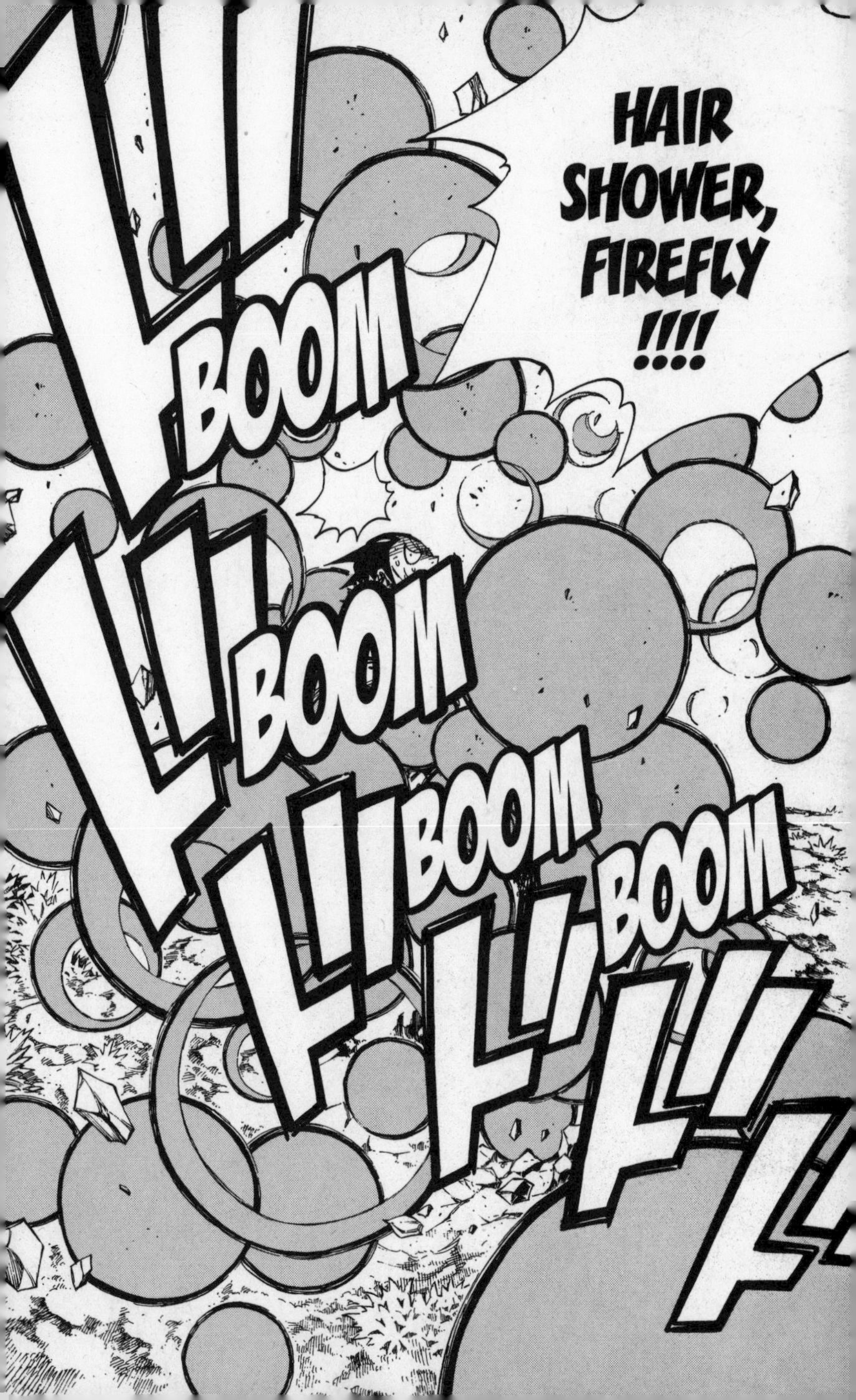
HAIR SHOWER, FIREFLY!!!!
BOOM
BOOM
BOOM
BOOM

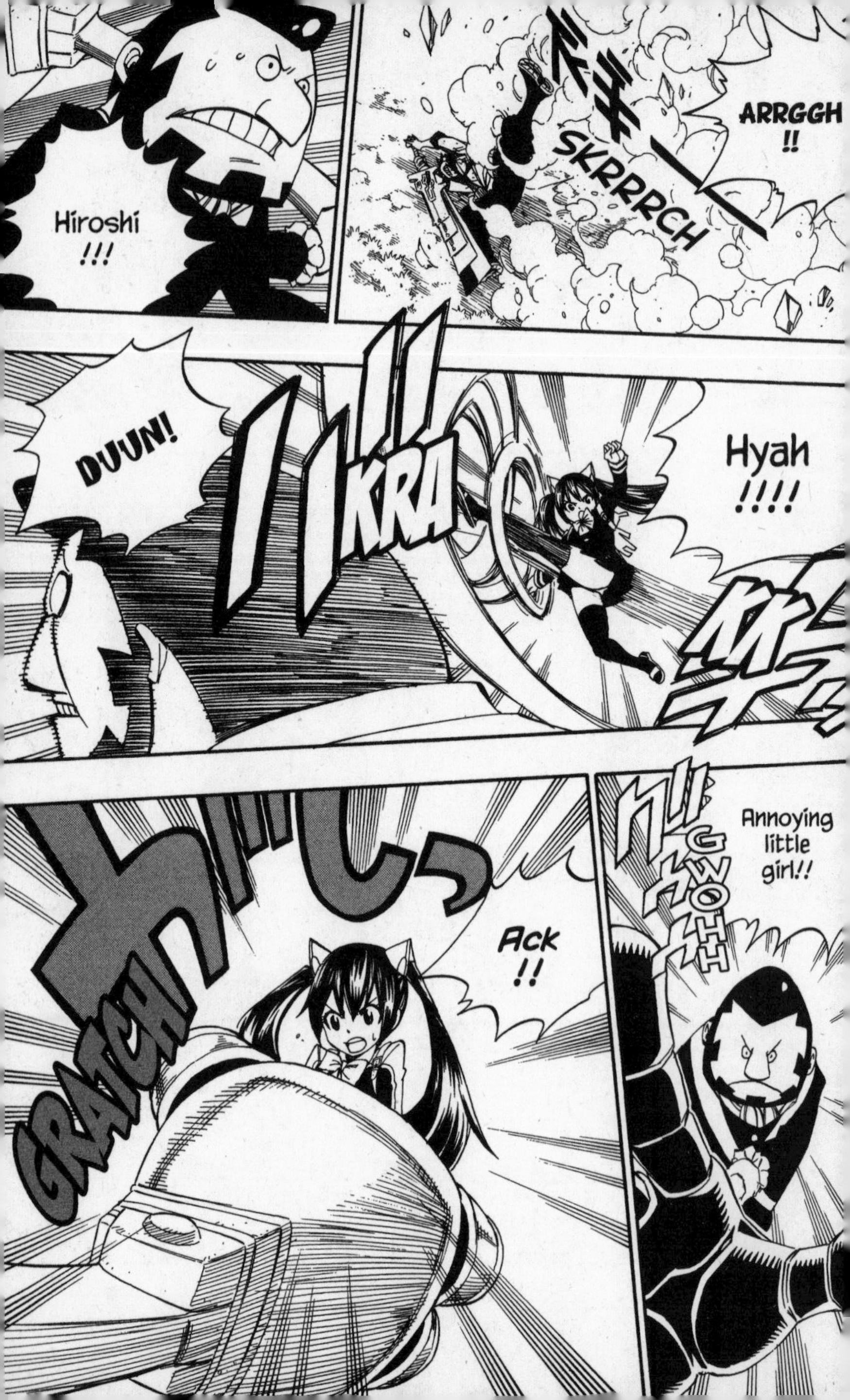
ARRGGH!!
SKRRRCH
Hiroshi!!!
Hyah!!!!
KRA
DUUN!
Annoying little girl!!
GWOHH
Ack!!
GRATCH

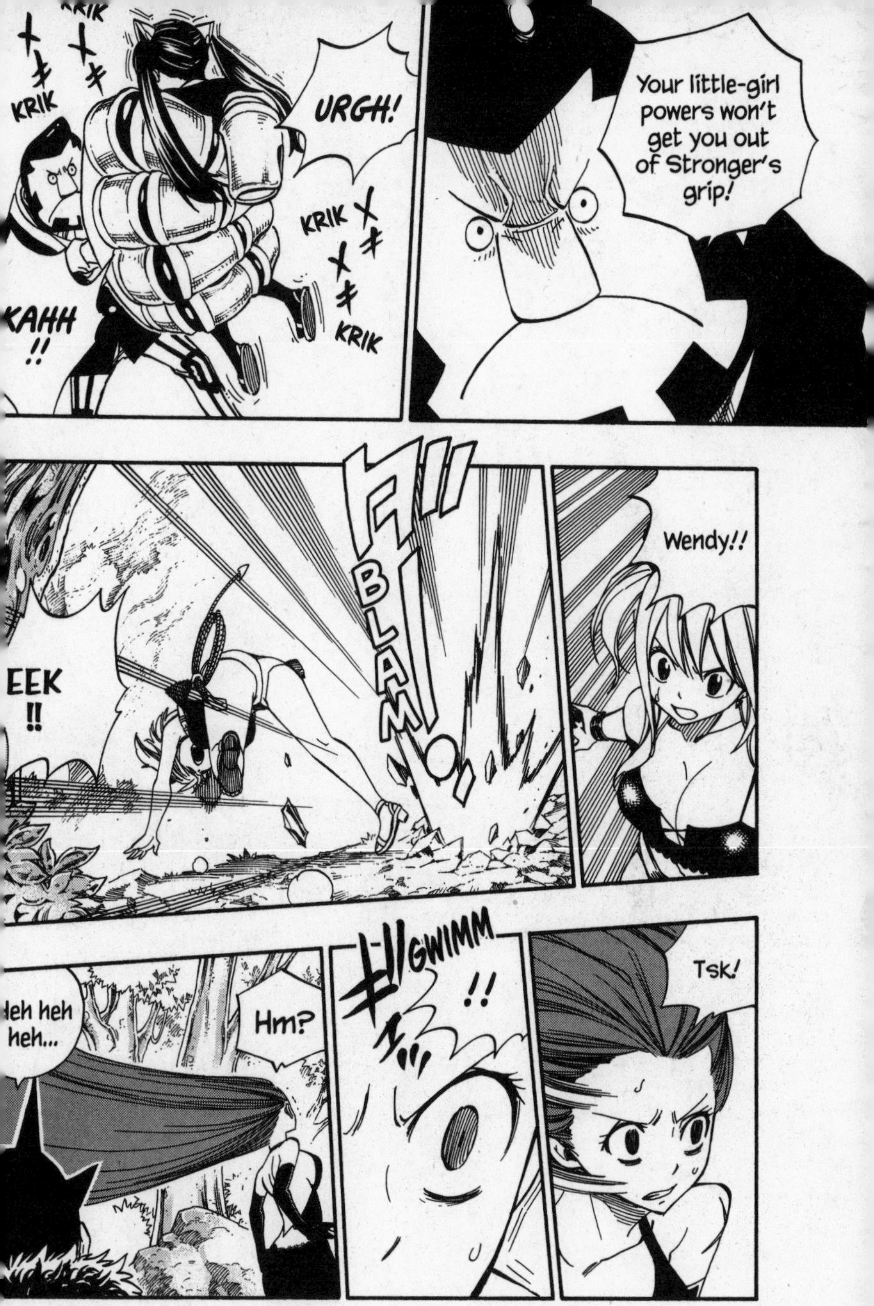
Your little-girl powers won't get you out of Stronger's grip!
URGH!
KRIK
KRIK
KRIK
KRIK
KAHH!!
Wendy!!
BLAM
EEK!!
Tsk!
GWIMM
!!
Hm?
eh heh heh...

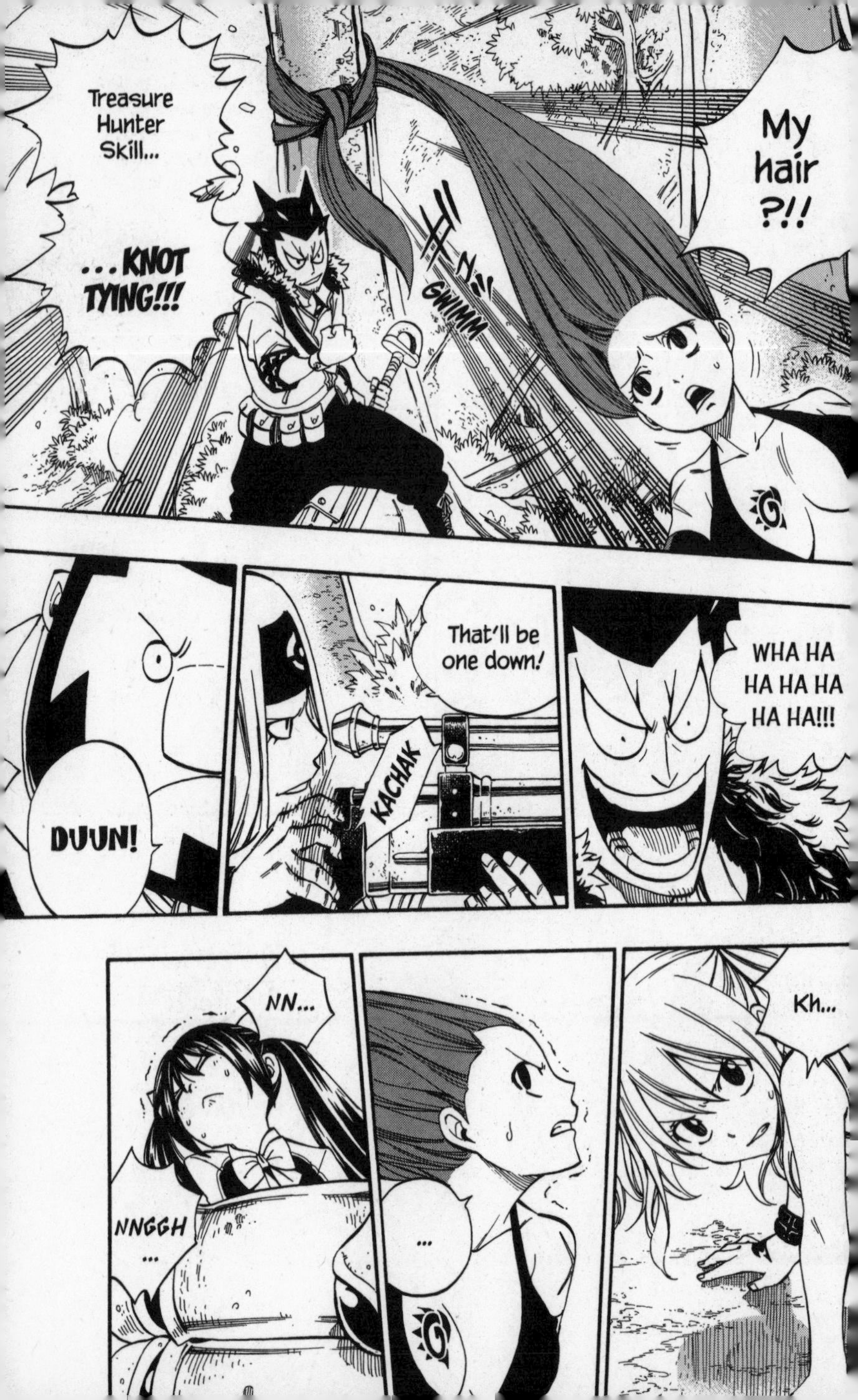
My hair ?!!
GWIMM
Treasure Hunter Skill...
...KNOT TYING!!!
WHA HA HA HA HA HA HA!!!
That'll be one down!
KACHAK
DUUN!
Kh...
...
NN...
NNGGH ...

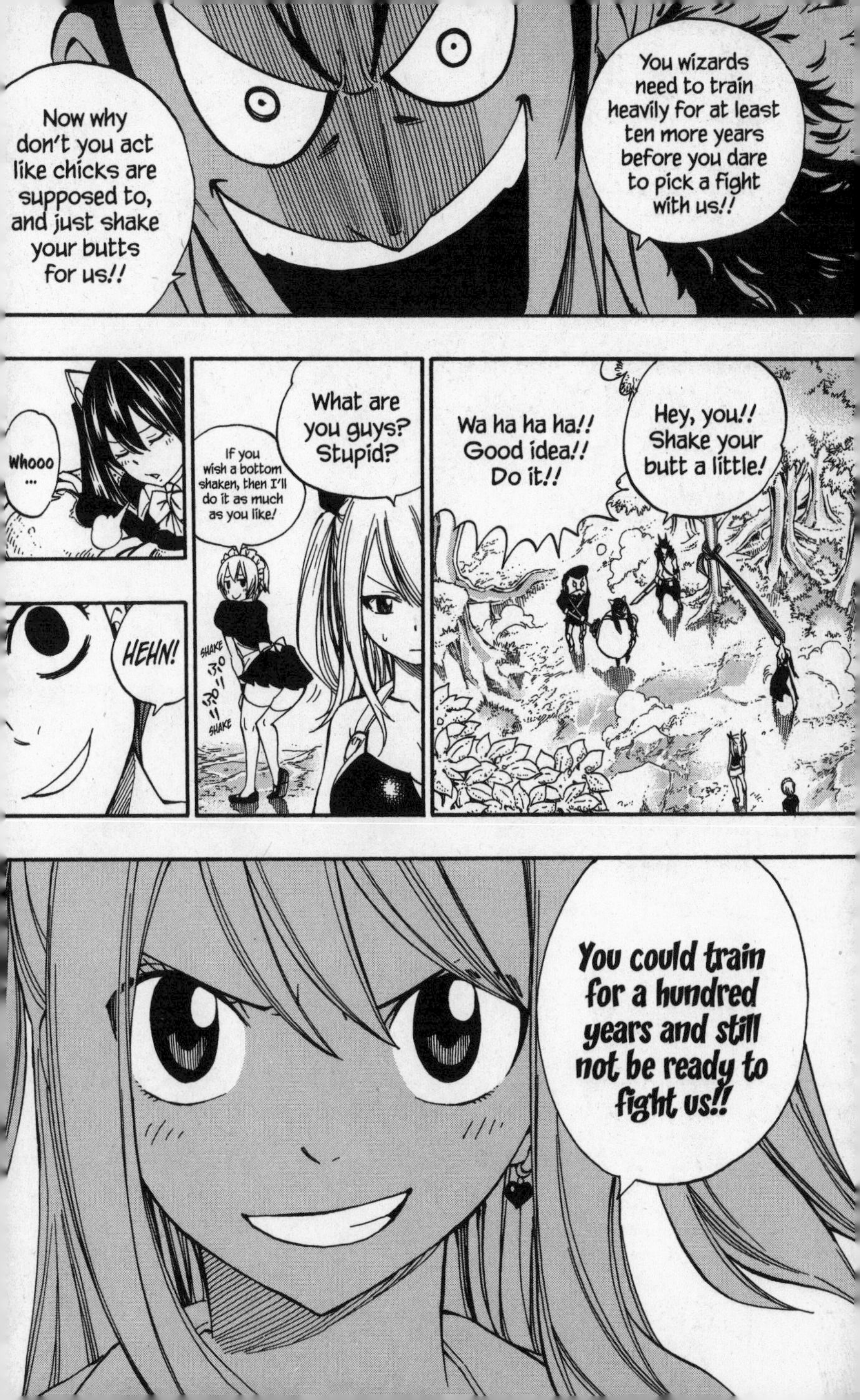

You wizards need to train heavily for at least ten more years before you dare to pick a fight with us!!
Now why don't you act like chicks are supposed to, and just shake your butts for us!!
Hey, you!! Shake your butt a little!
Wa ha ha ha!! Good idea!! Do it!!
What are you guys? Stupid?
If you wish a bottom shaken, then I'll do it as much as you like!
SHAKE
SHAKE
Whooo ...
HEHN!
You could train for a hundred years and still not be ready to fight us!!

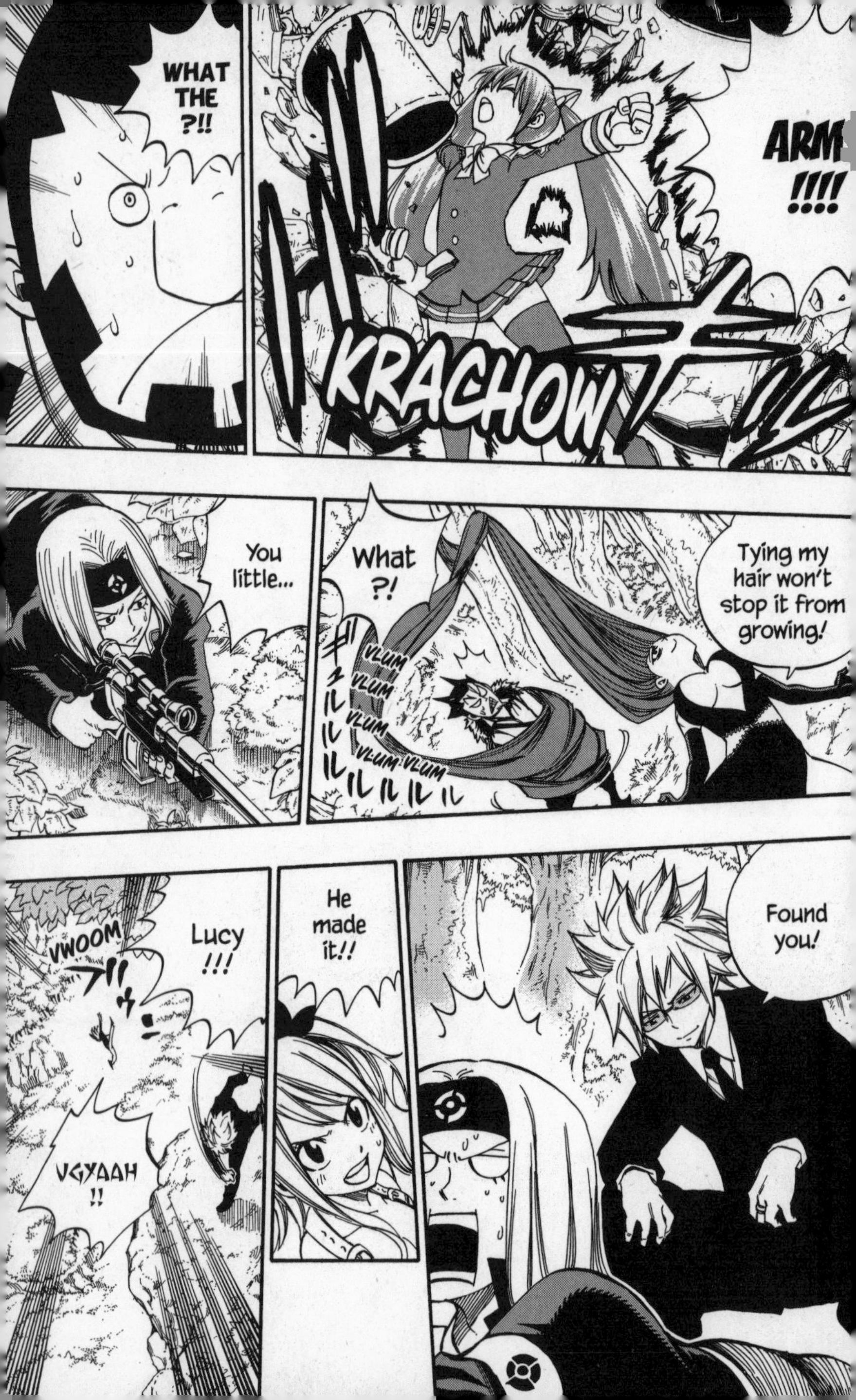
ARM !!!!
KRACHOW
WHAT THE ?!!
Tying my hair won't stop it from growing!
What ?!
VLUM VLUM VLUM VLUM VLUM
You little...
Found you!
He made it!!
Lucy !!!
VWOOM
UGYAAH !!

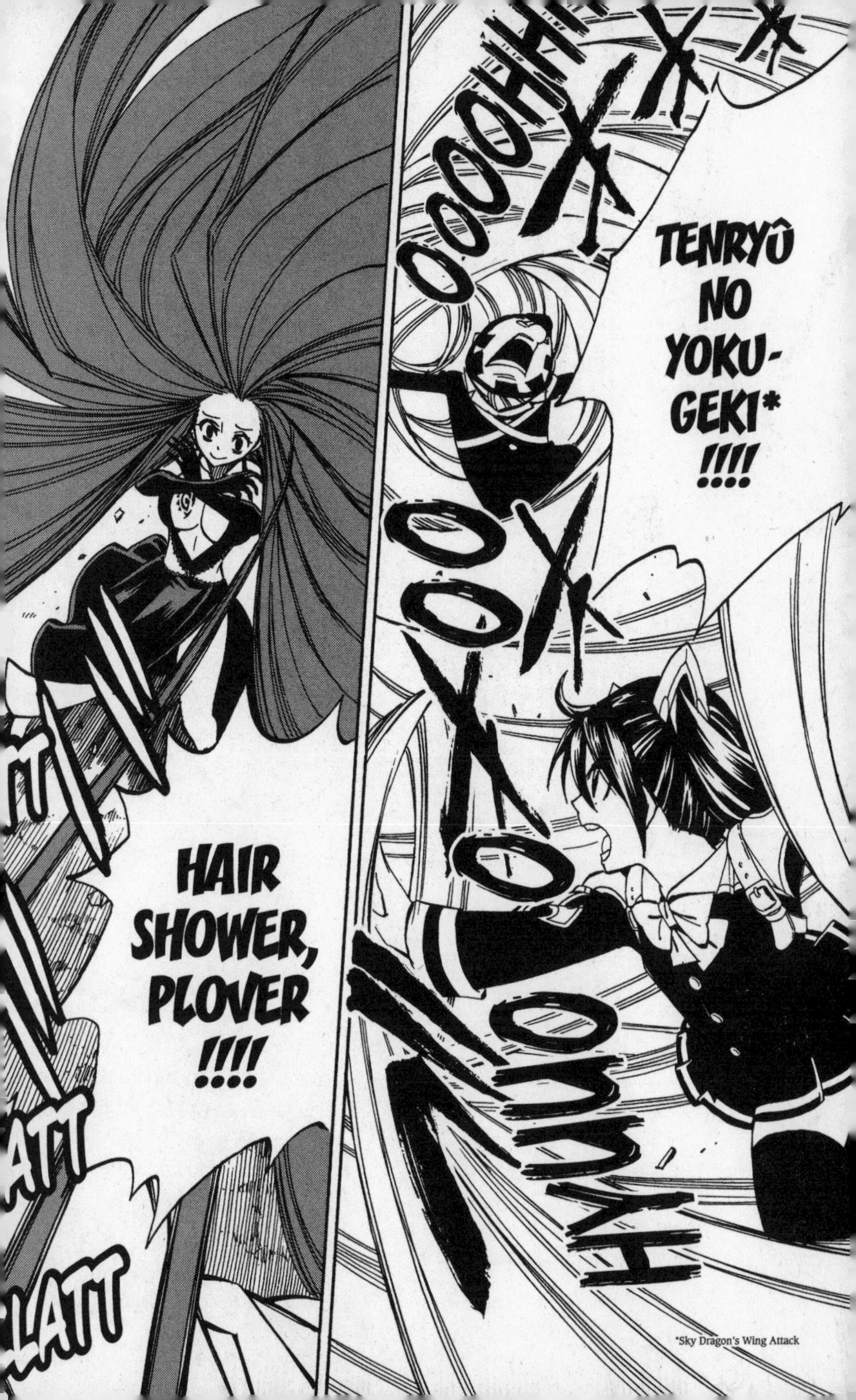
TENRYÛ NO YOKU-GEKI* !!!!
HAIR SHOWER, PLOVER !!!!
*Sky Dragon's Wing Attack

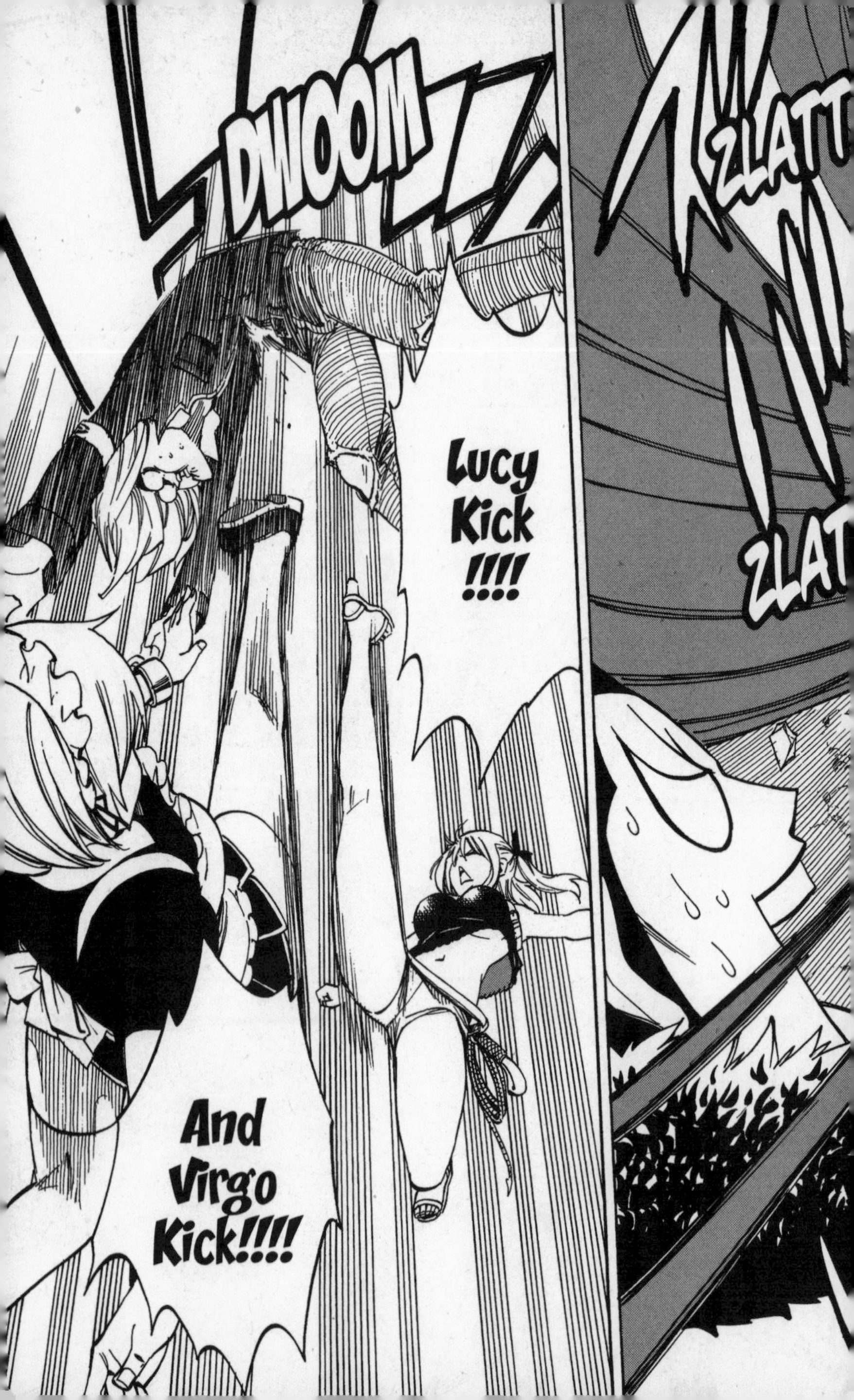
ZLATT
ZLAT
DWOOM
Lucy Kick!!!!
And Virgo Kick!!!!

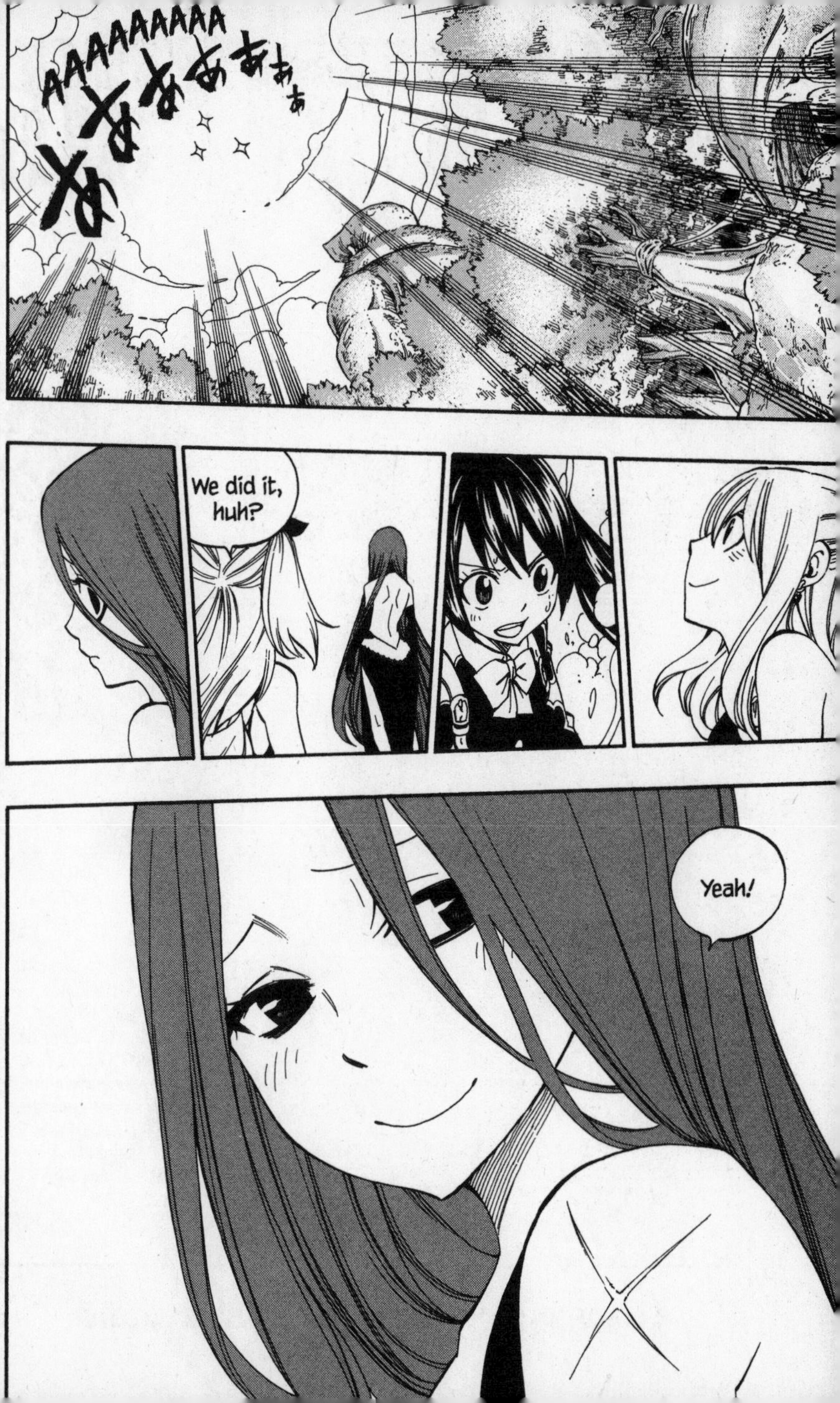
AAAAAAAAA
We did it, huh?
Yeah!

FAIRY TAIL

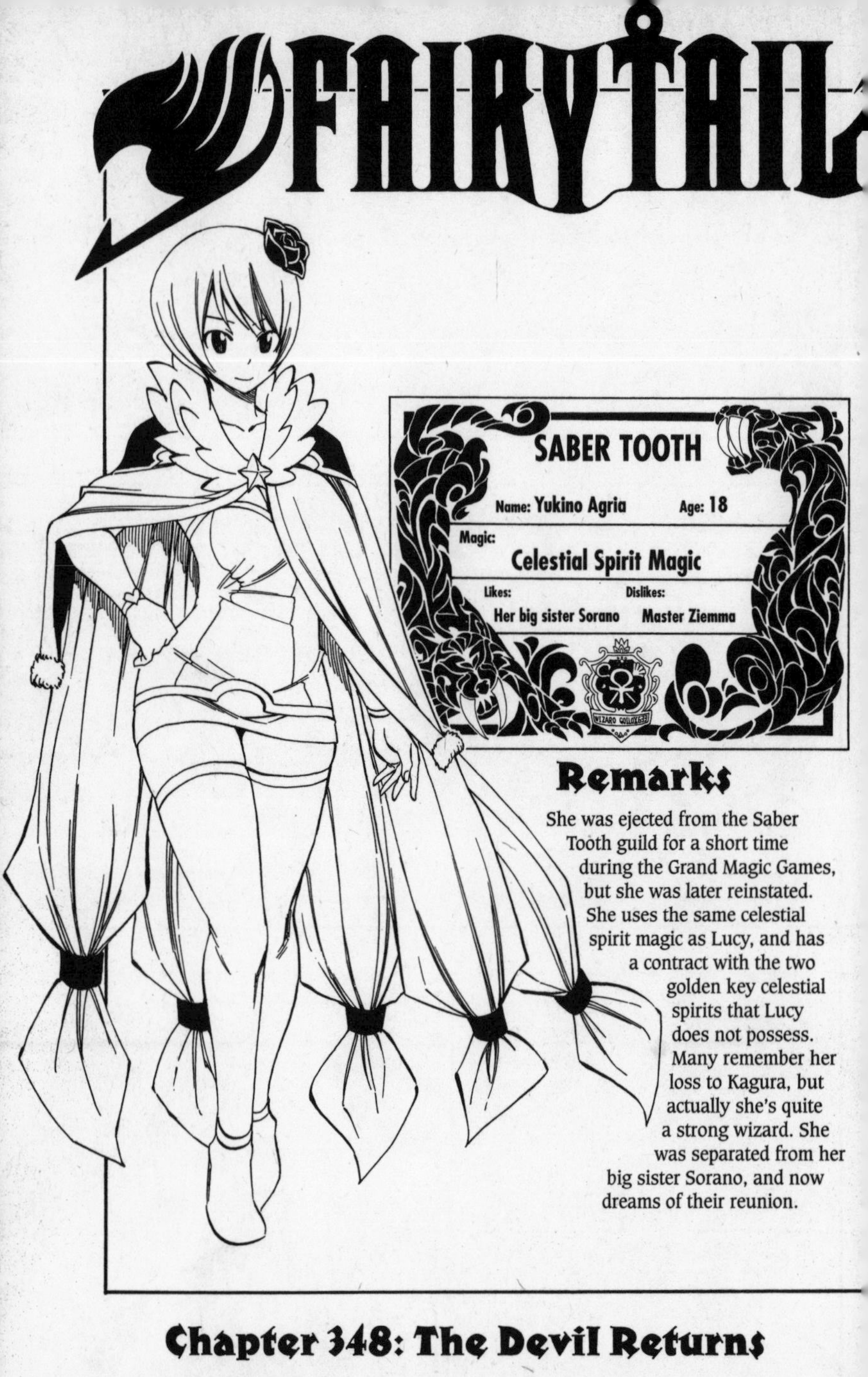

SABER TOOTH

Name: Yukino Agria **Age:** 18

Magic: Celestial Spirit Magic

Likes: Her big sister Sorano

Dislikes: Master Ziemma

Remarks

She was ejected from the Saber Tooth guild for a short time during the Grand Magic Games, but she was later reinstated. She uses the same celestial spirit magic as Lucy, and has a contract with the two golden key celestial spirits that Lucy does not possess. Many remember her loss to Kagura, but actually she's quite a strong wizard. She was separated from her big sister Sorano, and now dreams of their reunion.

Chapter 348: The Devil Returns

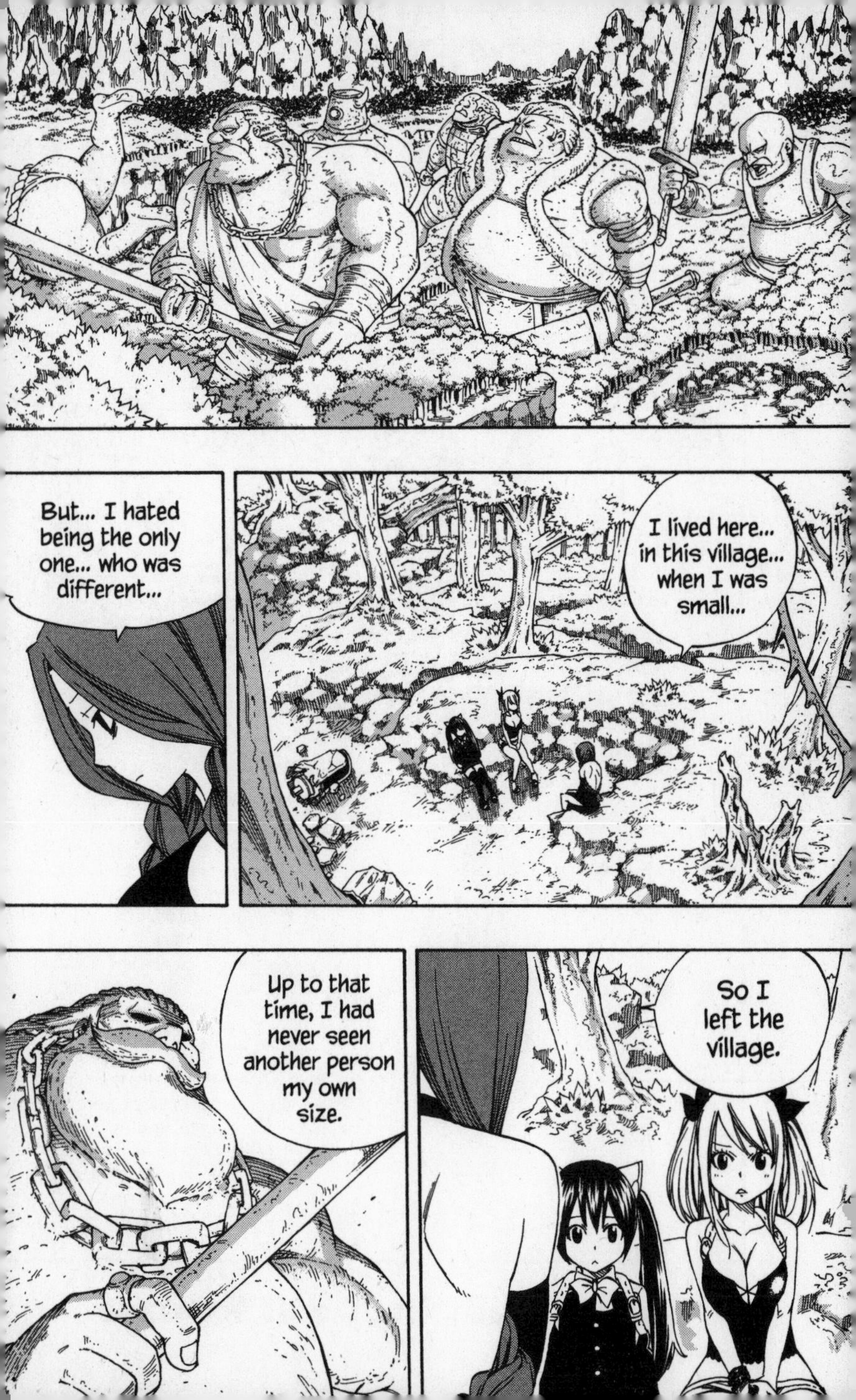
I lived here... in this village... when I was small...
But... I hated being the only one... who was different...
So I left the village.
Up to that time, I had never seen another person my own size.

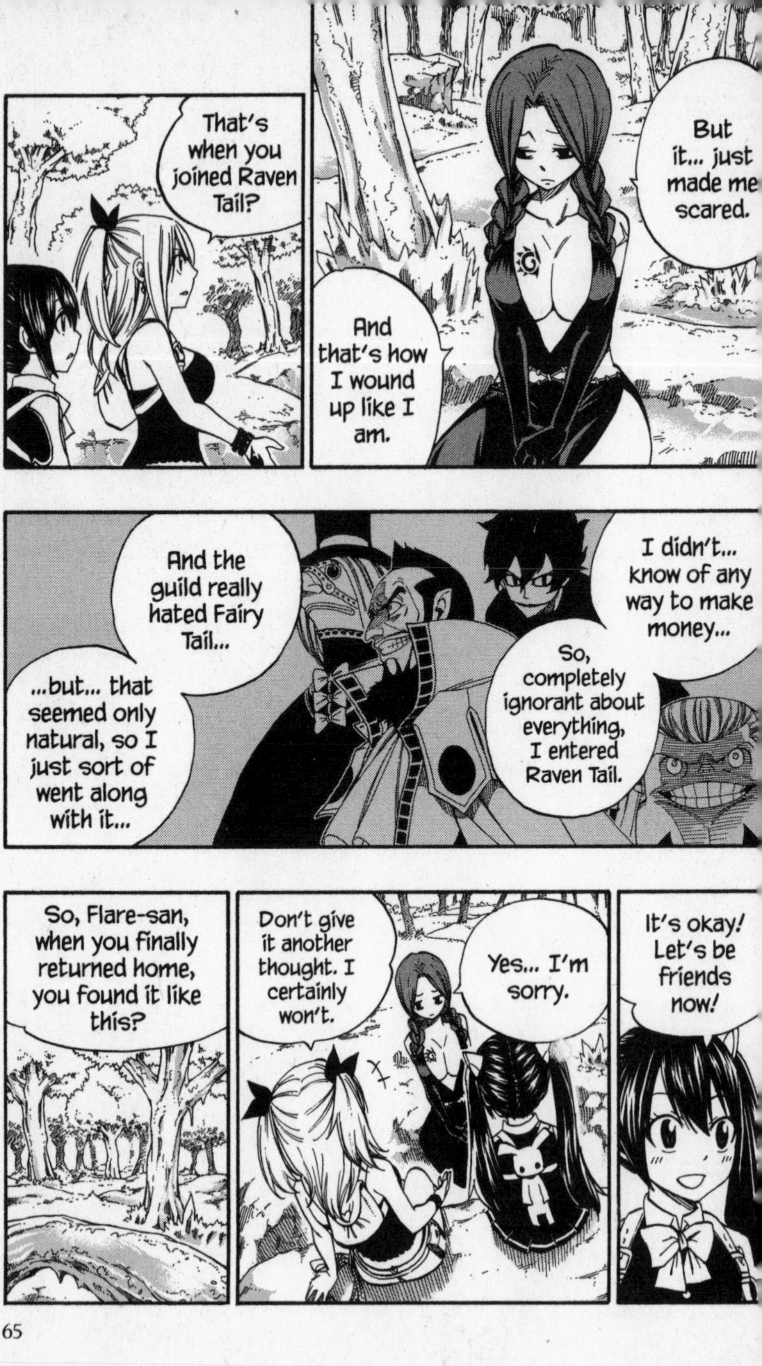
But it... just made me scared.
And that's how I wound up like I am.
That's when you joined Raven Tail?
I didn't... know of any way to make money...
So, completely ignorant about everything, I entered Raven Tail.
And the guild really hated Fairy Tail...
...but... that seemed only natural, so I just sort of went along with it...
It's okay! Let's be friends now!
Yes... I'm sorry.
Don't give it another thought. I certainly won't.
So, Flare-san, when you finally returned home, you found it like this?

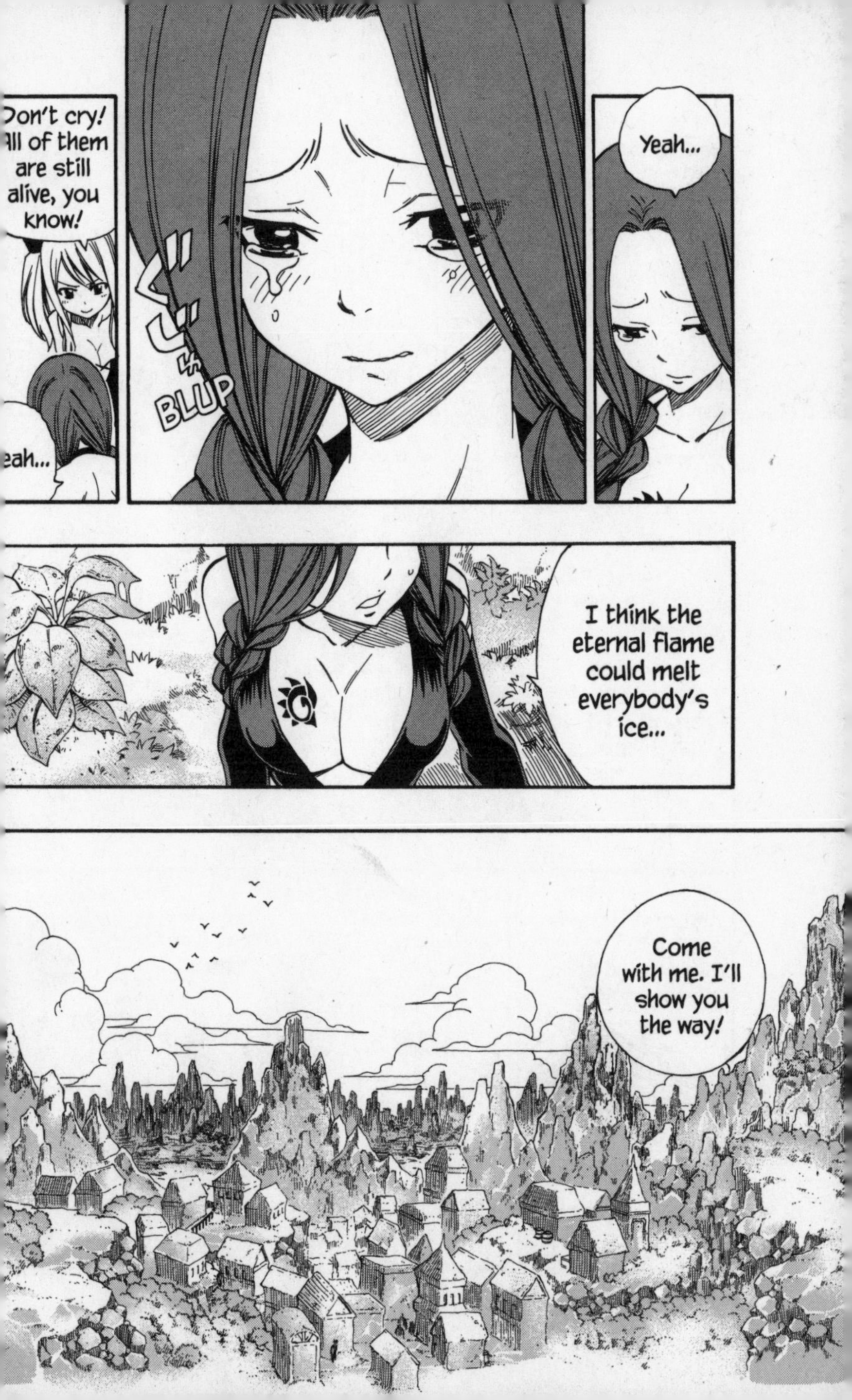
Yeah...
BLUP
Don't cry! All of them are still alive, you know!
eah...
I think the eternal flame could melt everybody's ice...
Come with me. I'll show you the way!

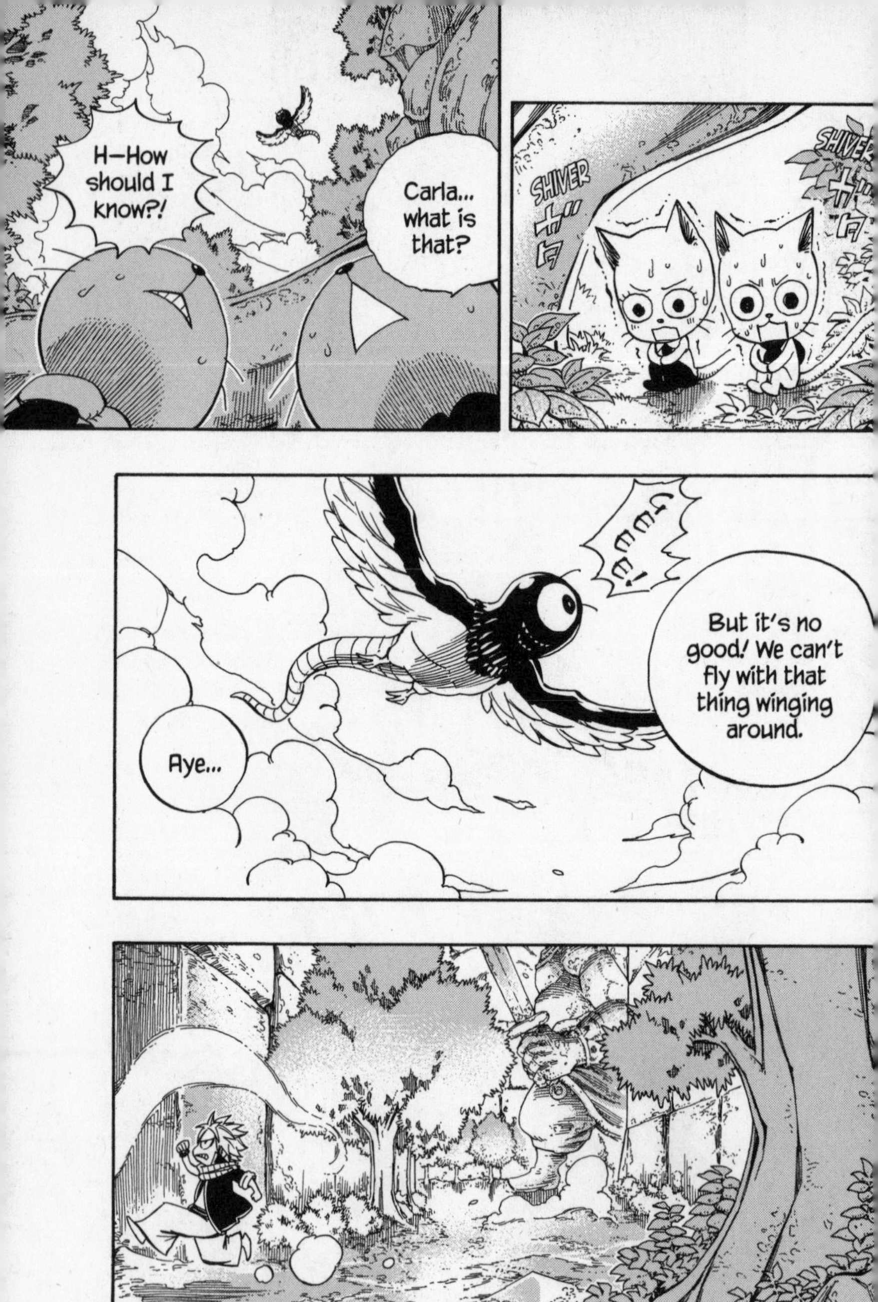
SHIVER
SHIVER
Carla... what is that?
H—How should I know?!
GEEEE!
But it's no good! We can't fly with that thing winging around.
Aye...

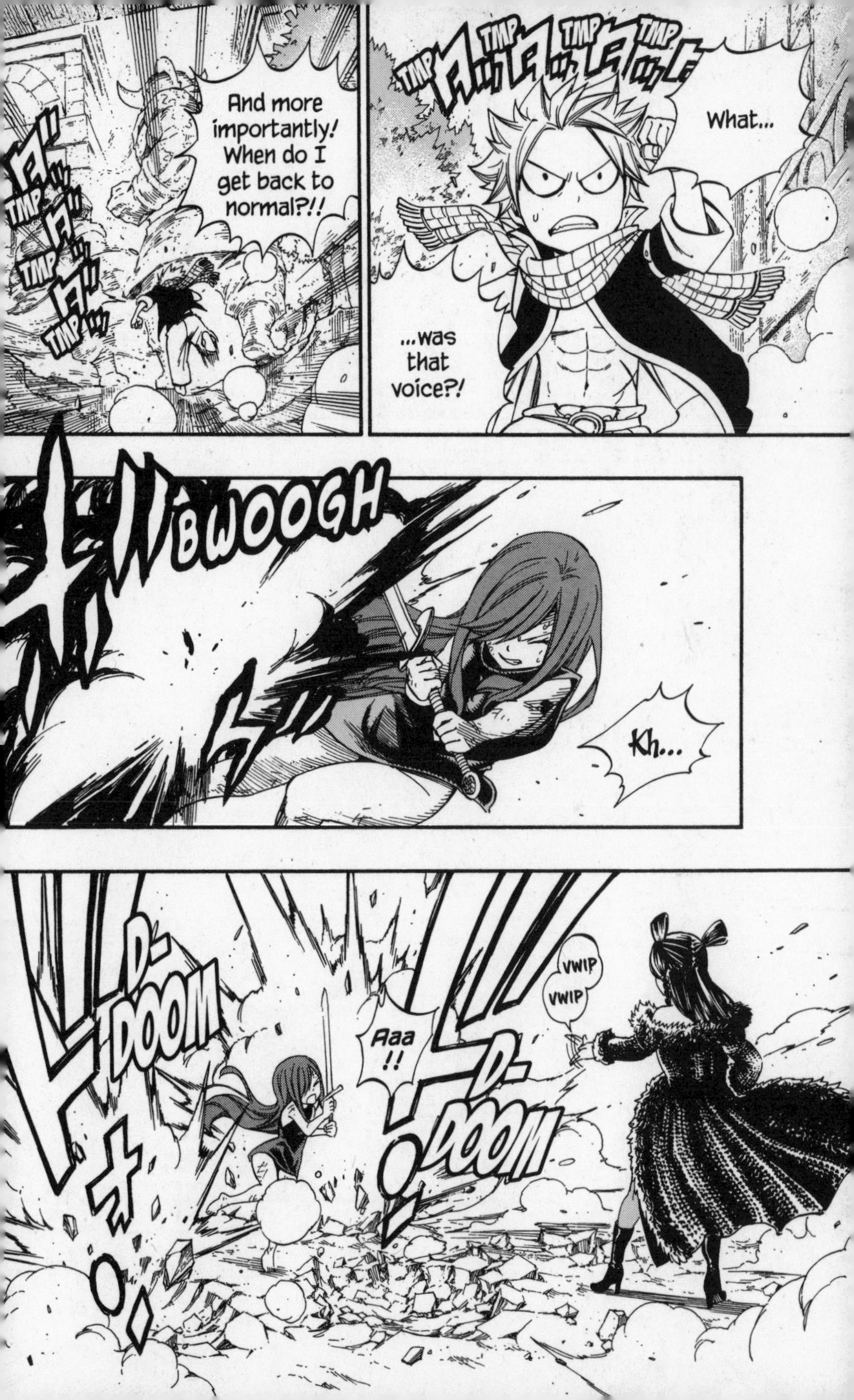
TMP TMP TMP TMP
What...
...was that voice?!
And more importantly! When do I get back to normal?!!
TMP TMP TMP
BWOOGH
Kh...
VWIP VWIP
Aaa !!
D-DOOM
D-DOOM

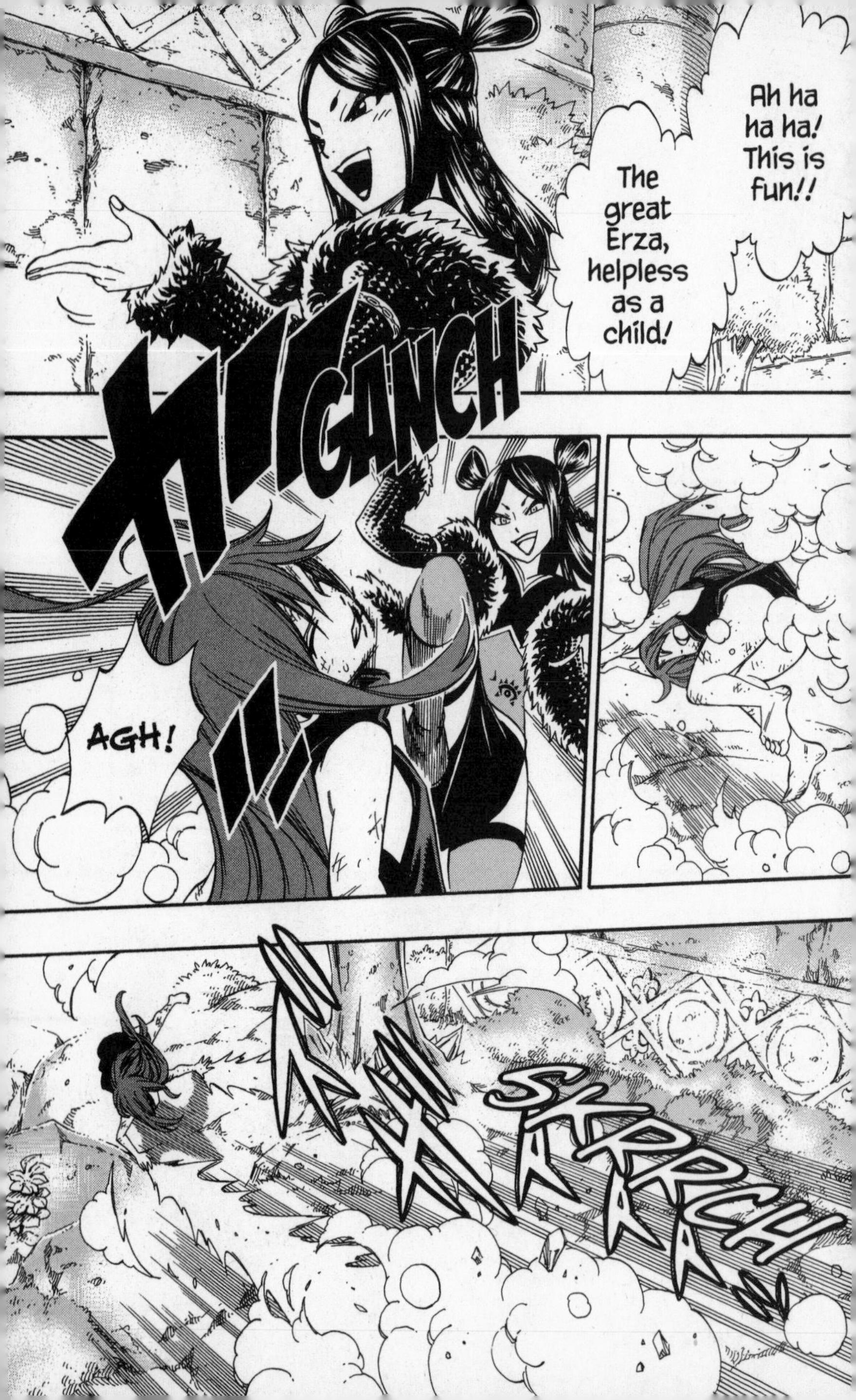
Ah ha ha ha! This is fun!!
The great Erza, helpless as a child!
GANCH
AGH!
SKRRCH

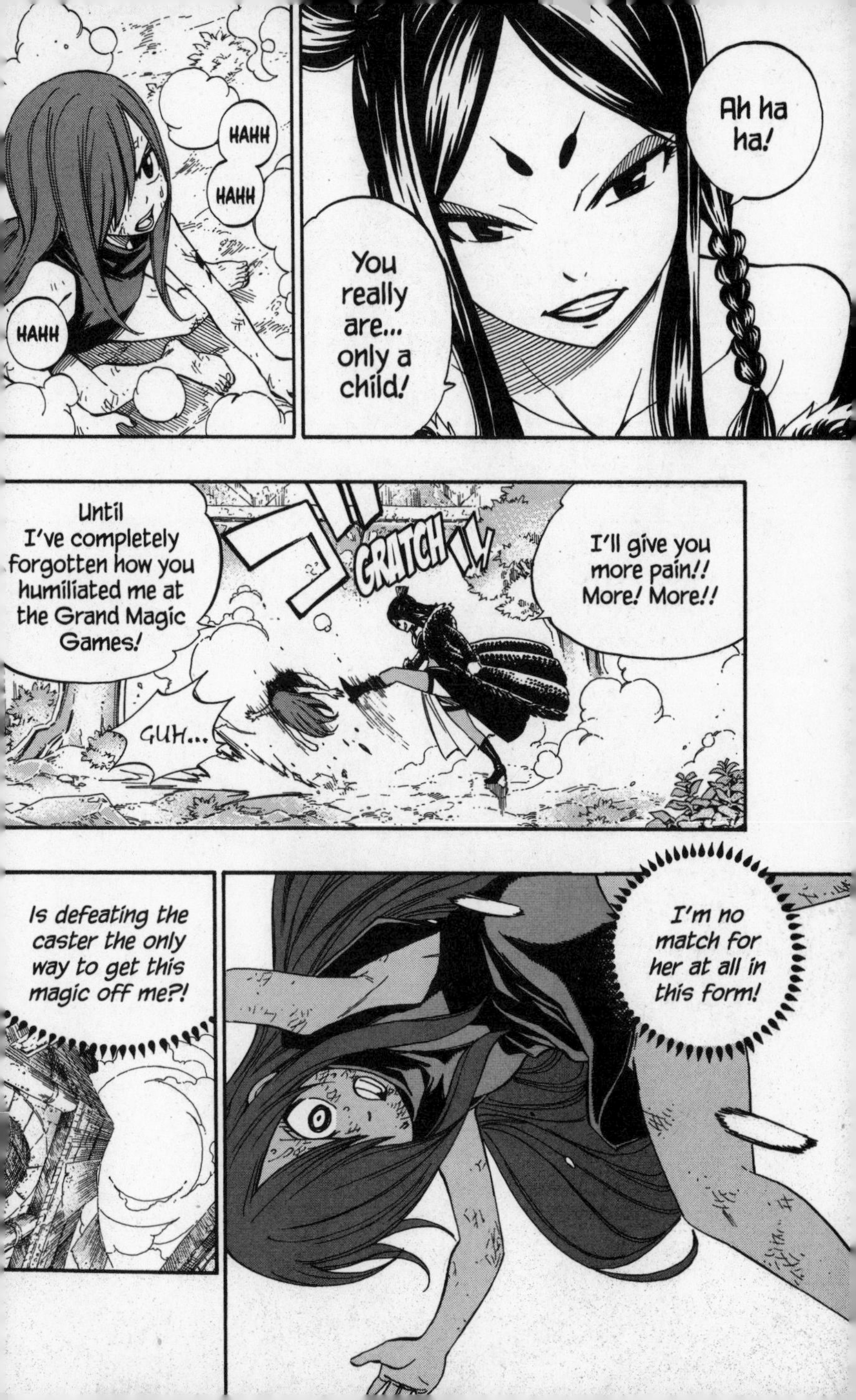
Ah ha ha!
You really are... only a child!
HAHH
HAHH
HAHH
I'll give you more pain!! More! More!!
GRATCH
Until I've completely forgotten how you humiliated me at the Grand Magic Games!
GUH...
I'm no match for her at all in this form!
Is defeating the caster the only way to get this magic off me?!

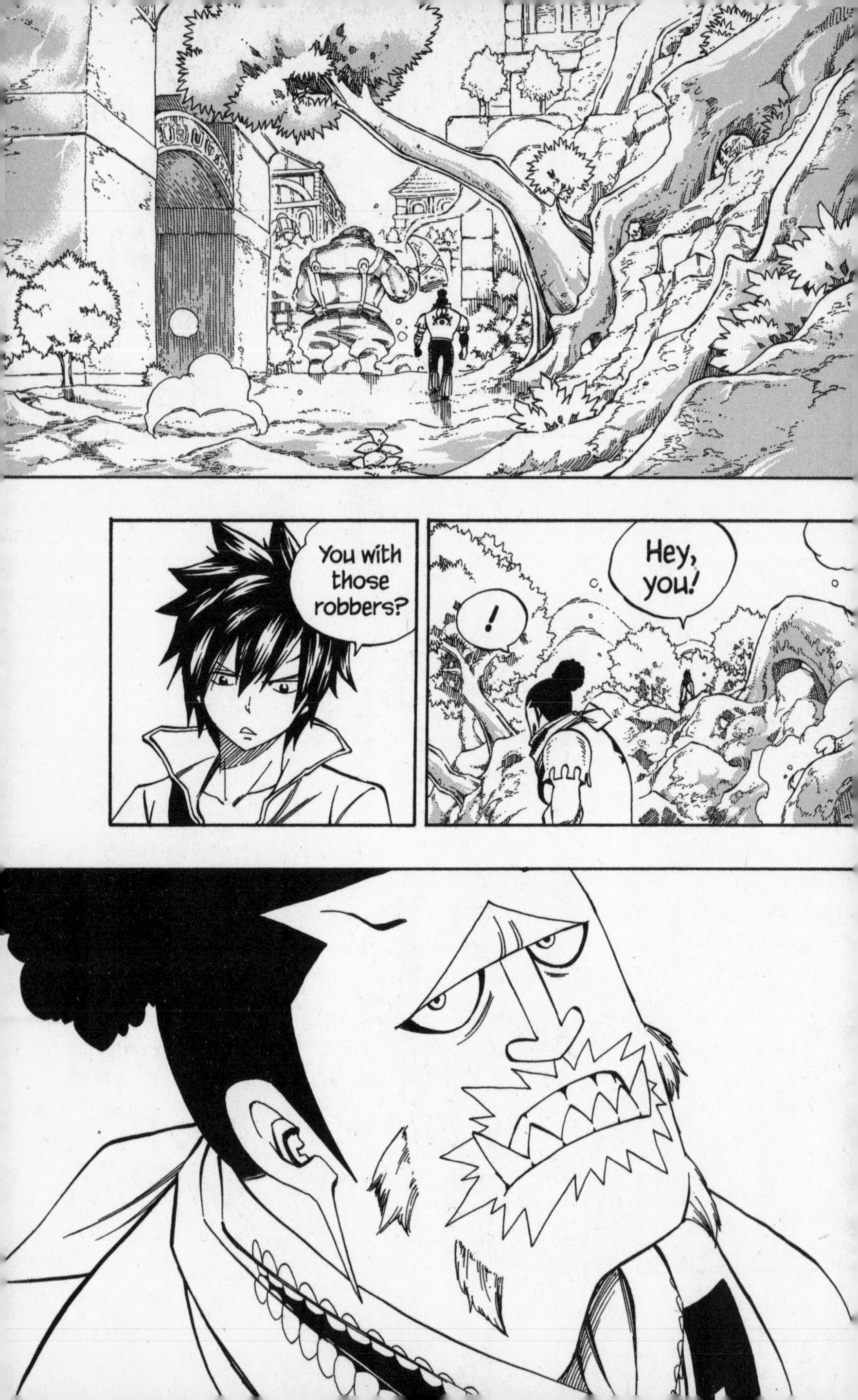
Hey, you!
!
You with those robbers?

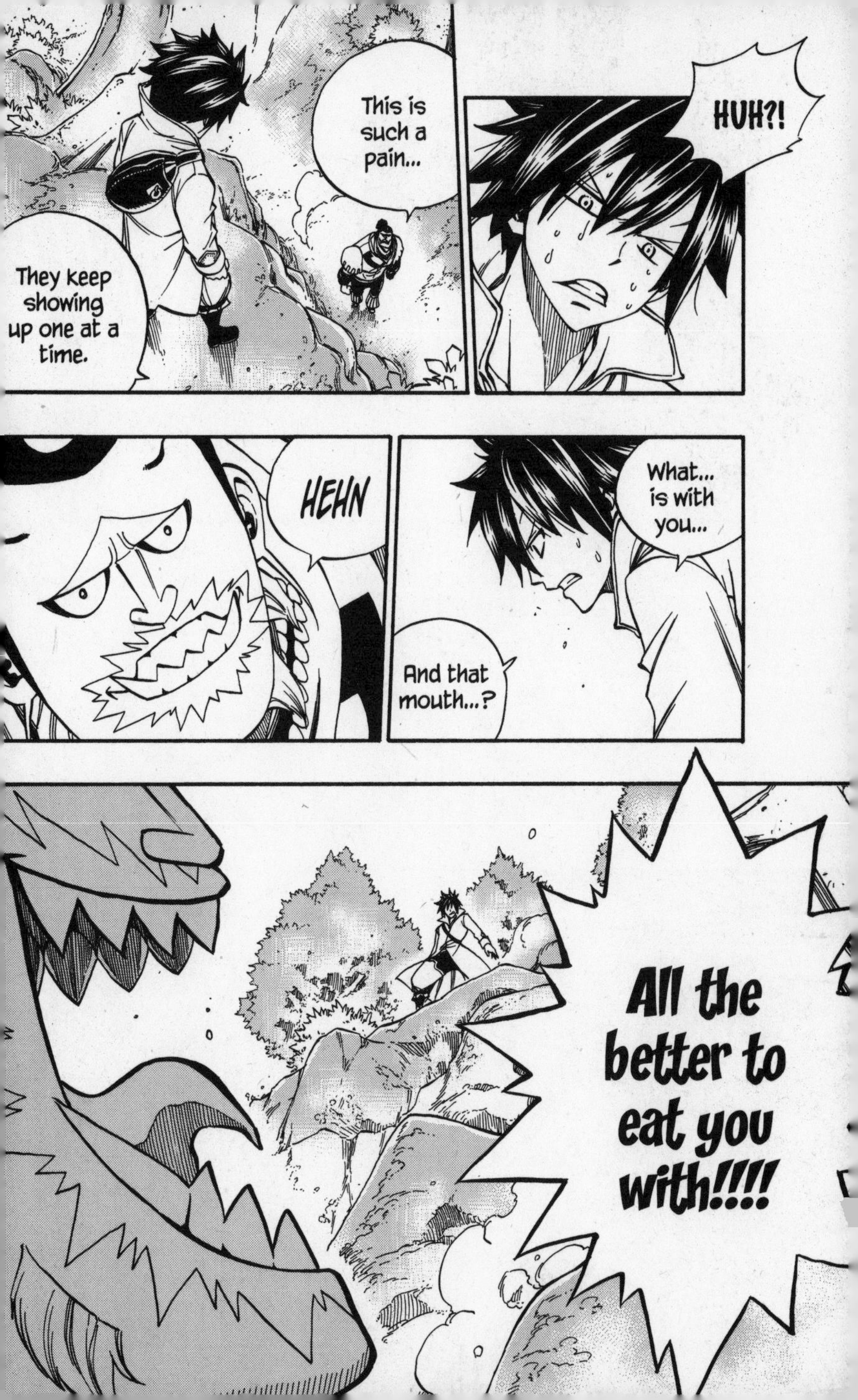
HUH?!
This is such a pain...
They keep showing up one at a time.
What... is with you...
And that mouth...?
HEHN
All the better to eat you with!!!!

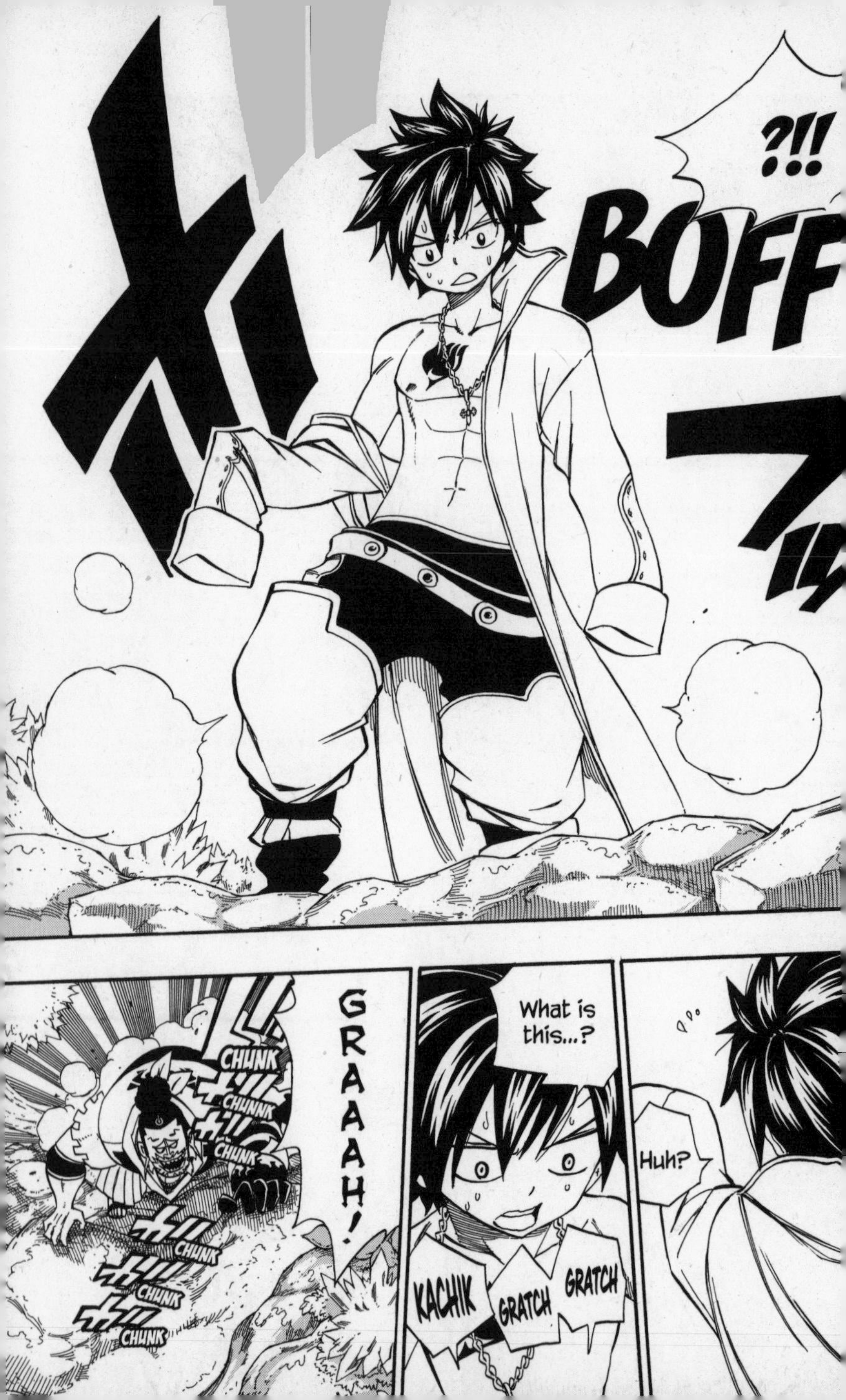
?!!
BOFF
Huh?
What is this...?
KACHIK
GRATCH
GRATCH
GRAAAH!
CHUNK
CHUNNK
CHUNK
CHUNK
CHUNK
CHUNK

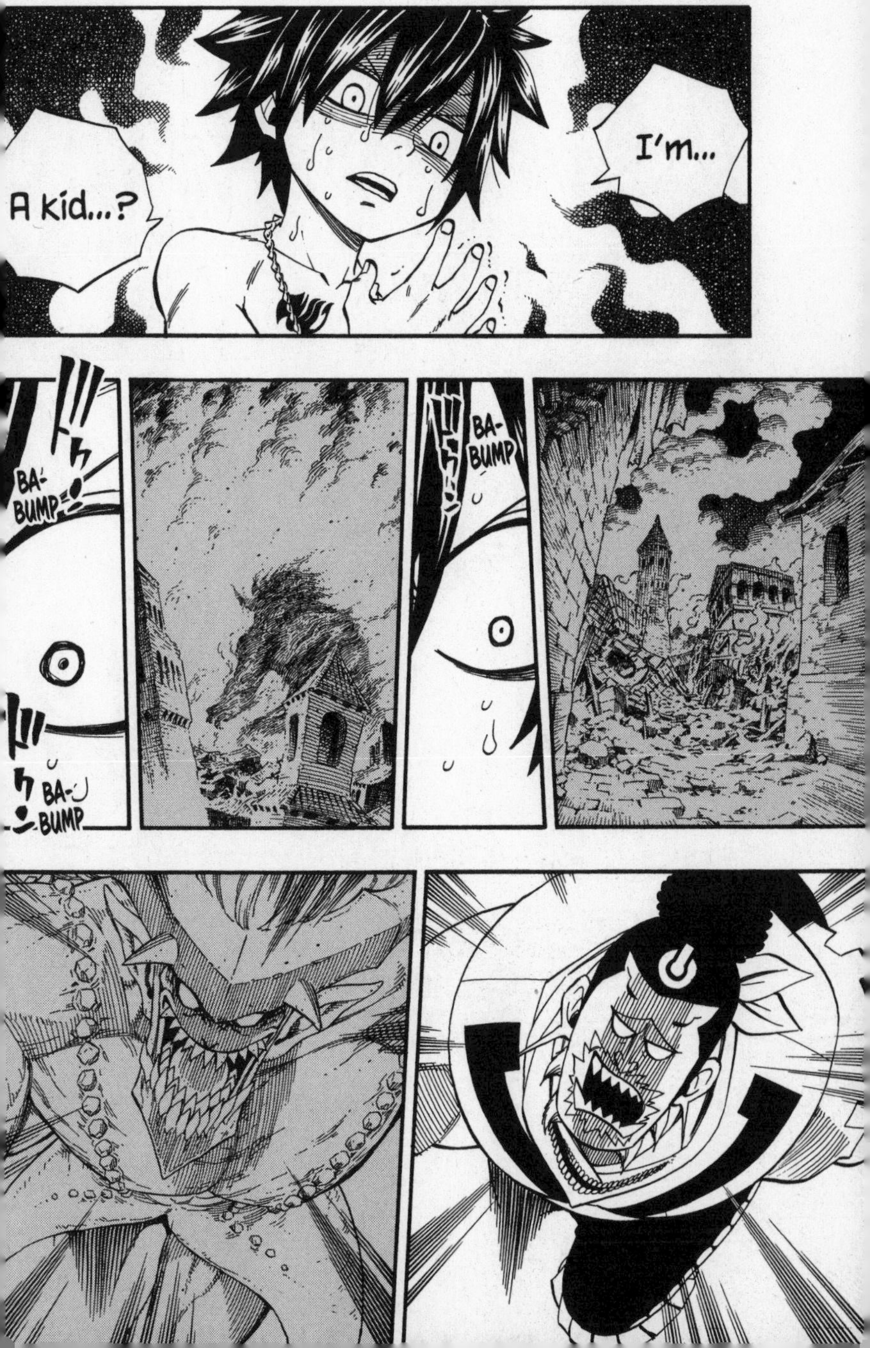

I'm...
A kid...?
BA-BUMP
BA-BUMP
BA-BUMP

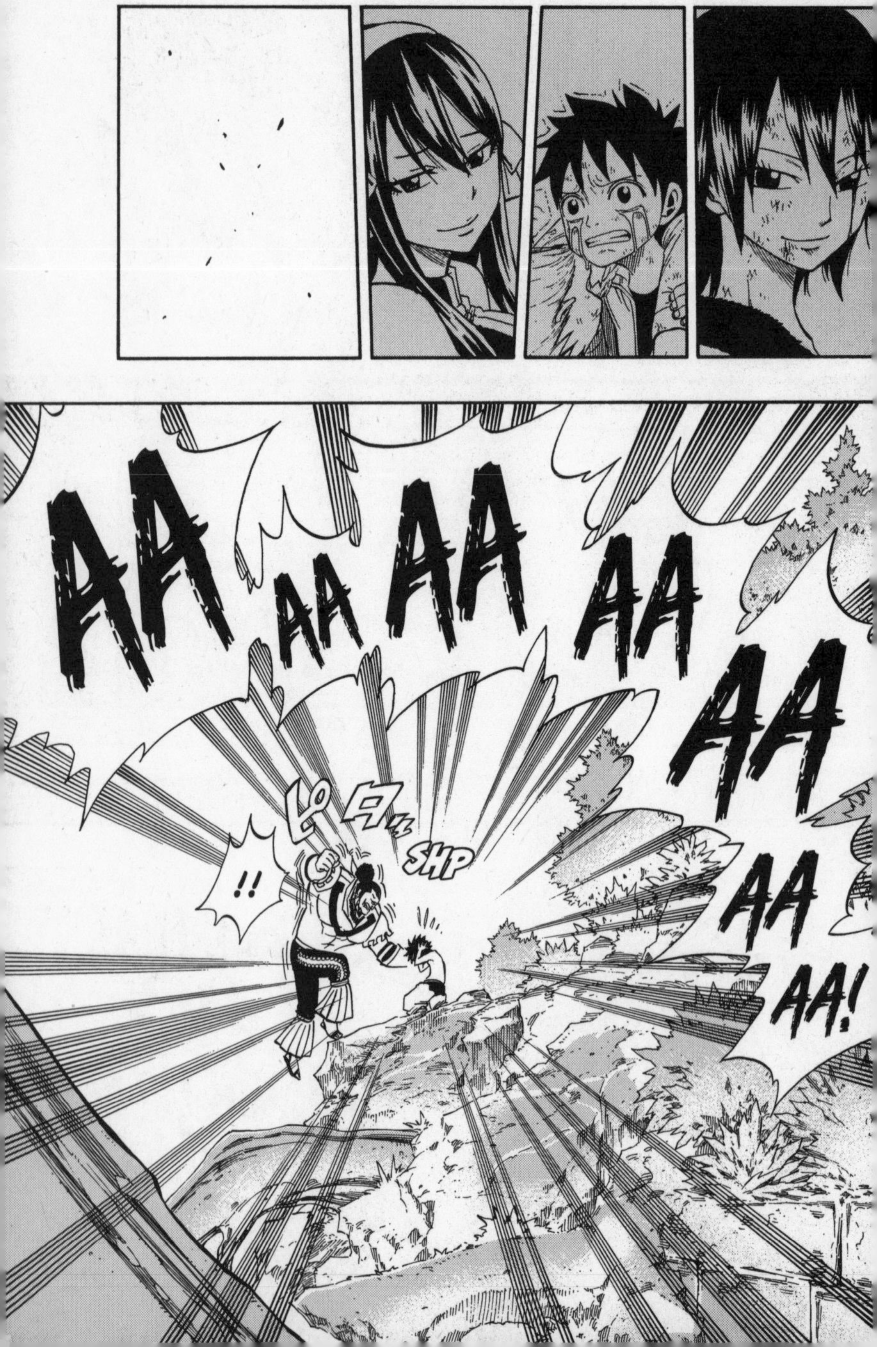
AA AA AA AA AA AA AA AA!
ピタ
SHP
!!

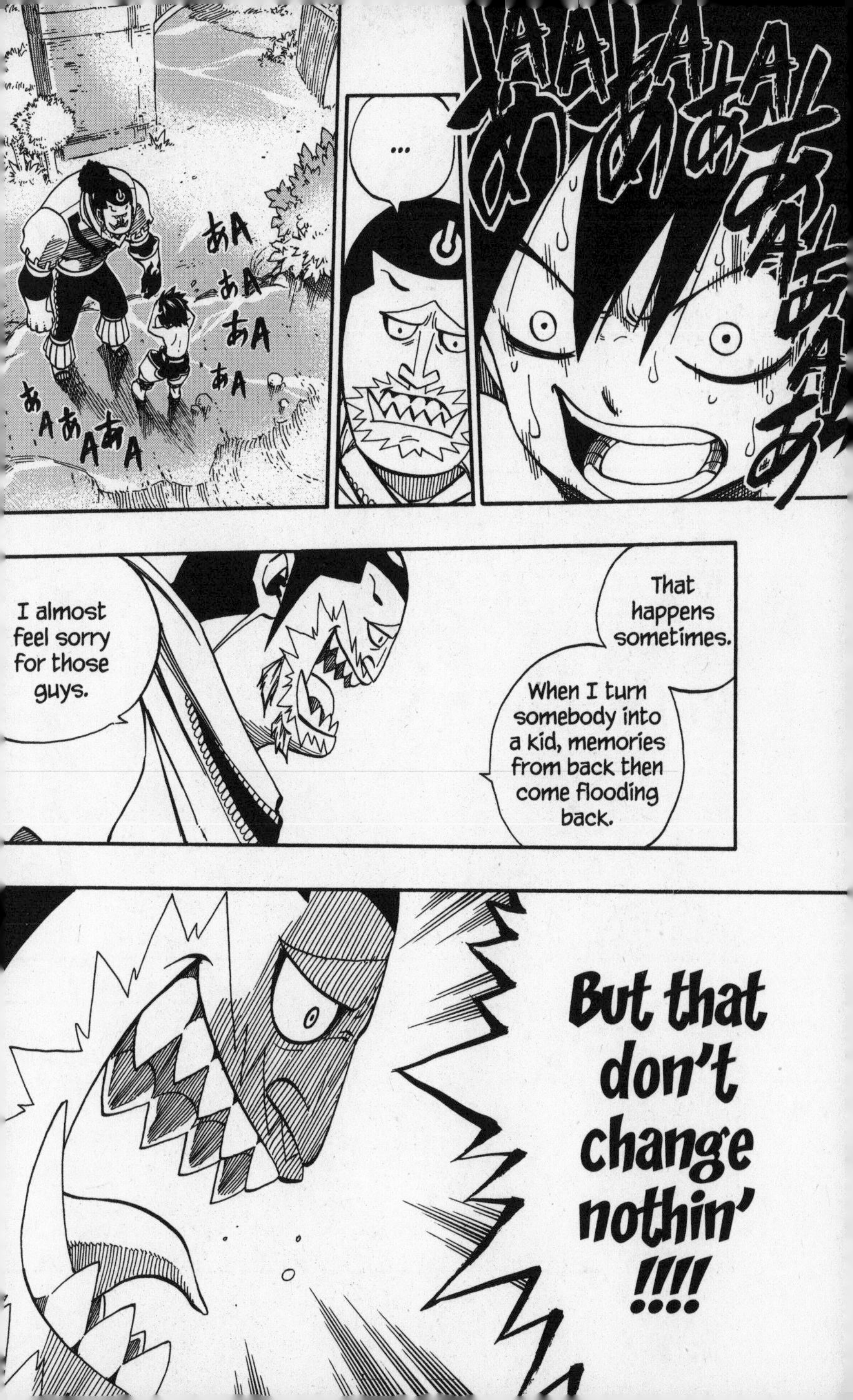

あAあAあAあAあAあ
...
あA あA あA あA
あA あA あA
That happens sometimes.
When I turn somebody into a kid, memories from back then come flooding back.
I almost feel sorry for those guys.
But that don't change nothin'!!!!

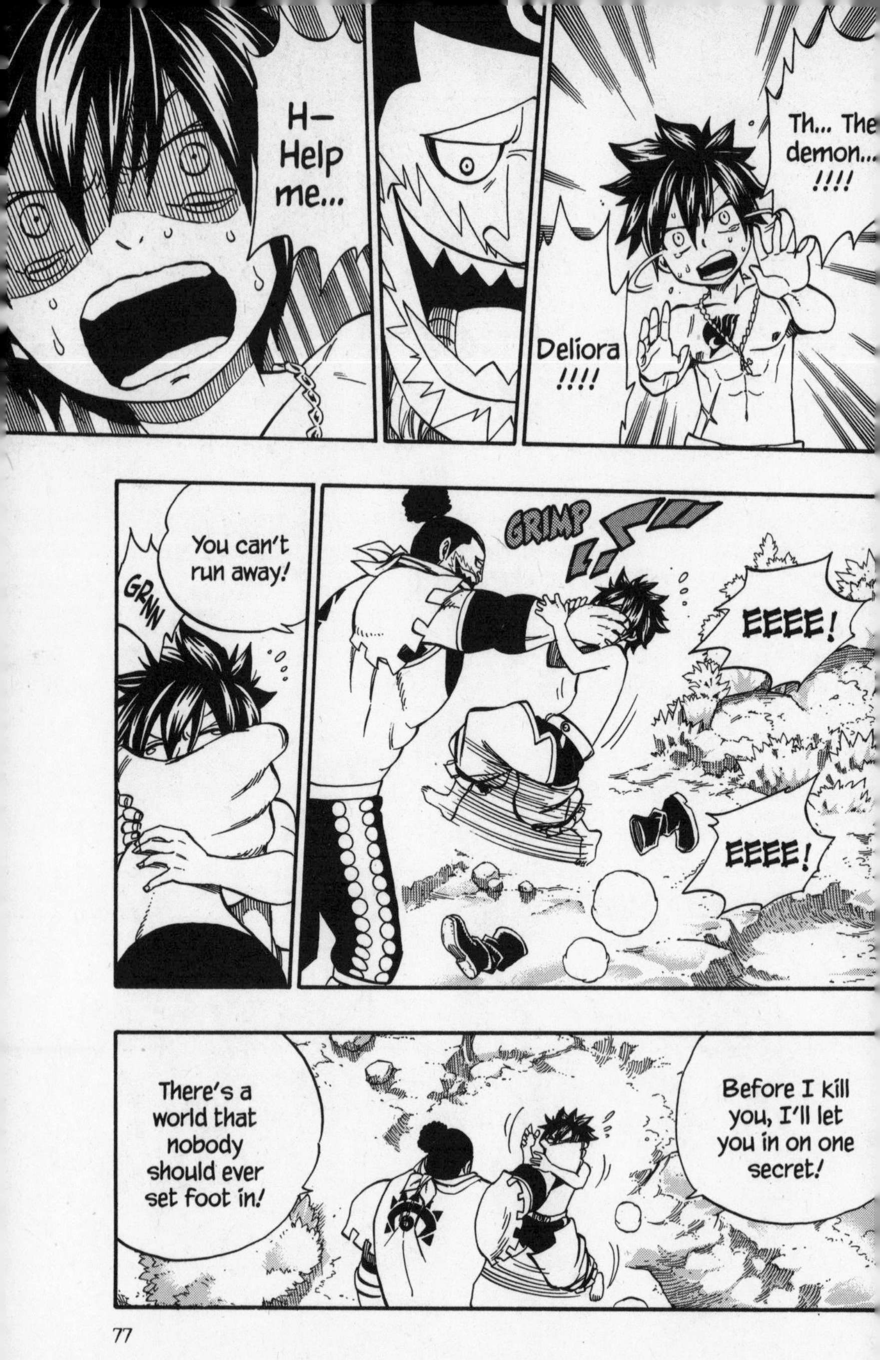
Th... The demon... !!!!
Deliora !!!!
H— Help me...
GRIMP
EEEE!
EEEE!
You can't run away!
GRNN
Before I kill you, I'll let you in on one secret!
There's a world that nobody should ever set foot in!

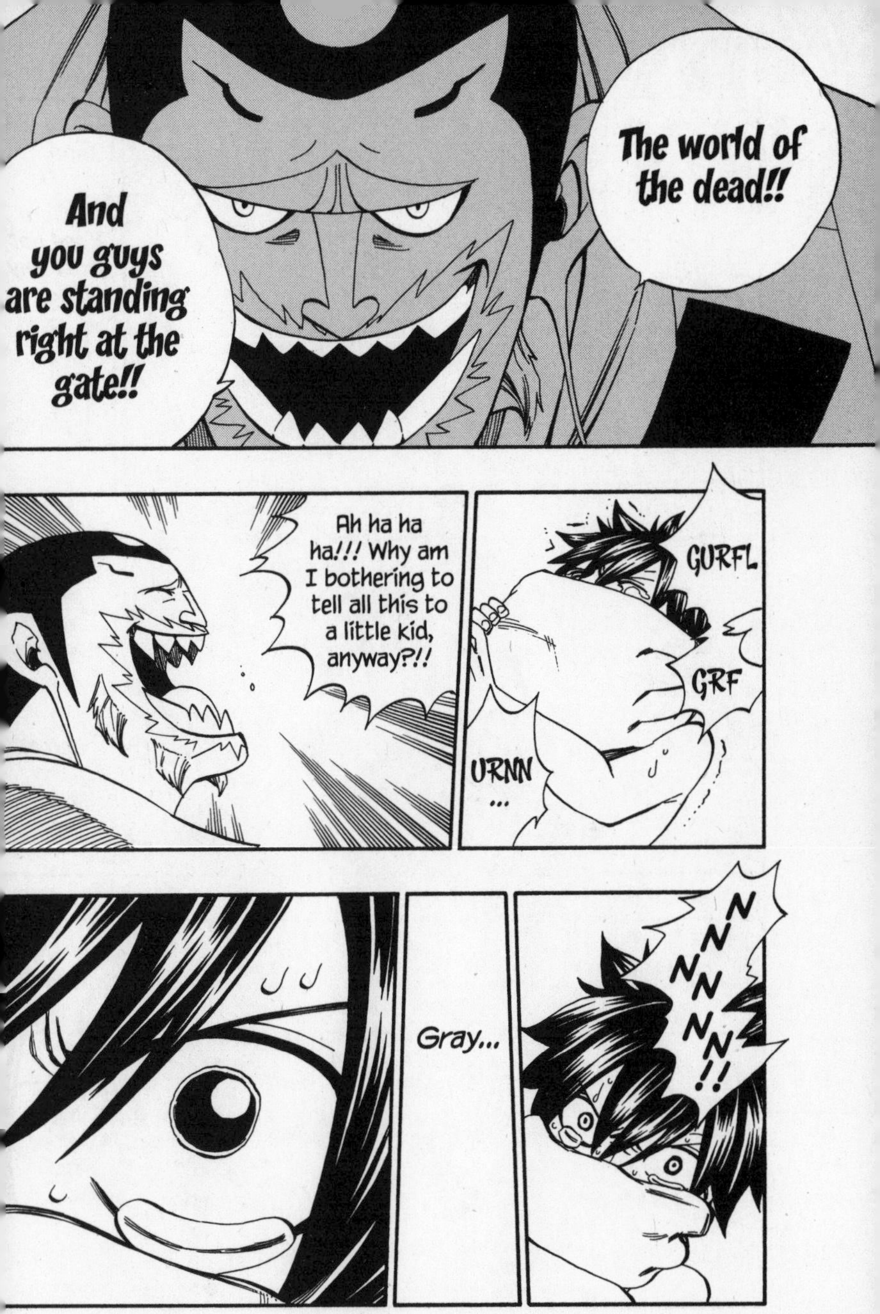
The world of the dead!!
And you guys are standing right at the gate!!
GURFL
GRF
URNN...
Ah ha ha ha!!! Why am I bothering to tell all this to a little kid, anyway?!!
NNNNNN!!
Gray...

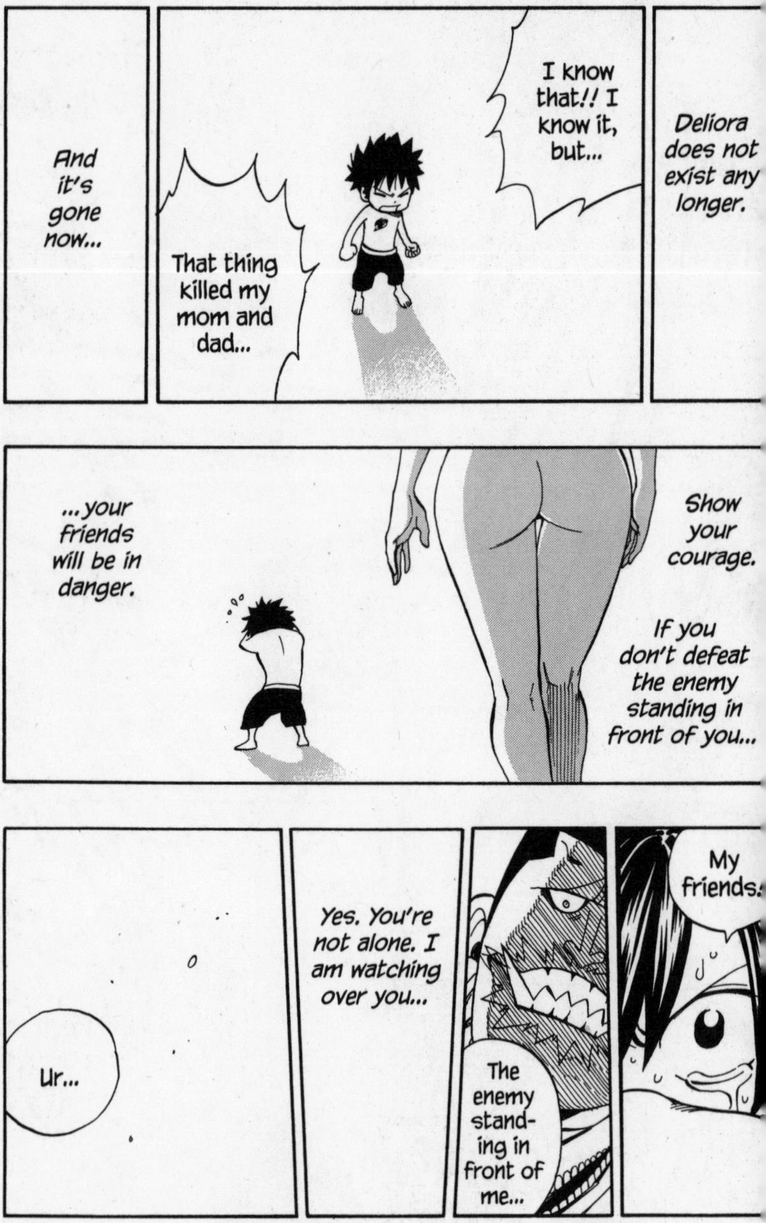
Deliora does not exist any longer.
I know that!! I know it, but...
That thing killed my mom and dad...
And it's gone now...
Show your courage.
If you don't defeat the enemy standing in front of you...
...your friends will be in danger.
My friends
The enemy stand-ing in front of me...
Yes. You're not alone. I am watching over you...
Ur...

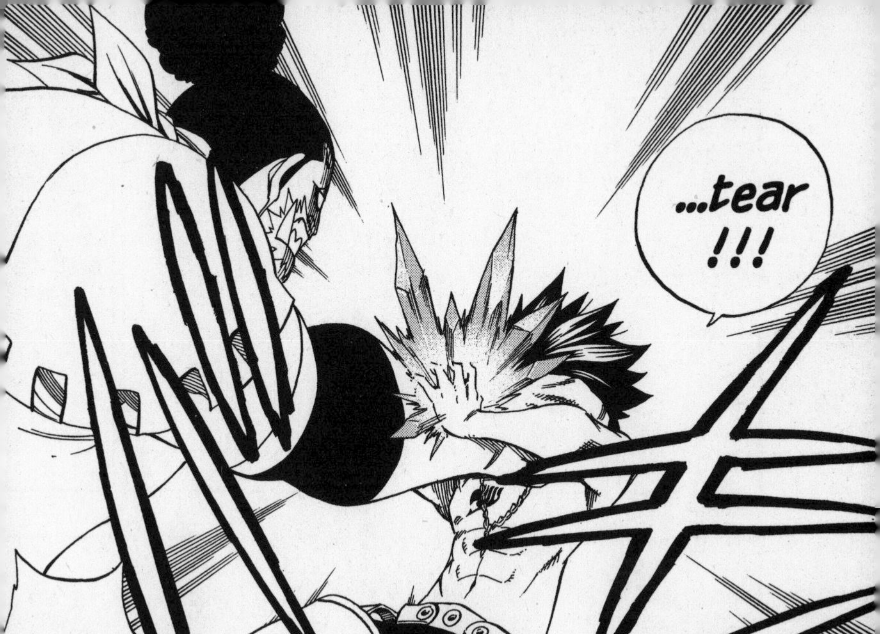
...tear !!!
GAH!
PACHIKK

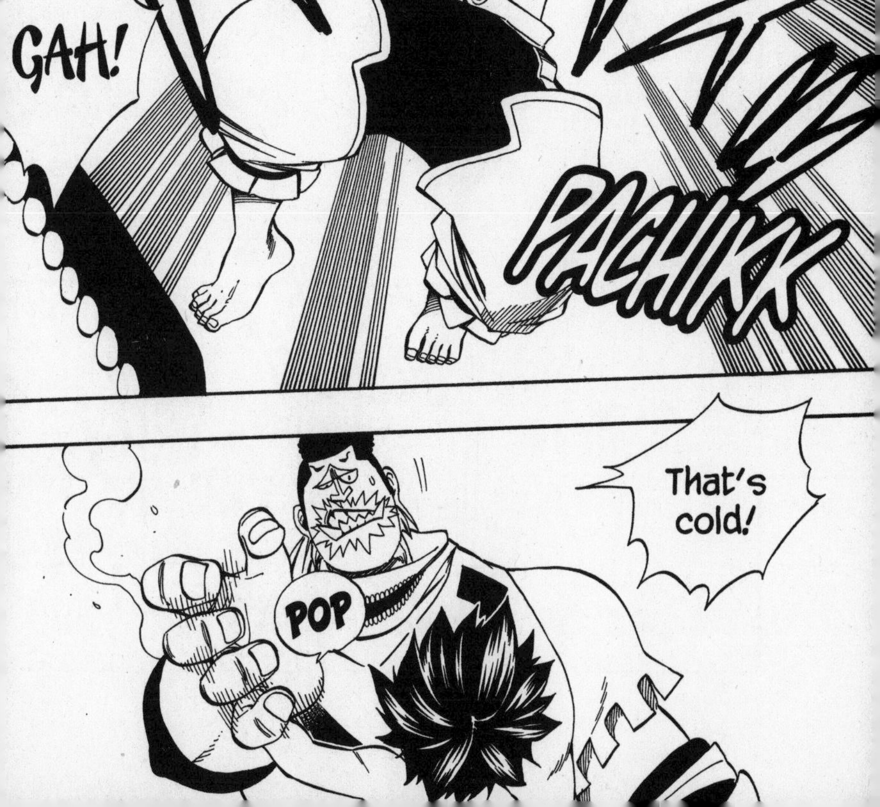
That's cold!
POP

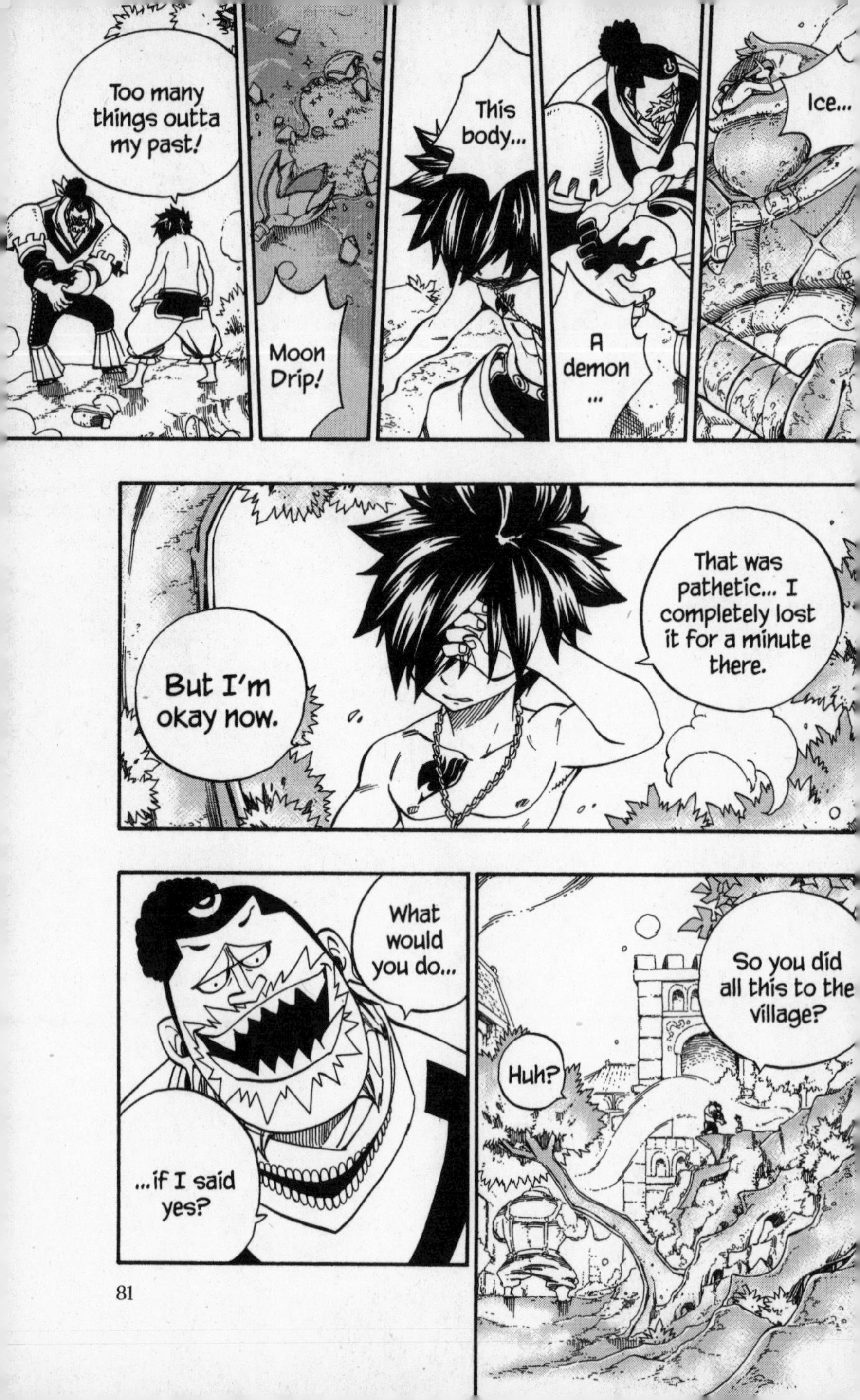
Ice...
A demon ...
This body...
Moon Drip!
Too many things outta my past!
That was pathetic... I completely lost it for a minute there.
But I'm okay now.
So you did all this to the village?
Huh?
What would you do...
...if I said yes?

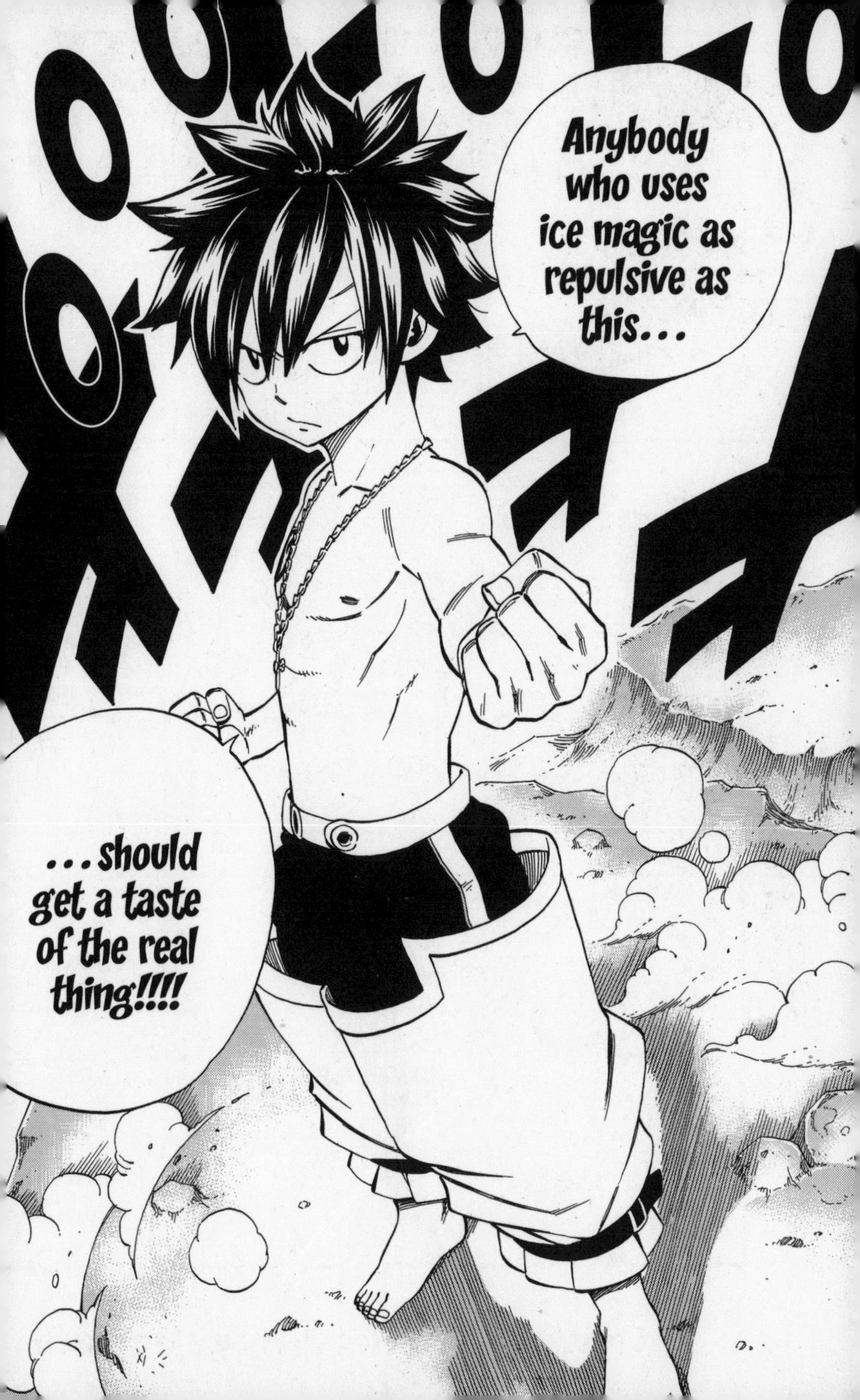
Anybody who uses ice magic as repulsive as this...
...should get a taste of the real thing!!!!

FAIRYTAIL

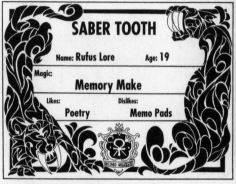

SABER TOOTH

Name: Rufus Lore   **Age:** 19

Magic:

Memory Make

Likes: **Dislikes:**

Poetry   Memo Pads

Remarks

A Memory Maker wizard whose nickname is "the Troubadour who Sings to the Red Moon." Memory Make can be used to instantly memorize any magic the wizard sees and change it into a new kind of magic. It can also be employed to manipulate people's memories in a variety of ways, but that wasn't demonstrated during the Grand Magic Games. Realizing there are many similarities between himself and Fairy Tail's Fried, Rufus is considering taking this opportunity to change his image now that he has returned to Saber Tooth.

Chapter 349: The Demon Doriath

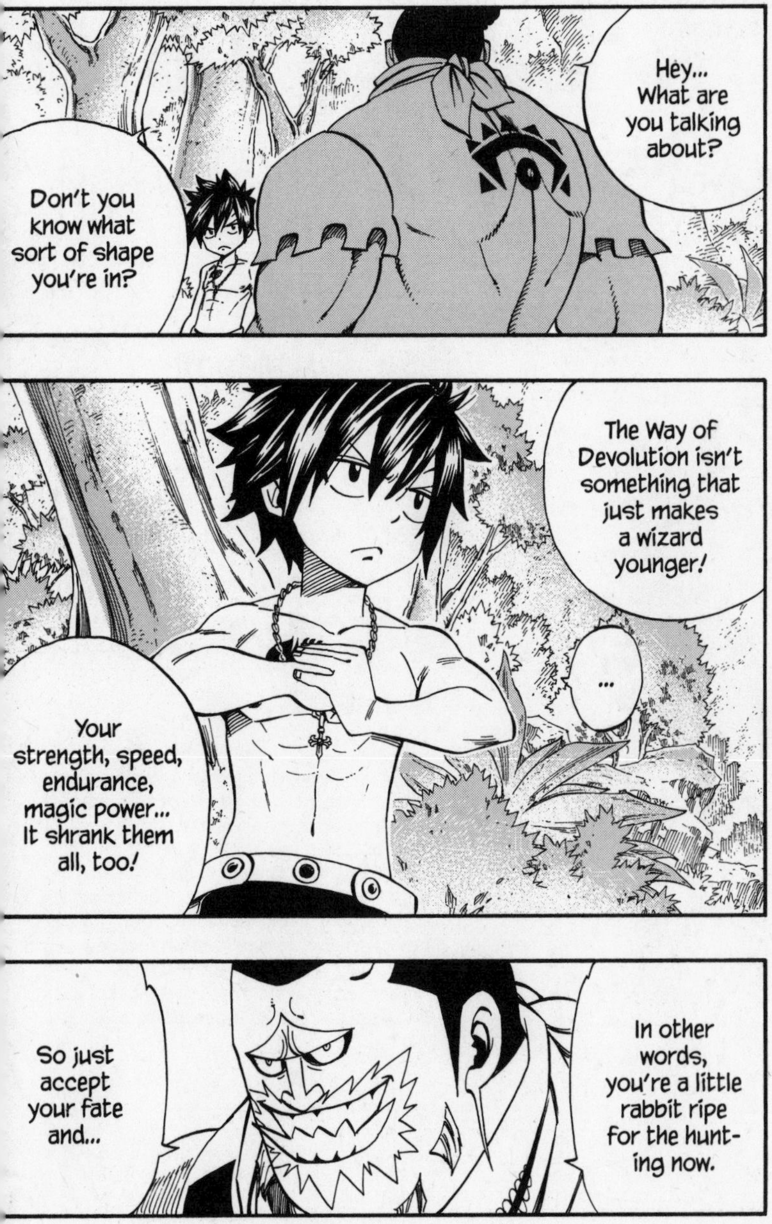
Hey... What are you talking about?
Don't you know what sort of shape you're in?
The Way of Devolution isn't something that just makes a wizard younger!
...
Your strength, speed, endurance, magic power... It shrank them all, too!
In other words, you're a little rabbit ripe for the hunting now.
So just accept your fate and...

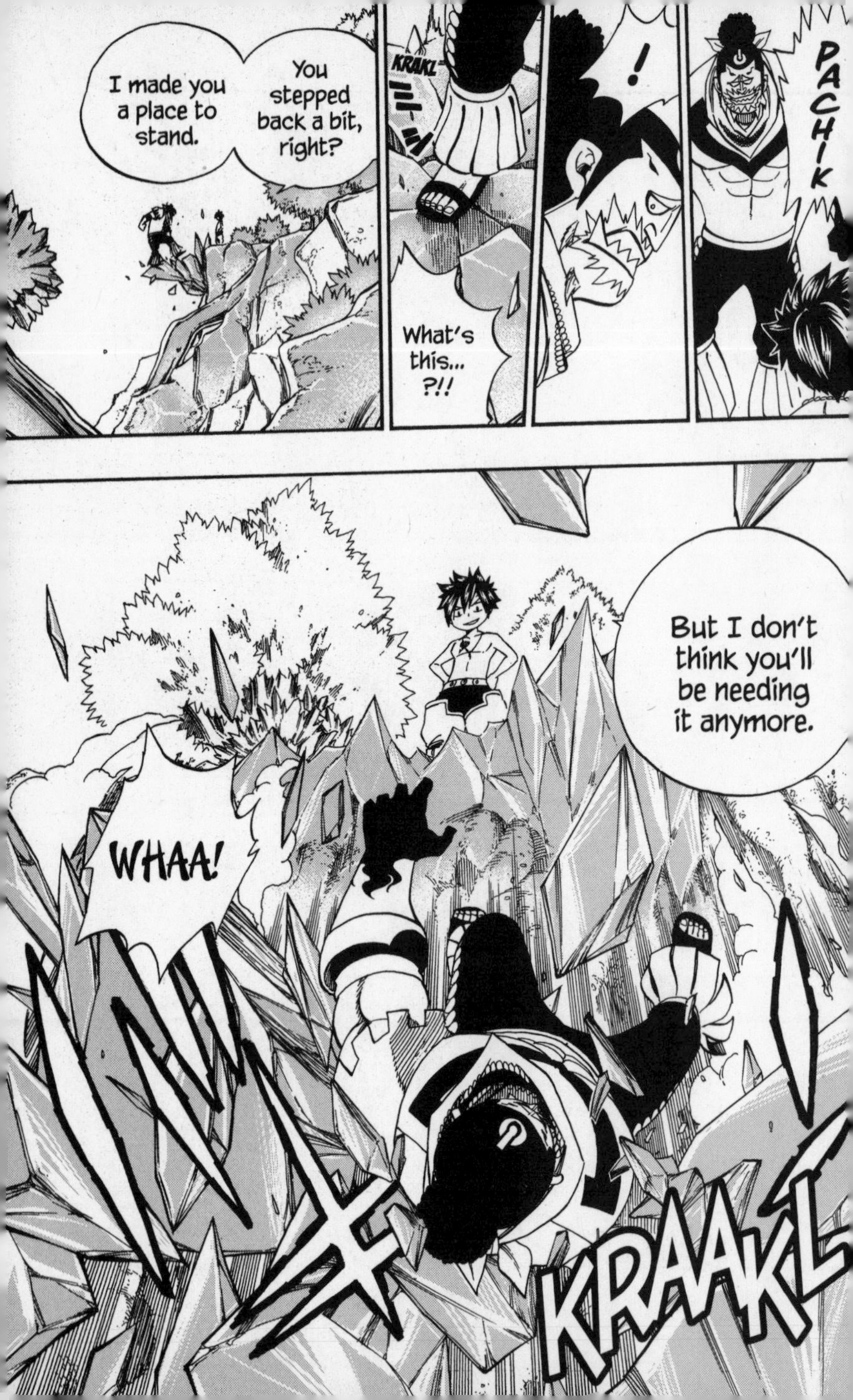
PACHIK
!
KRAKL
What's this... ?!!
You stepped back a bit, right?
I made you a place to stand.
But I don't think you'll be needing it anymore.
WHAA!
KRAAKL

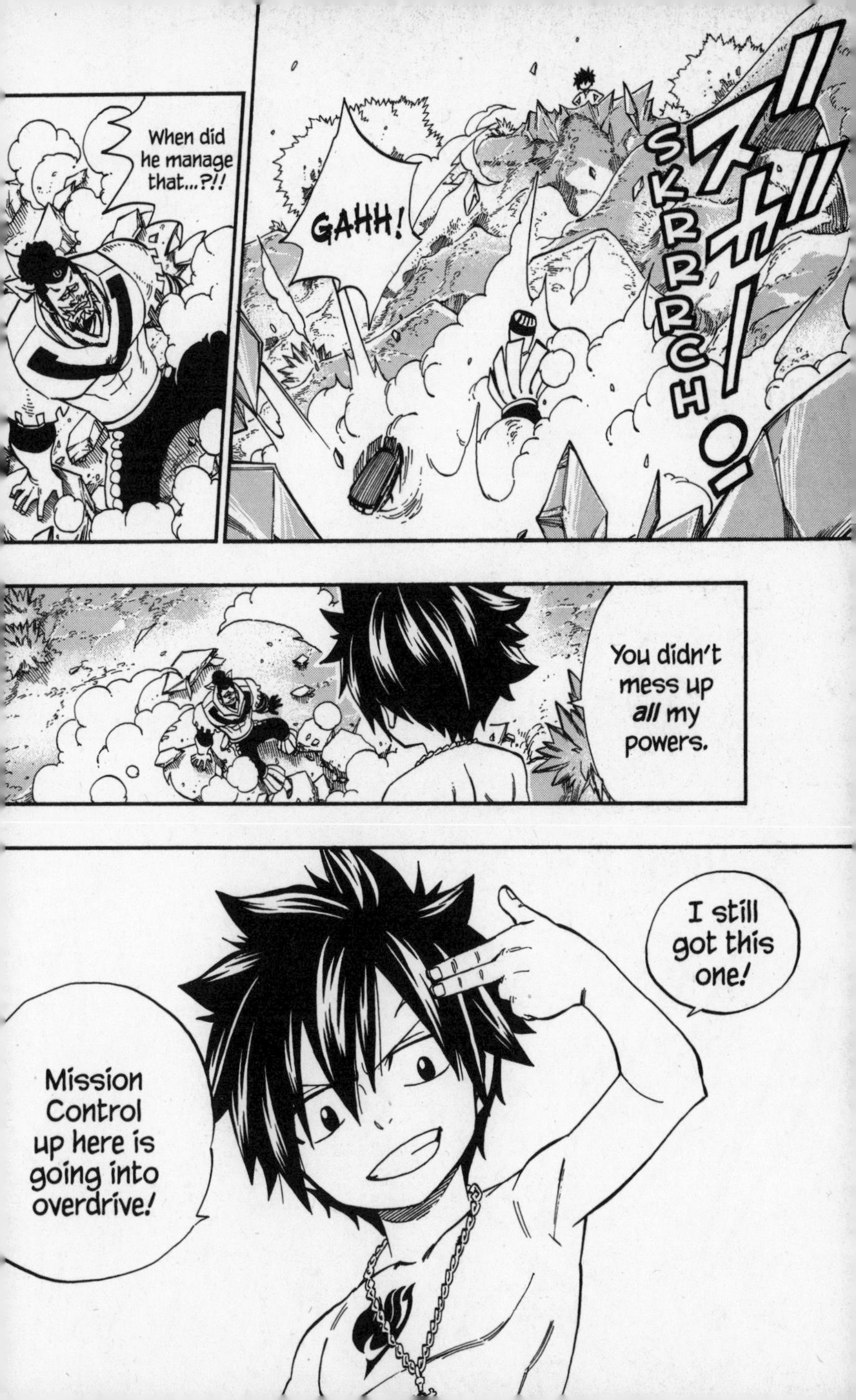
GAHH!
SKRRRCH
When did he manage that...?!!
You didn't mess up *all* my powers.
I still got this one!
Mission Control up here is going into overdrive!

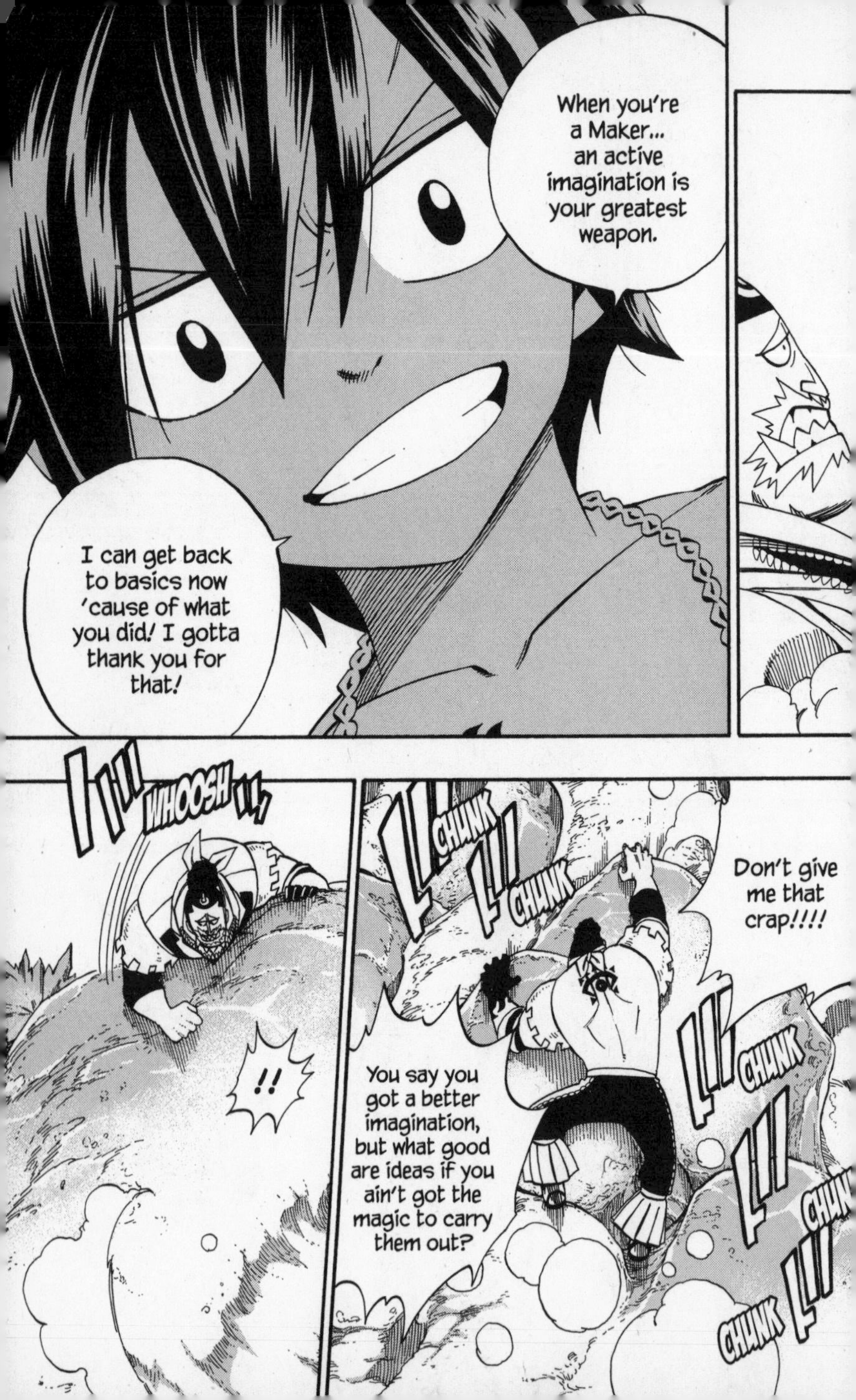

When you're a Maker... an active imagination is your greatest weapon.
I can get back to basics now 'cause of what you did! I gotta thank you for that!
Don't give me that crap!!!!
CHUNK
CHUNK
CHUNK
You say you got a better imagination, but what good are ideas if you ain't got the magic to carry them out?
CHUNK
WHOOSH
!!

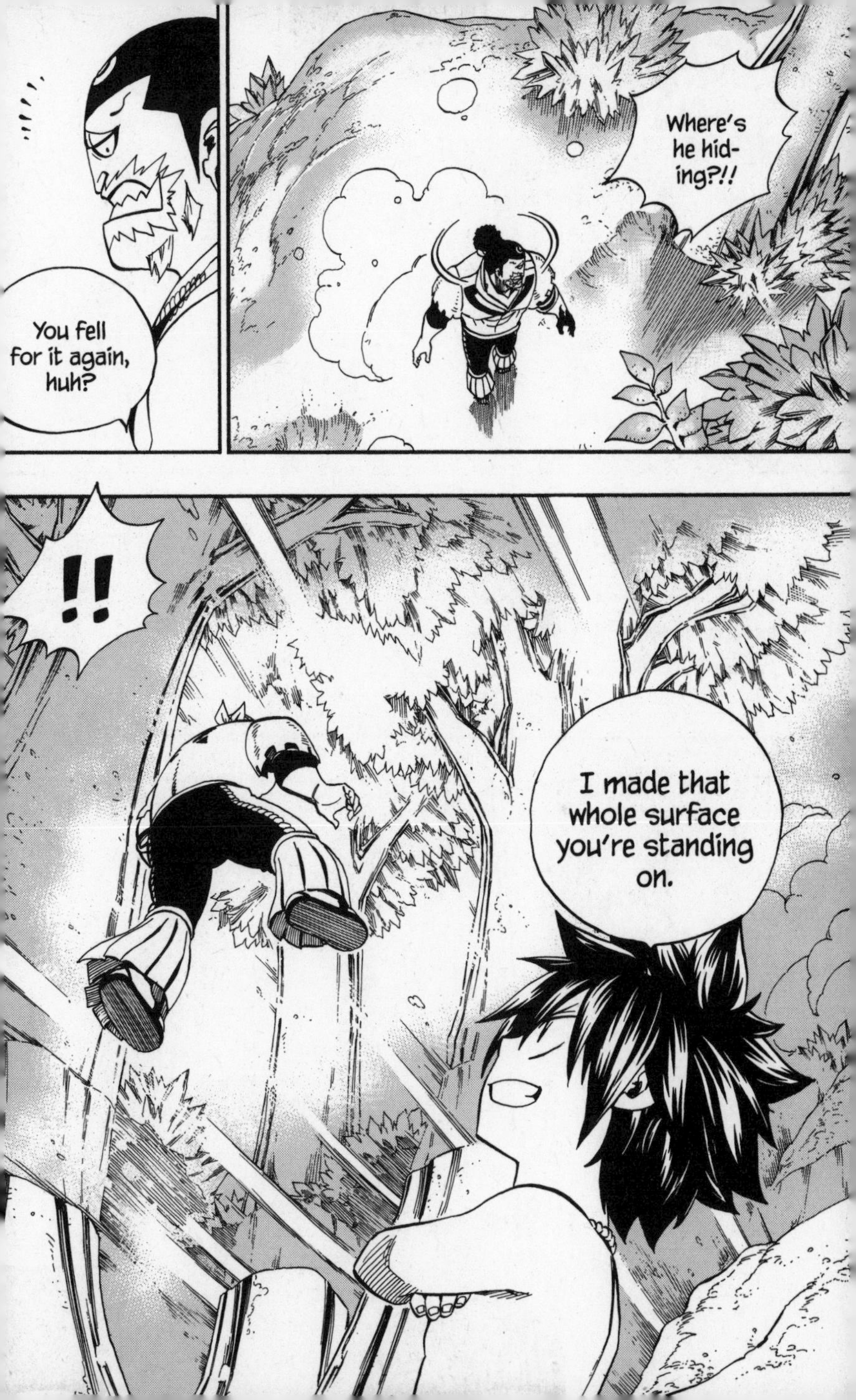
Where's he hid-ing?!!
You fell for it again, huh?
!!
I made that whole surface you're standing on.

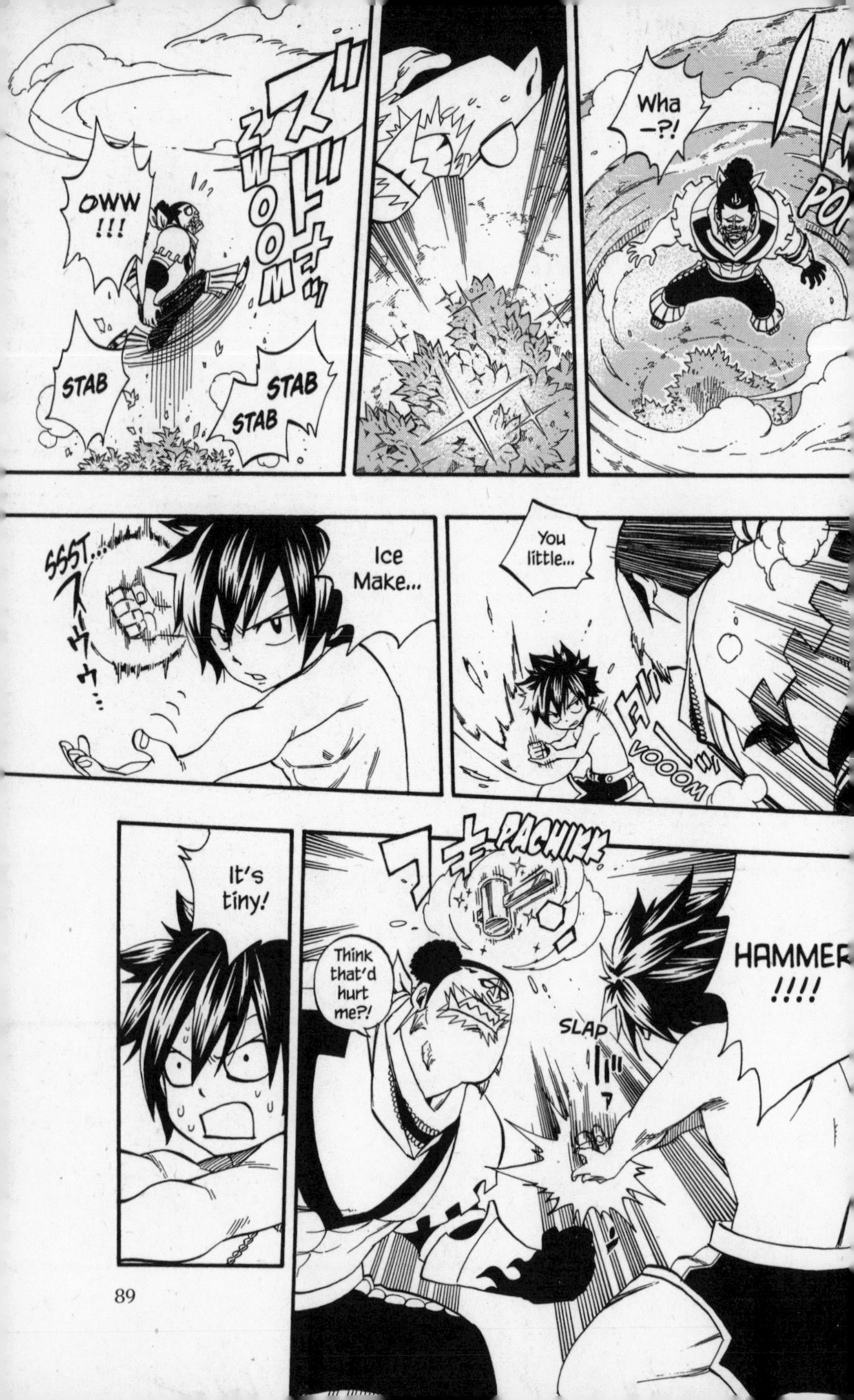
Wha
—?!
PO
ZWOOOM
OWW
!!!
STAB
STAB
STAB
You
little...
VOOOM
Ice
Make...
SSST...
PACHIKK
HAMMER
!!!!
Think
that'd
hurt
me?!
SLAP
It's
tiny!

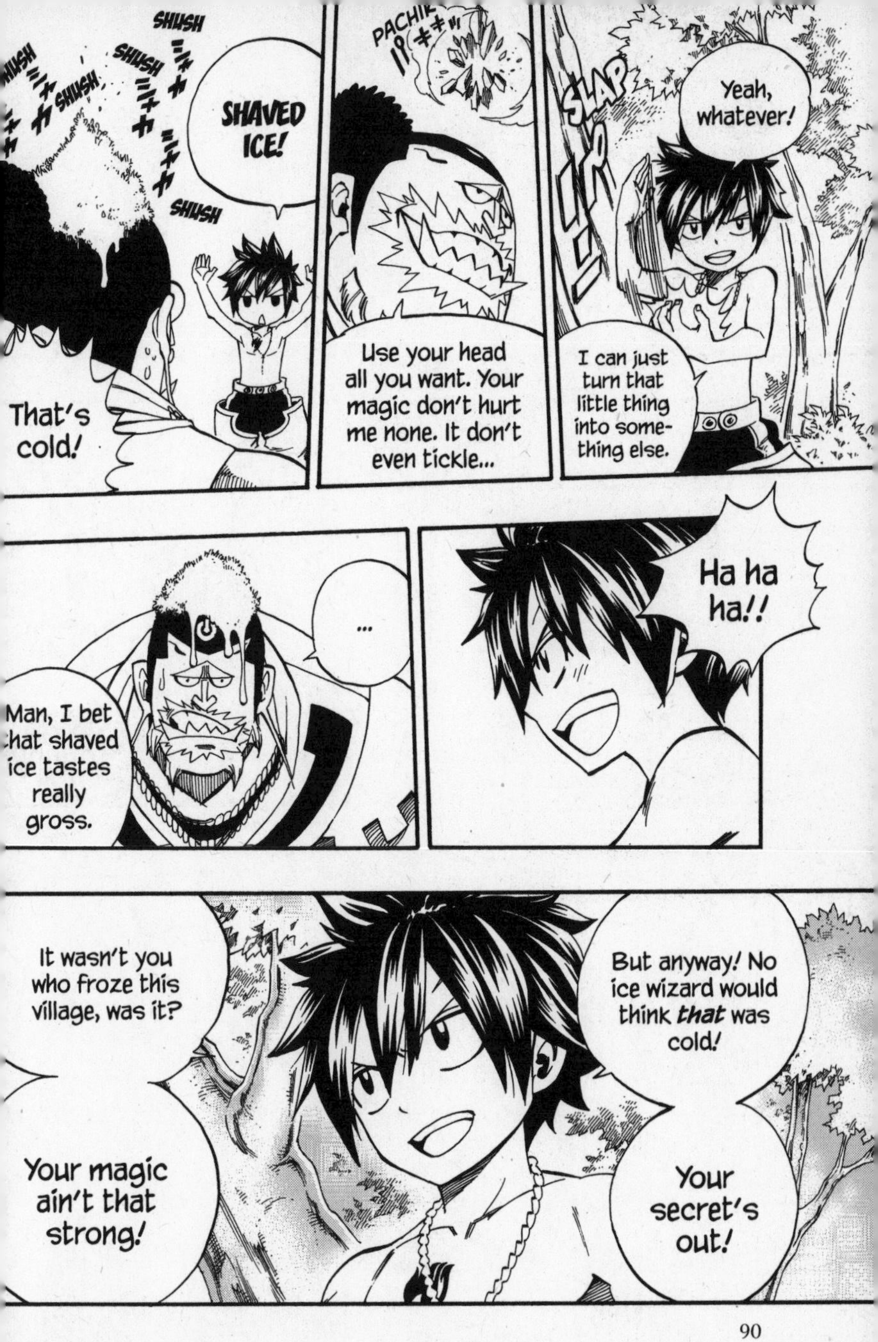
SLAP
Yeah, whatever!
I can just turn that little thing into something else.
PACHIR
Use your head all you want. Your magic don't hurt me none. It don't even tickle...
SHUSH
SHAVED ICE!
SHUSH
SHUSH
SHUSH
SHUSH
That's cold!
Ha ha ha!!
...
Man, I bet that shaved ice tastes really gross.
But anyway! No ice wizard would think *that* was cold!
Your secret's out!
It wasn't you who froze this village, was it?
Your magic ain't that strong!

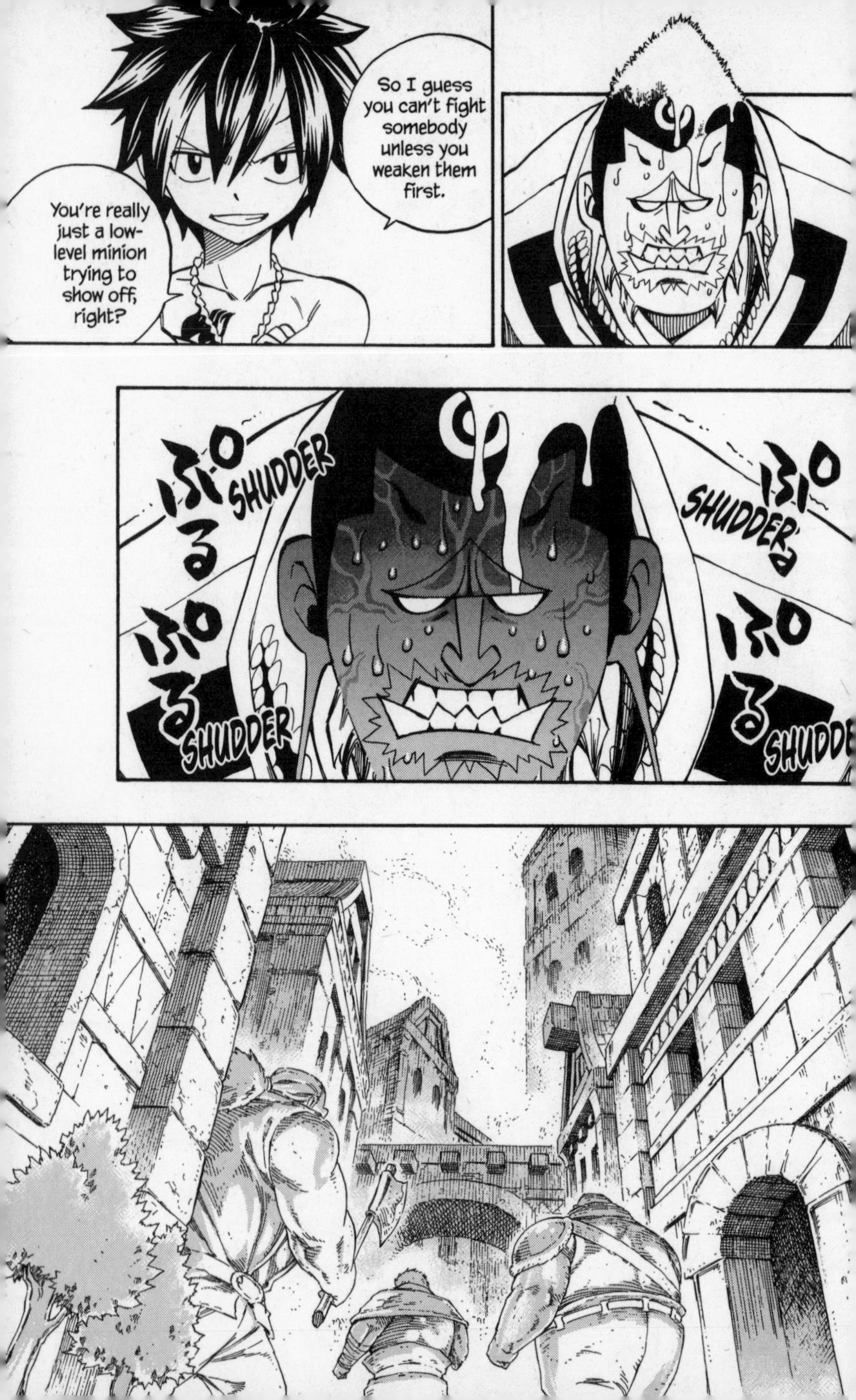

So I guess you can't fight somebody unless you weaken them first.
You're really just a low-level minion trying to show off, right?
ぶる SHUDDER
ぶる SHUDDER
ぶる SHUDDER
ぶる SHUDDER

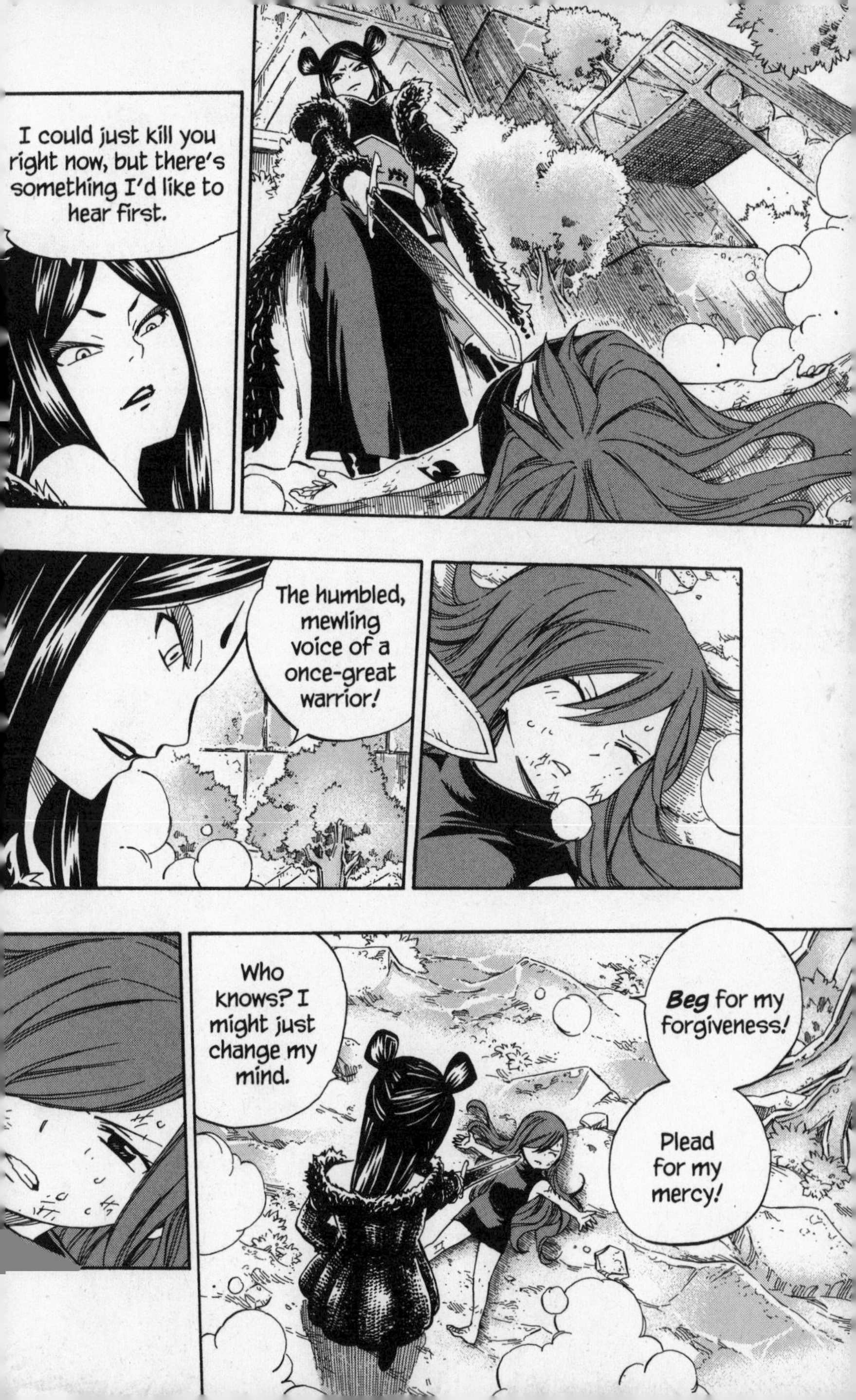
I could just kill you right now, but there's something I'd like to hear first.
The humbled, mewling voice of a once-great warrior!
Beg for my forgiveness!
Who knows? I might just change my mind.
Plead for my mercy!

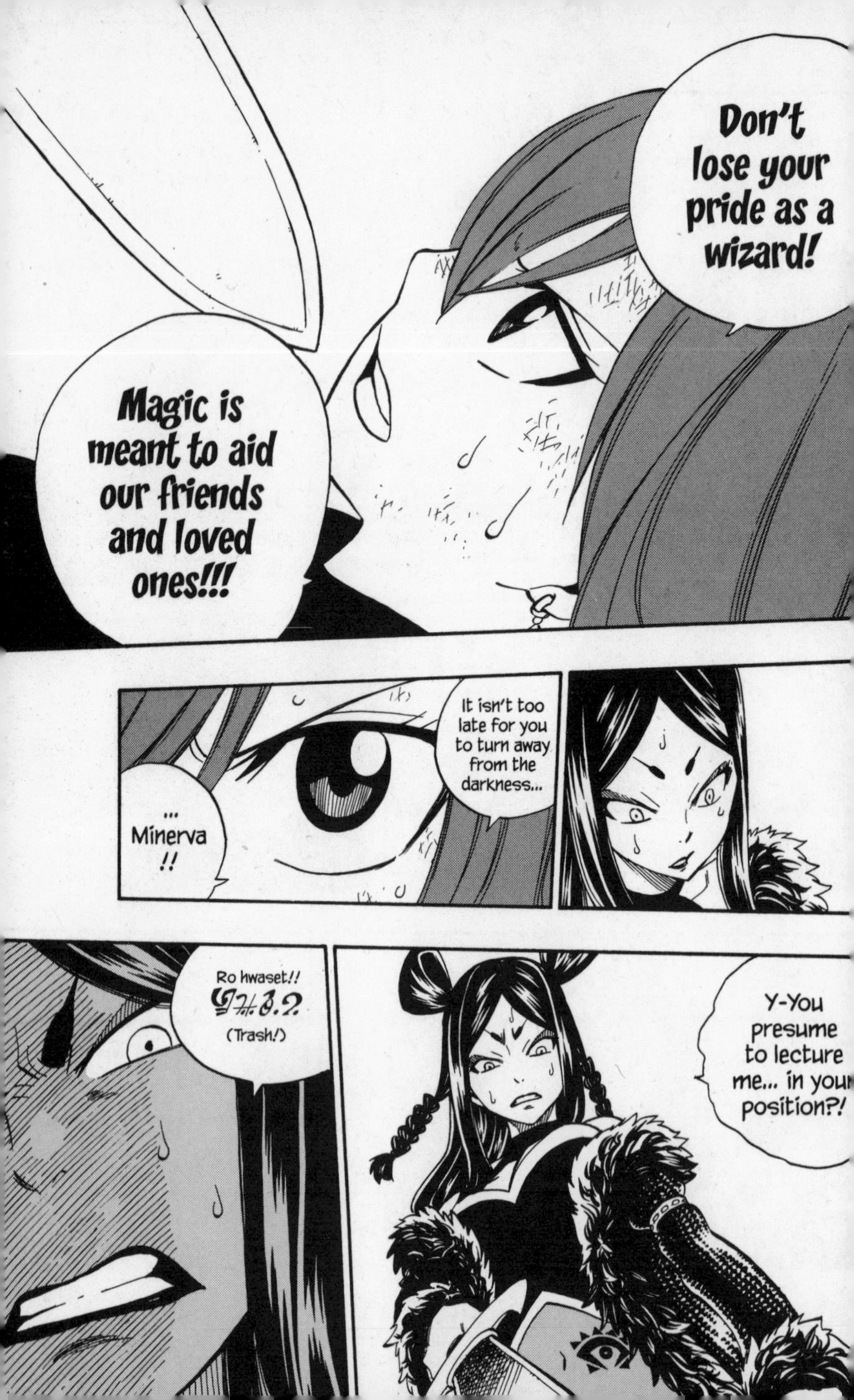
Don't lose your pride as a wizard!
Magic is meant to aid our friends and loved ones!!!
It isn't too late for you to turn away from the darkness...
... Minerva !!
Y-You presume to lecture me... in your position?!
Ro hwaset!!
(Trash!)

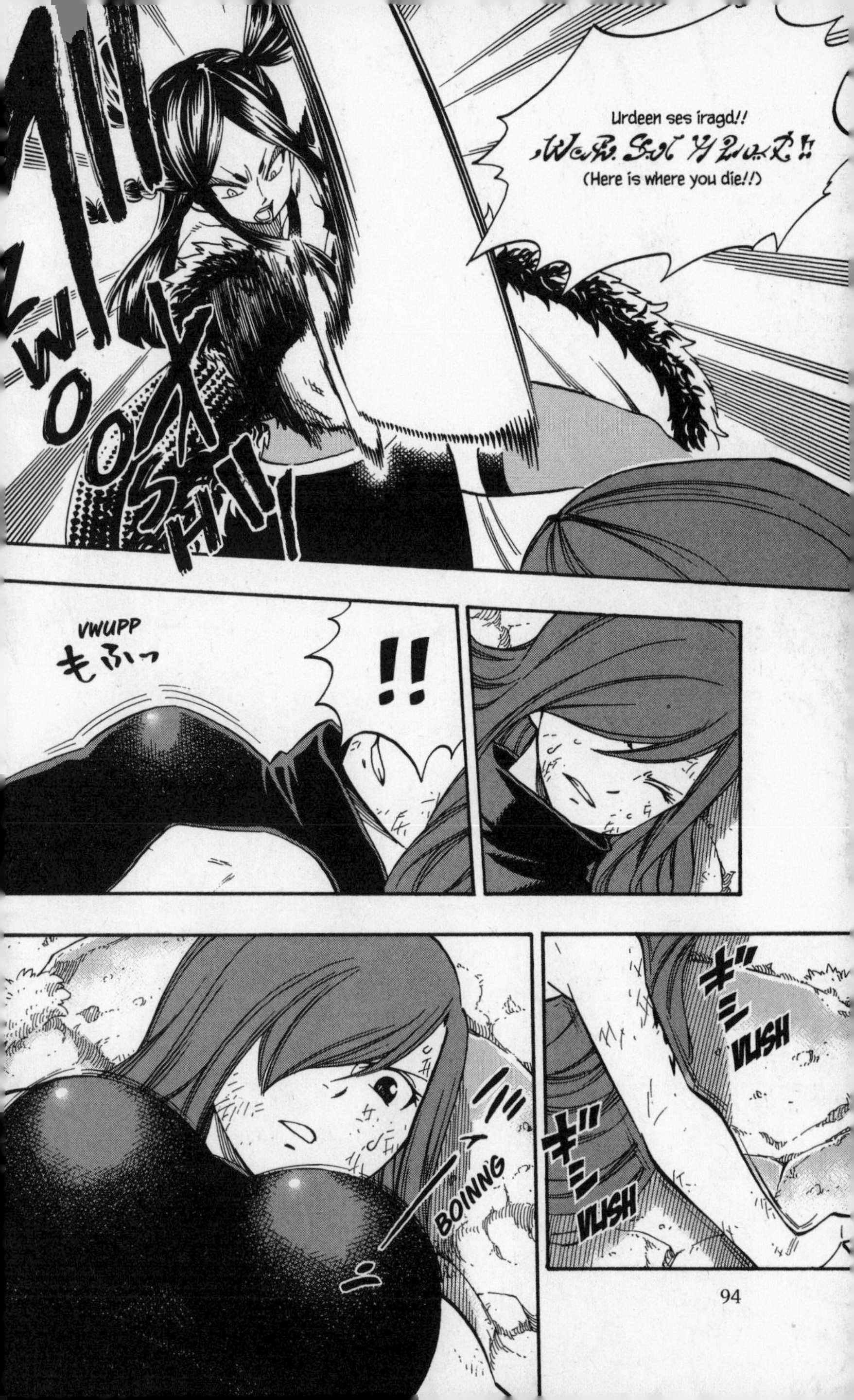
Urdeen ses iragd!!
(Here is where you die!!)
ZWOOSH!!
!!
VWUPP
もふっ
ギシ
VLISH
ギシ
VLISH
BOINNG

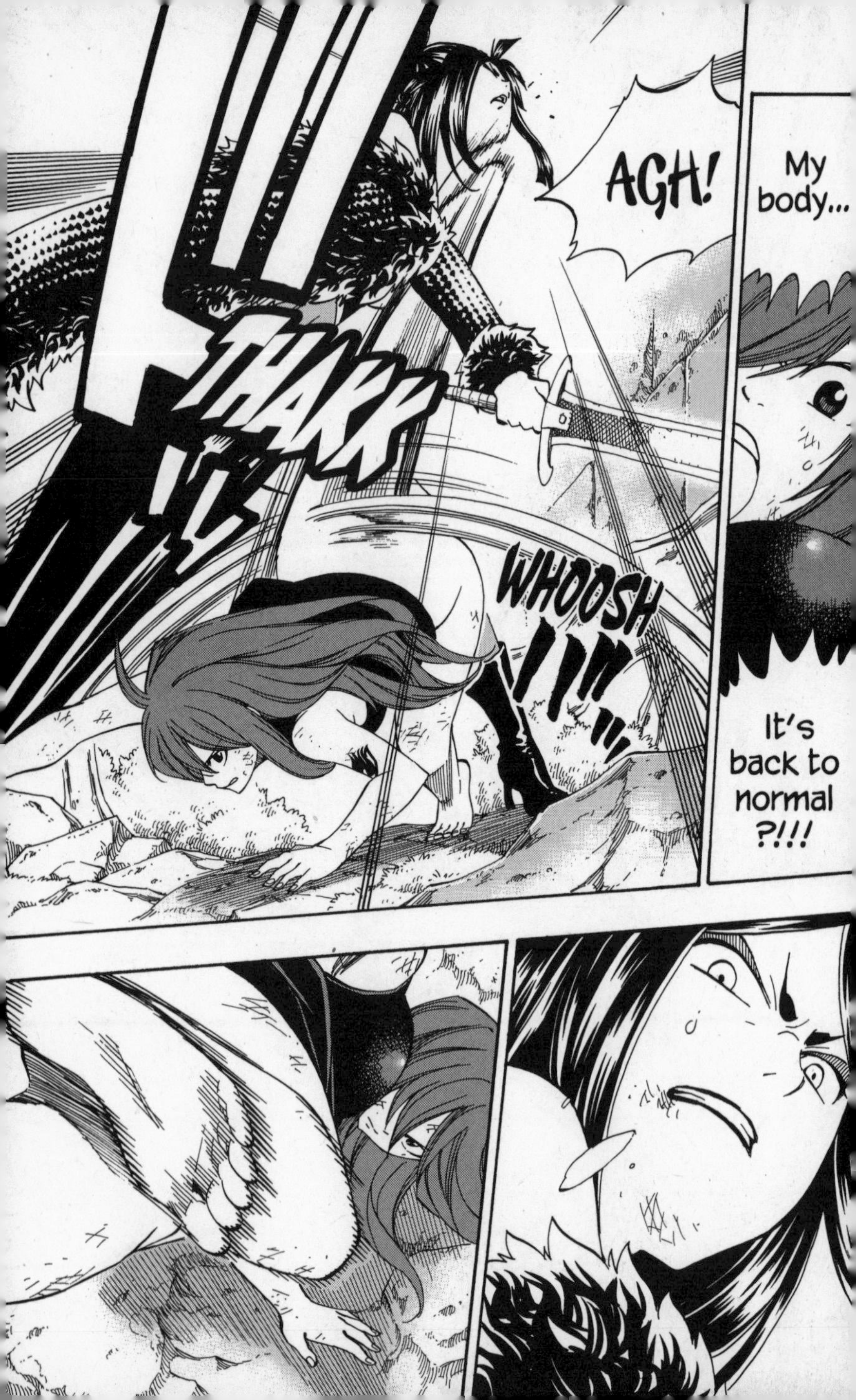
My body...
It's back to normal ?!!!
AGH!
THAKK
WHOOSH

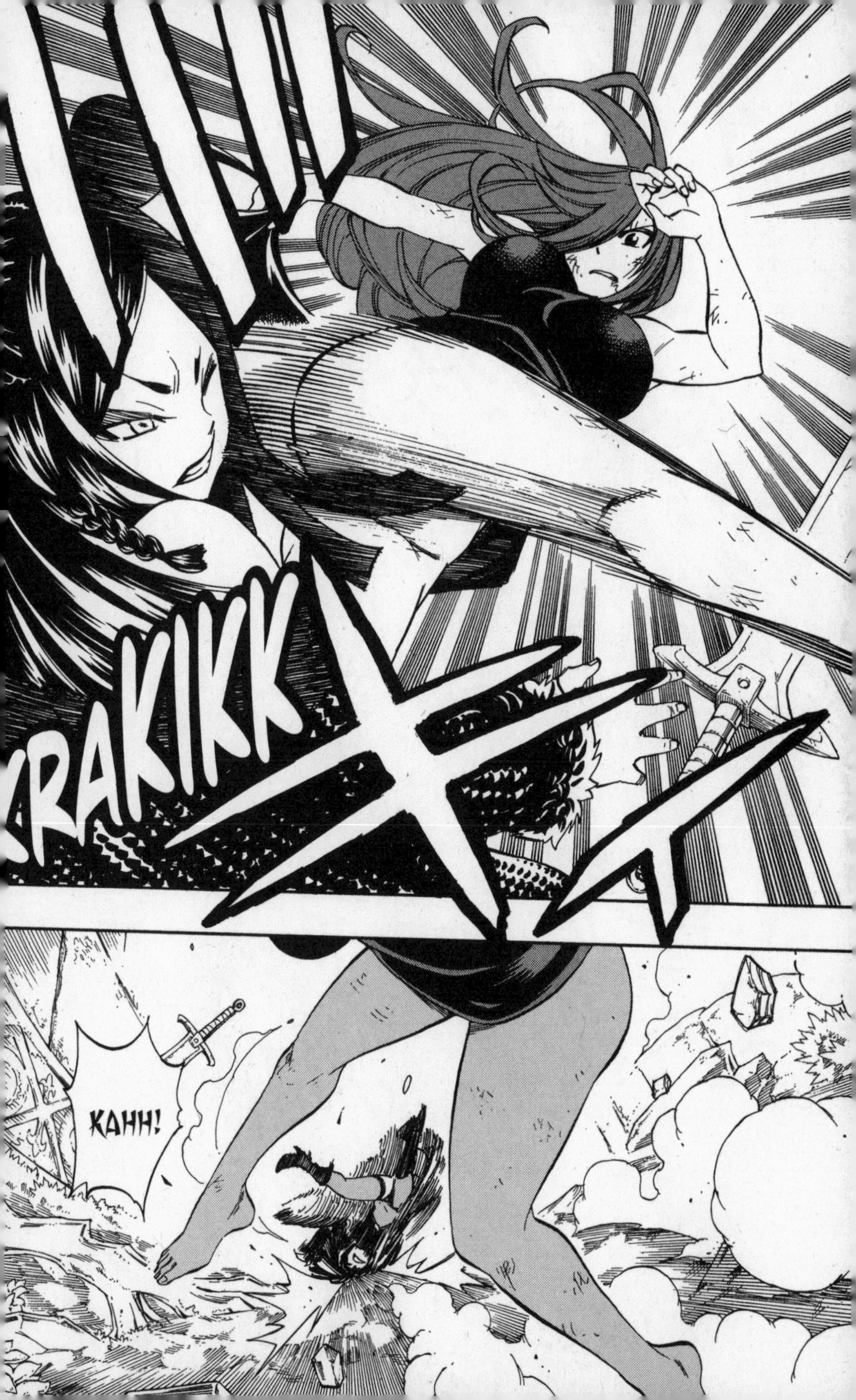
KRAKIKK
KAHH!

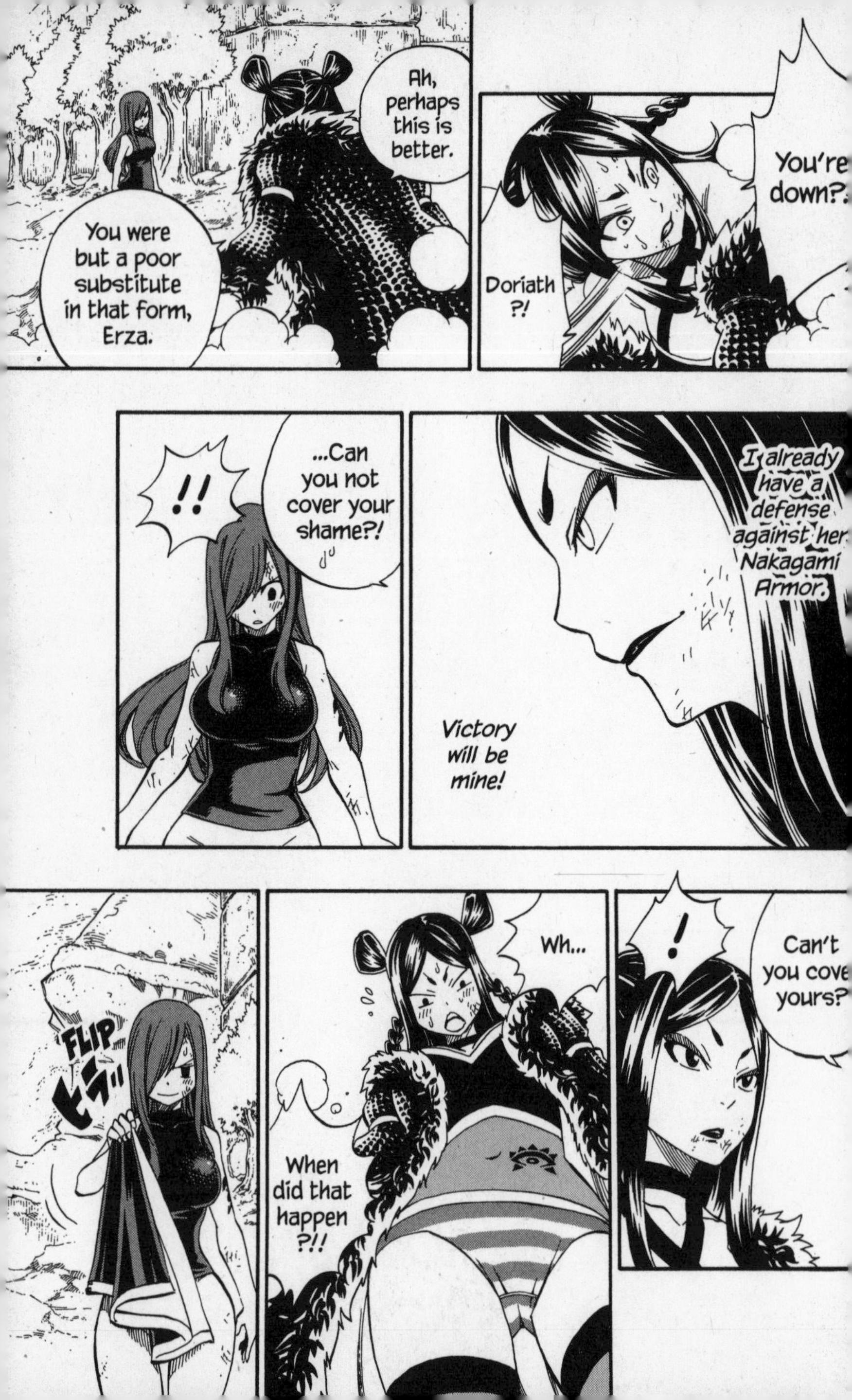
You're down?!
Doriath ?!
Ah, perhaps this is better.
You were but a poor substitute in that form, Erza.
I already have a defense against her Nakagami Armor.
Victory will be mine!
!!
...Can you not cover your shame?!
!
Can't you cove yours?
Wh...
When did that happen ?!!
FLIP

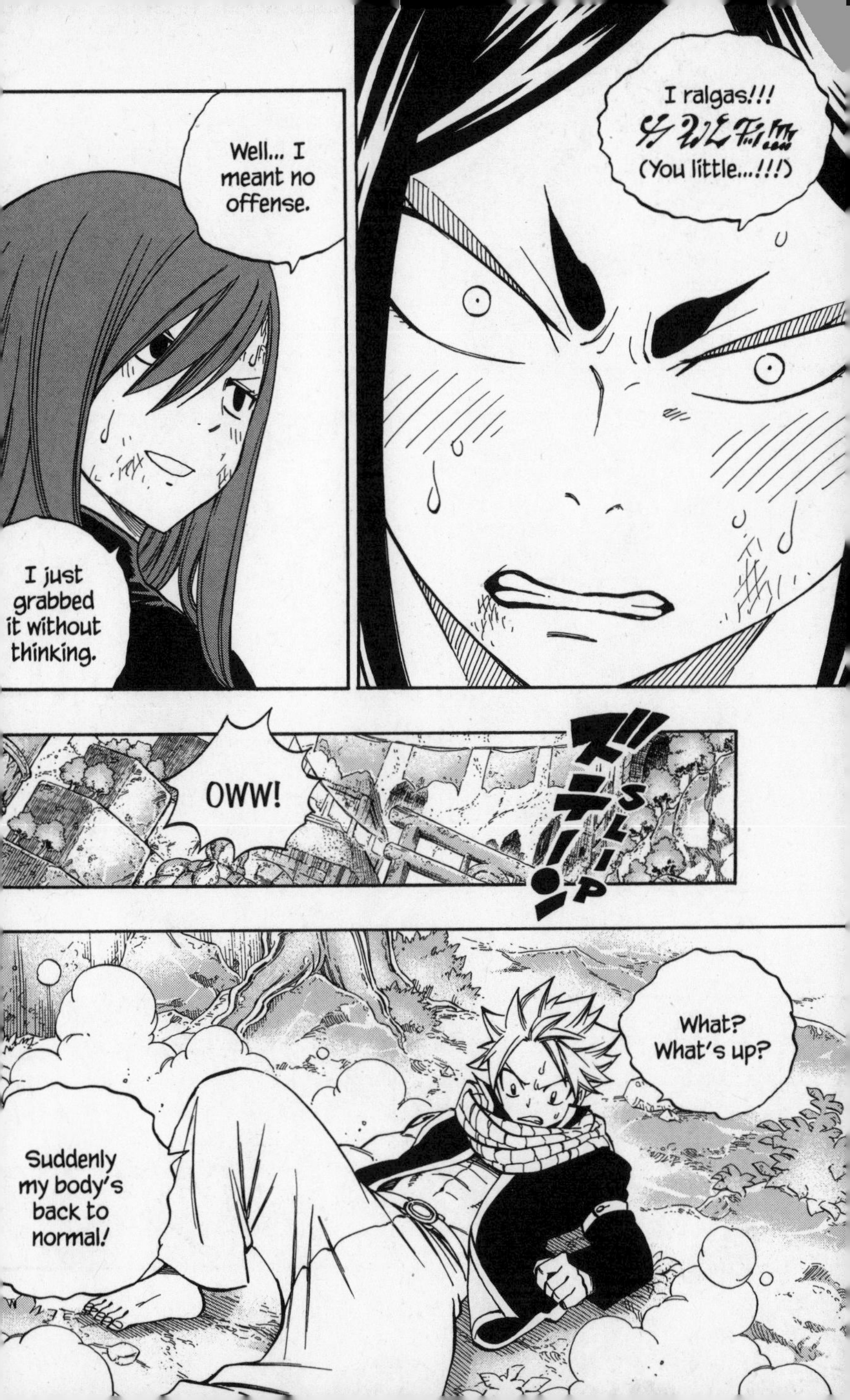
I ralgas!!!
(You little...!!!)
Well... I meant no offense.
I just grabbed it without thinking.
OWW!
SLIP
What? What's up?
Suddenly my body's back to normal!

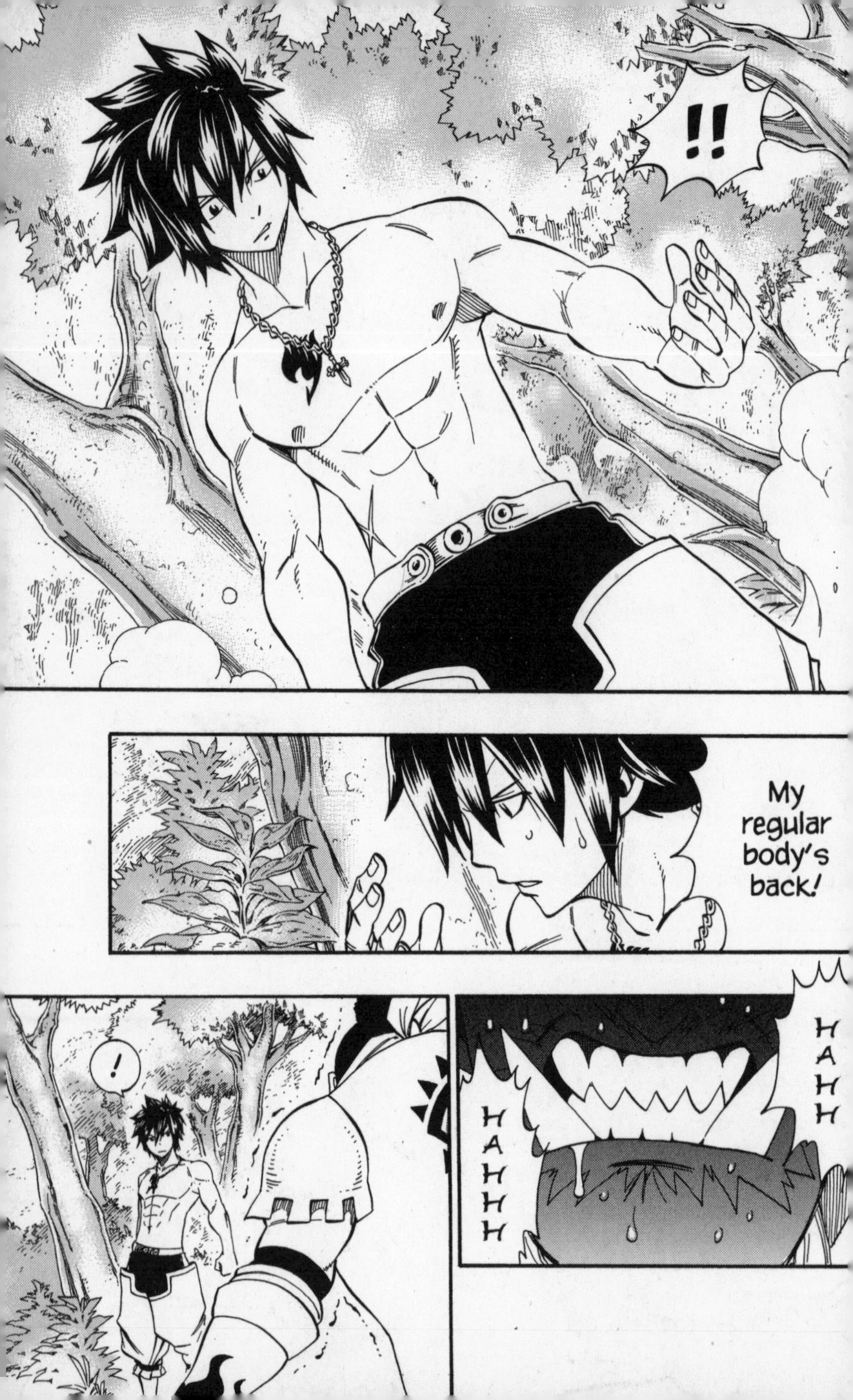
!!
My regular body's back!
HAHH
HAHH
!

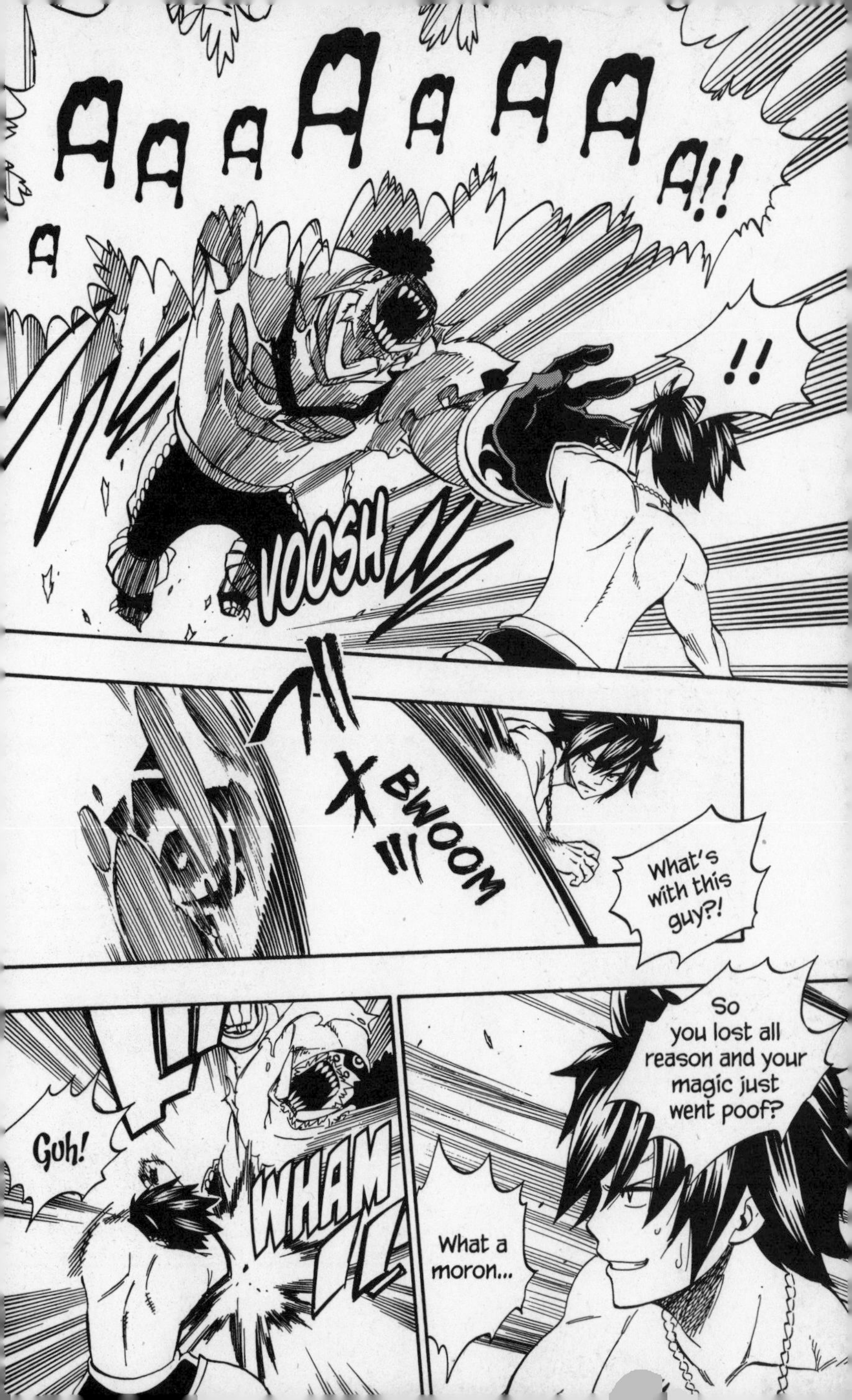
AAAAAAAAA!!
!!
VOOSH
What's with this guy?!
BWOOM
So you lost all reason and your magic just went poof?
What a moron...
WHAM
Guh!

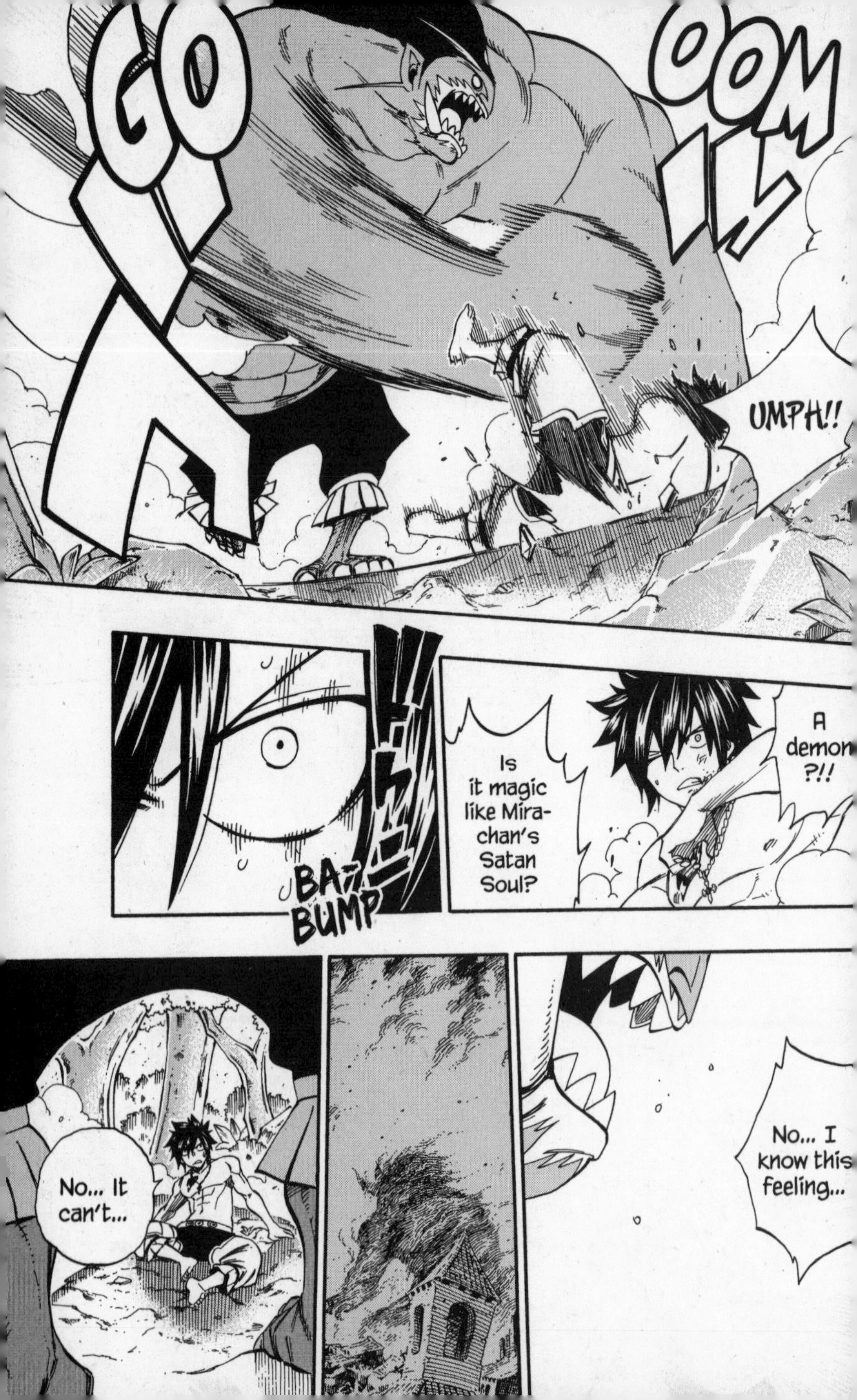
GO OOM
UMPH!!
A demon?!!
Is it magic like Mira-chan's Satan Soul?
BA-BUMP
No... I know this feeling...
No... It can't...

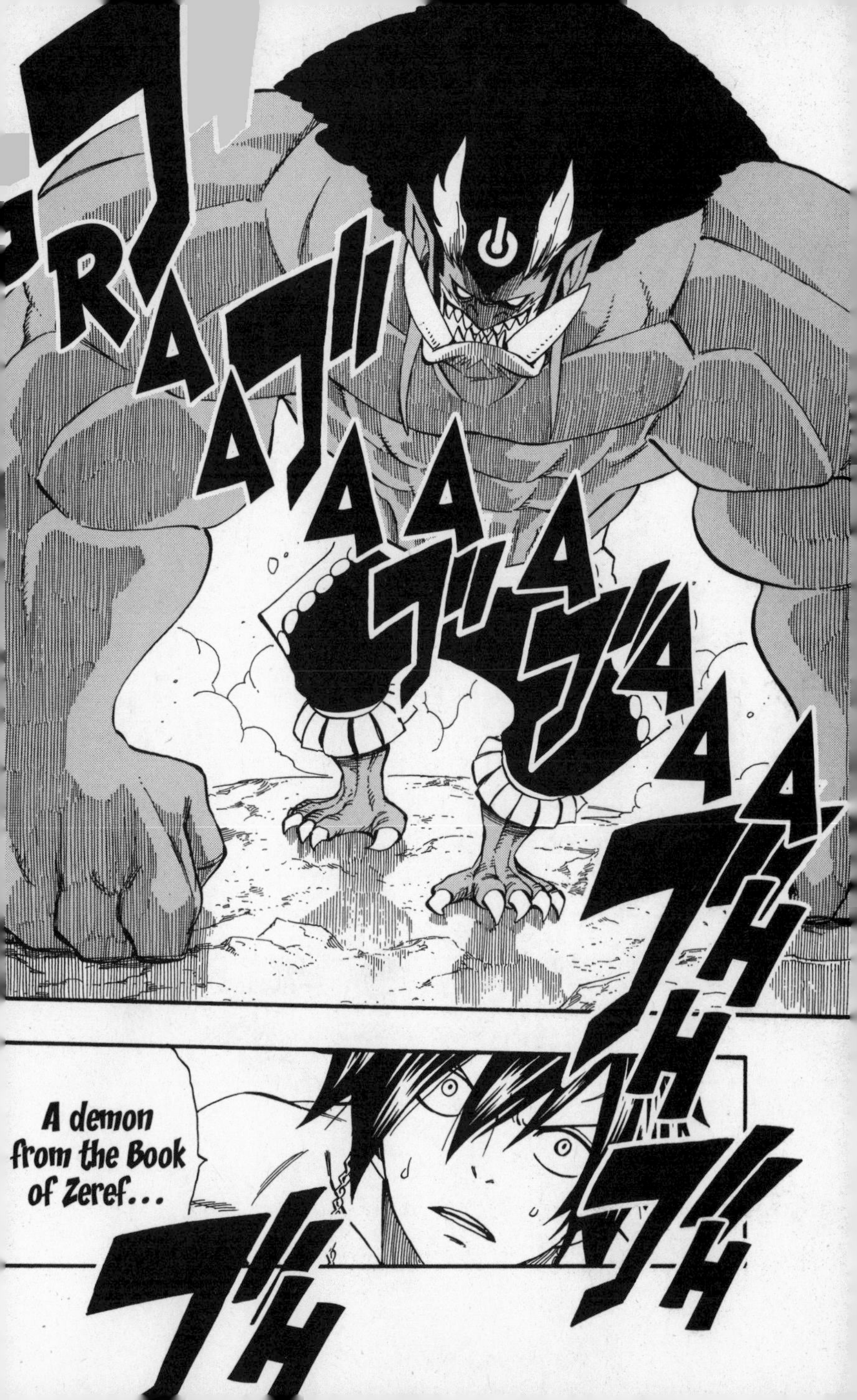
A demon from the Book of Zeref...

FAIRY TAIL

Chapter 350: Gray vs. Doriath

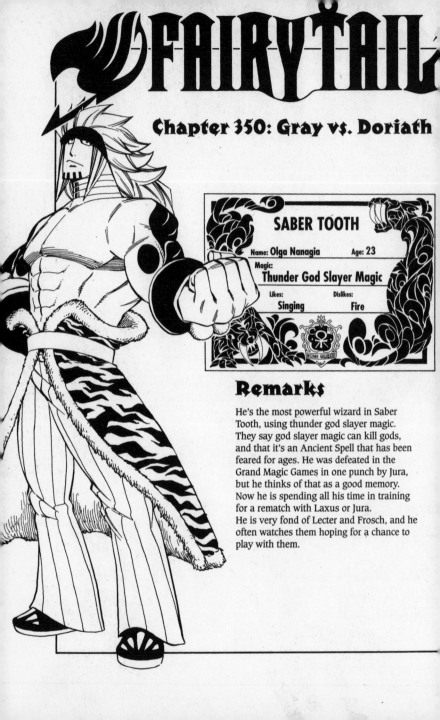

SABER TOOTH

Name: Olga Nanagia   **Age:** 23

Magic:
Thunder God Slayer Magic

Likes: **Dislikes:**
Singing   **Fire**

Remarks

He's the most powerful wizard in Saber
Tooth, using thunder god slayer magic.
They say god slayer magic can kill gods,
and that it's an Ancient Spell that has been
feared for ages. He was defeated in the
Grand Magic Games in one punch by Jura,
but he thinks of that as a good memory.
Now he is spending all his time in training
for a rematch with Laxus or Jura.
He is very fond of Lecter and Frosch, and he
often watches them hoping for a chance to
play with them.

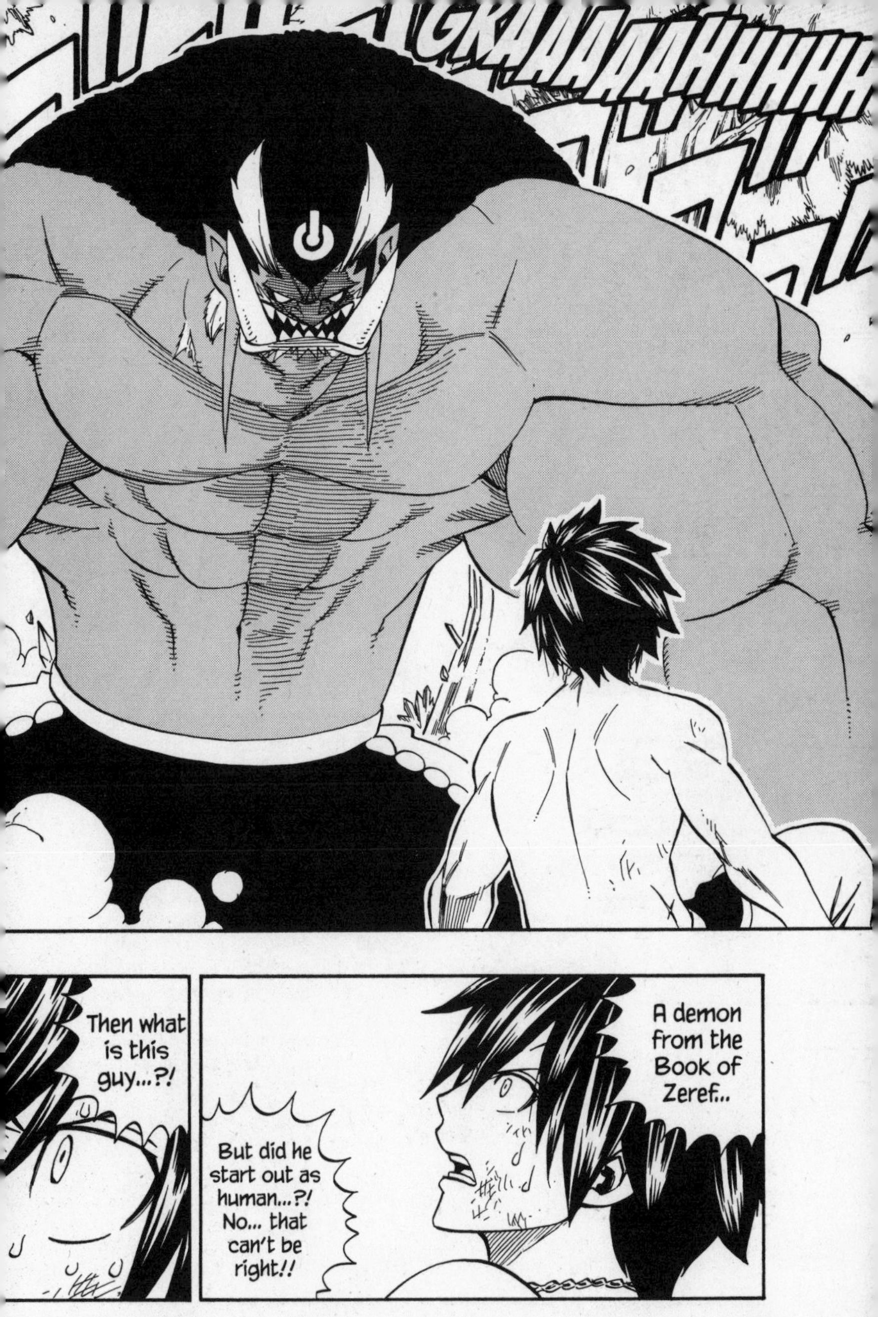
GRAAAAAHHHHH
A demon from the Book of Zeref...
But did he start out as human...?! No... that can't be right!!
Then what is this guy...?!

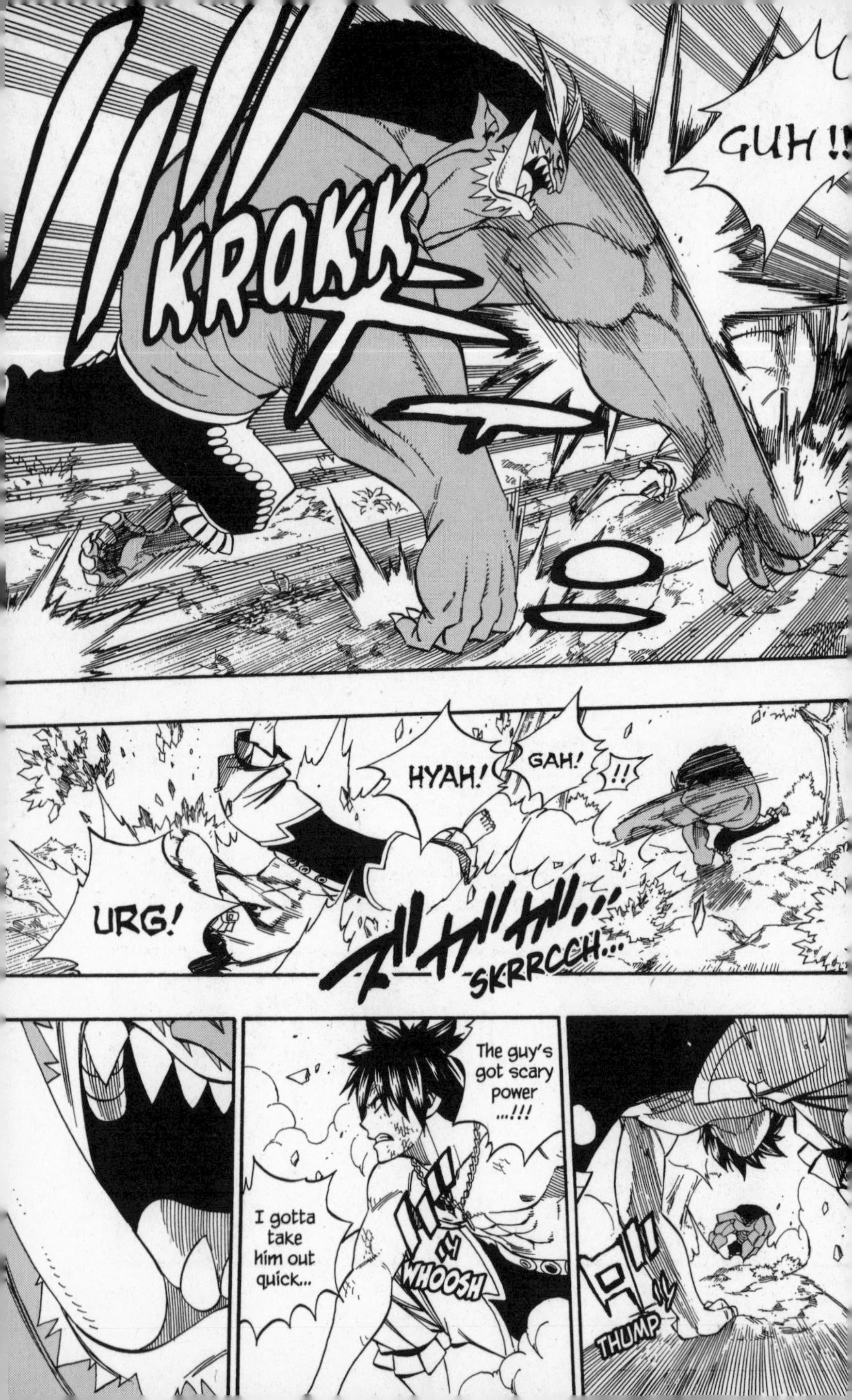
GUH!!
KRAKK
!!
GAH!
HYAH!
URG!
SKRRCCH...
THUMP
The guy's got scary power ...!!!
WHOOSH
I gotta take him out quick...

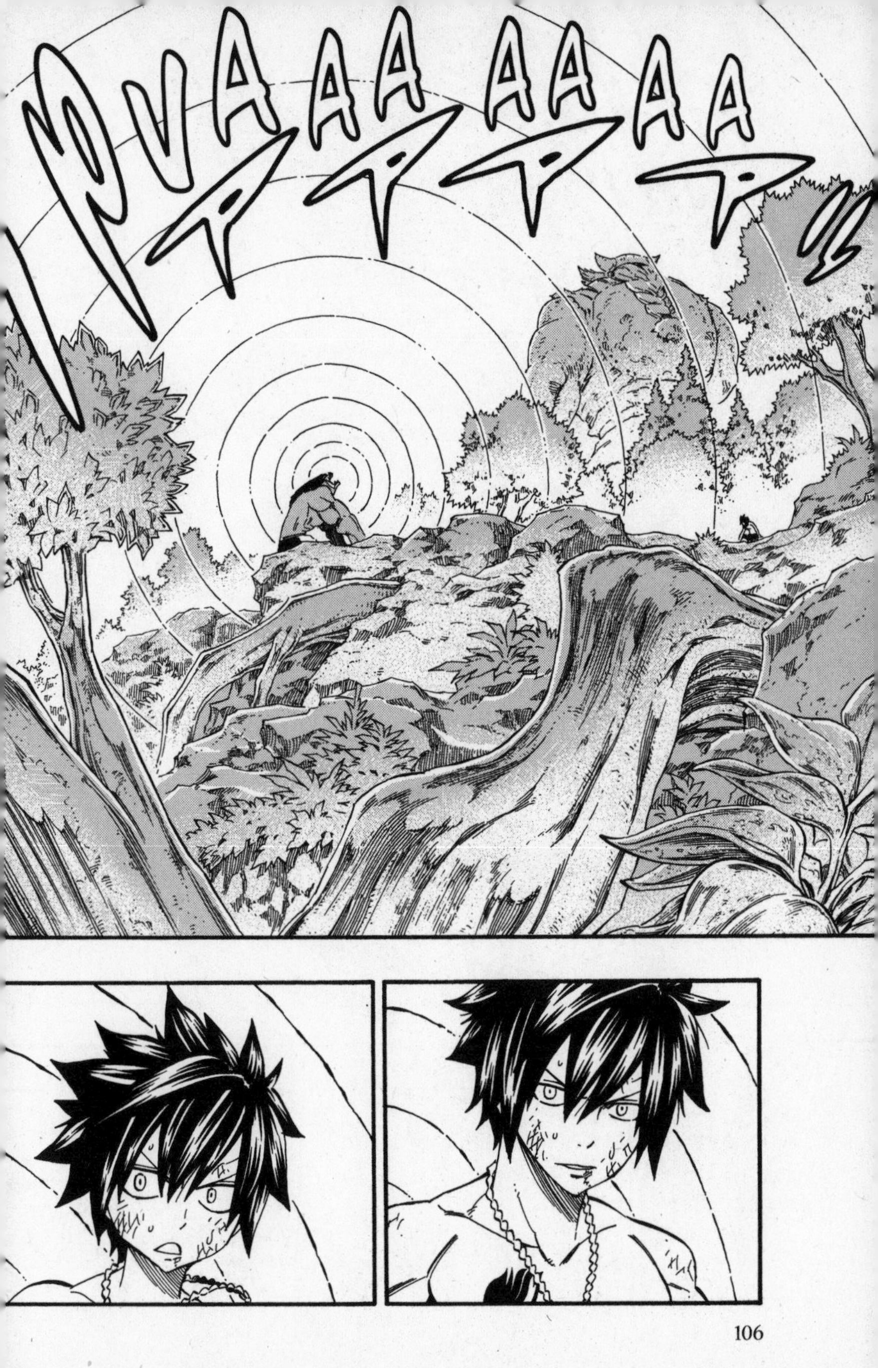

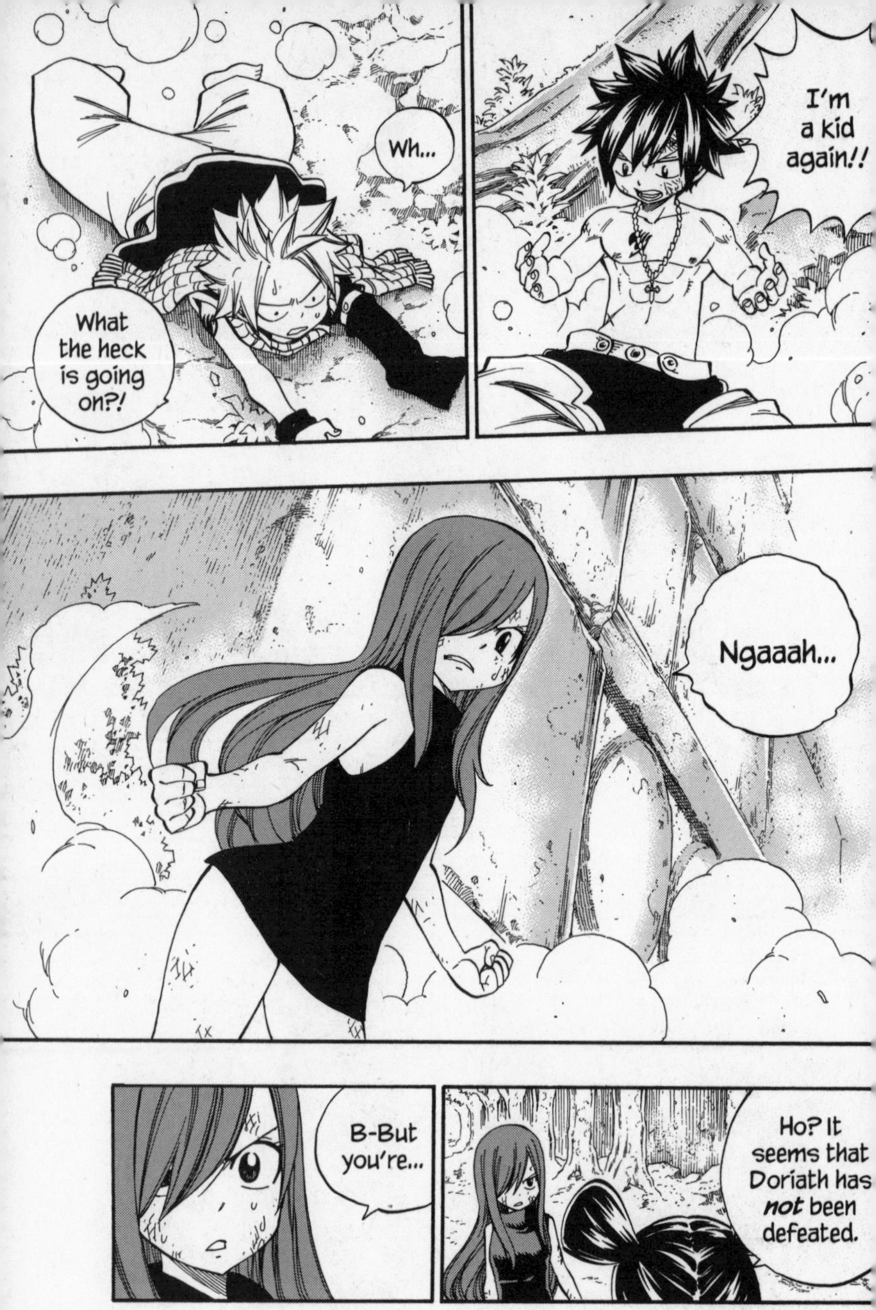
I'm a kid again!!
Wh...
What the heck is going on?!
Ngaaah...
Ho? It seems that Doriath has *not* been defeated.
B-But you're...

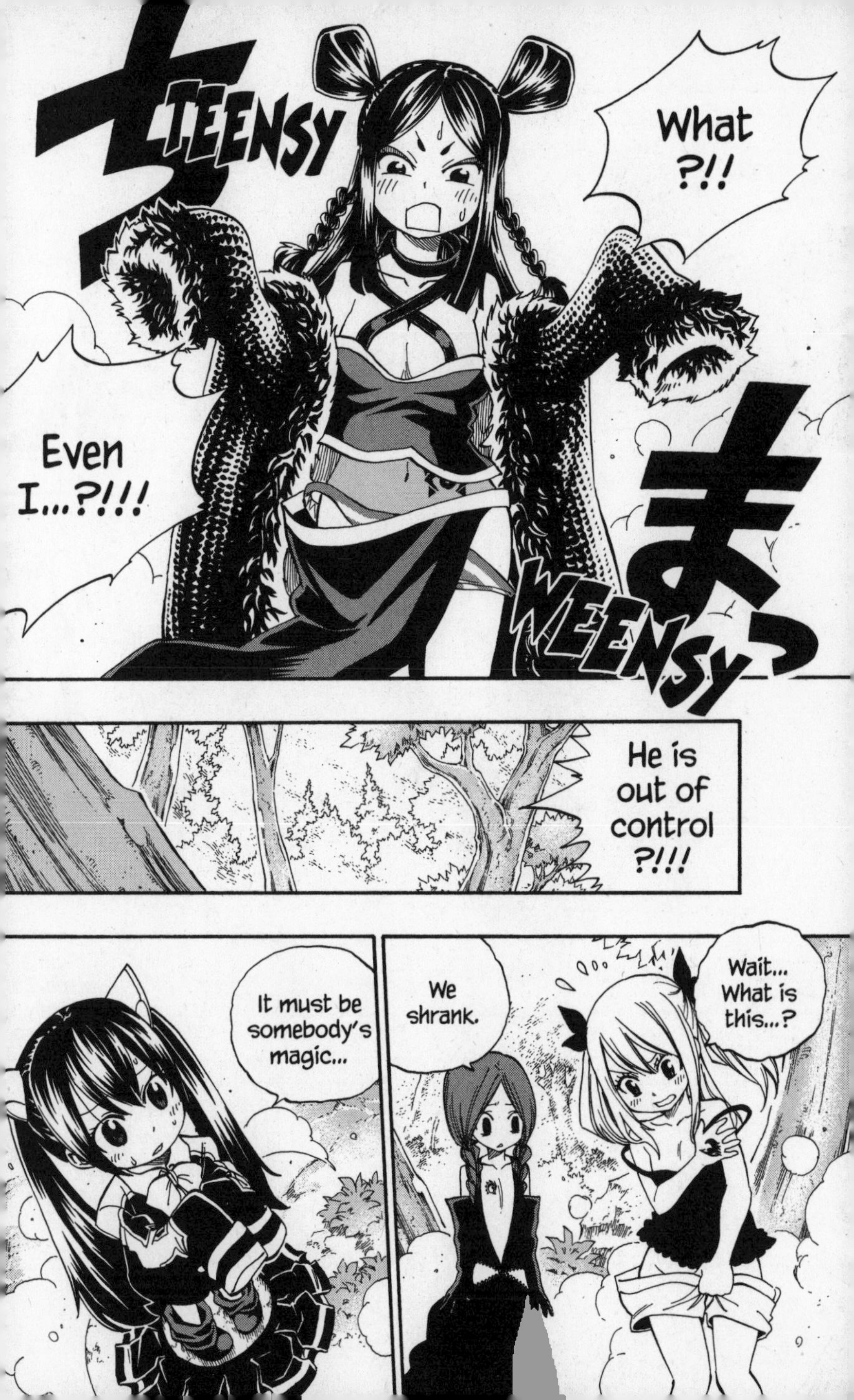

What ?!!
TEENSY
WEENSY
Even I...?!!!
He is out of control ?!!!
Wait... What is this...?
We shrank.
It must be somebody's magic...

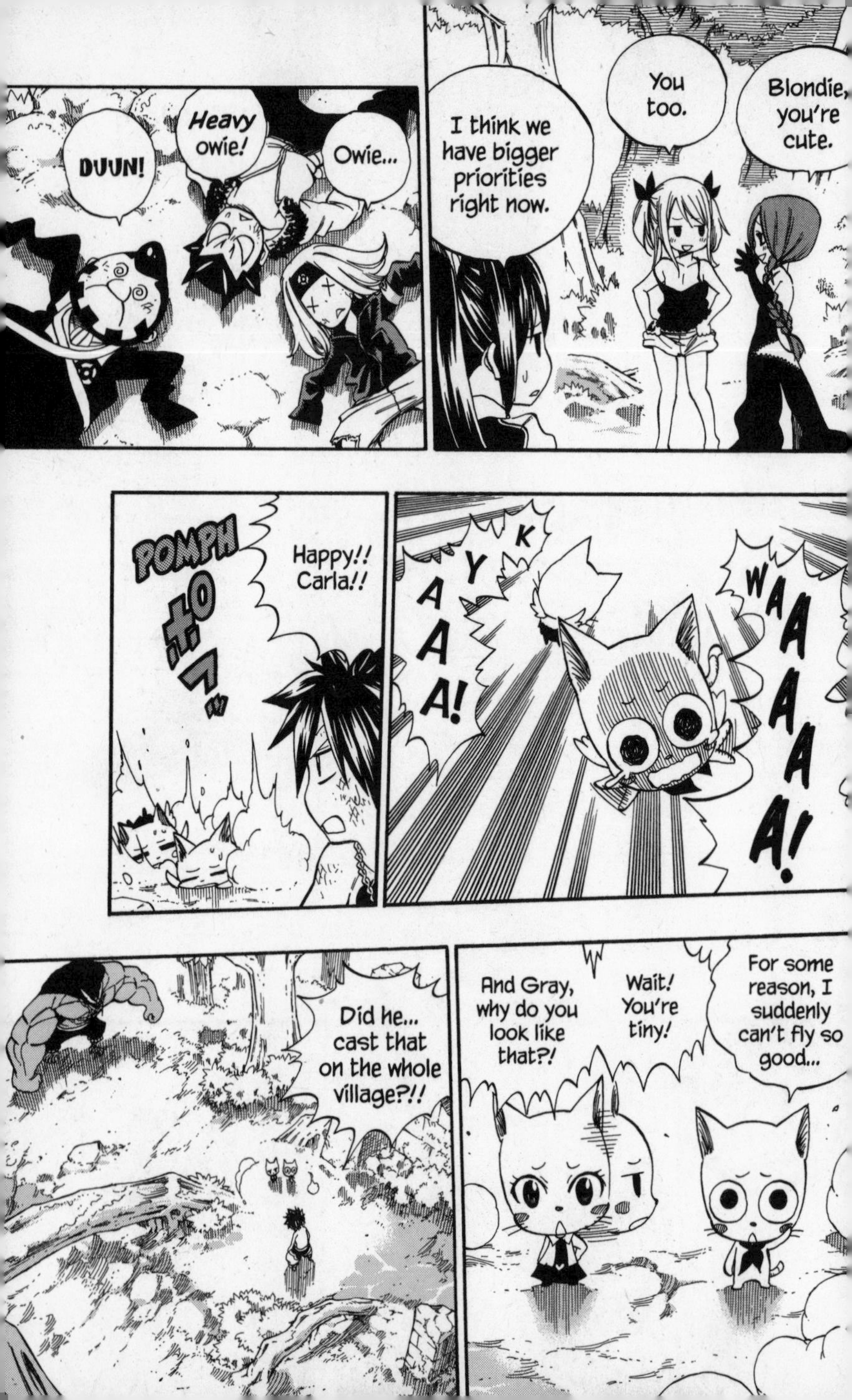
Blondie, you're cute.
You too.
I think we have bigger priorities right now.
Owie...
Heavy owie!
DUUN!
WAAAAAAA!
KYAAAA!
Happy!! Carla!!
POMPH
For some reason, I suddenly can't fly so good...
Wait! You're tiny!
And Gray, why do you look like that?!
Did he... cast that on the whole village?!!

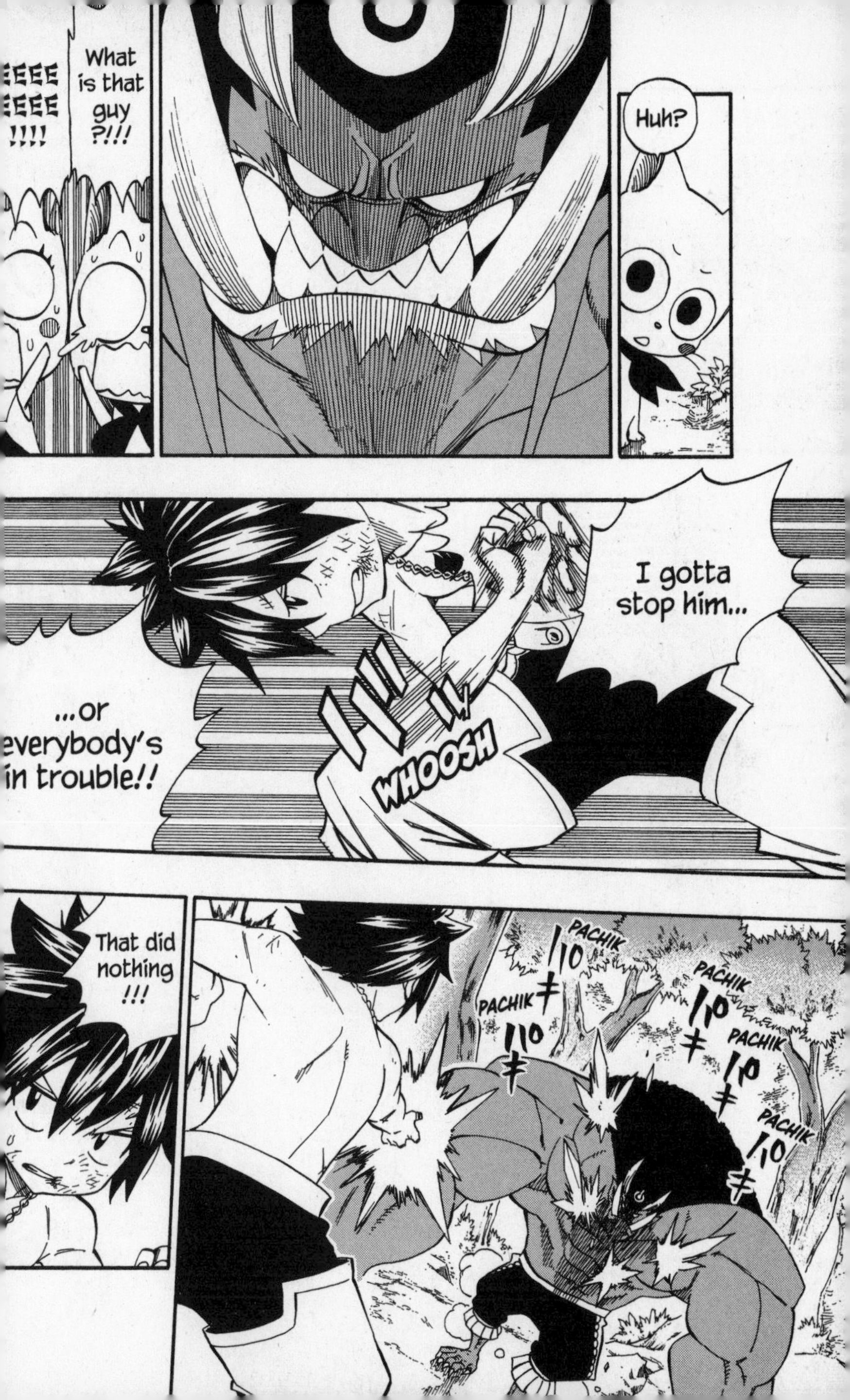
Huh?
What is that guy?!!!
EEEE EEEE !!!!
I gotta stop him...
WHOOSH
...or everybody's in trouble!!
PACHIK
PACHIK
PACHIK
PACHIK
PACHIK
That did nothing!!!

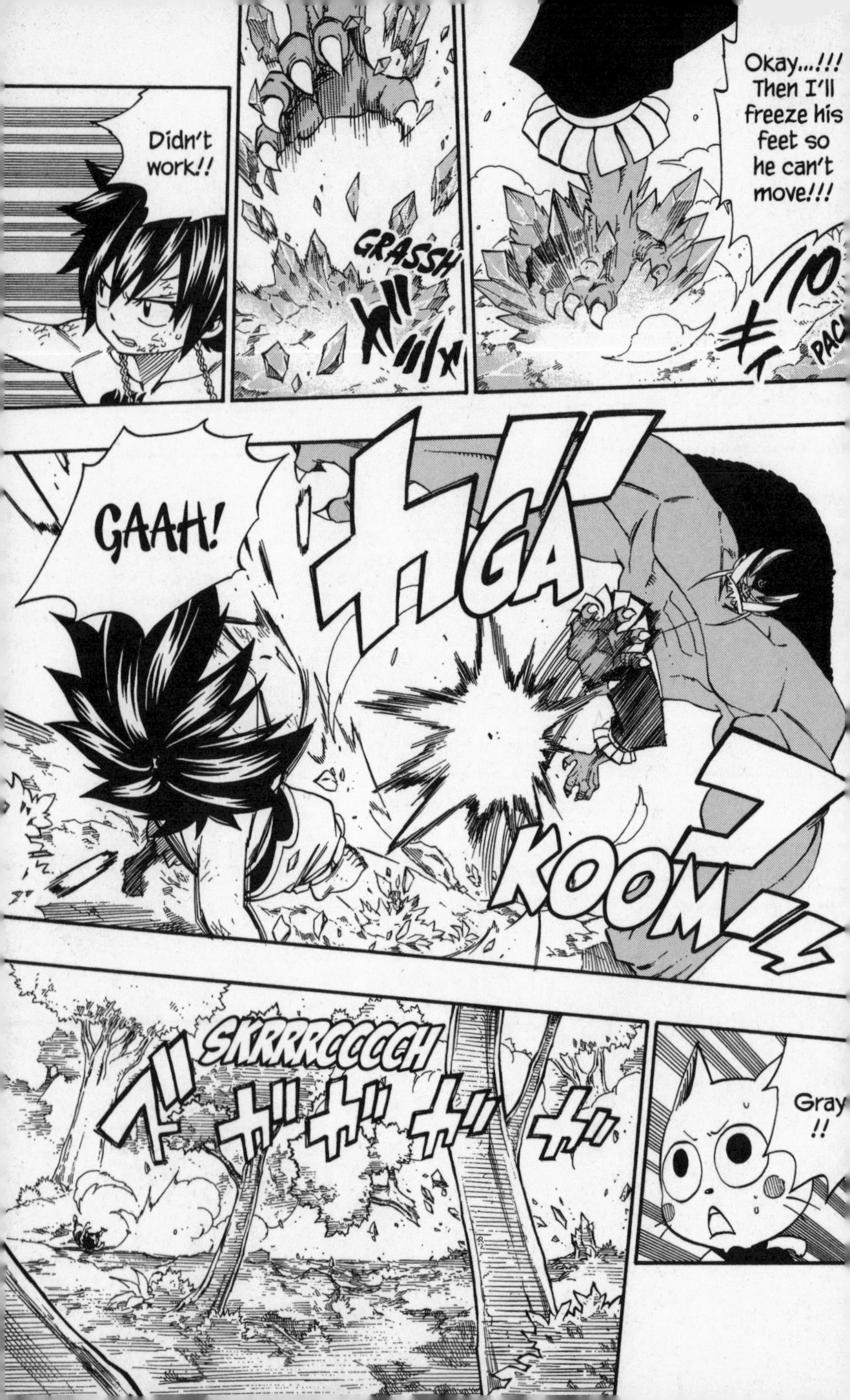
Okay...!!! Then I'll freeze his feet so he can't move!!!
PAC
GRASSH
Didn't work!!
GAAH!
GA
KOOM
Gray !!
SKRRRCCCCH

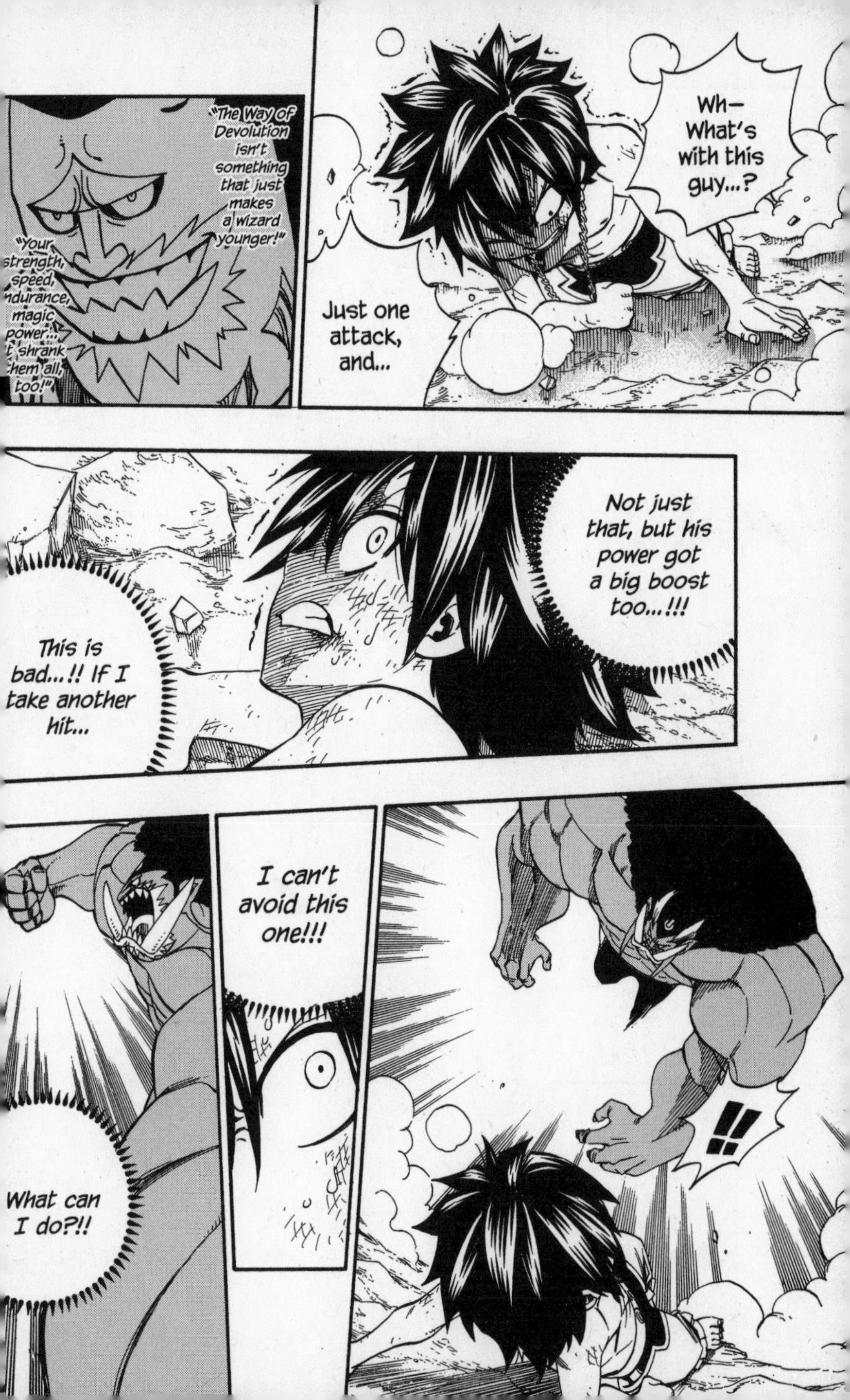
Wh– What's with this guy...?
Just one attack, and...
"The Way of Devolution isn't something that just makes a wizard younger!"
"Your strength, speed, ndurance, magic power... t shrank hem all, too!"
Not just that, but his power got a big boost too...!!!
This is bad...!! If I take another hit...
!!
I can't avoid this one!!!
What can I do?!!

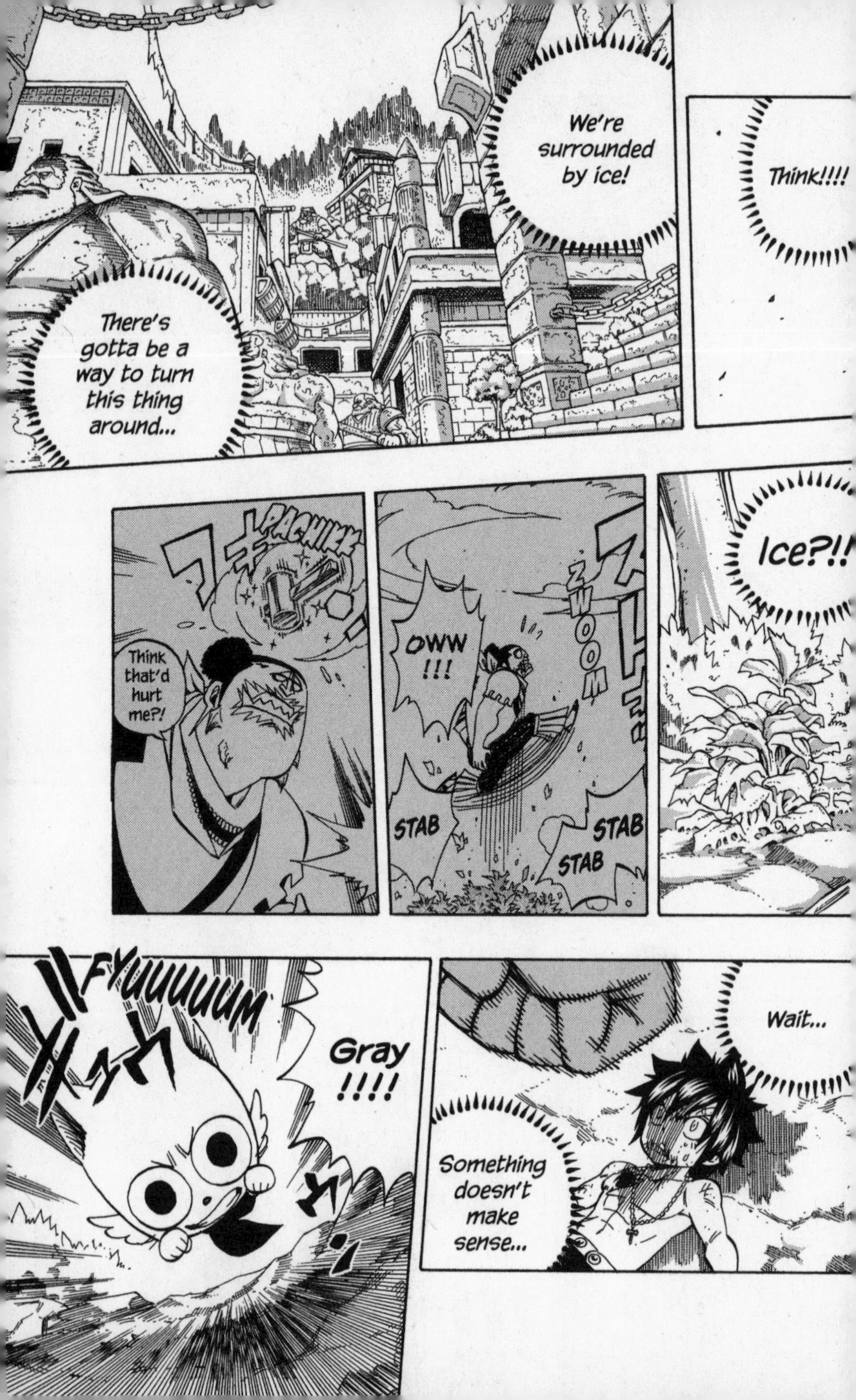
Think!!!!
We're surrounded by ice!
There's gotta be a way to turn this thing around...
Ice?!!
ZWOOM
OWW !!!
STAB
STAB
STAB
PACHINK
Think that'd hurt me?!
Wait...
Something doesn't make sense...
Gray !!!!
FYUUUUUM

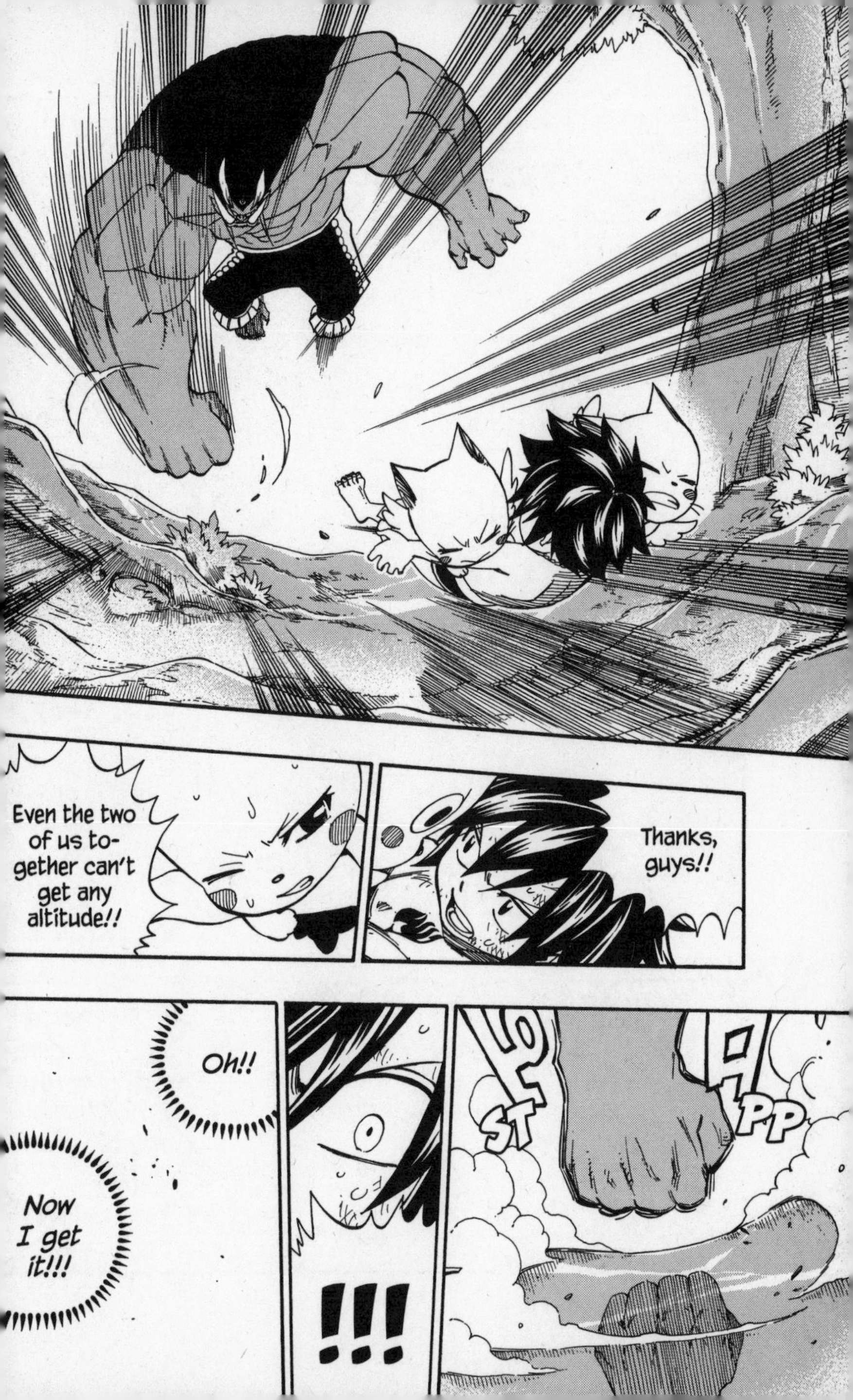
Thanks, guys!!
Even the two of us to-gether can't get any altitude!!
!!!
Oh!!
Now I get it!!!

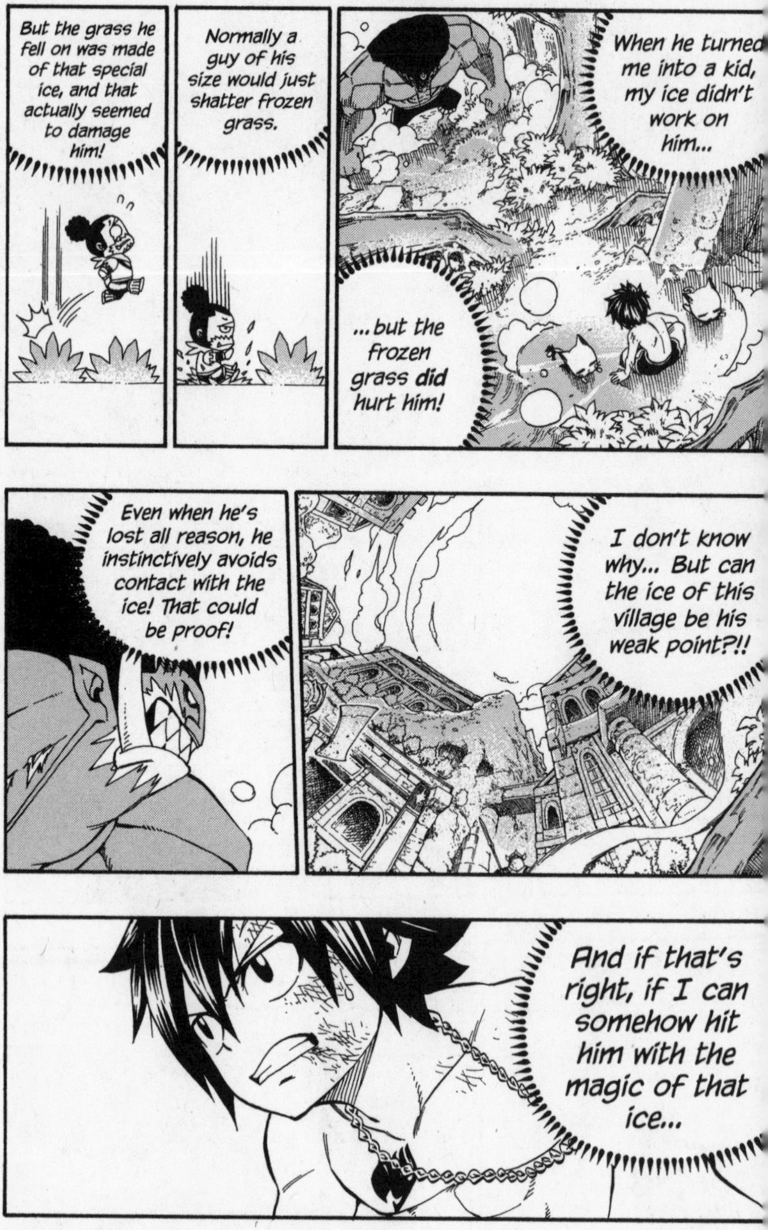
When he turned me into a kid, my ice didn't work on him...
...but the frozen grass did hurt him!
Normally a guy of his size would just shatter frozen grass.
But the grass he fell on was made of that special ice, and that actually seemed to damage him!
I don't know why... But can the ice of this village be his weak point?!!
Even when he's lost all reason, he instinctively avoids contact with the ice! That could be proof!
And if that's right, if I can somehow hit him with the magic of that ice...

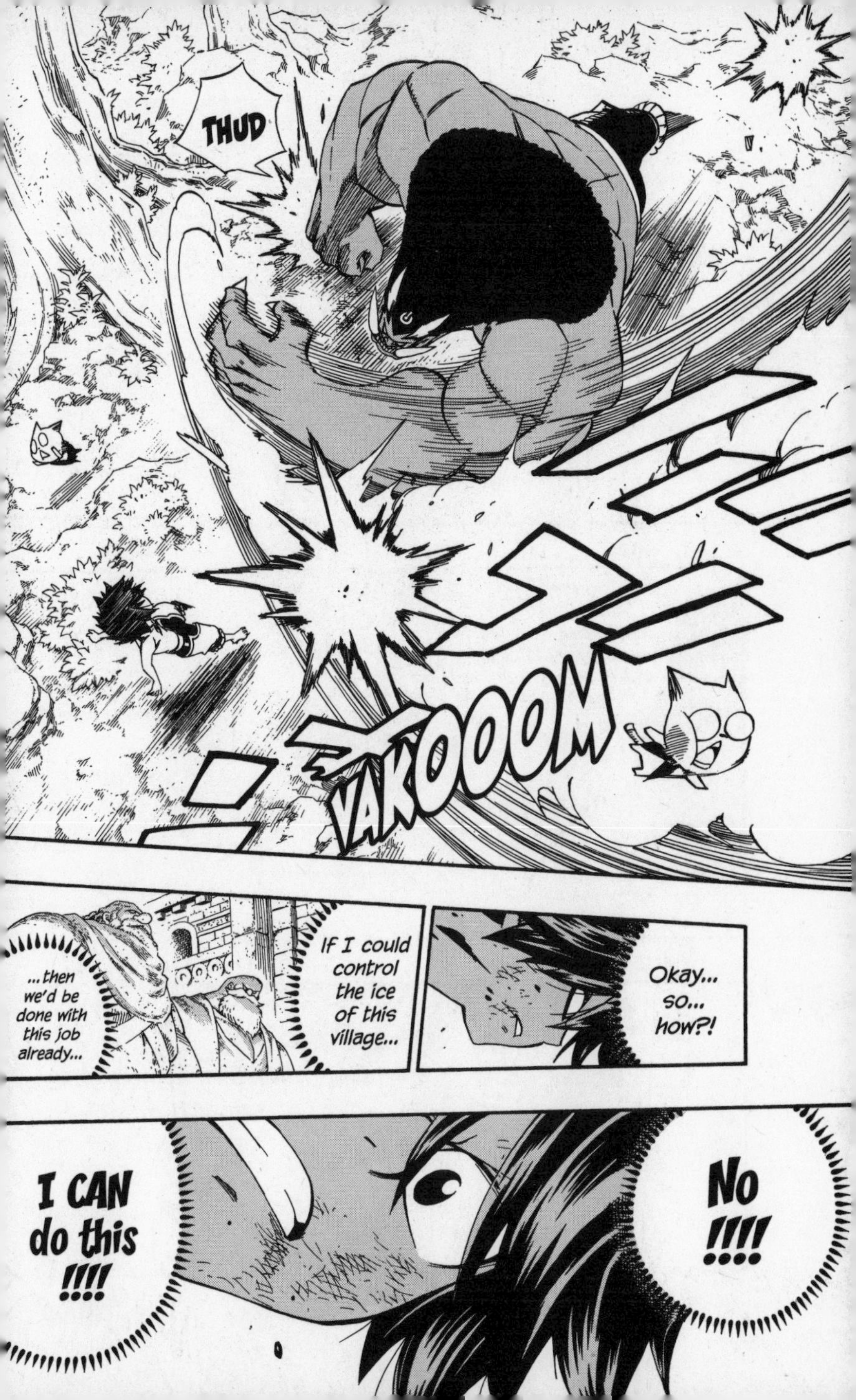
THUD
VAKOOOM
Okay... so... how?!
If I could control the ice of this village...
...then we'd be done with this job already...
No!!!!
I CAN do this!!!!

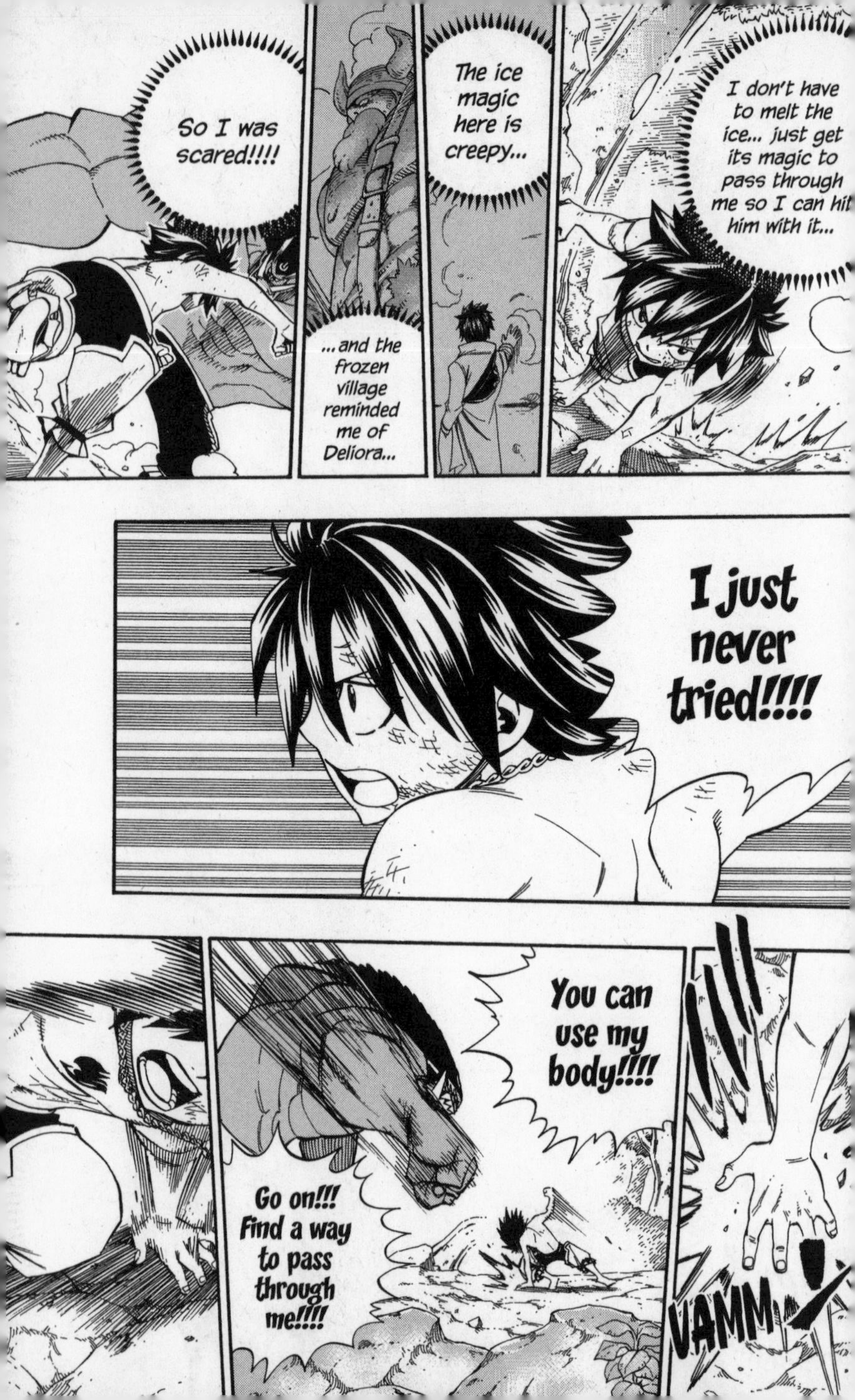
I don't have to melt the ice... just get its magic to pass through me so I can hit him with it...
The ice magic here is creepy...
...and the frozen village reminded me of Deliora...
So I was scared!!!!
I just never tried!!!!
VAMM
You can use my body!!!!
Go on!!! Find a way to pass through me!!!!

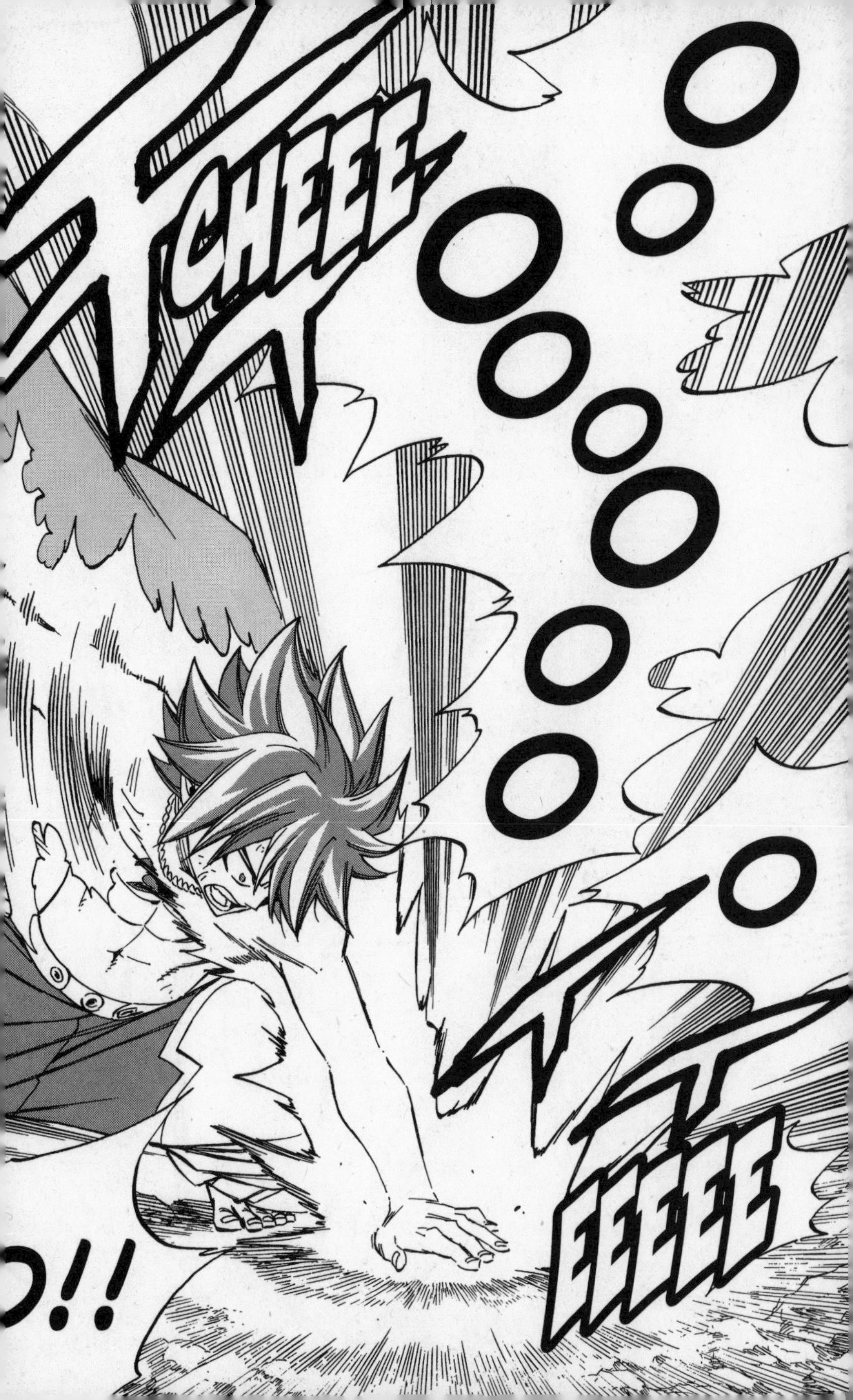

CHEEE
OOOOOOOOOO
EEEEE
O!!

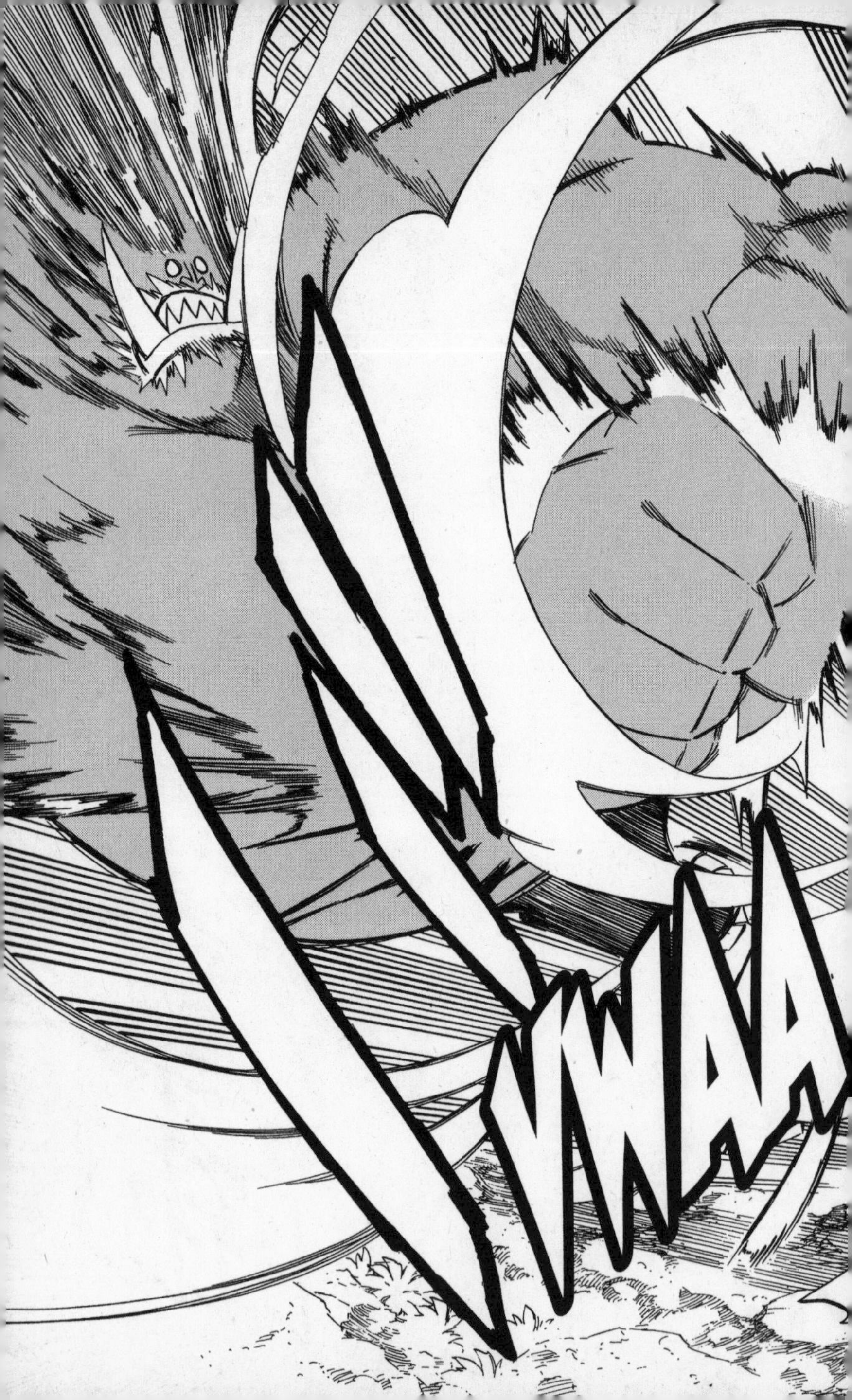
VWAA

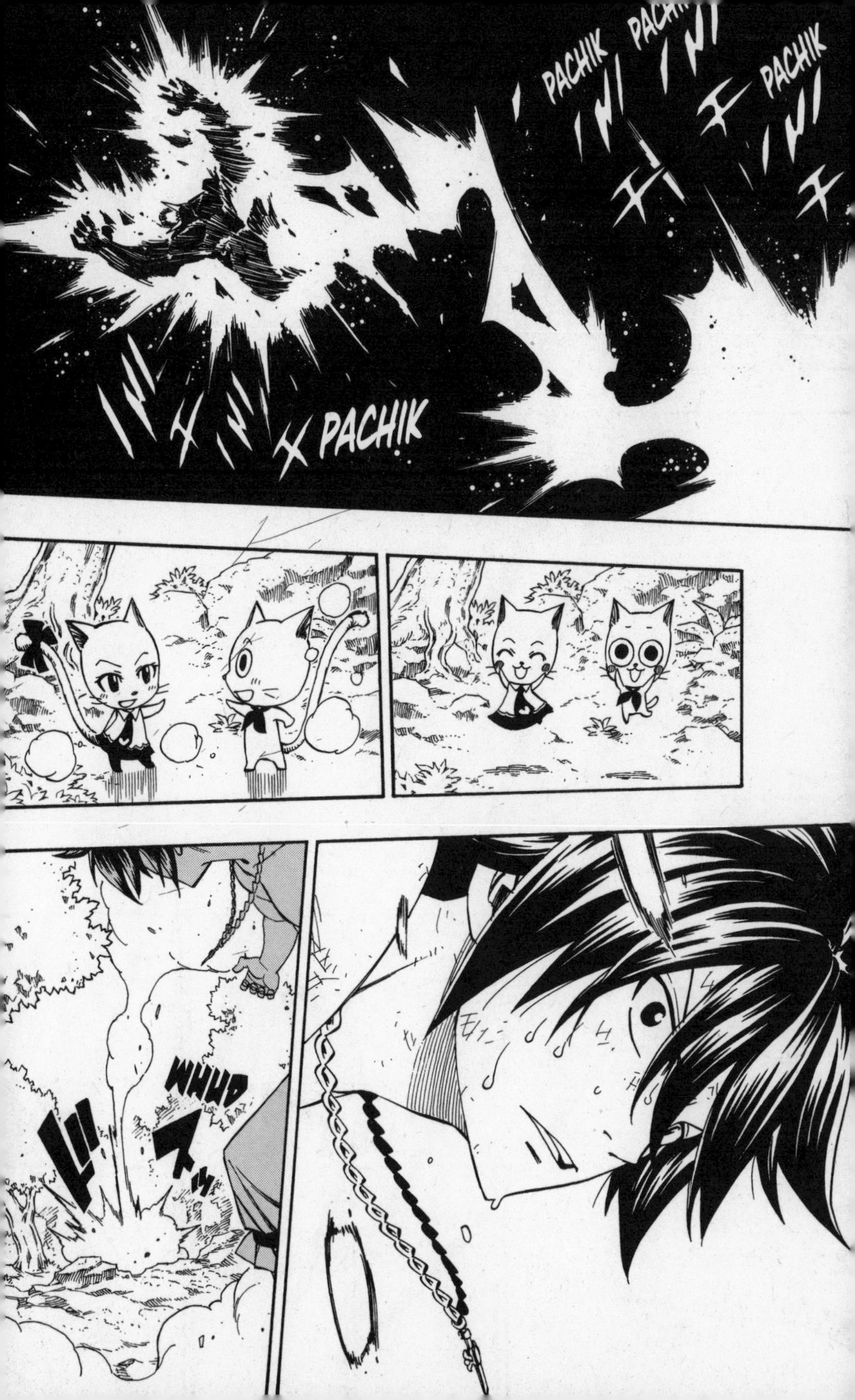
PACHIK
PACHI
PACHIK
PACHIK
WHUD

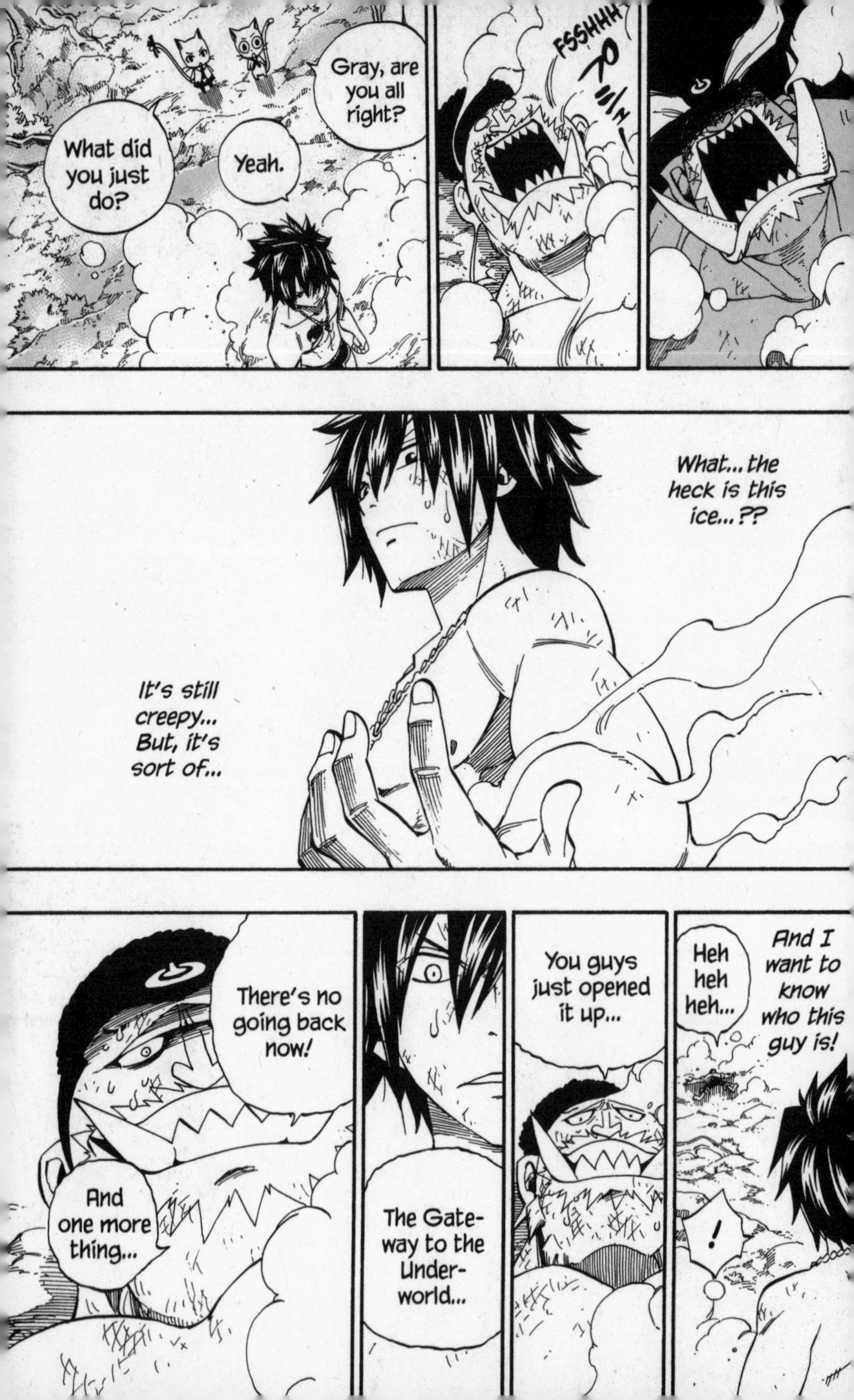
FSSHHH
Gray, are you all right?
Yeah.
What did you just do?
What... the heck is this ice...??
It's still creepy... But, it's sort of...
And I want to know who this guy is!
Heh heh heh...
!
You guys just opened it up...
The Gate-way to the Under-world...
There's no going back now!
And one more thing...

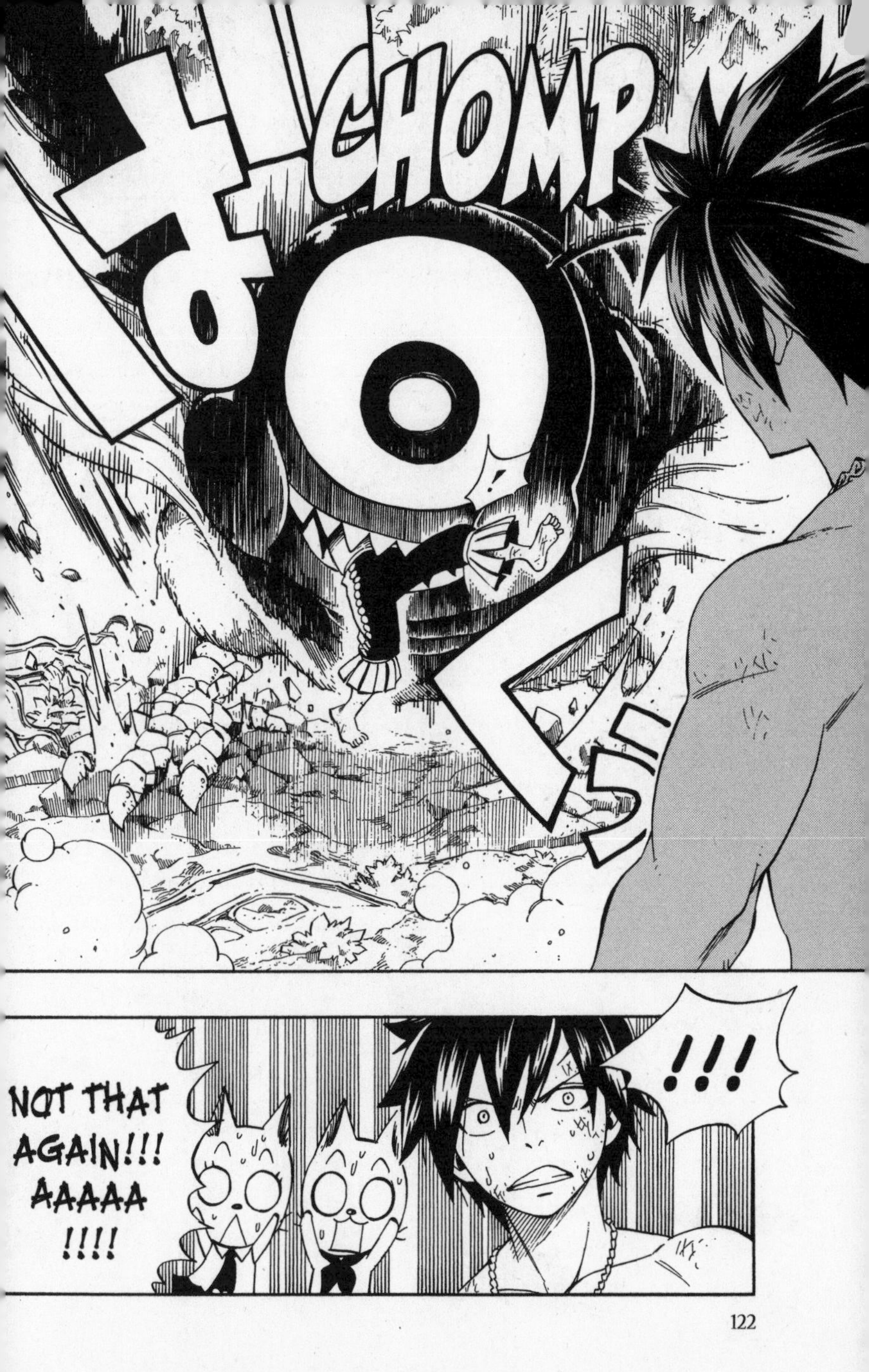
CHOMP
!!!
NOT THAT AGAIN!!! AAAAA !!!!

FAIRY TAIL

Chapter 351: Eternal Flame

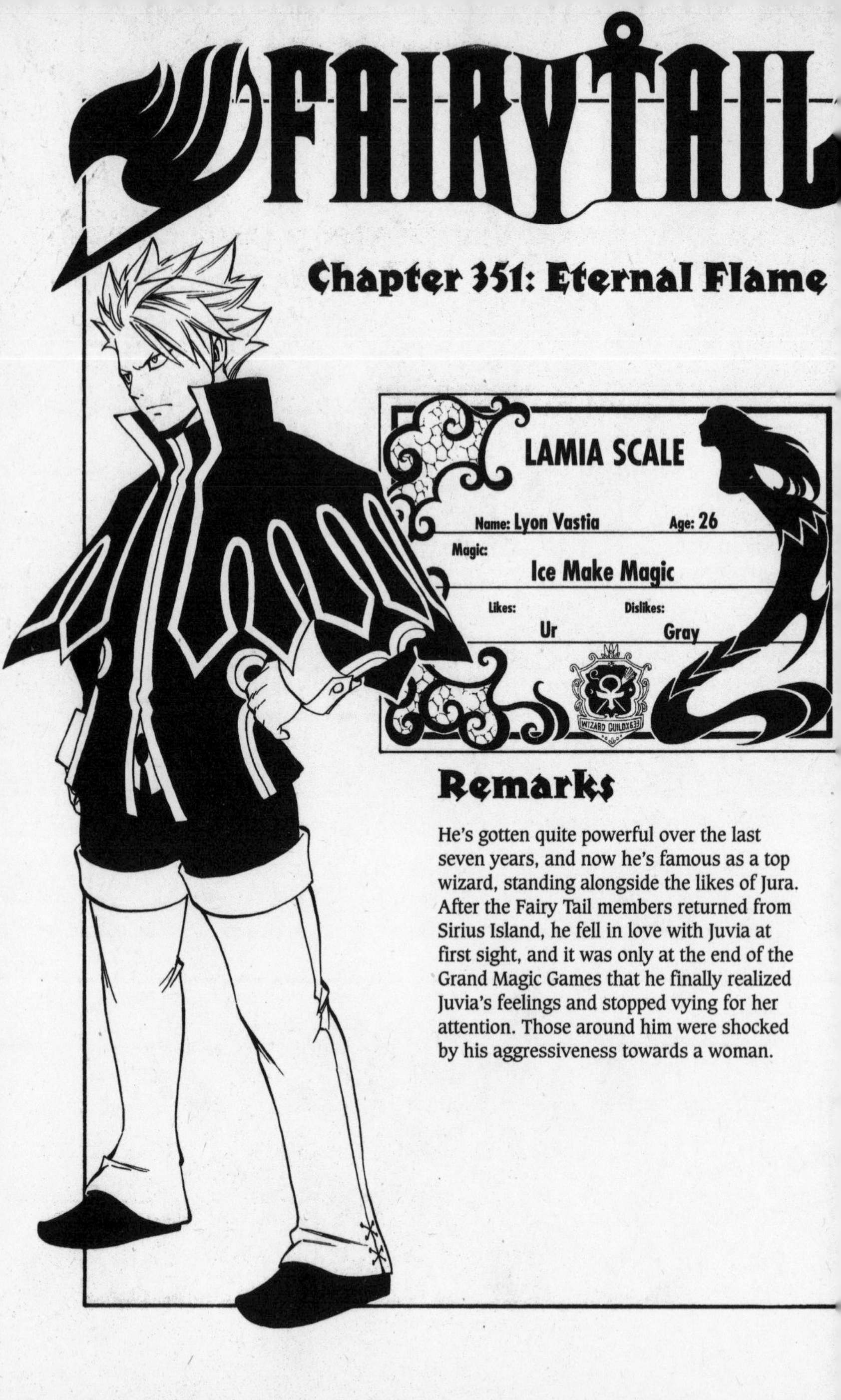

LAMIA SCALE

Name: Lyon Vastia **Age:** 26

Magic: Ice Make Magic

Likes: Ur **Dislikes:** Gray

WIZARD GUILD×633

Remarks

He's gotten quite powerful over the last seven years, and now he's famous as a top wizard, standing alongside the likes of Jura. After the Fairy Tail members returned from Sirius Island, he fell in love with Juvia at first sight, and it was only at the end of the Grand Magic Games that he finally realized Juvia's feelings and stopped vying for her attention. Those around him were shocked by his aggressiveness towards a woman.

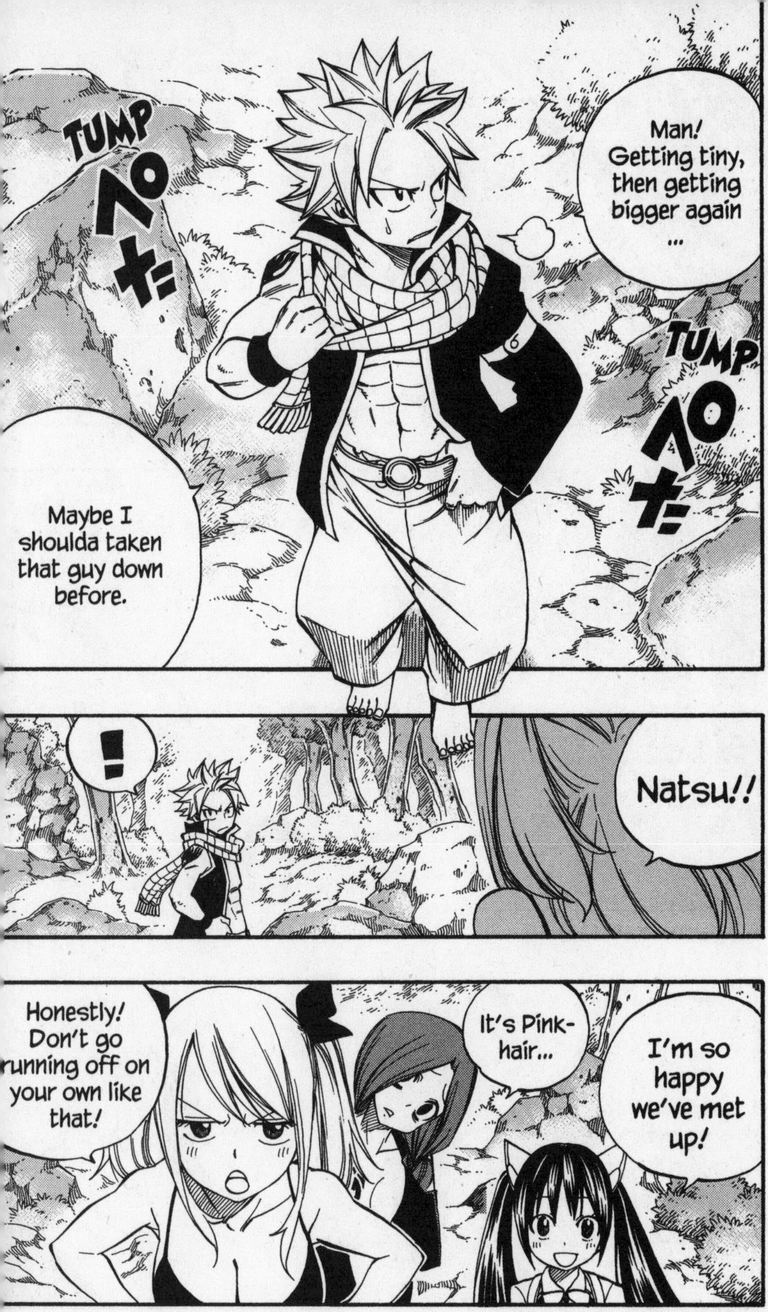

Man! Getting tiny, then getting bigger again ...
TUMP
TUMP
Maybe I shoulda taken that guy down before.
Natsu!!
!
I'm so happy we've met up!
It's Pink-hair...
Honestly! Don't go running off on your own like that!

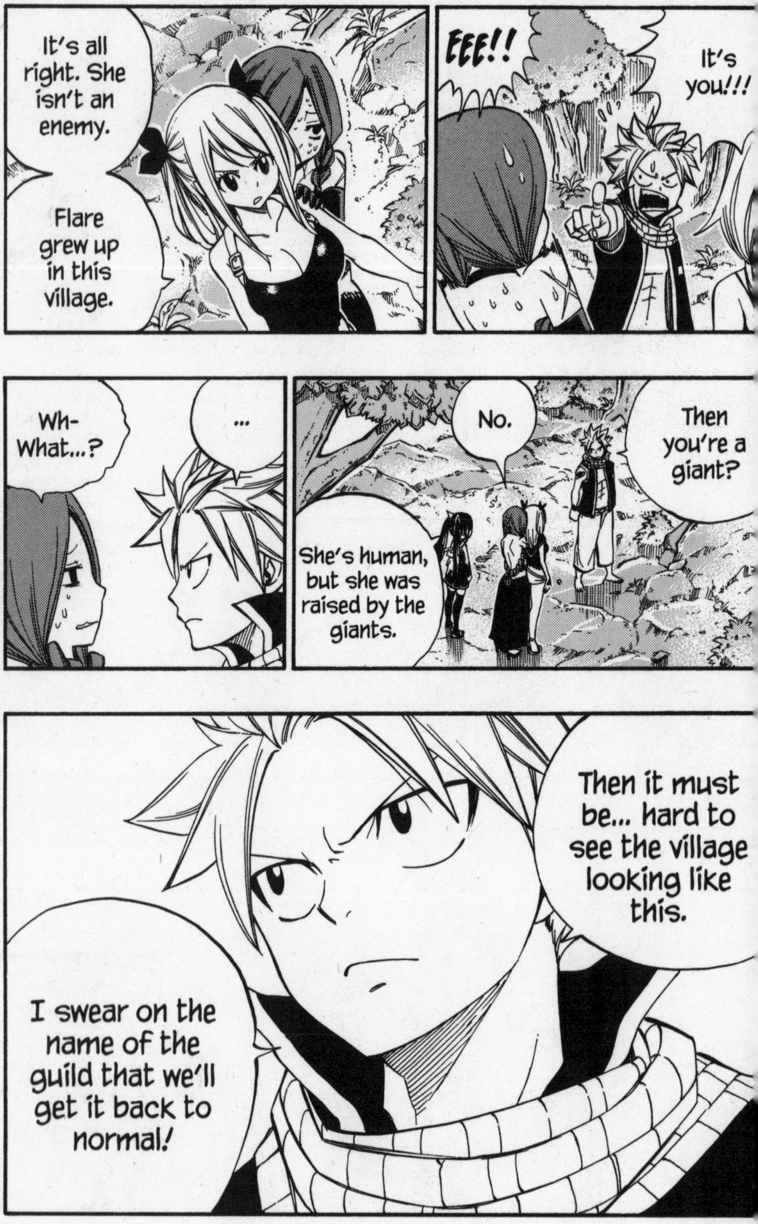
EEE!!
It's you!!!
It's all right. She isn't an enemy.
Flare grew up in this village.
Then you're a giant?
No.
She's human, but she was raised by the giants.
...
Wh- What...?
Then it must be... hard to see the village looking like this.
I swear on the name of the guild that we'll get it back to normal!

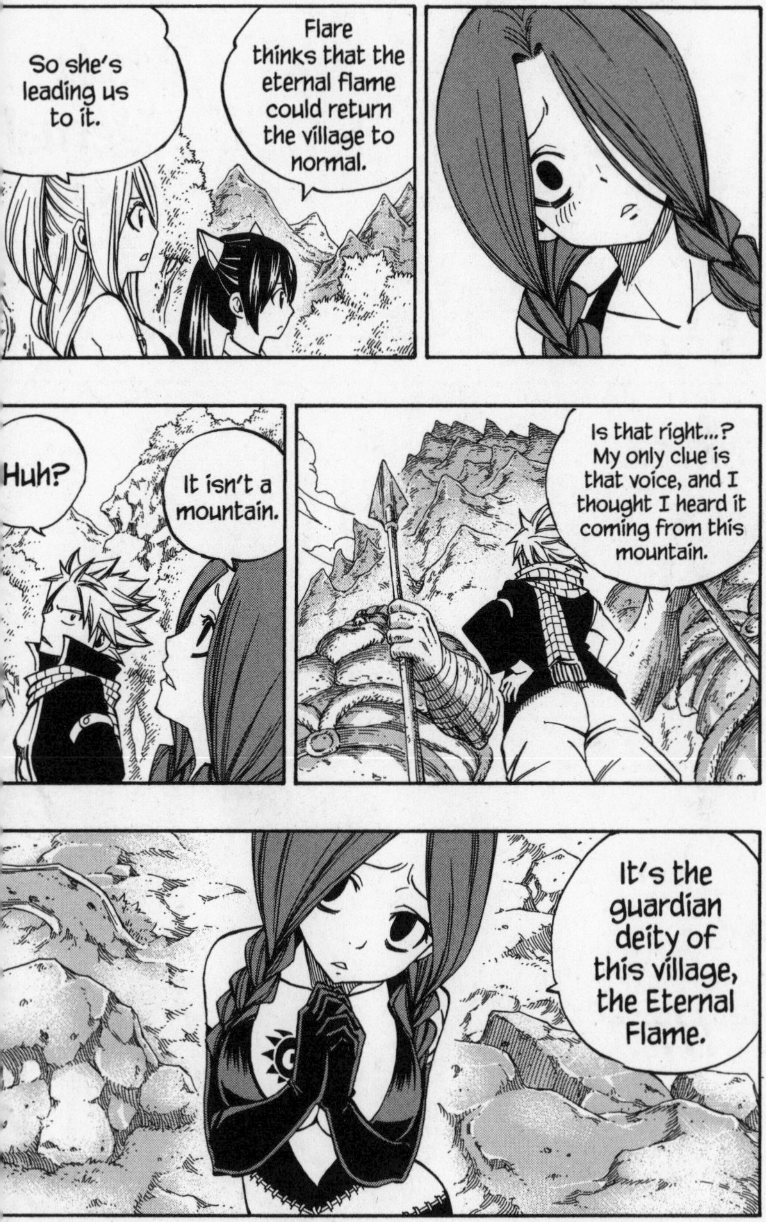
Flare thinks that the eternal flame could return the village to normal.
So she's leading us to it.
Is that right...? My only clue is that voice, and I thought I heard it coming from this mountain.
It isn't a mountain.
Huh?
It's the guardian deity of this village, the Eternal Flame.

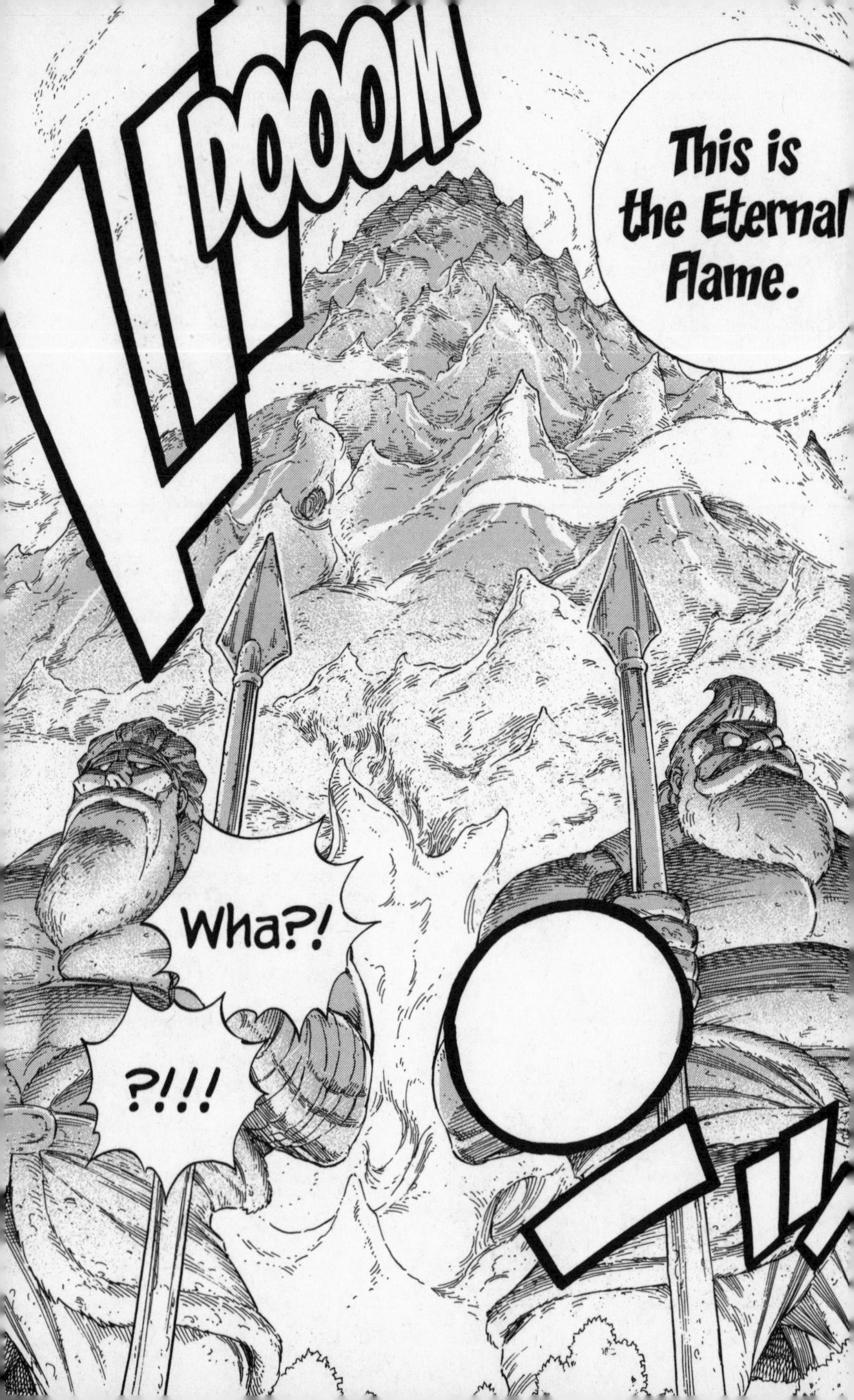
This is the Eternal Flame.
DOOOM
Wha?!
?!!!

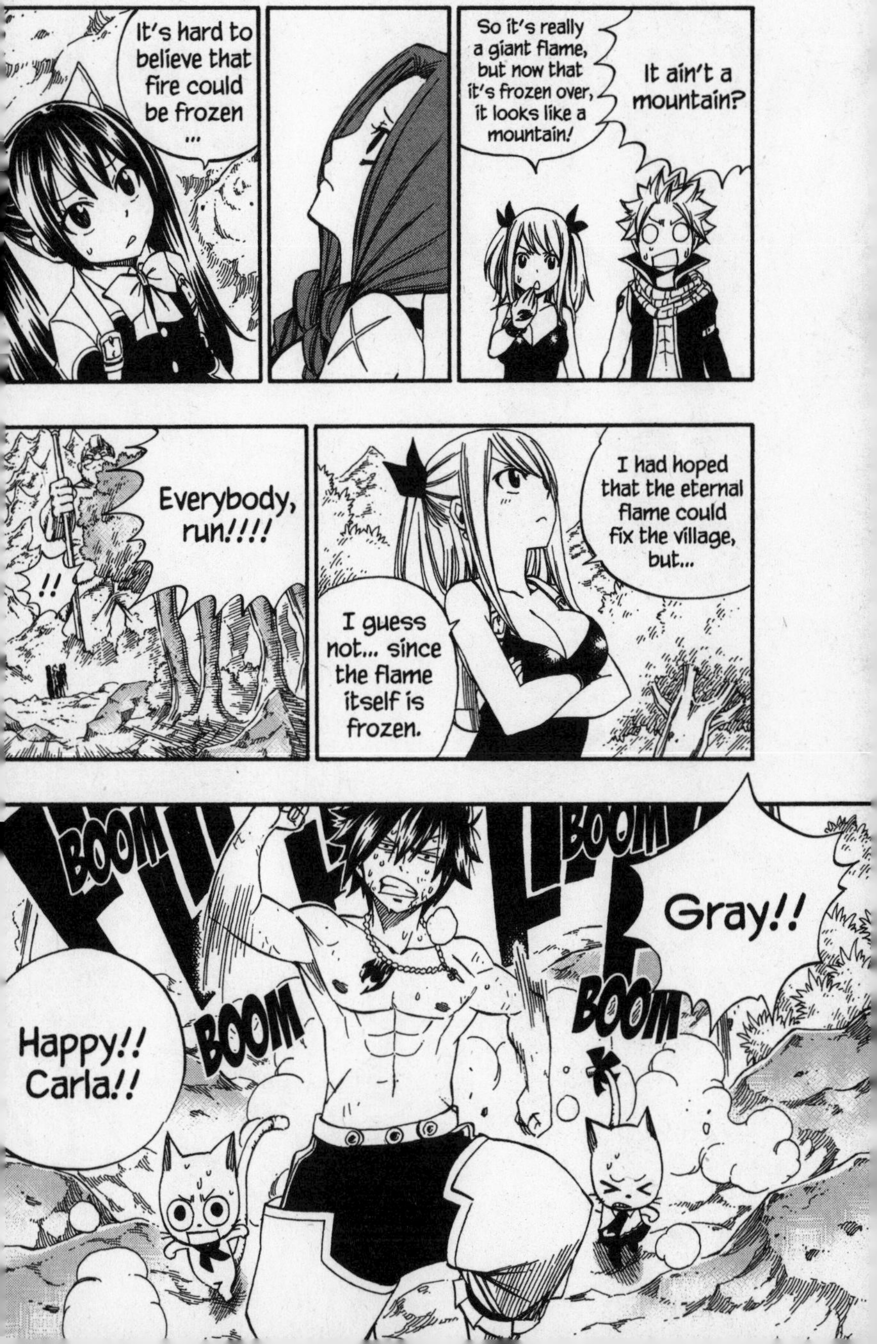
It ain't a mountain?
So it's really a giant flame, but now that it's frozen over, it looks like a mountain!
It's hard to believe that fire could be frozen ...
I had hoped that the eternal flame could fix the village, but...
I guess not... since the flame itself is frozen.
Everybody, run!!!!
!!
BOOM
Gray!!
BOOM
BOOM
BOOM
Happy!! Carla!!

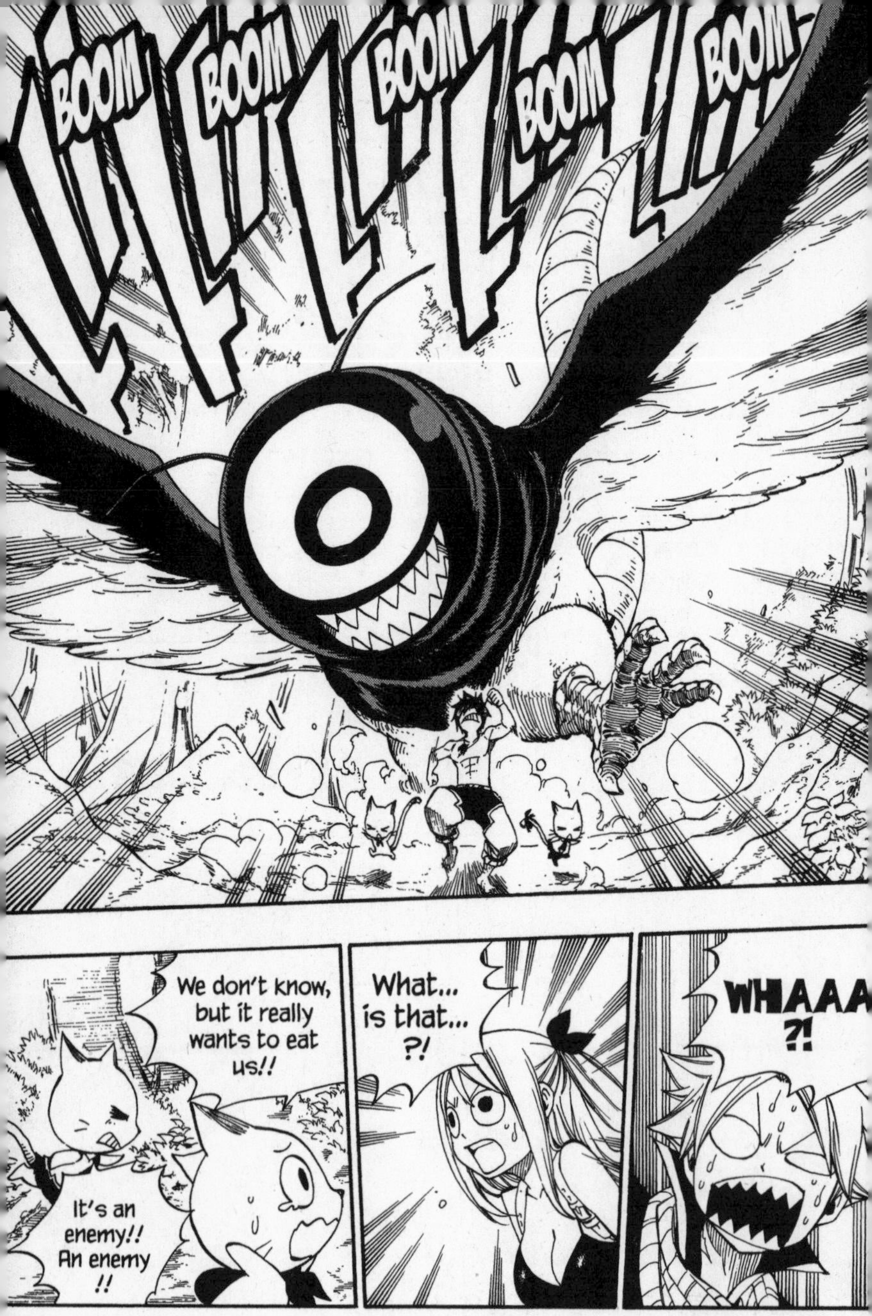
BOOM
BOOM
BOOM
BOOM
BOOM
WHAAA ?!
What... is that... ?!
We don't know, but it really wants to eat us!!
It's an enemy!! An enemy !!

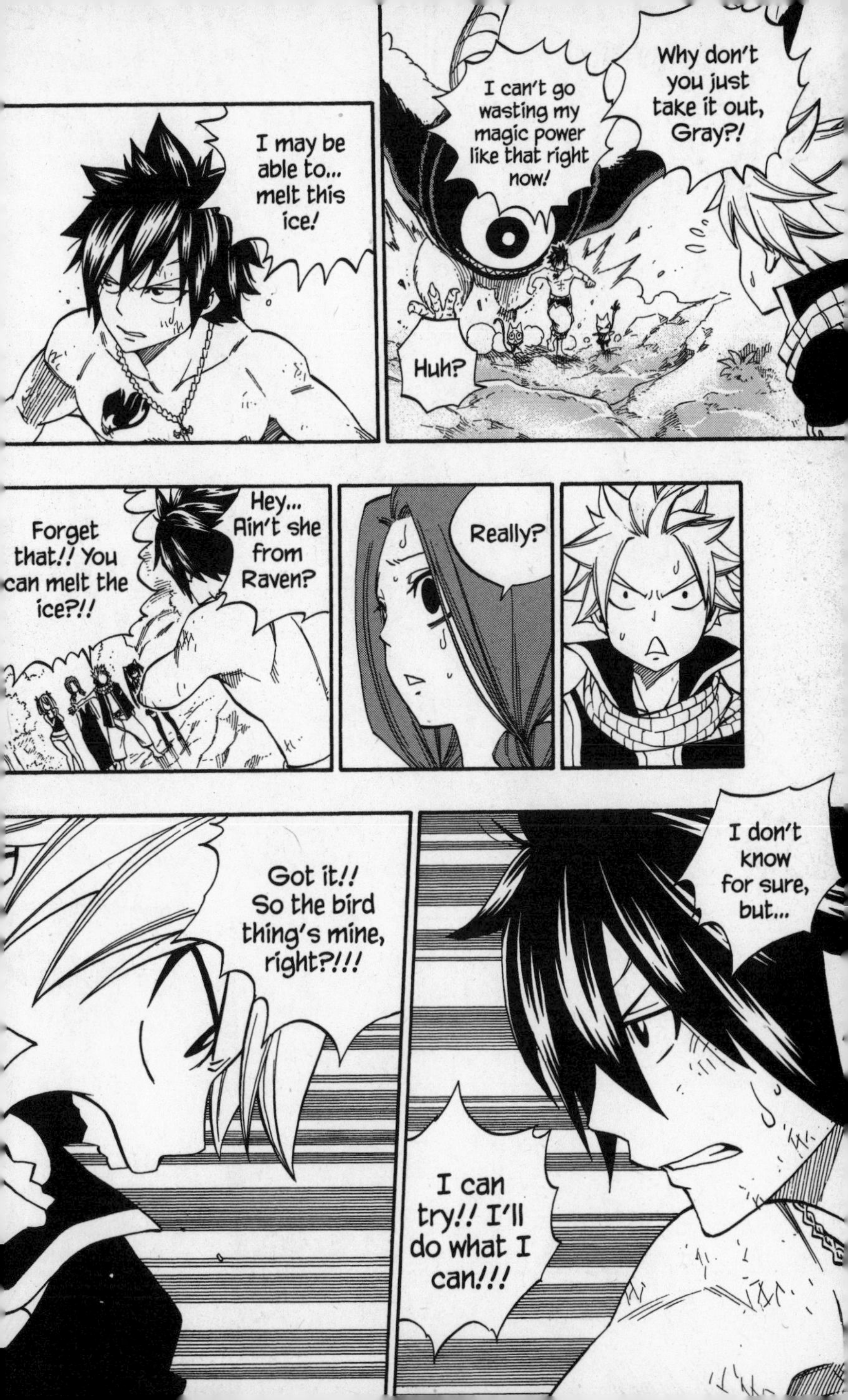
Why don't you just take it out, Gray?!
I can't go wasting my magic power like that right now!
Huh?
I may be able to... melt this ice!
Really?
Hey... Ain't she from Raven?
Forget that!! You can melt the ice?!!
I don't know for sure, but...
I can try!! I'll do what I can!!!
Got it!! So the bird thing's mine, right?!!!

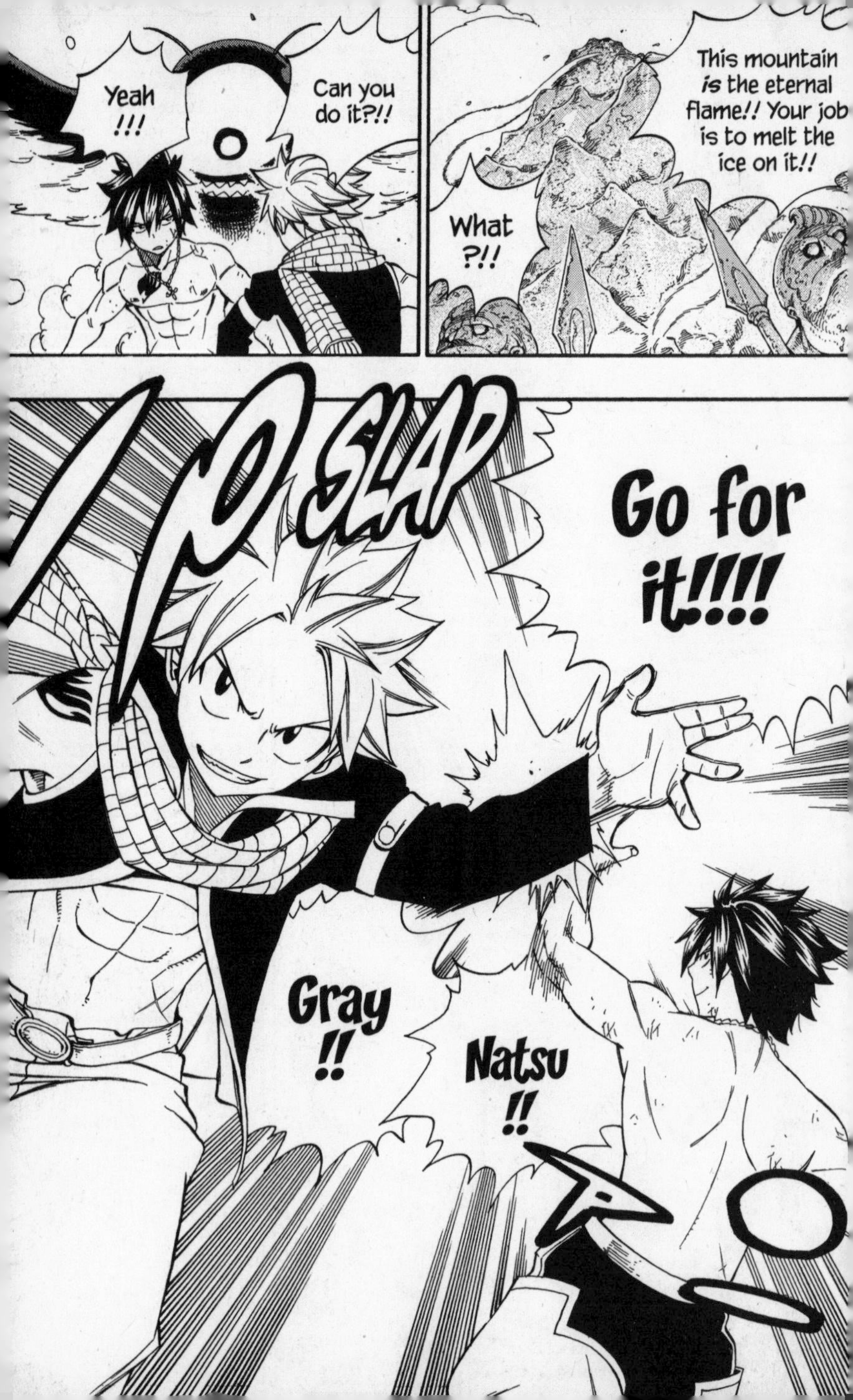
This mountain *is* the eternal flame!! Your job is to melt the ice on it!!
What ?!!
Can you do it?!!
Yeah !!!
Go for it!!!!
SLAP
Natsu !!
Gray !!

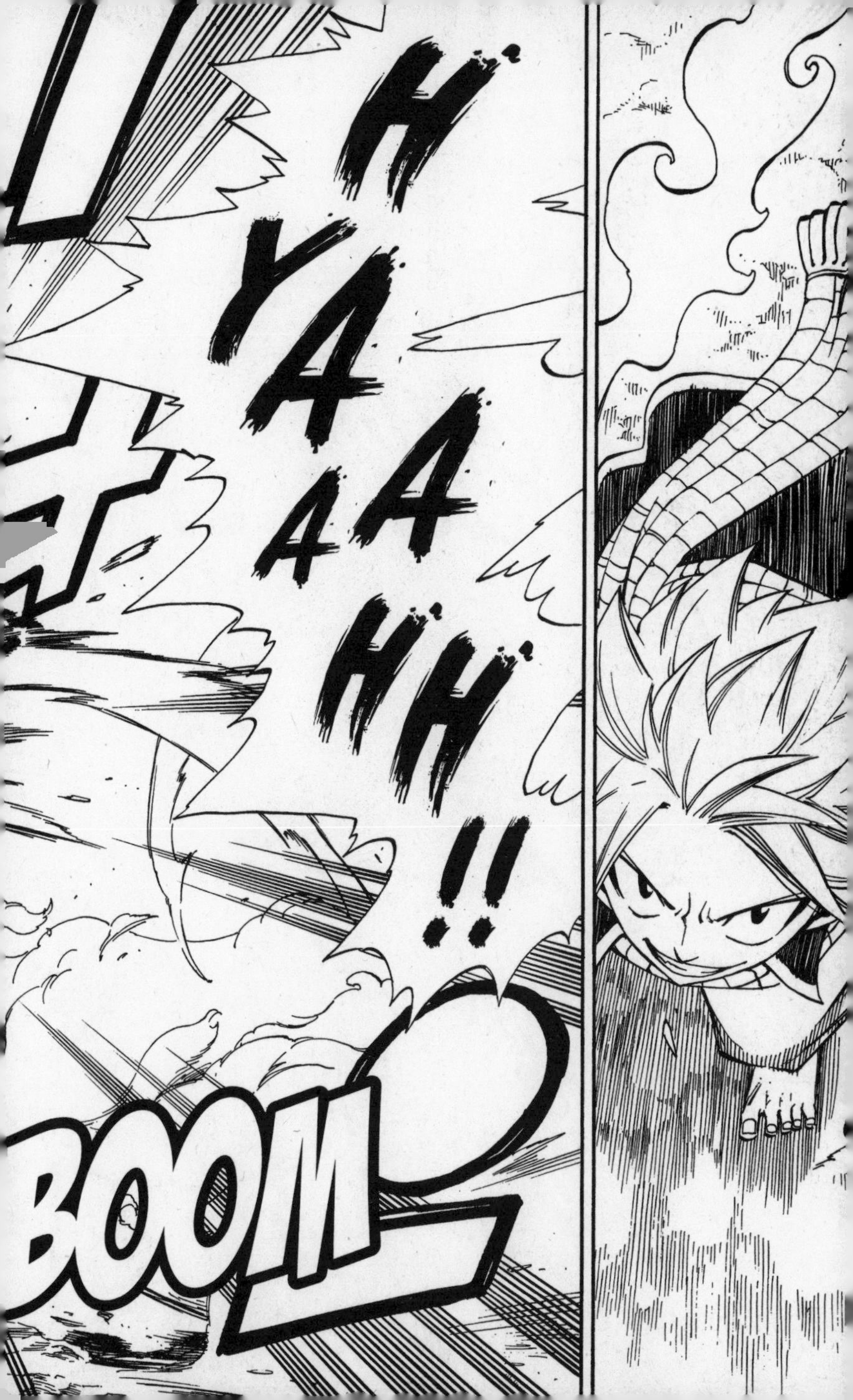
HYAAAAHH!!
BOOM

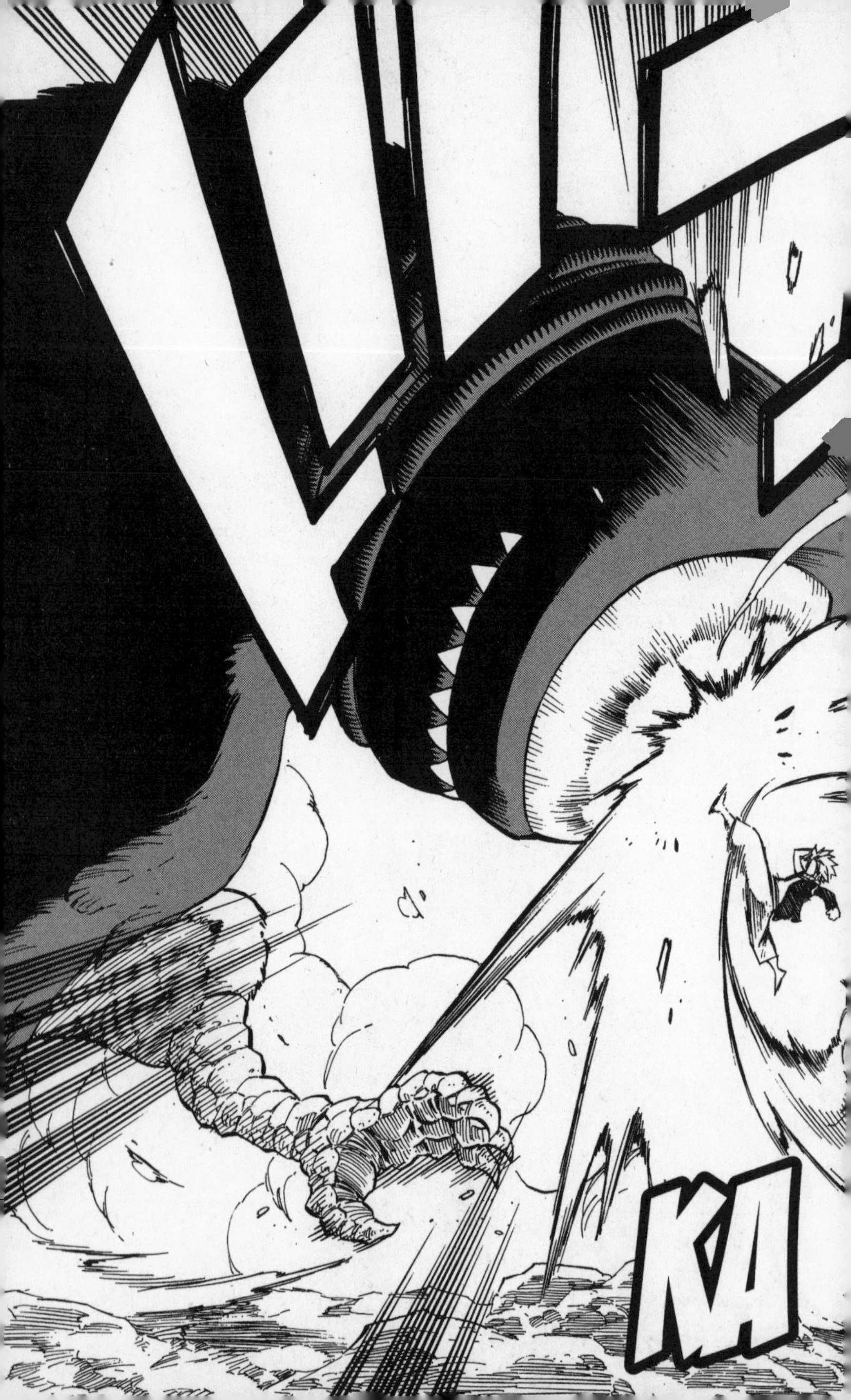
KA

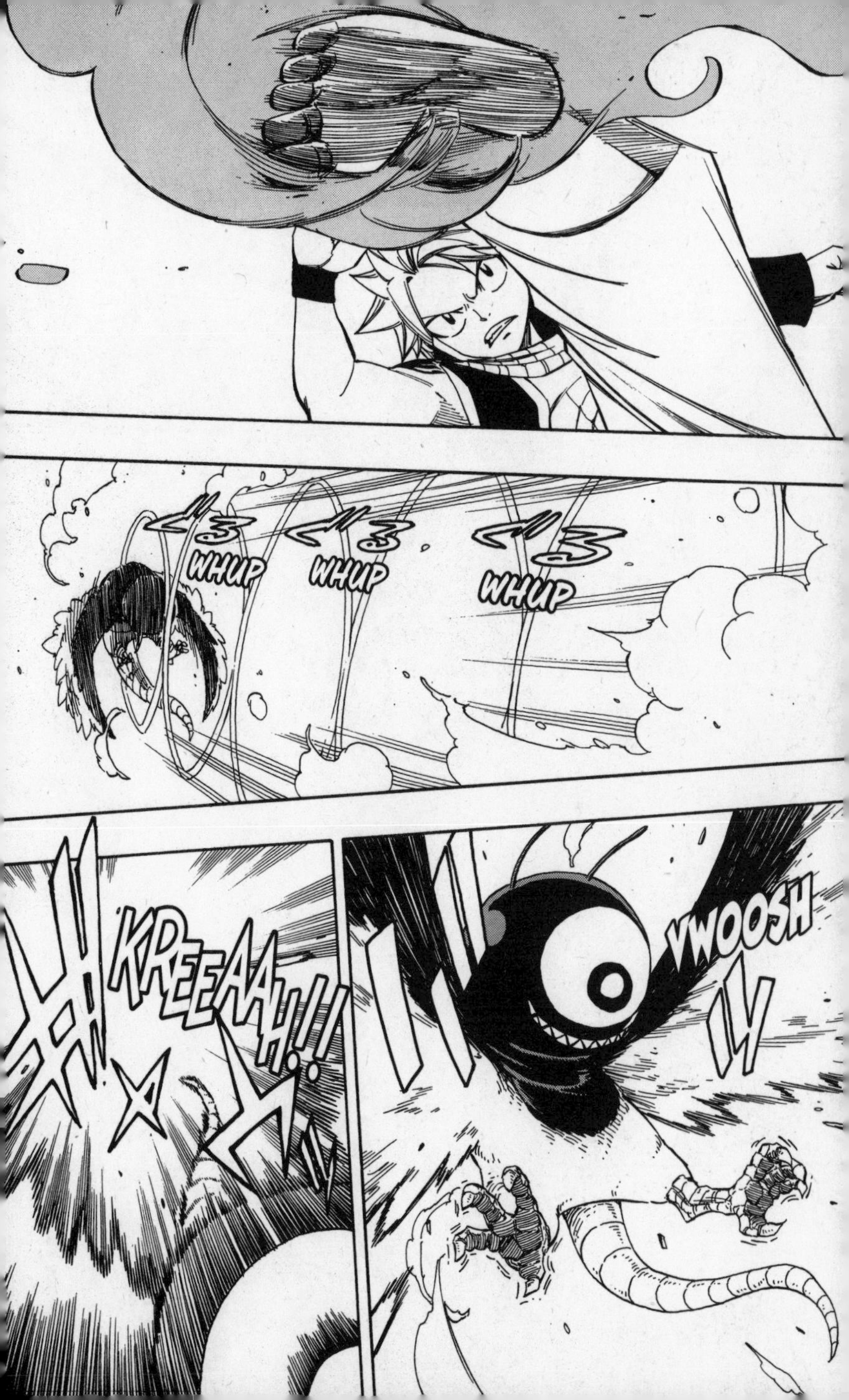
WHUP
WHUP
WHUP
VWOOSH
KREEAAH!!!

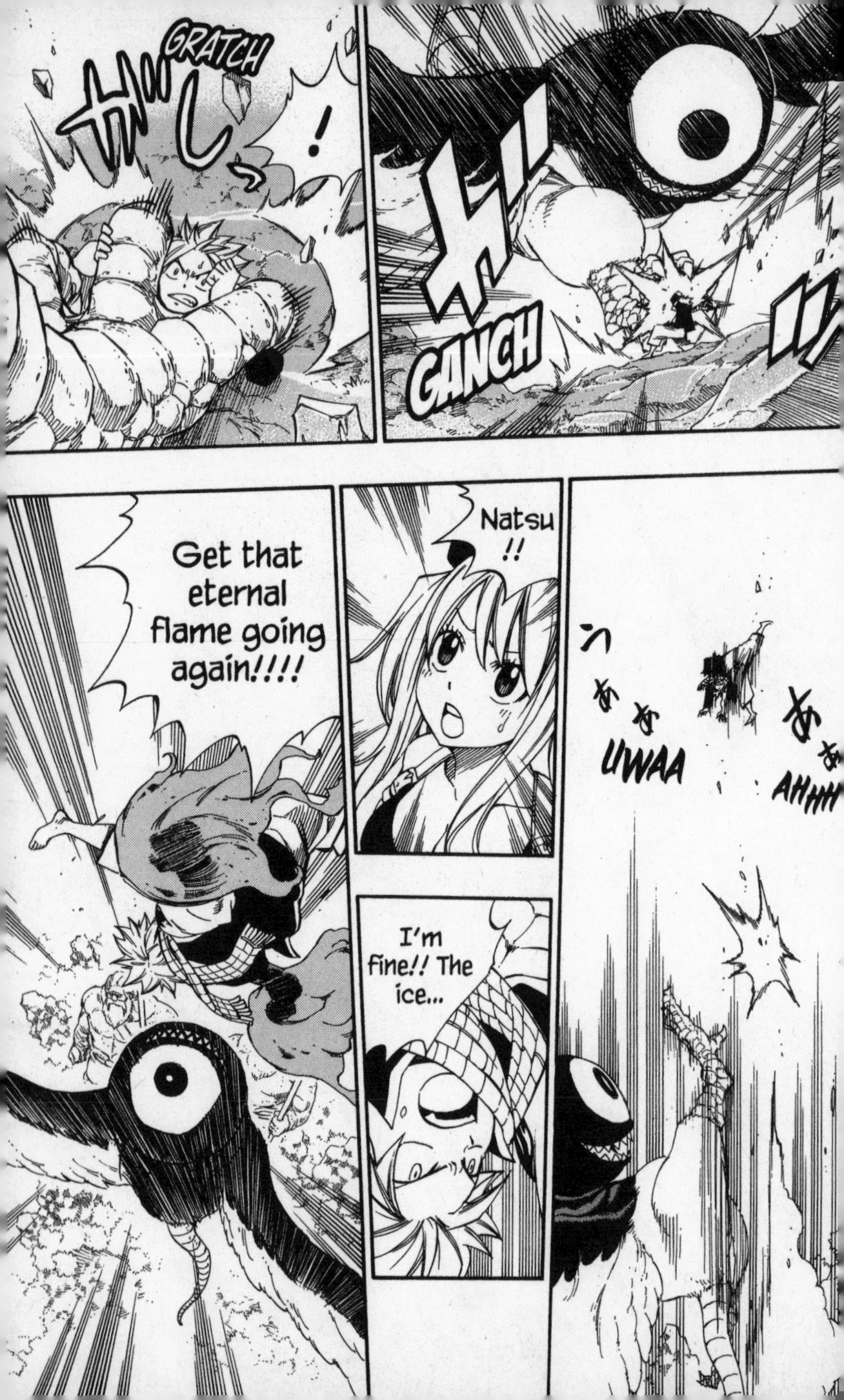
GANCH
GRATCH
!
UWAA
AHHH
Natsu!!
I'm fine!! The ice...
Get that eternal flame going again!!!!

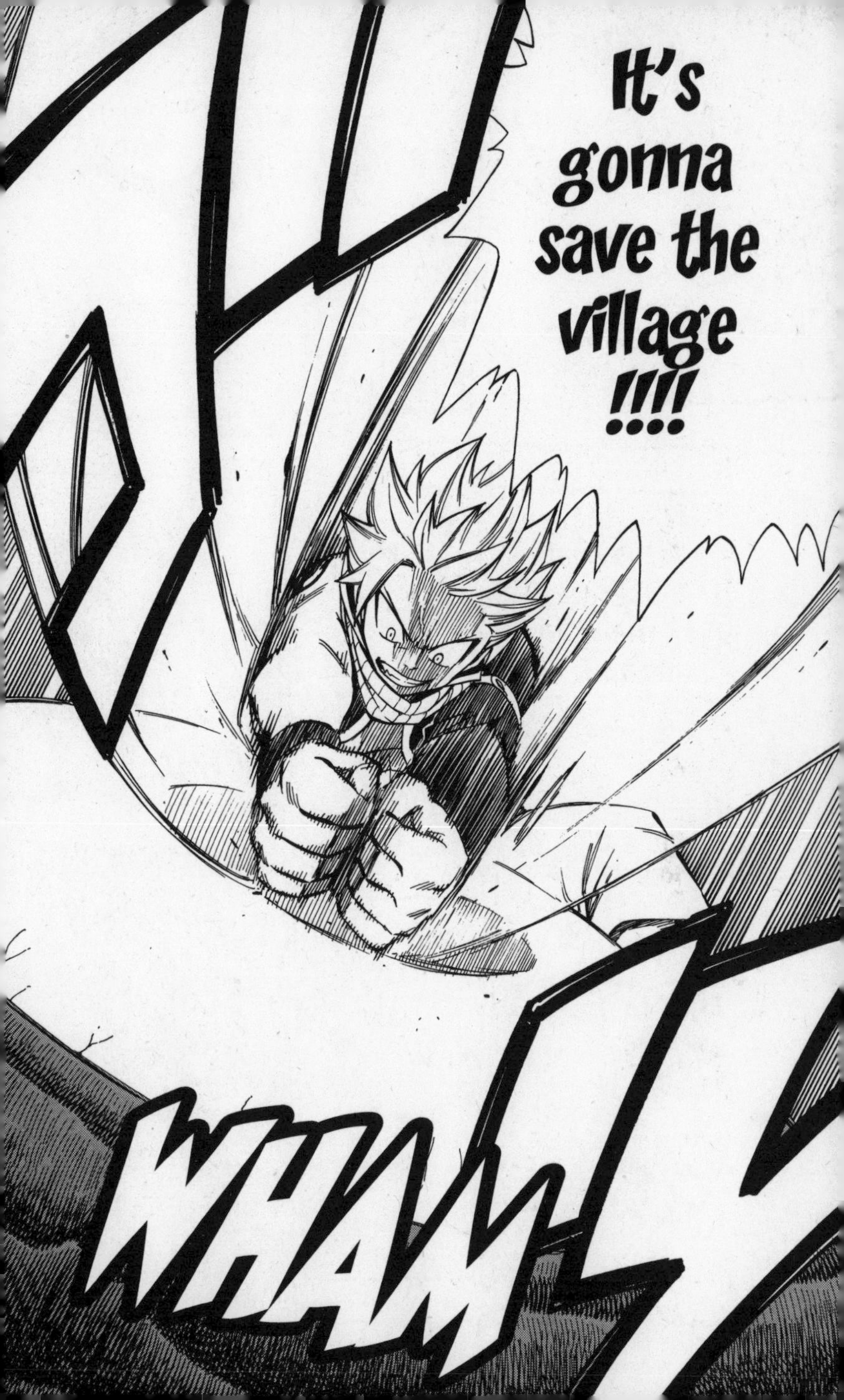
It's gonna save the village !!!!
WHAM

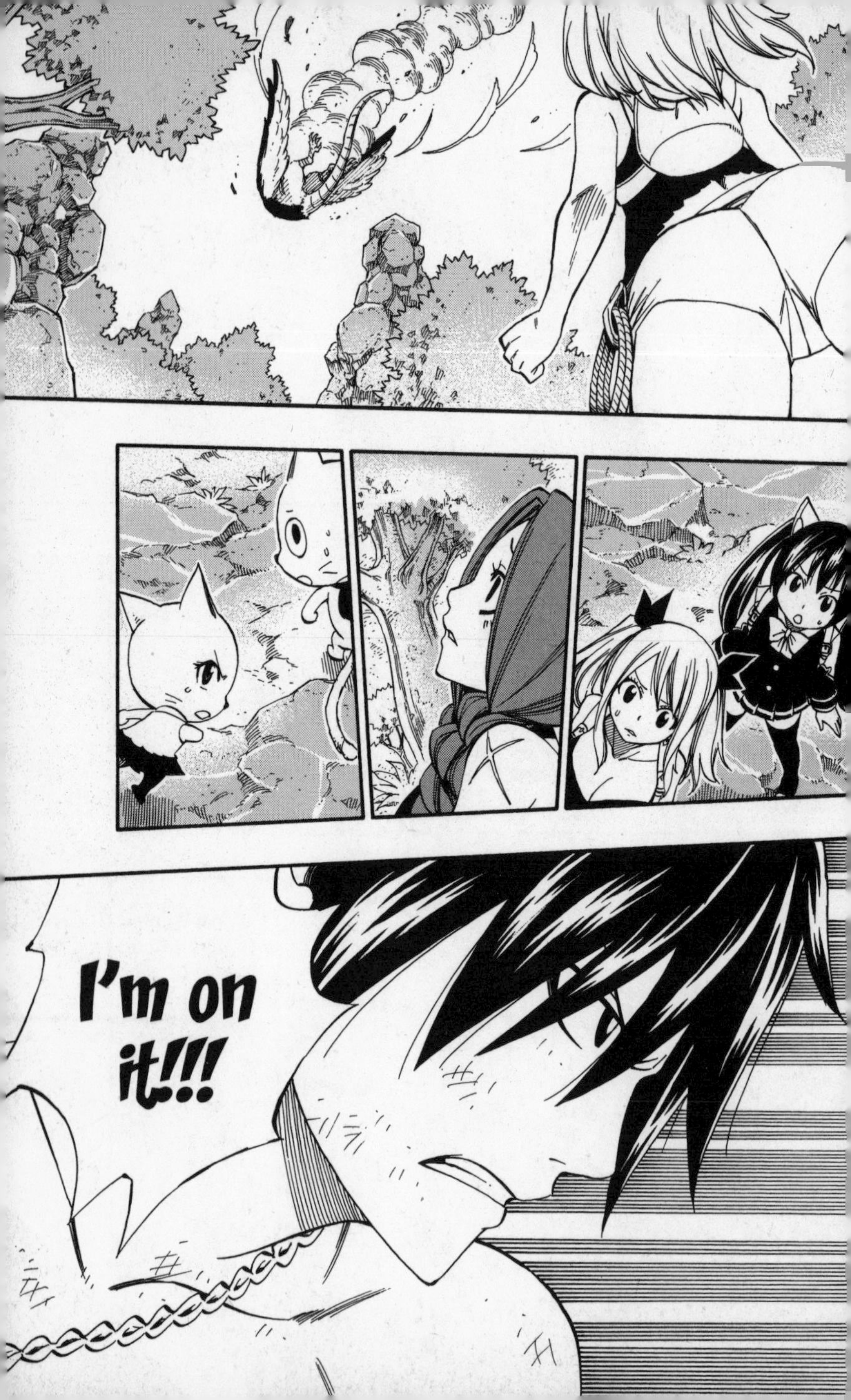
I'm on it!!!

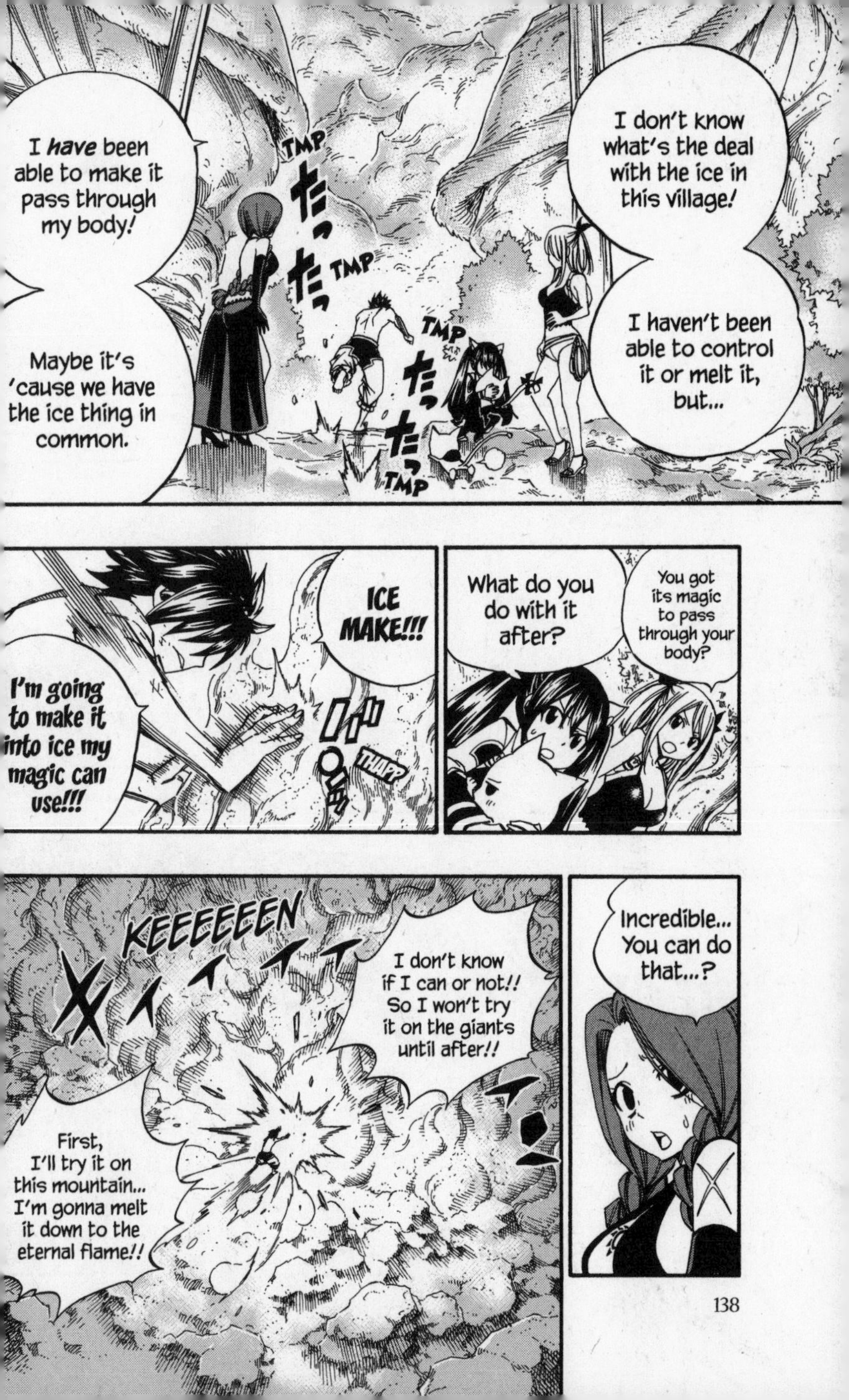
I don't know what's the deal with the ice in this village!
I haven't been able to control it or melt it, but...
TMP
TMP
TMP
TMP
I *have* been able to make it pass through my body!
Maybe it's 'cause we have the ice thing in common.
You got its magic to pass through your body?
What do you do with it after?
ICE MAKE!!!
THAPP
I'm going to make it into ice my magic can use!!!
Incredible... You can do that...?
KEEEEEEEN
I don't know if I can or not!! So I won't try it on the giants until after!!
First, I'll try it on this mountain... I'm gonna melt it down to the eternal flame!!

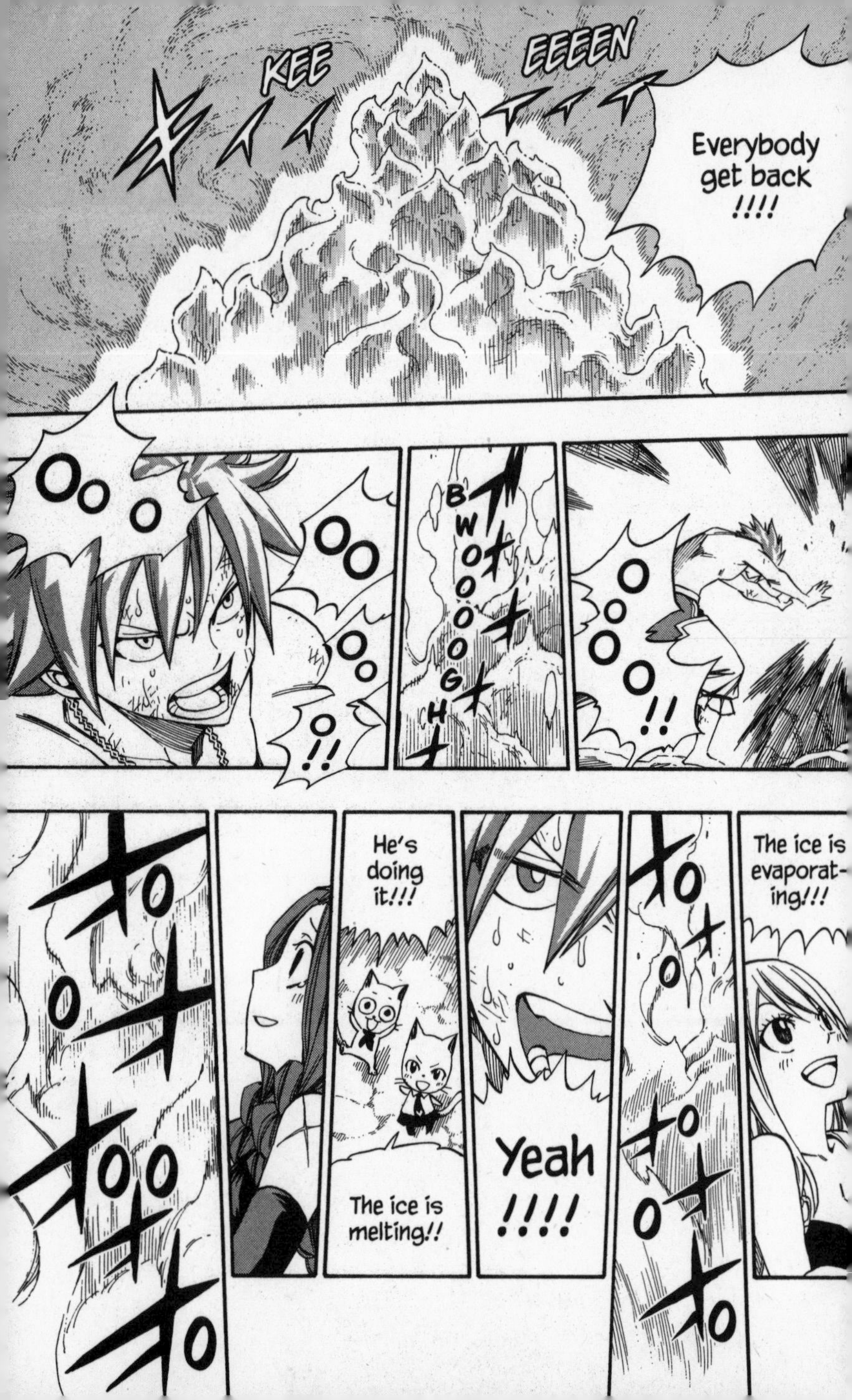
Everybody get back!!!!
KEE EEEEN
OOOOO!!
BWOOOOOOGH
OooOOOOO!!
The ice is evaporating!!!
OOOO
Yeah!!!!
He's doing it!!!
The ice is melting!!
OOOOO

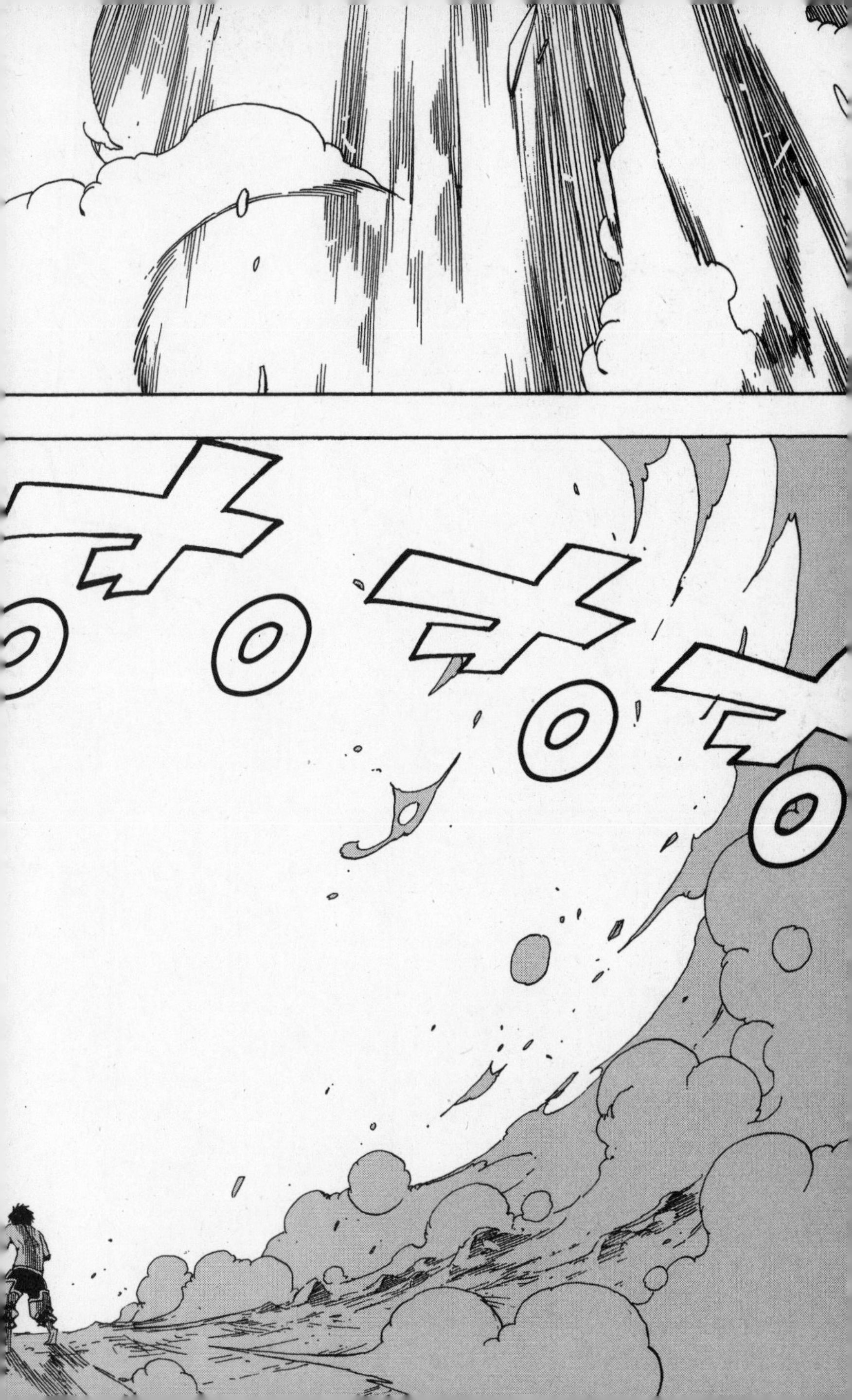

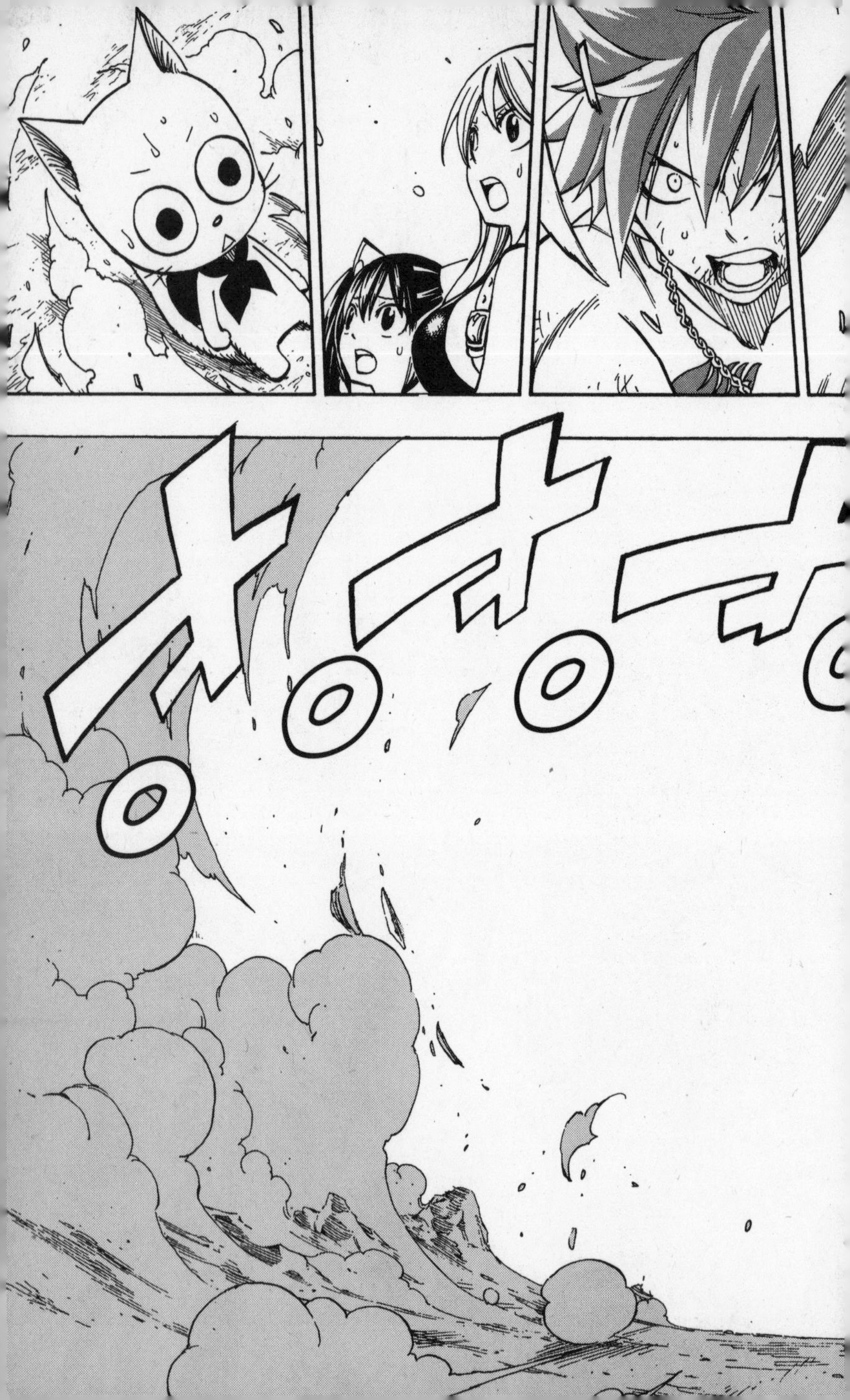
オオオ

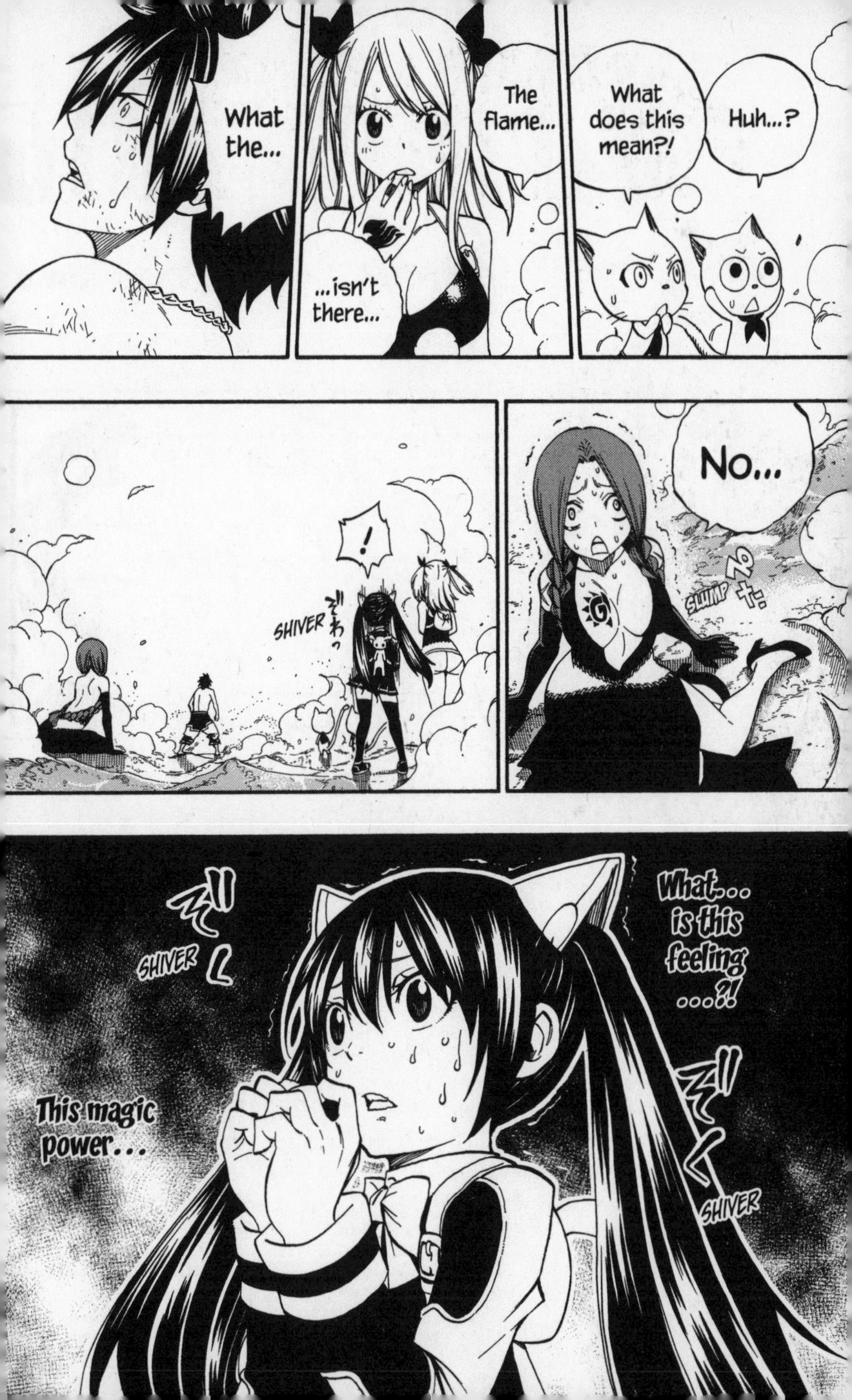
Huh...?
What does this mean?!
The flame...
...isn't there...
What the...
No...
SLUMP
!
SHIVER
What... is this feeling...?!
SHIVER
SHIVER
This magic power...

FAIRY TAIL

Chapter 352: Voice of the Flame

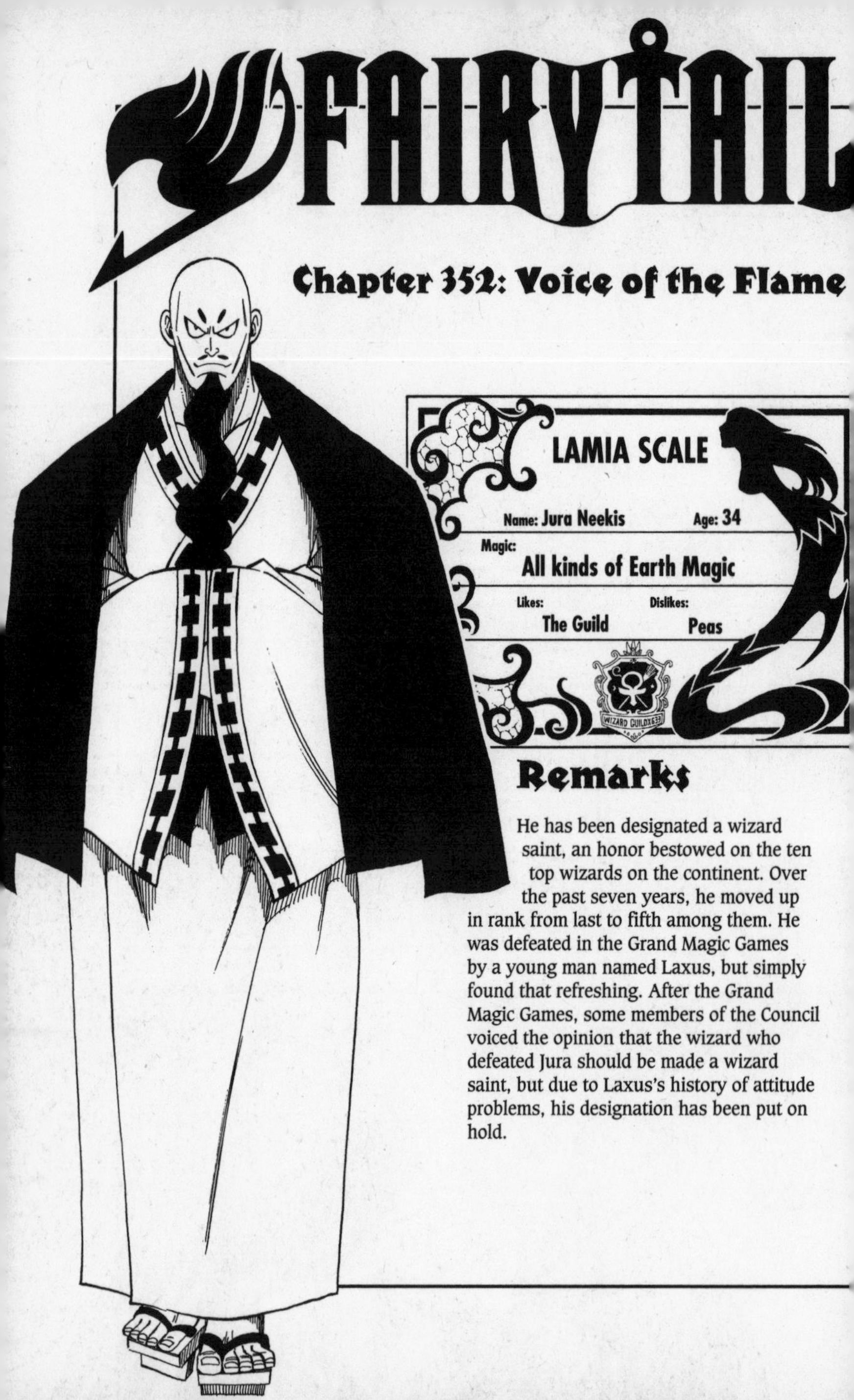

LAMIA SCALE

Name: Jura Neekis **Age:** 34

Magic: All kinds of Earth Magic

Likes: The Guild **Dislikes:** Peas

WIZARD GUILD×633

Remarks

He has been designated a wizard saint, an honor bestowed on the ten top wizards on the continent. Over the past seven years, he moved up in rank from last to fifth among them. He was defeated in the Grand Magic Games by a young man named Laxus, but simply found that refreshing. After the Grand Magic Games, some members of the Council voiced the opinion that the wizard who defeated Jura should be made a wizard saint, but due to Laxus's history of attitude problems, his designation has been put on hold.

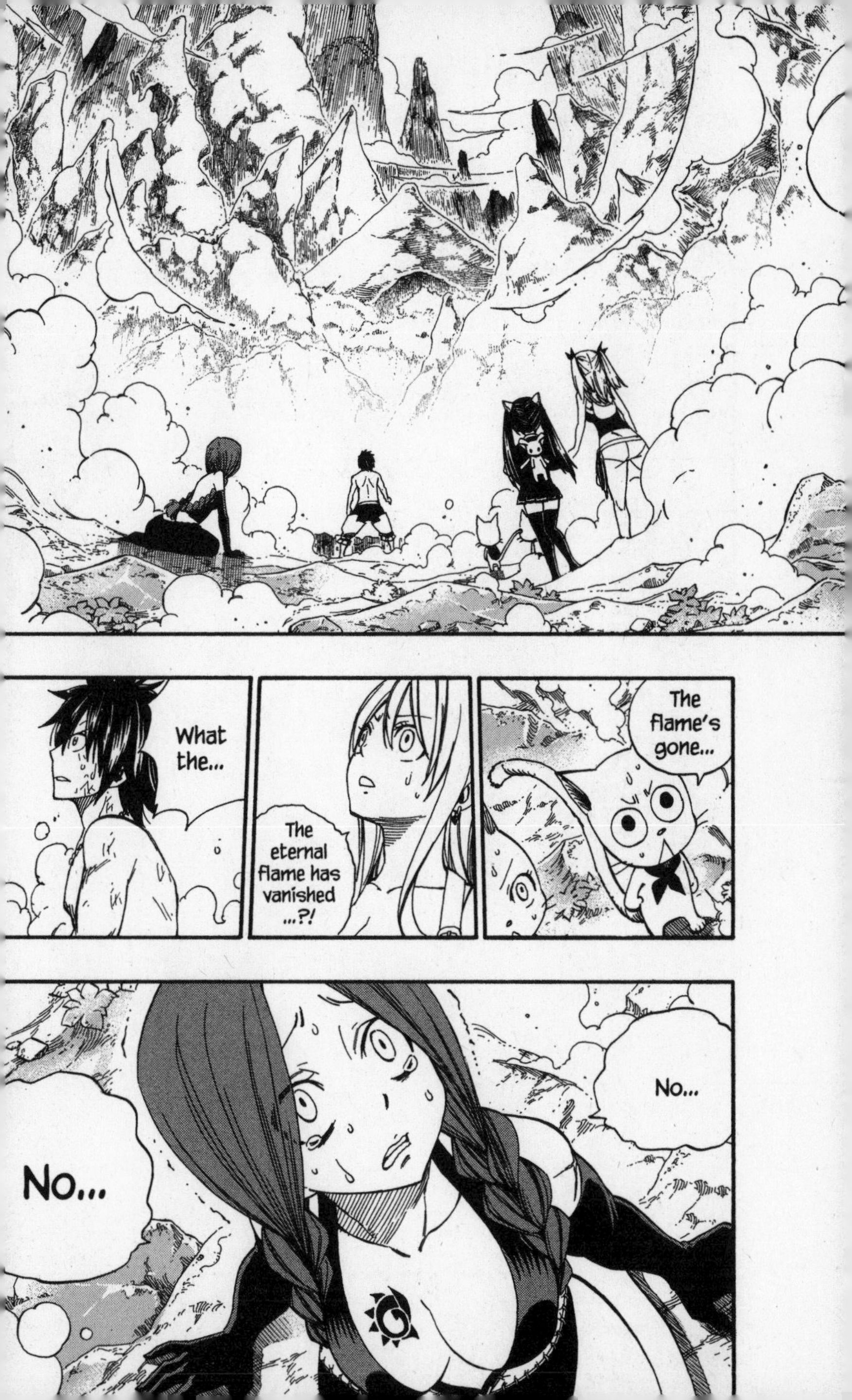
The flame's gone...
The eternal flame has vanished ...?!
What the...
No...
No...

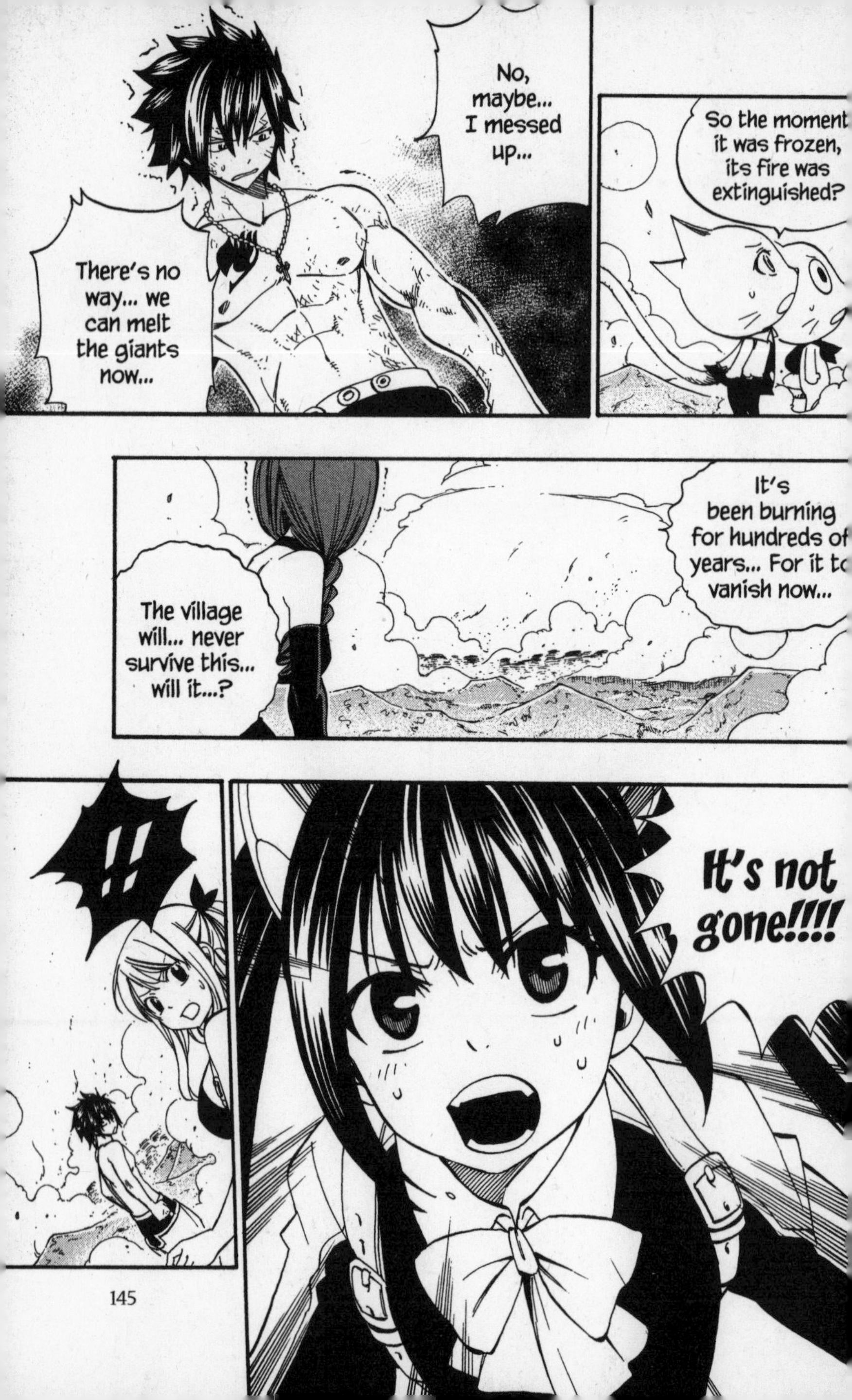
So the moment it was frozen, its fire was extinguished?
No, maybe... I messed up...
There's no way... we can melt the giants now...
It's been burning for hundreds of years... For it to vanish now...
The village will... never survive this... will it...?
It's not gone!!!!
!!

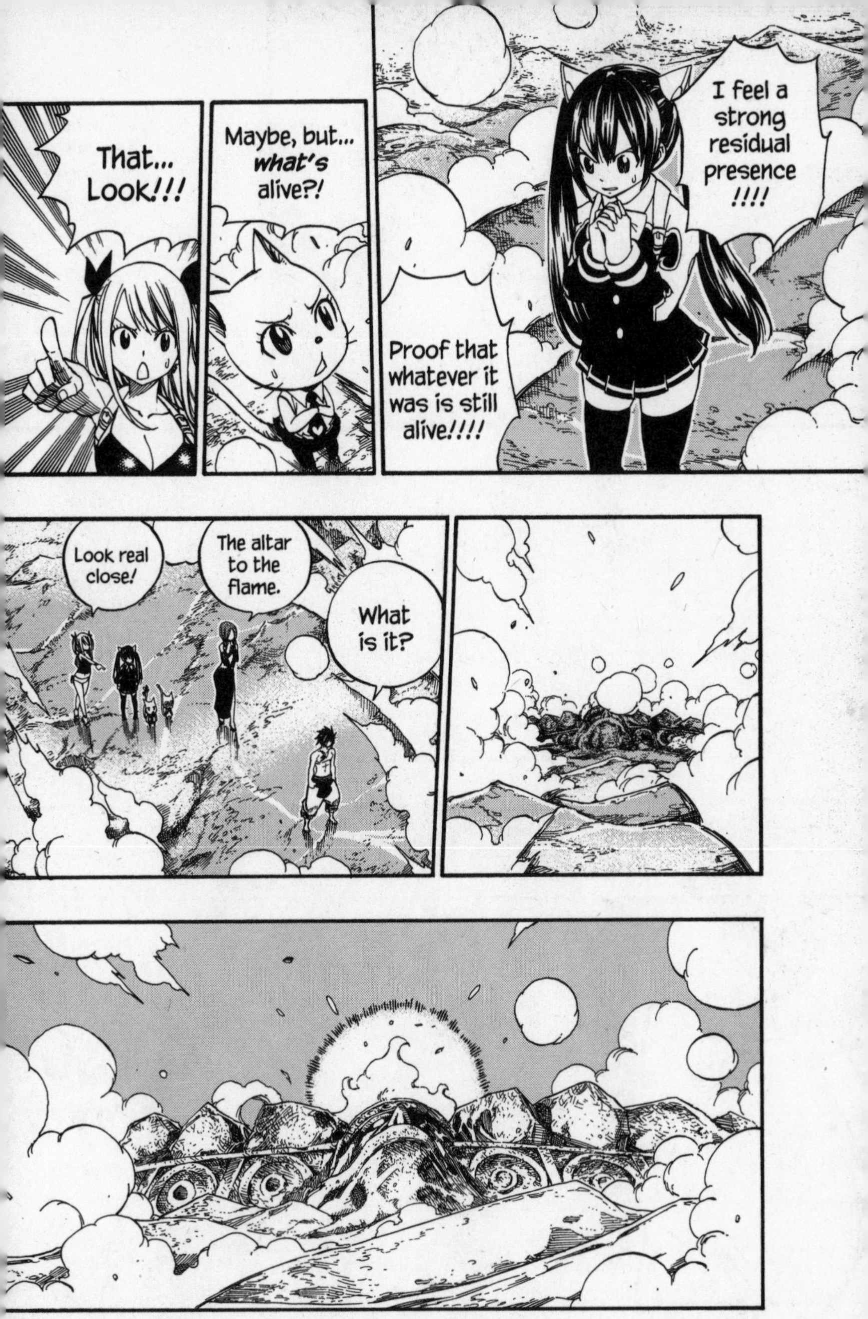
I feel a strong residual presence!!!!
Proof that whatever it was is still alive!!!!
Maybe, but... *what's* alive?!
That... Look!!!
What is it?
The altar to the flame.
Look real close!

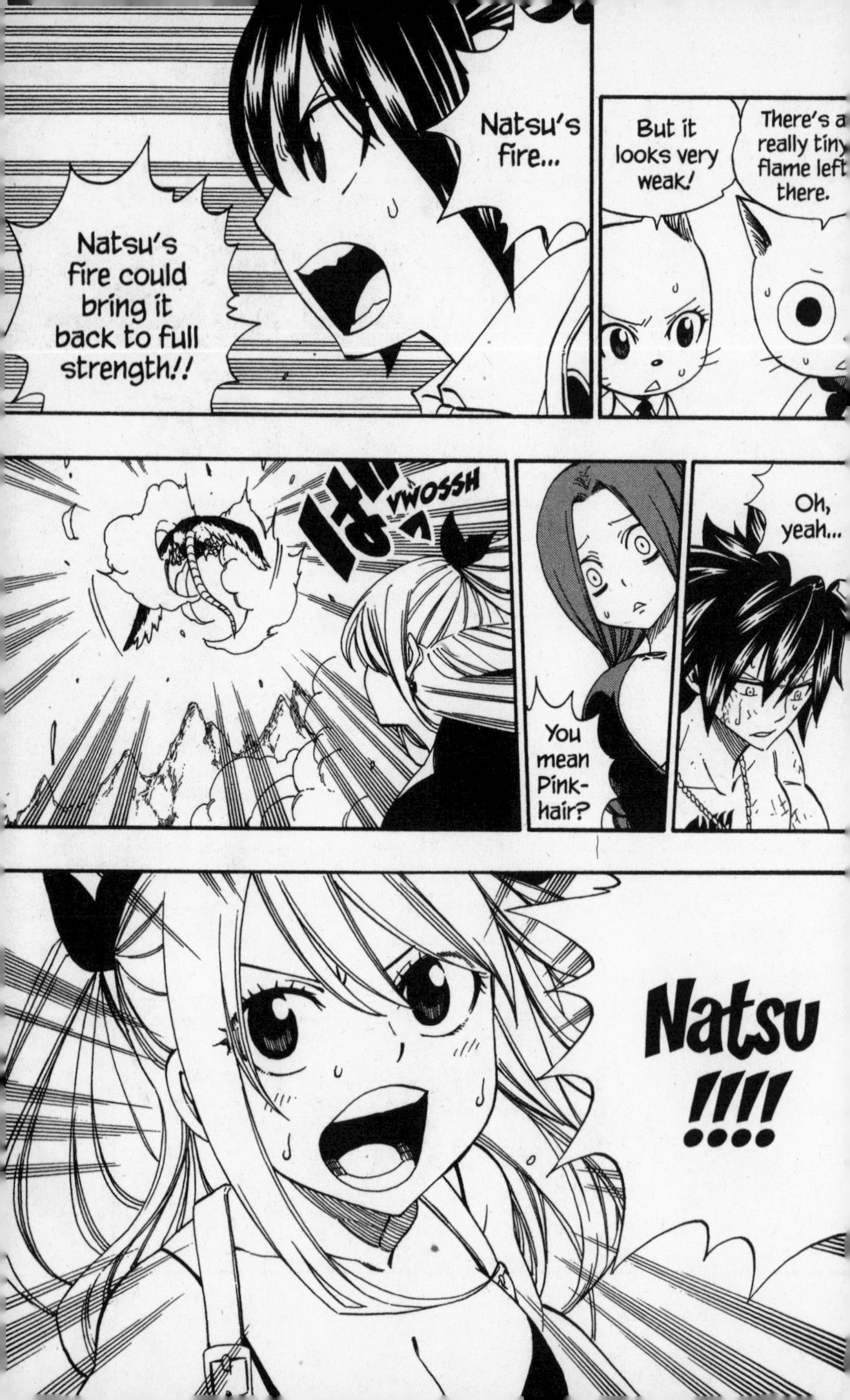
There's a really tiny flame left there.
But it looks very weak!
Natsu's fire...
Natsu's fire could bring it back to full strength!!
Oh, yeah...
You mean Pink-hair?
VWOSSH
Natsu!!!!

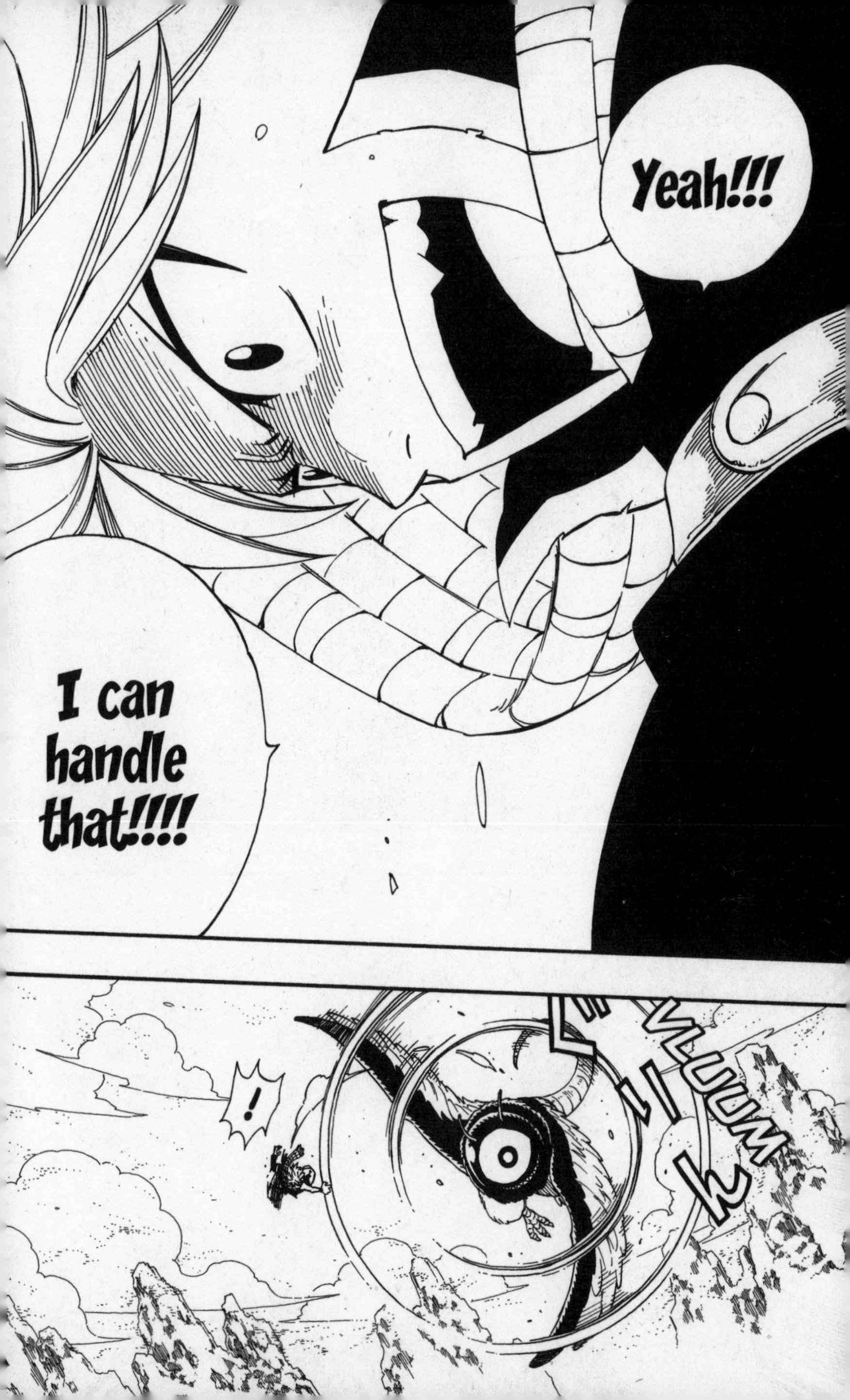
Yeah!!!
I can handle that!!!!
!

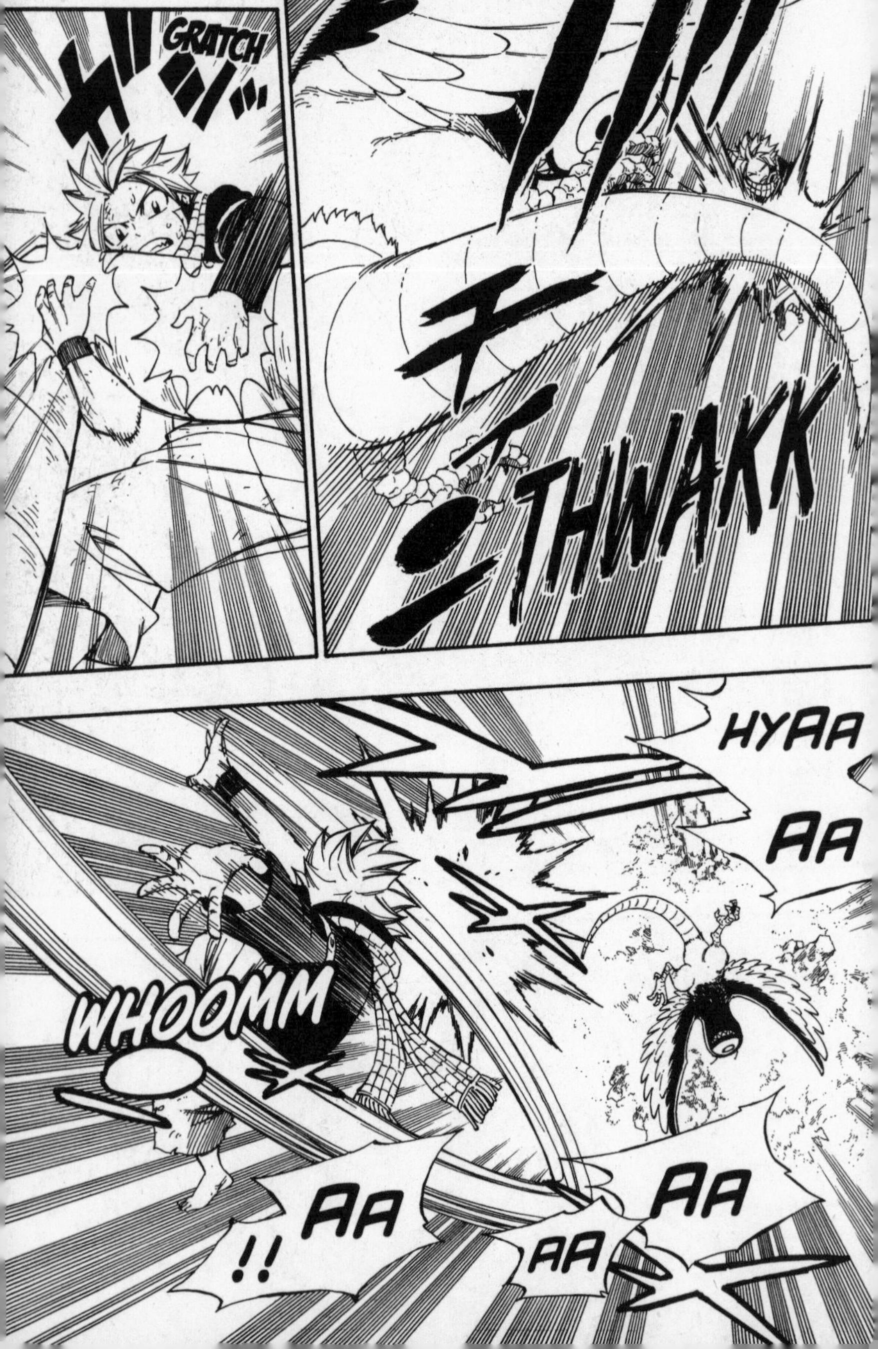
THWAKK
GRATCH
HYAA
AA
AA
AA
AA
WHOOMM
!!

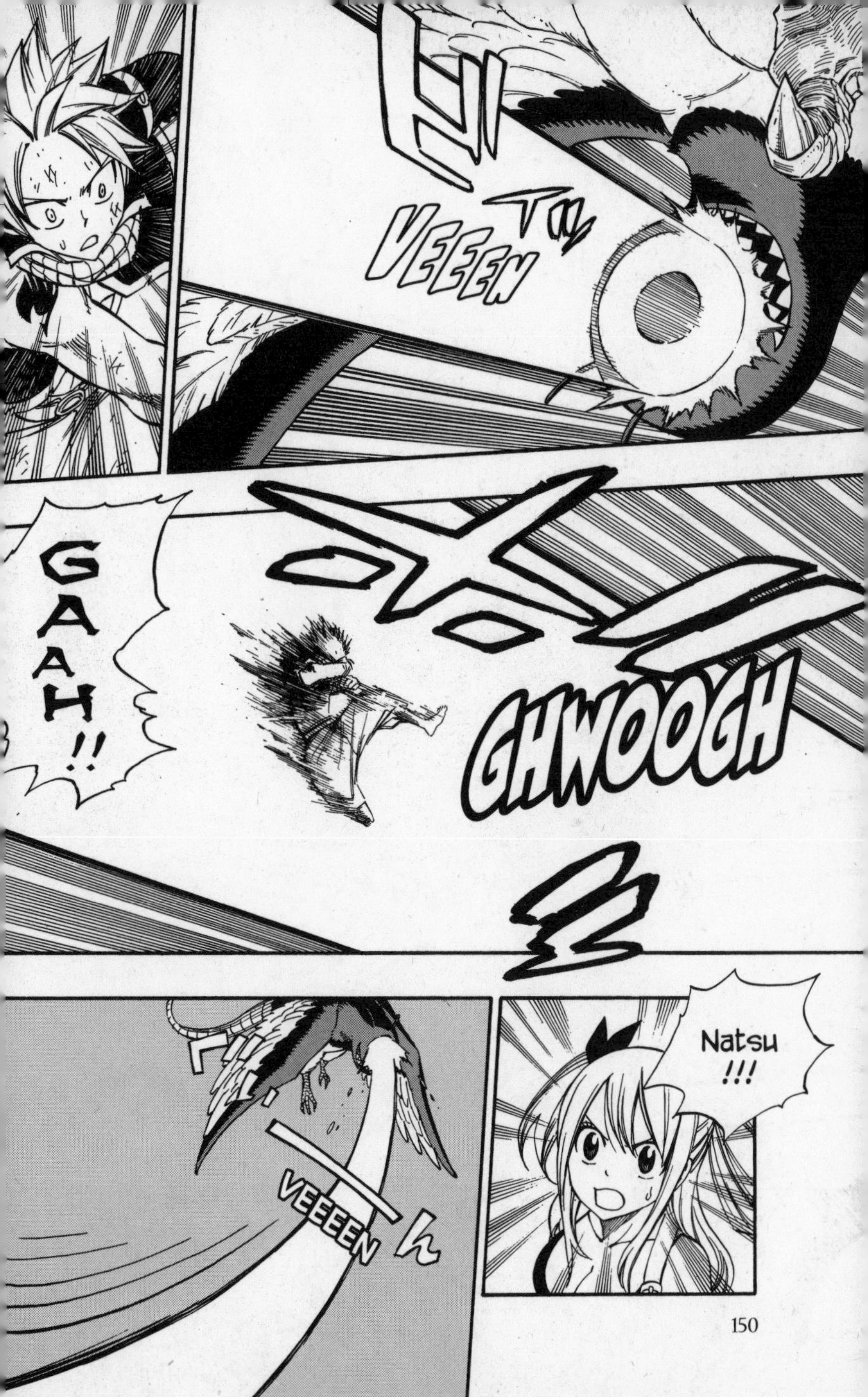
VEEEN
GHWOOGH
GAAH!!
Natsu !!!
VEEEEN h

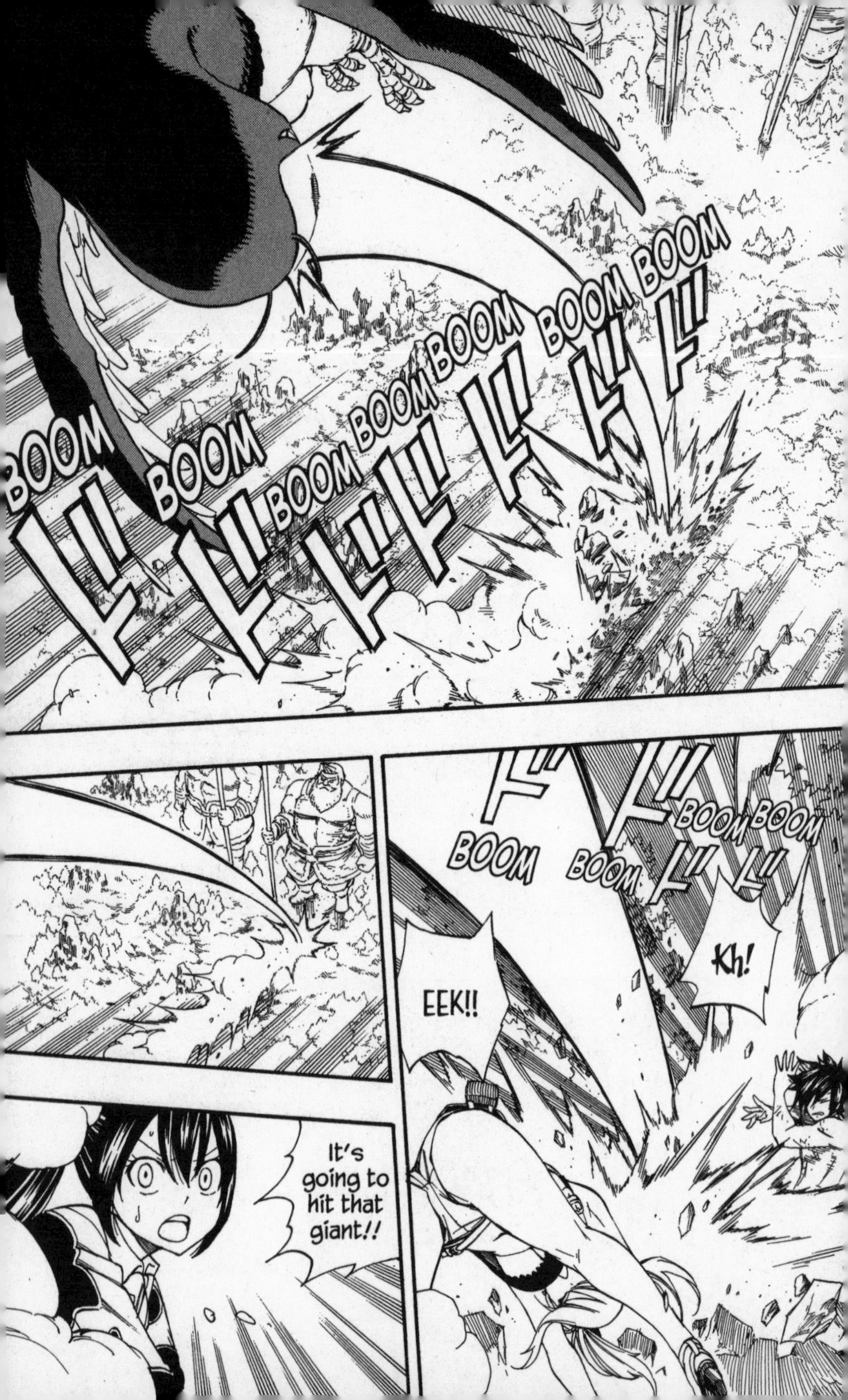
BOOM BOOM BOOM BOOM BOOM BOOM BOOM
ドドドドドドド
BOOM BOOM BOOM BOOM
ドドドド
Kh!
EEK!!
It's going to hit that giant!!

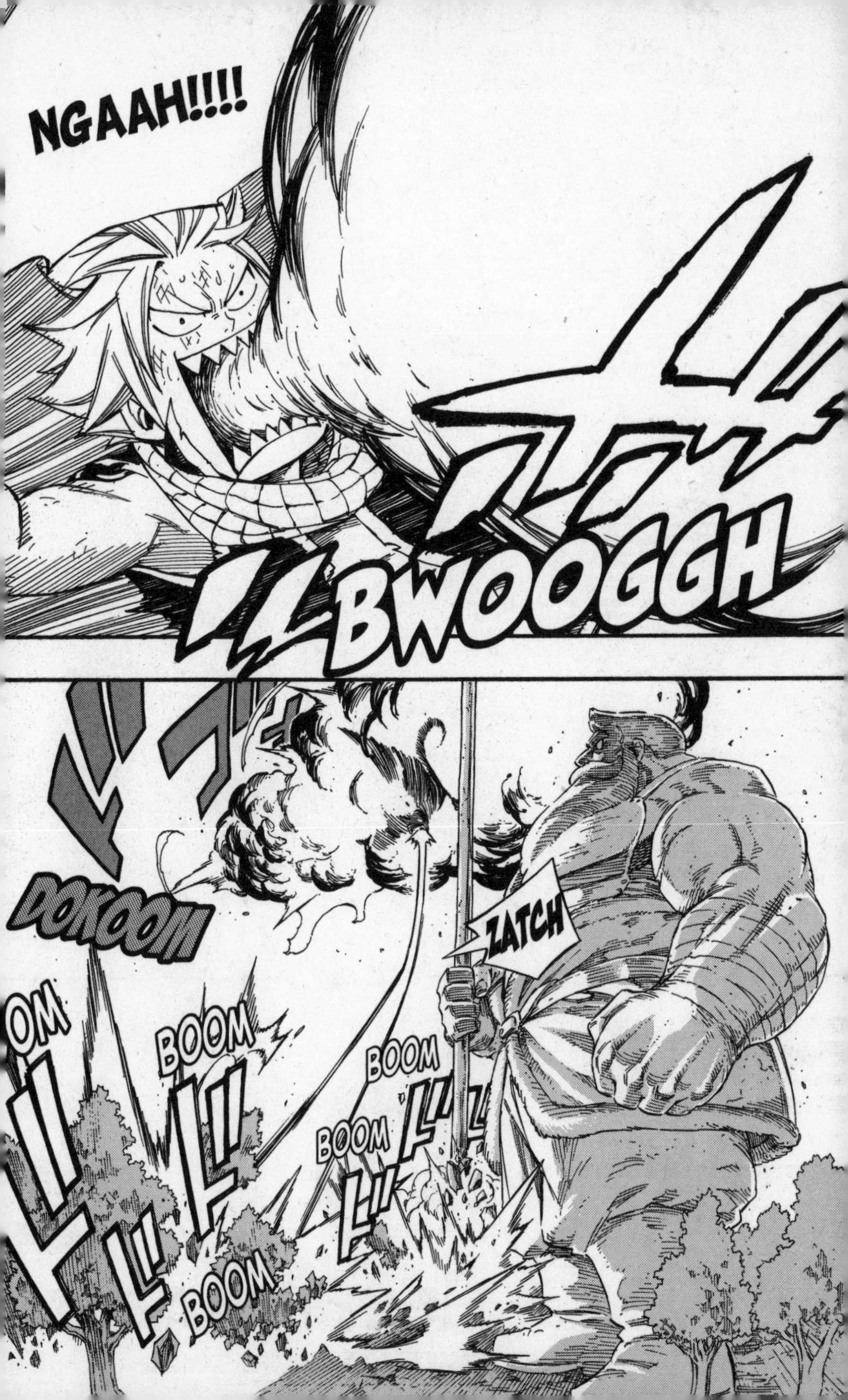
NGAAH!!!!
BWOOGGH
ZATCH
DOKOOM
BOOM
BOOM
BOOM
OM
BOOM

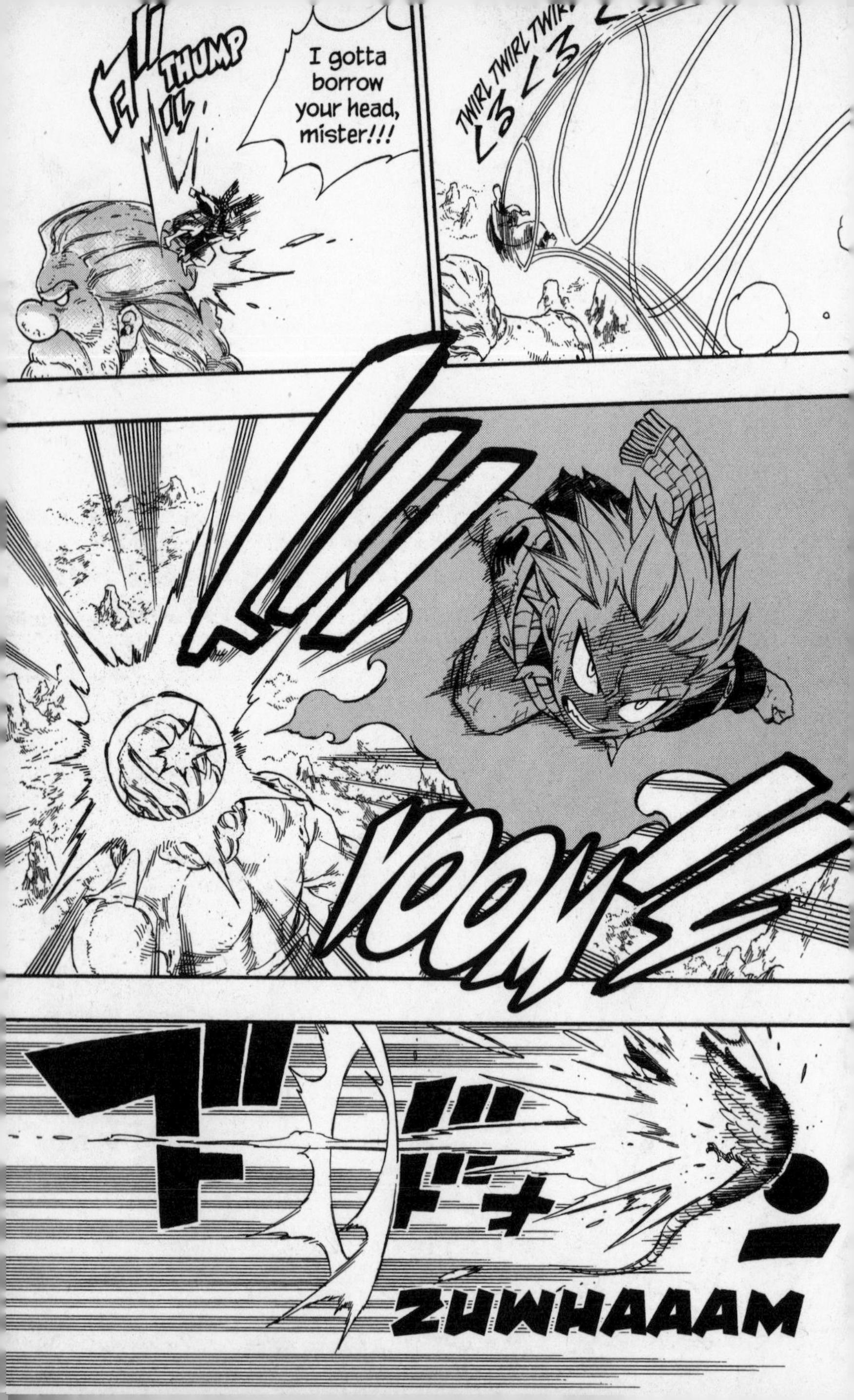
TWIRL TWIRL TWIRL
I gotta borrow your head, mister!!!
THUMP
VOOM
ZUWHAAAM

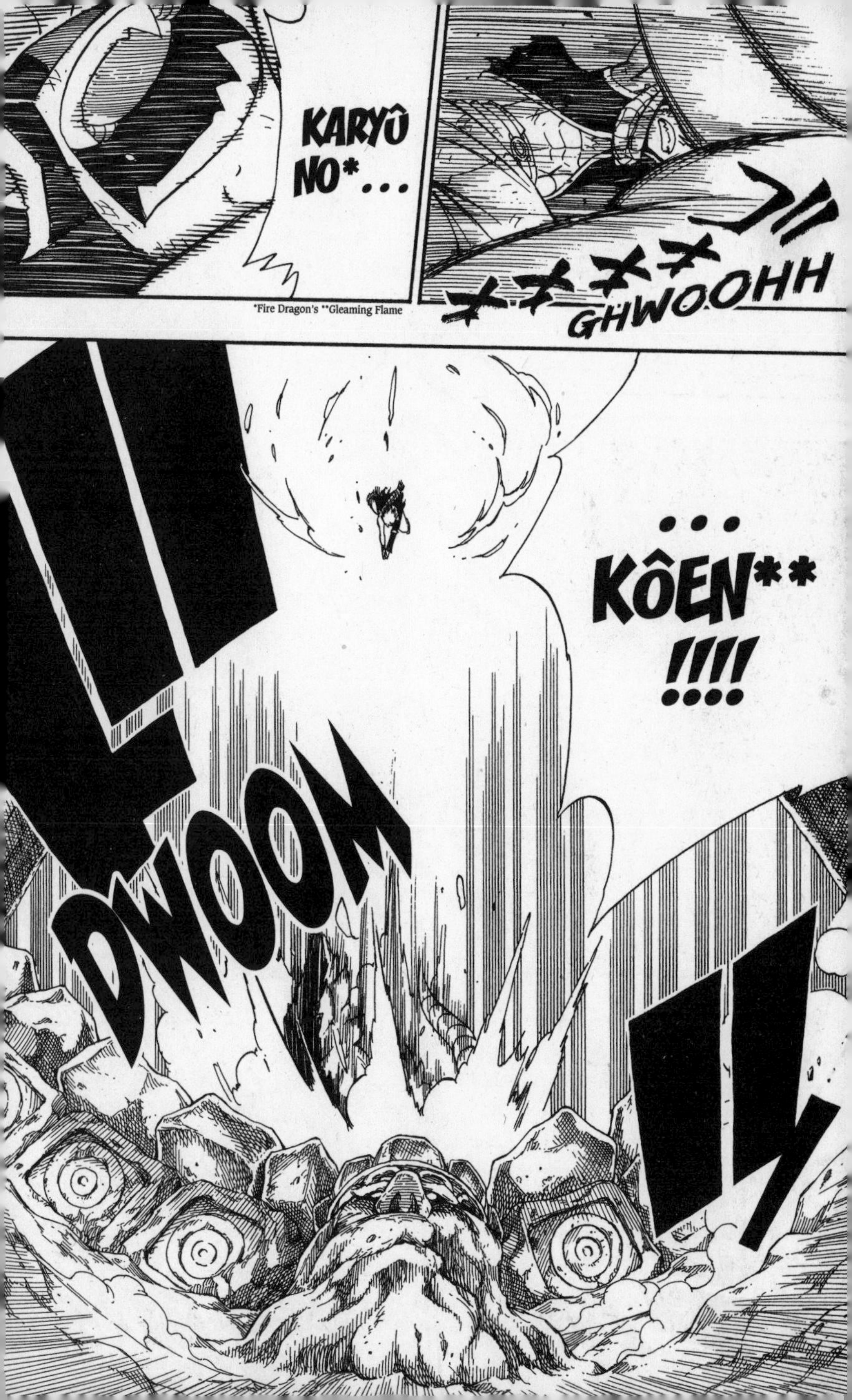
GHWOOHH
KARYÛ NO*...
...KÔEN** !!!!
DWOOM
*Fire Dragon's **Gleaming Flame

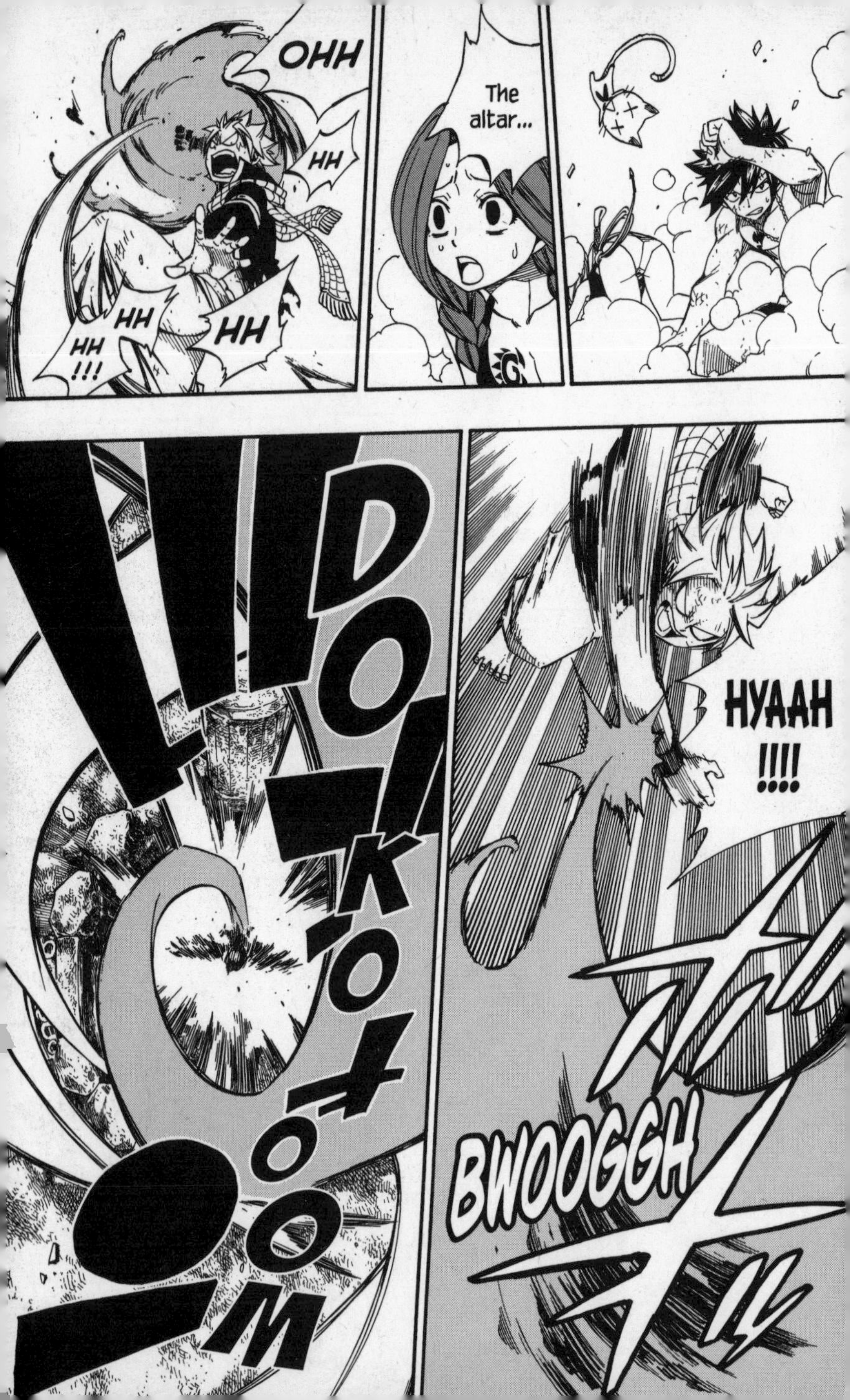

The altar...
OHH
HH
HH
HH
HH
!!!
HYAAH
!!!!
BWOOGGH
!!
DOKOOOOM
!!

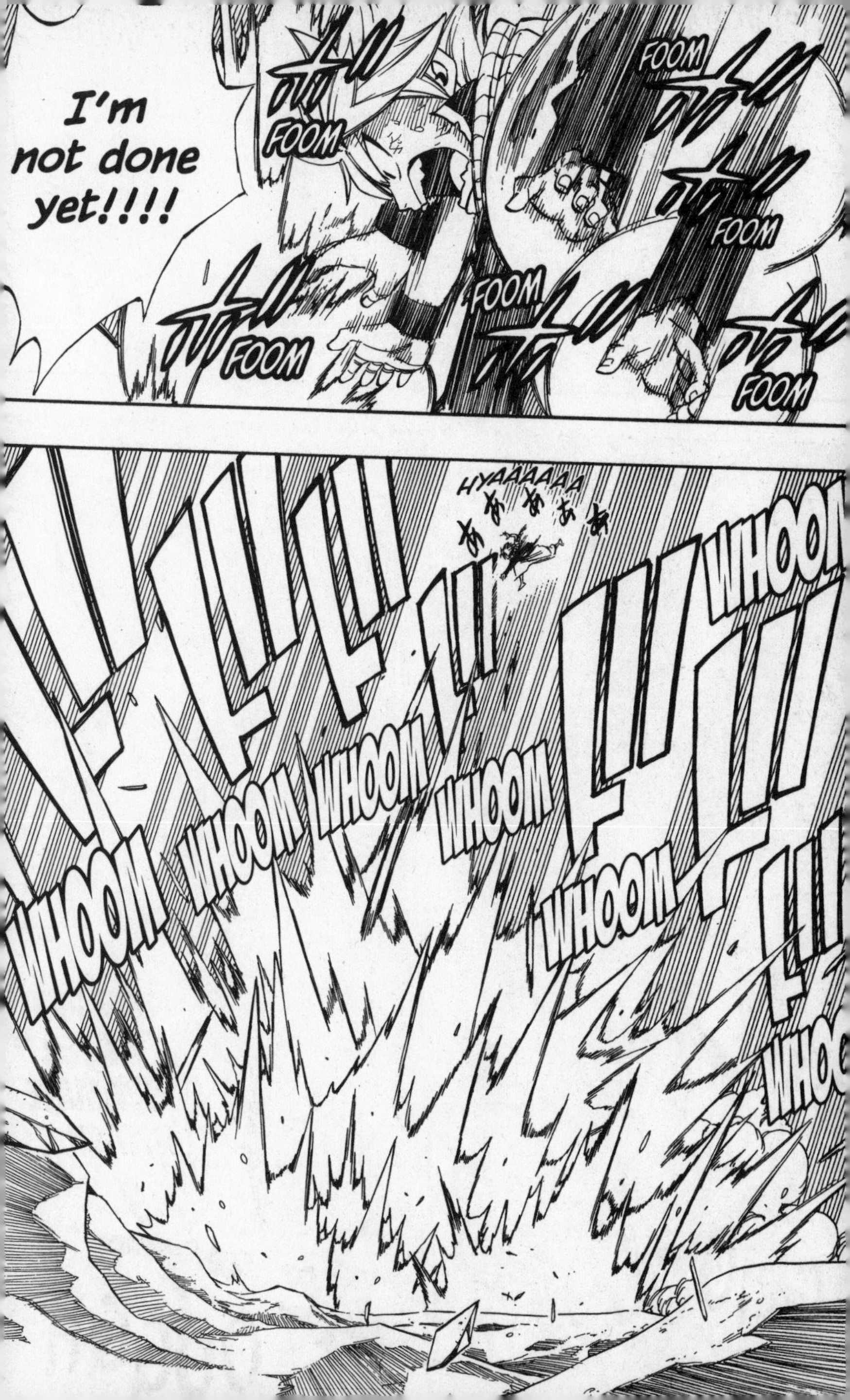

FOOM
FOOM
I'm not done yet!!!!
FOOM
FOOM
FOOM
FOOM
HYAAAAAA
WHOOM
WHOOM
WHOO
WHOOM
WHOOM
WHOOM
WHOOM
WHOOM

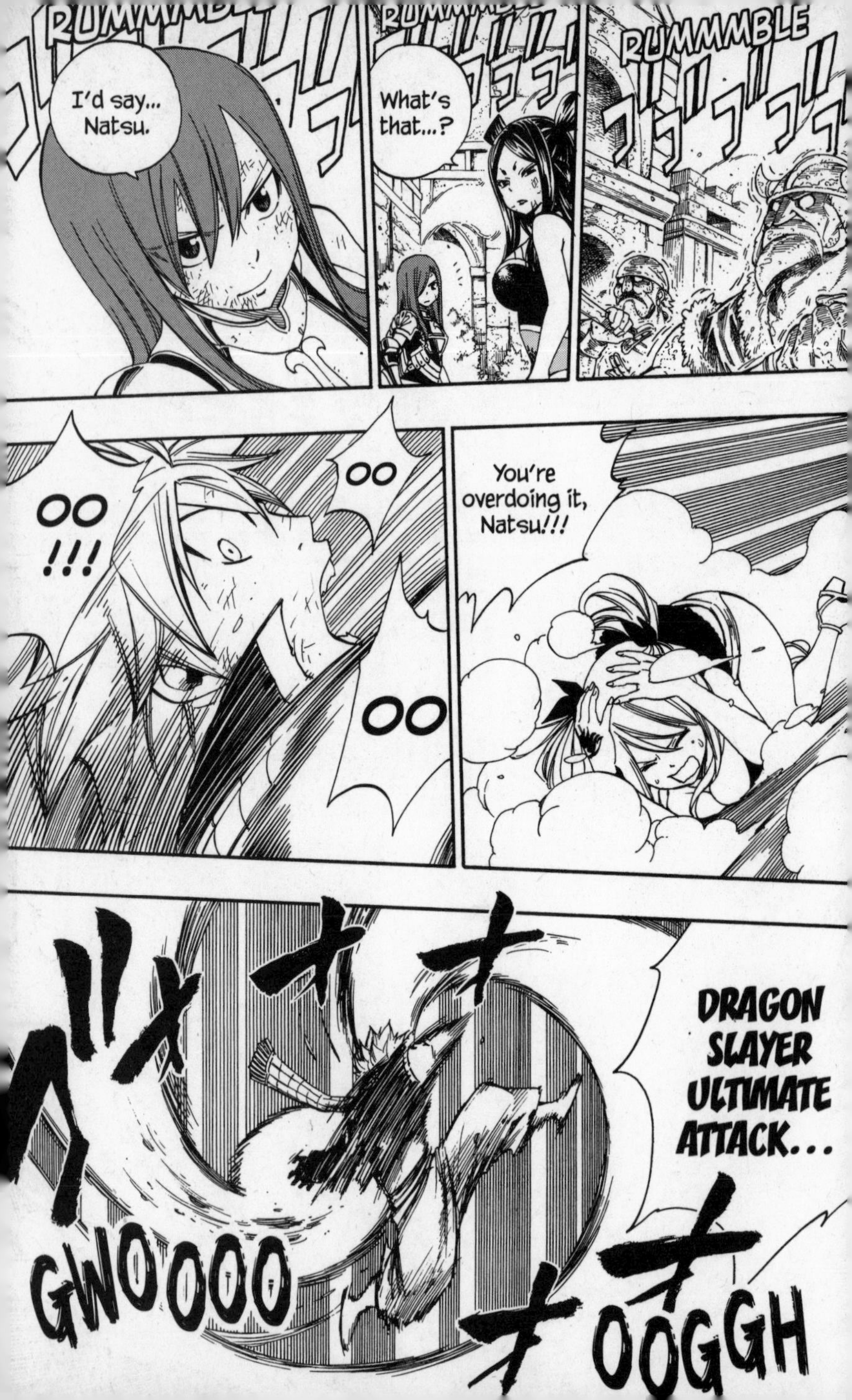
RUMMMBLE
What's that...?
I'd say... Natsu.
You're overdoing it, Natsu!!!
OO
OO !!!
OO
DRAGON SLAYER ULTIMATE ATTACK...
GWOOOO
OOGGH

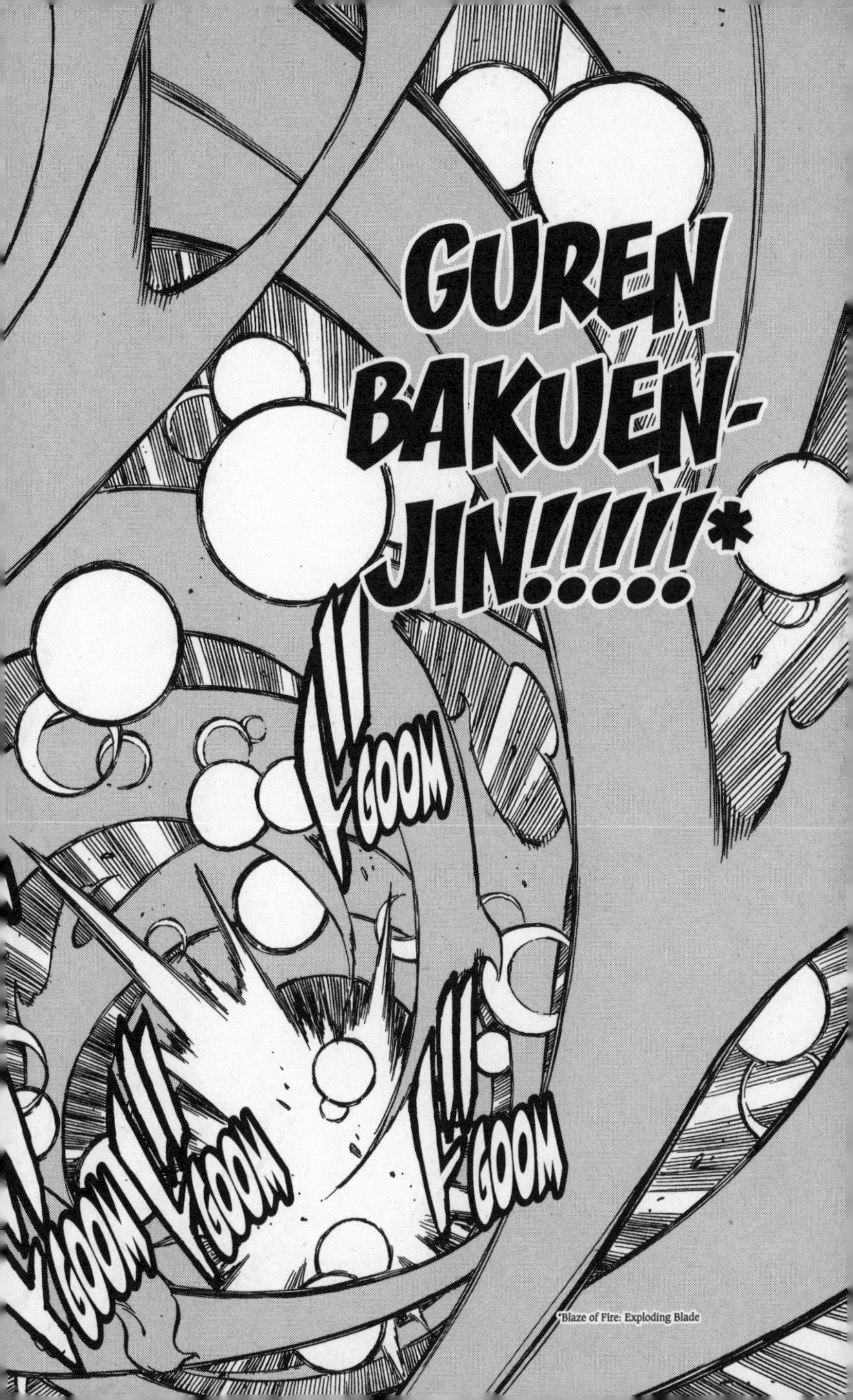
GUREN BAKUEN-JIN!!!!!!*
GOOM
GOOM
GOOM
GOOM!!
*Blaze of Fire: Exploding Blade

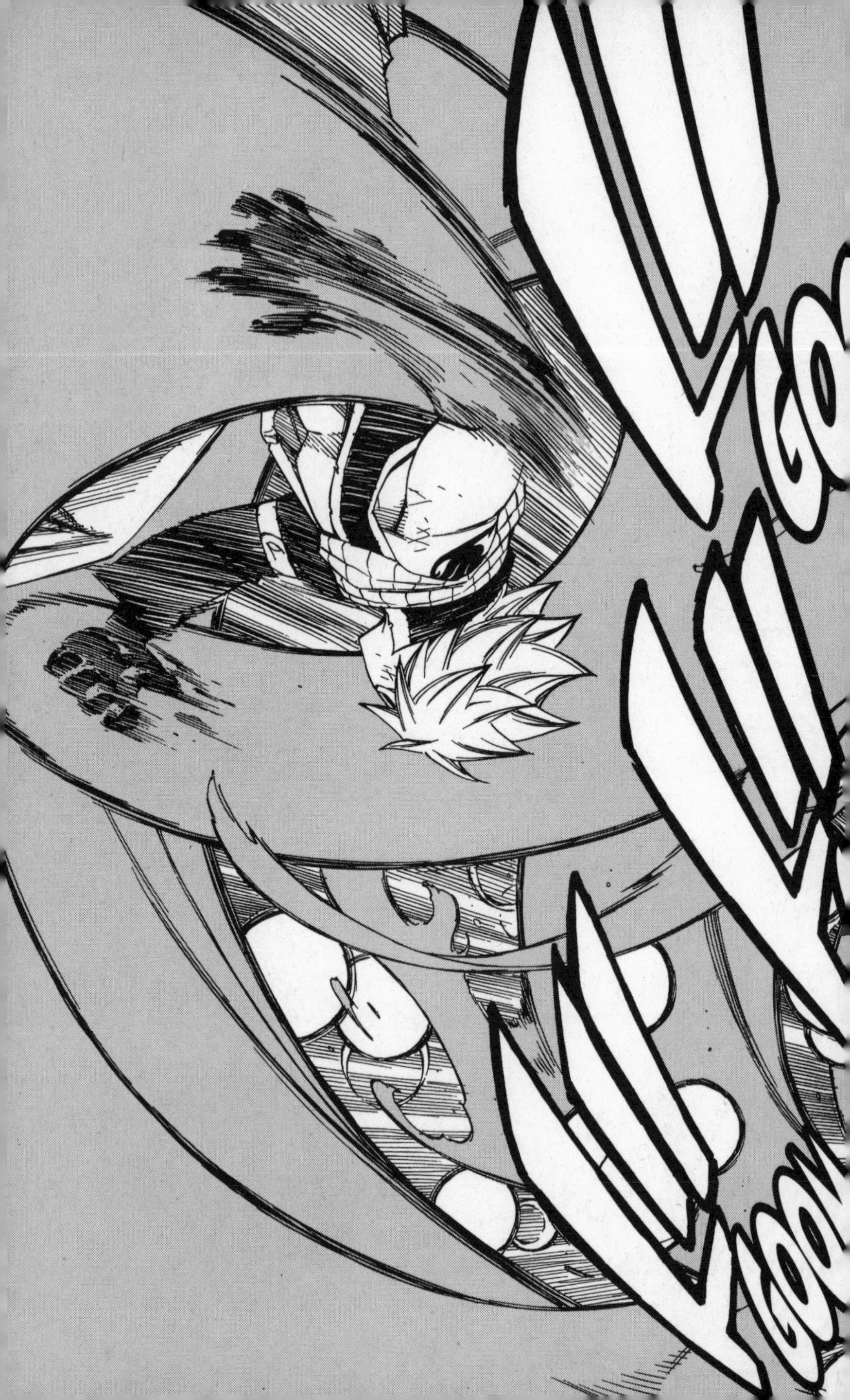

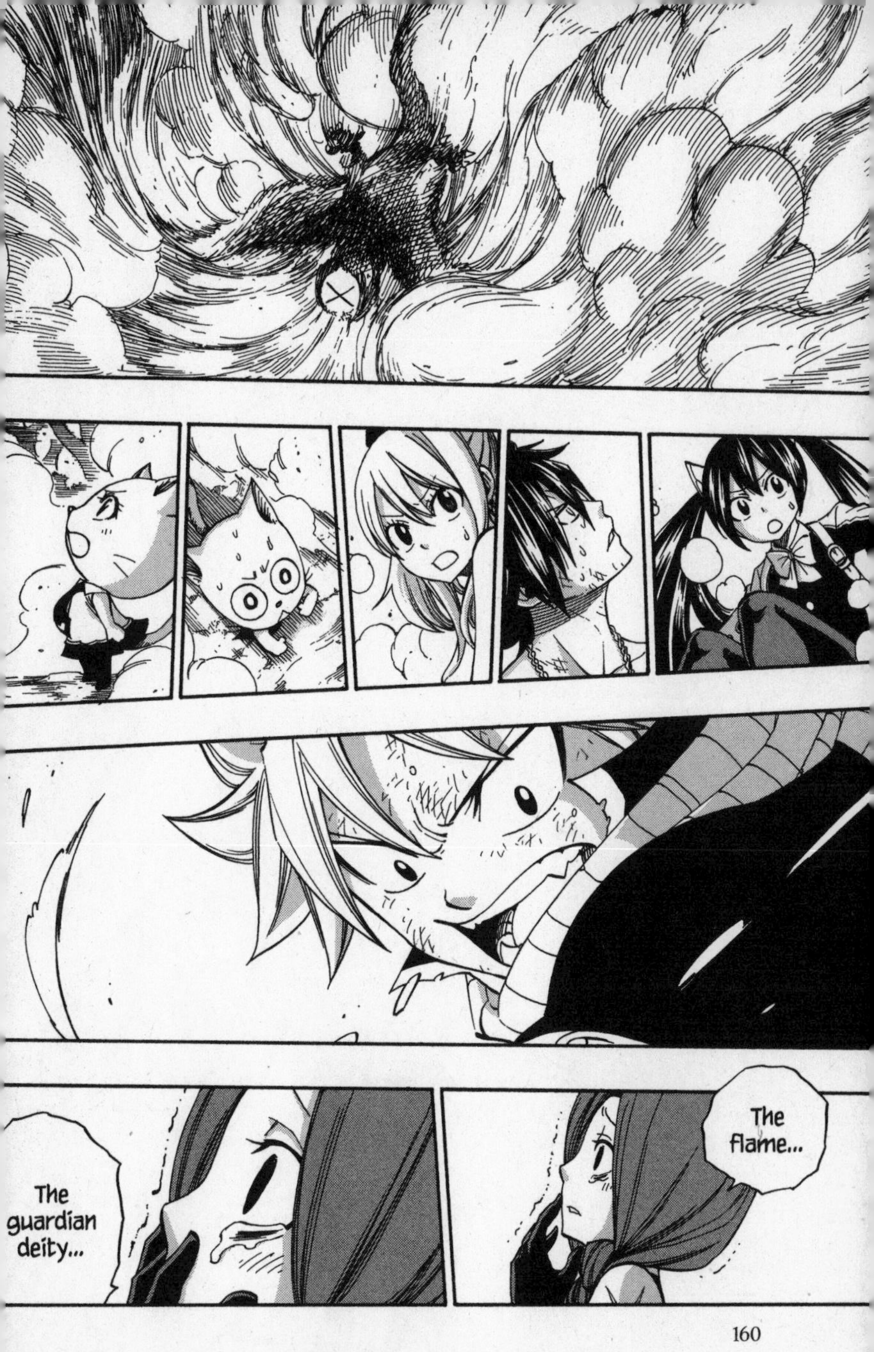
The flame...
The guardian deity...

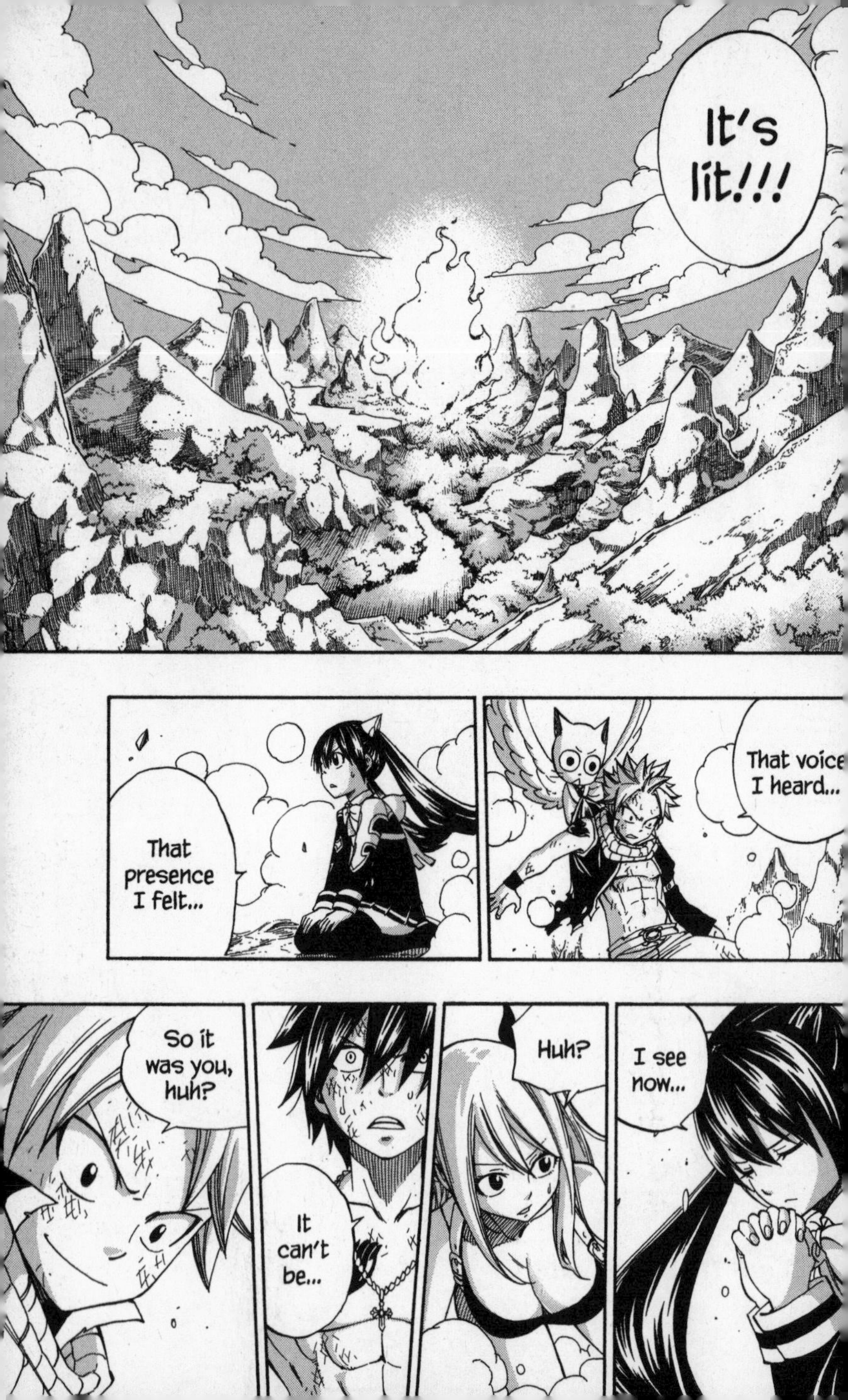
It's lit!!!
That voice I heard...
That presence I felt...
I see now...
Huh?
It can't be...
So it was you, huh?

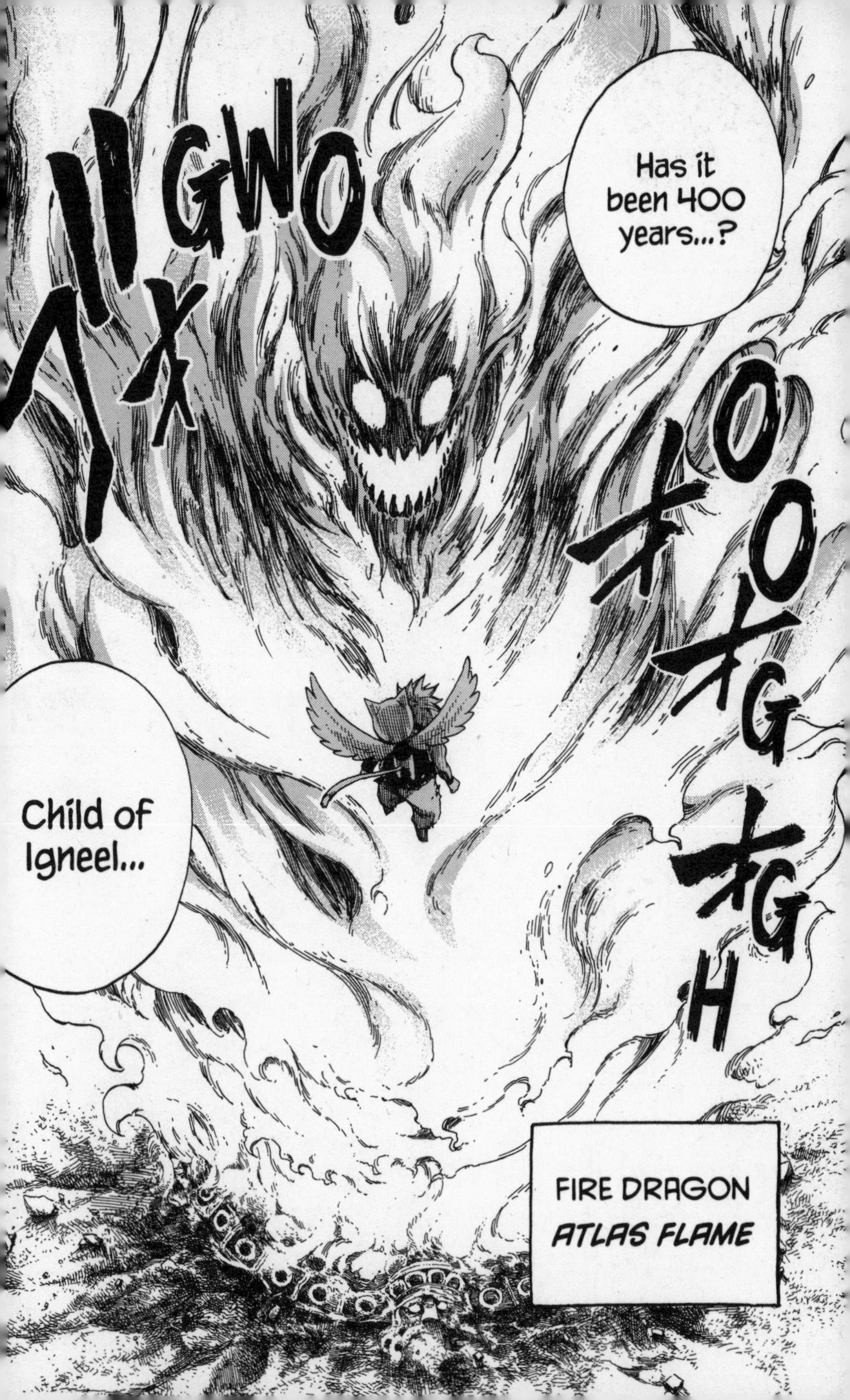

Has it been 400 years...?
GWO
Child of Igneel...
FIRE DRAGON
ATLAS FLAME

FAIRY TAIL

LAMIA SCALE

Name: Sherria Blendy   Age: 15

Magic:
Sky God Slayer Magic

Likes: Dislikes:
Love   Spicy foods

Remarks

Sherria is Sherry's cousin (daughter of Sherry's mother's little sister). Ever since Sherria was small, she always seemed to have more magic power than Sherry, and she even skipped some grades in her school of magic to graduate early. She taught herself god slayer magic from a book awarded her for academic excellence by the chairman of the Magic Council, Grand Doma. He never dreamed she would actually be able to put it into practice! She really likes Wendy, who she became friends with during the Grand Magic Games. They've gone out to have fun together (along with Carla) many times since.

Chapter 353: Demon Exorcist

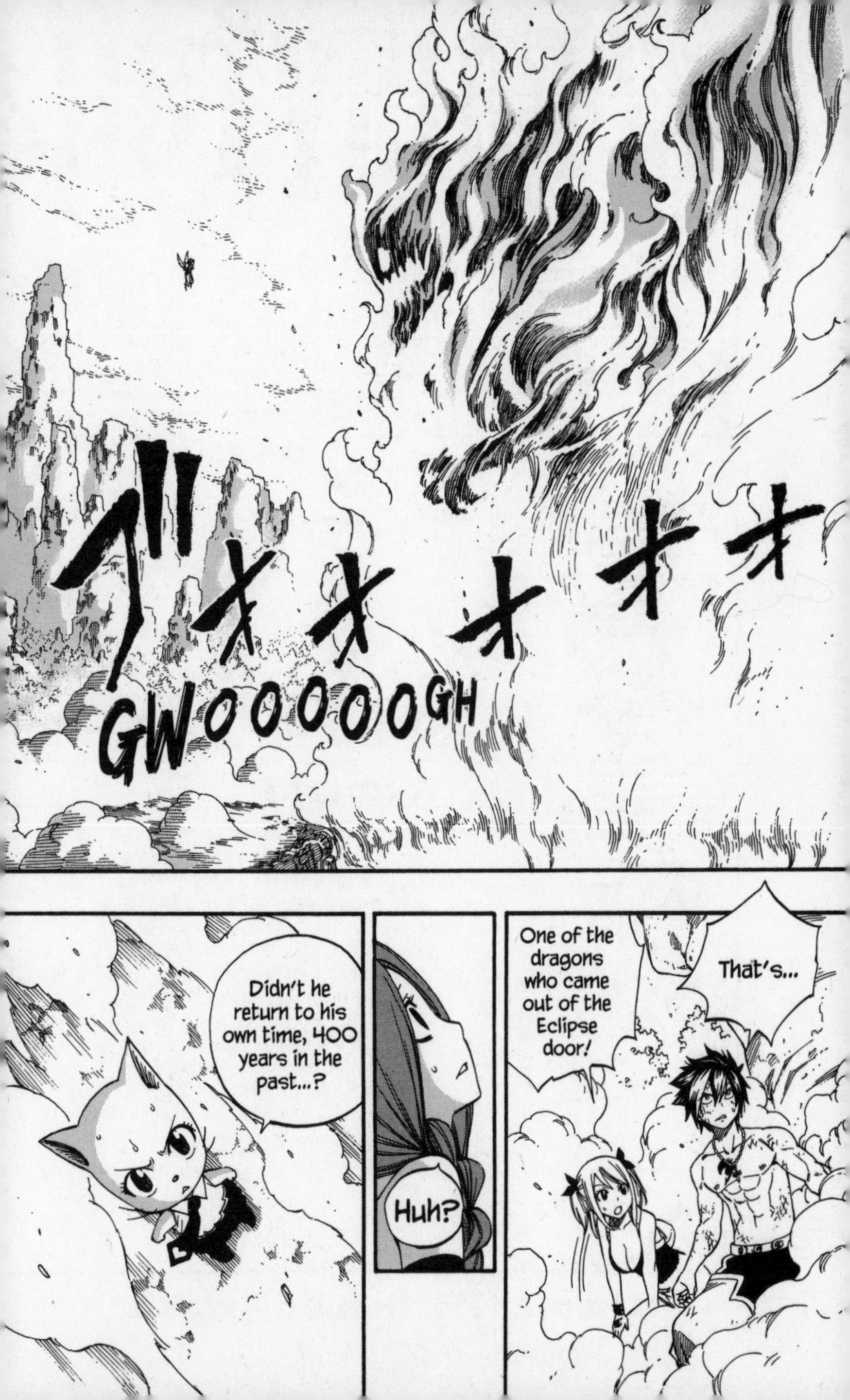
GWOOOOOGH
That's...
One of the dragons who came out of the Eclipse door!
Huh?
Didn't he return to his own time, 400 years in the past...?

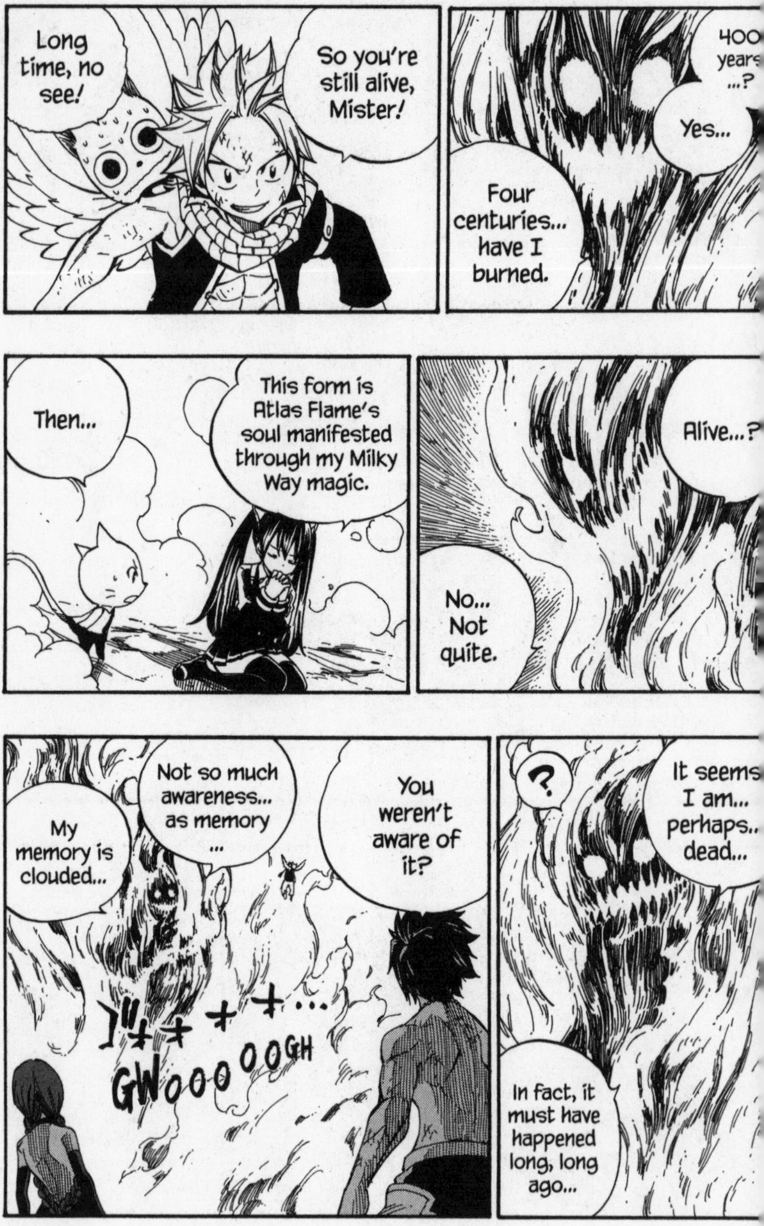

400 years ...?
Yes...
Four centuries... have I burned.
So you're still alive, Mister!
Long time, no see!
Alive...?
No... Not quite.
This form is Atlas Flame's soul manifested through my Milky Way magic.
Then...
It seems I am... perhaps... dead...
?
In fact, it must have happened long, long ago...
You weren't aware of it?
Not so much awareness... as memory ...
My memory is clouded...
GWOOOOOOGH

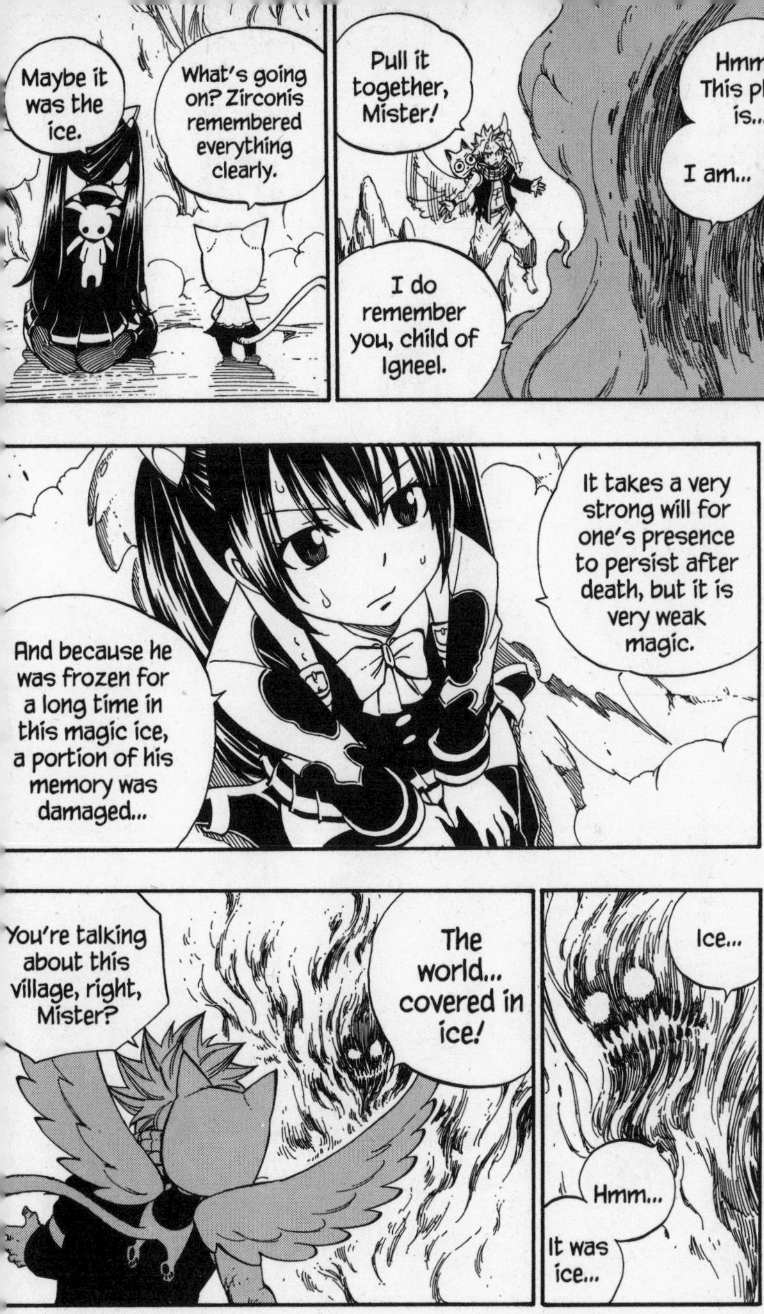
Hmm... This place is...
I am...
Pull it together, Mister!
I do remember you, child of Igneel.
What's going on? Zirconis remembered everything clearly.
Maybe it was the ice.
It takes a very strong will for one's presence to persist after death, but it is very weak magic.
And because he was frozen for a long time in this magic ice, a portion of his memory was damaged...
Ice...
Hmm...
It was ice...
The world... covered in ice!
You're talking about this village, right, Mister?

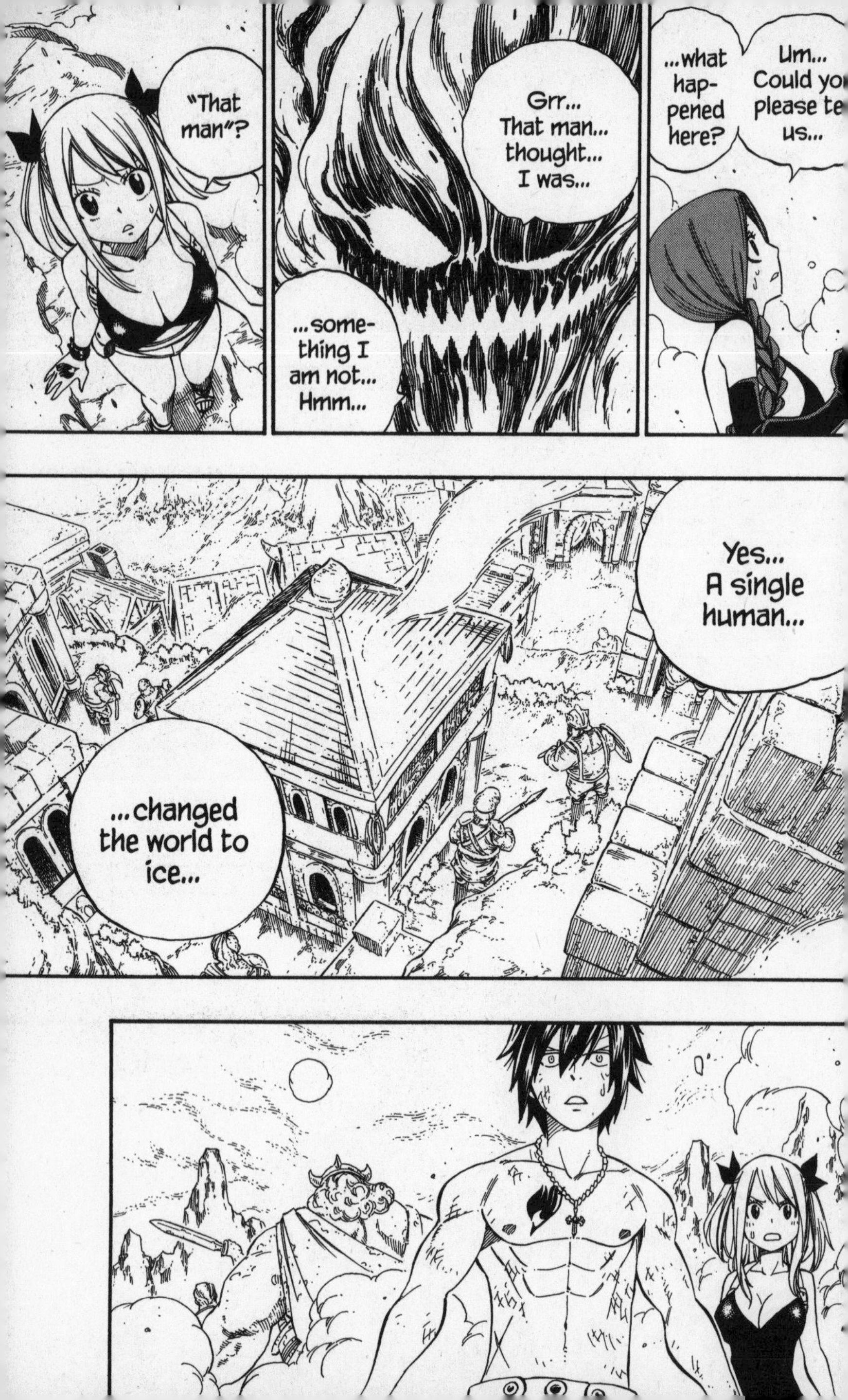
Um... Could yo please te us...
...what hap-pened here?
Grr... That man... thought... I was...
...some-thing I am not... Hmm...
"That man"?
Yes... A single human...
...changed the world to ice...

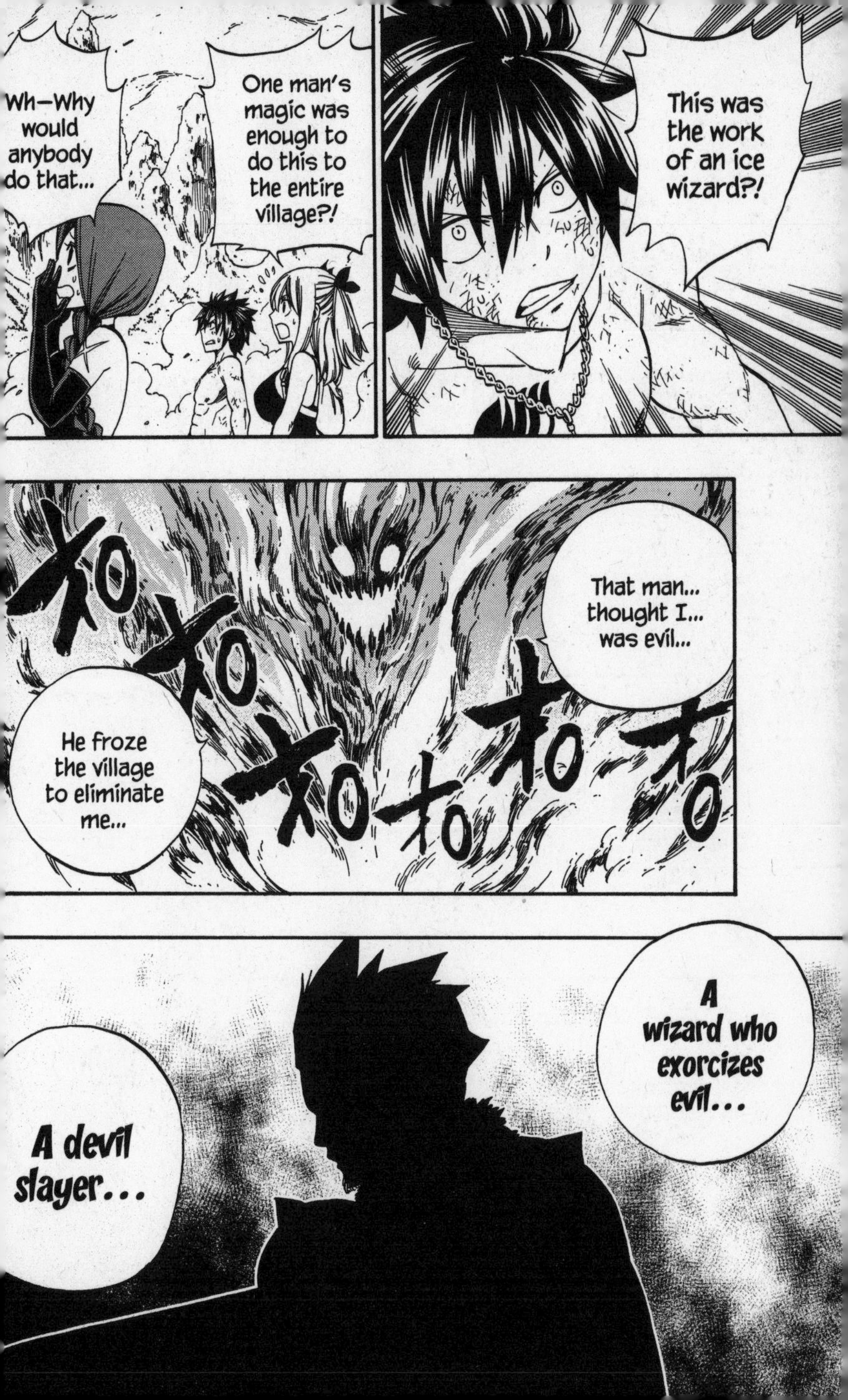
This was the work of an ice wizard?!
One man's magic was enough to do this to the entire village?!
Wh—Why would anybody do that...
That man... thought I... was evil...
He froze the village to eliminate me...
A wizard who exorcizes evil...
A devil slayer...

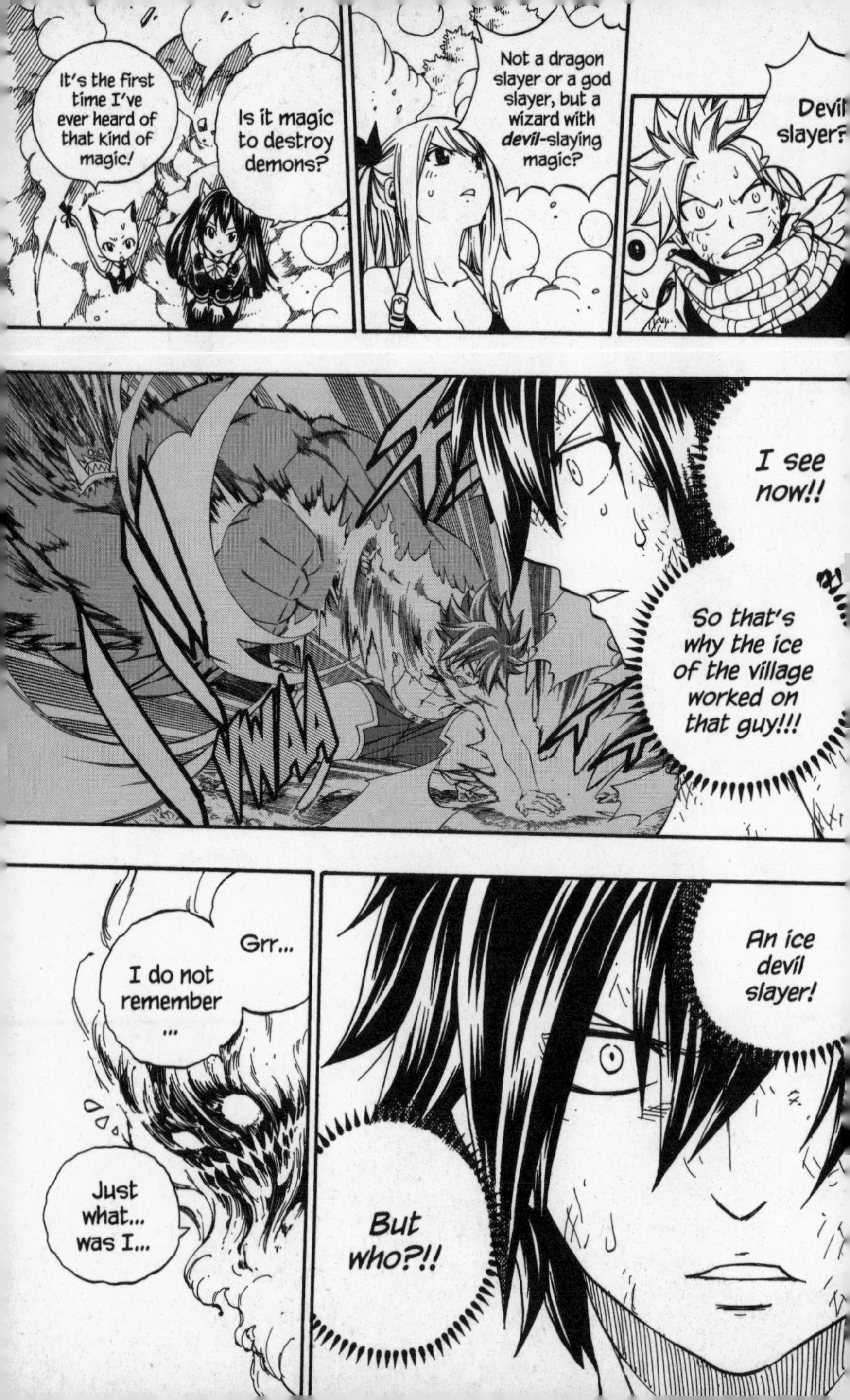
Devil slayer?
Not a dragon slayer or a god slayer, but a wizard with *devil*-slaying magic?
Is it magic to destroy demons?
It's the first time I've ever heard of that kind of magic!
I see now!!
So that's why the ice of the village worked on that guy!!!
An ice devil slayer!
But who?!!
Grr...
I do not remember ...
Just what... was I...

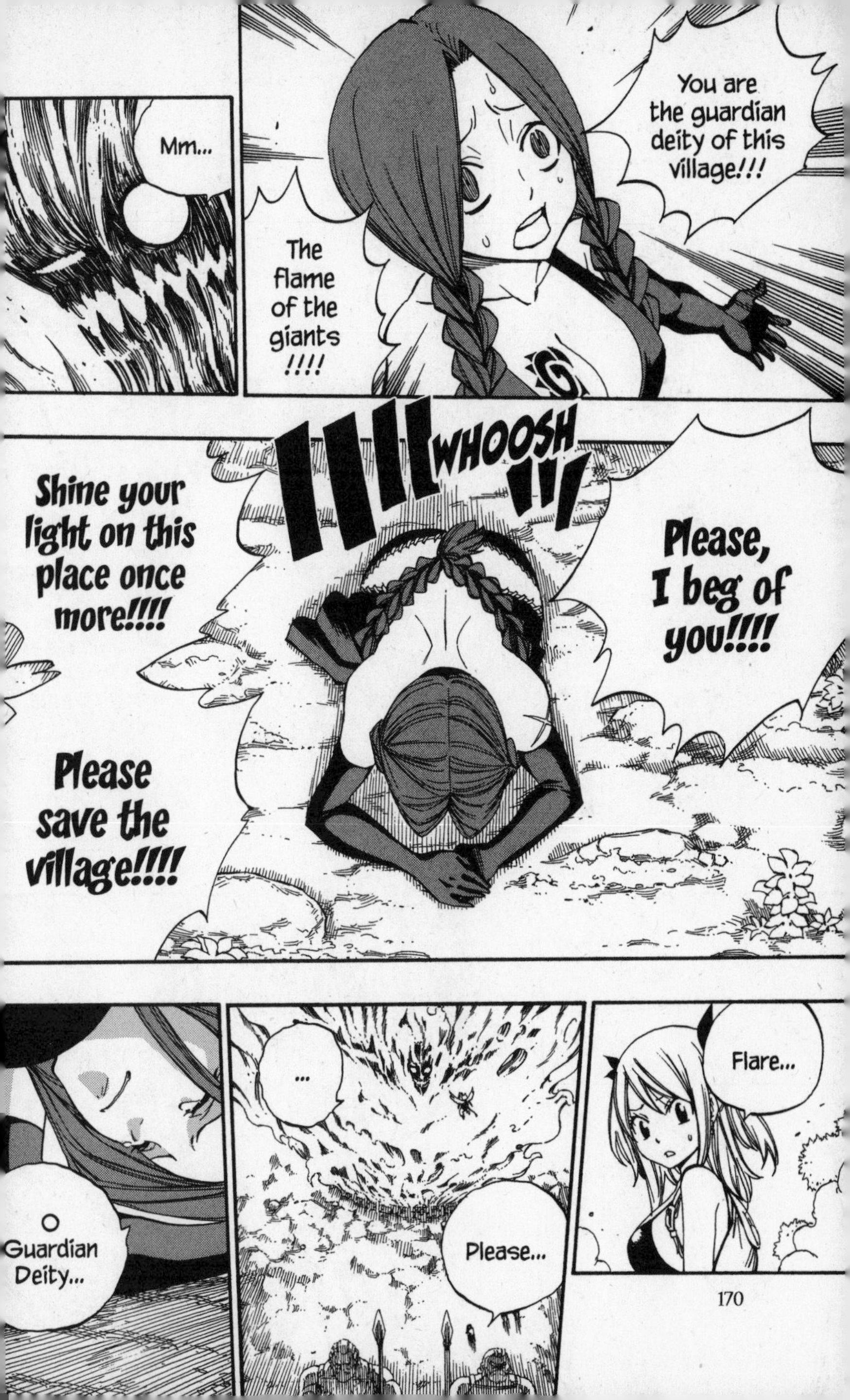

You are the guardian deity of this village!!!
The flame of the giants !!!!
Mm...
WHOOSH
Please, I beg of you!!!!
Shine your light on this place once more!!!!
Please save the village!!!!
Flare...
...
Please...
O Guardian Deity...

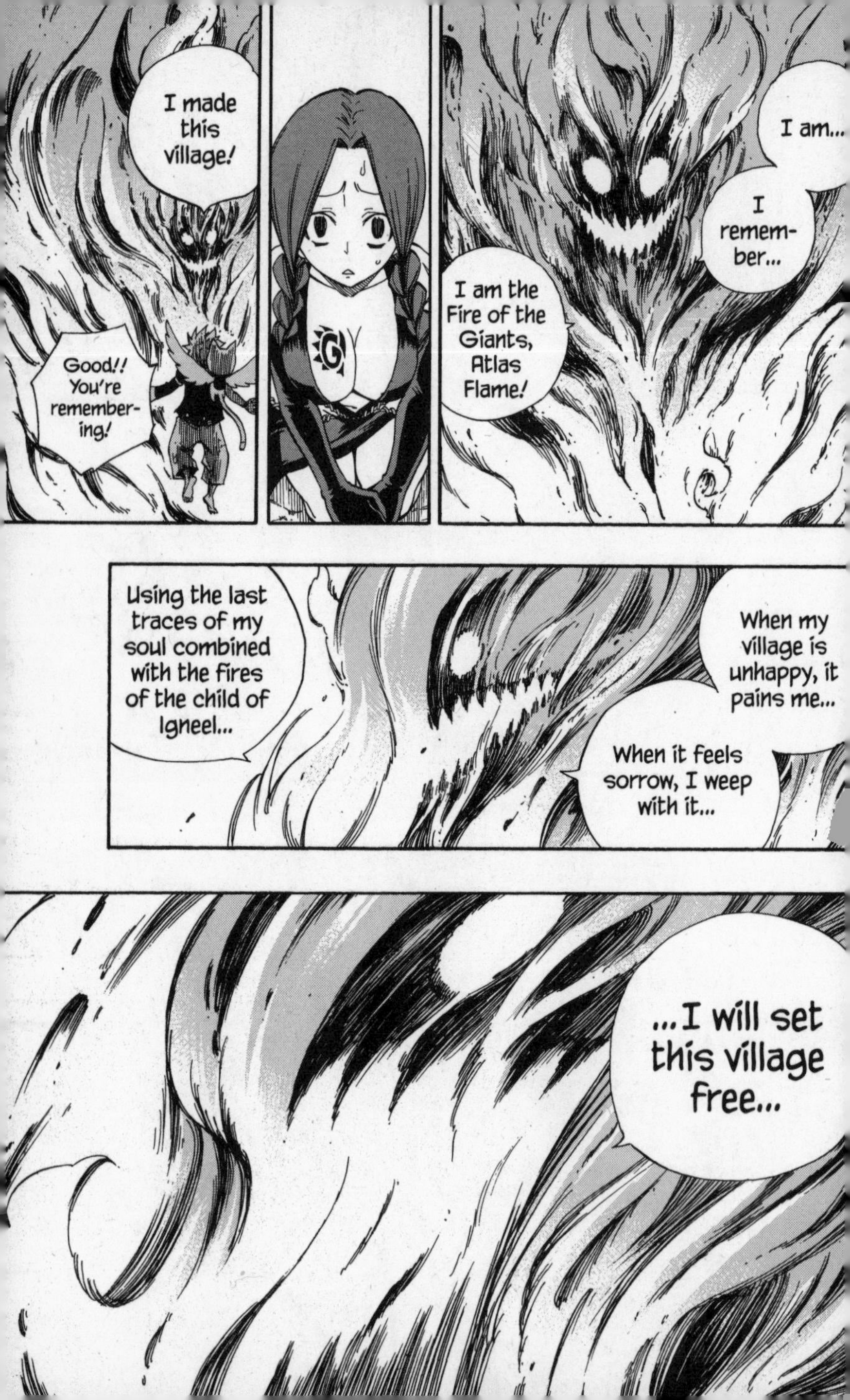
I am...
I remember...
I am the Fire of the Giants, Atlas Flame!
I made this village!
Good!! You're remembering!
When my village is unhappy, it pains me...
When it feels sorrow, I weep with it...
Using the last traces of my soul combined with the fires of the child of Igneel...
...I will set this village free...

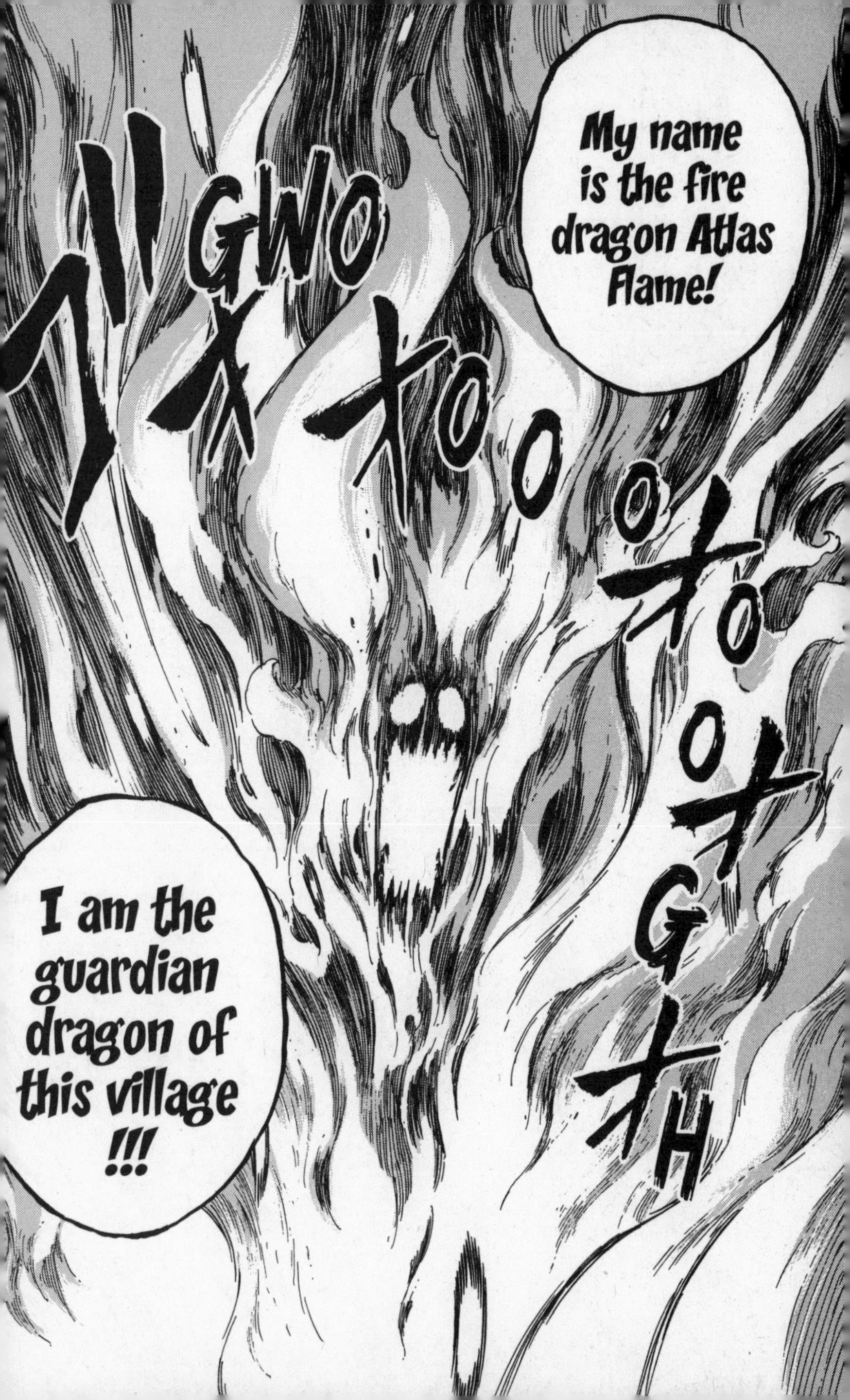
My name is the fire dragon Atlas Flame!
I am the guardian dragon of this village !!!

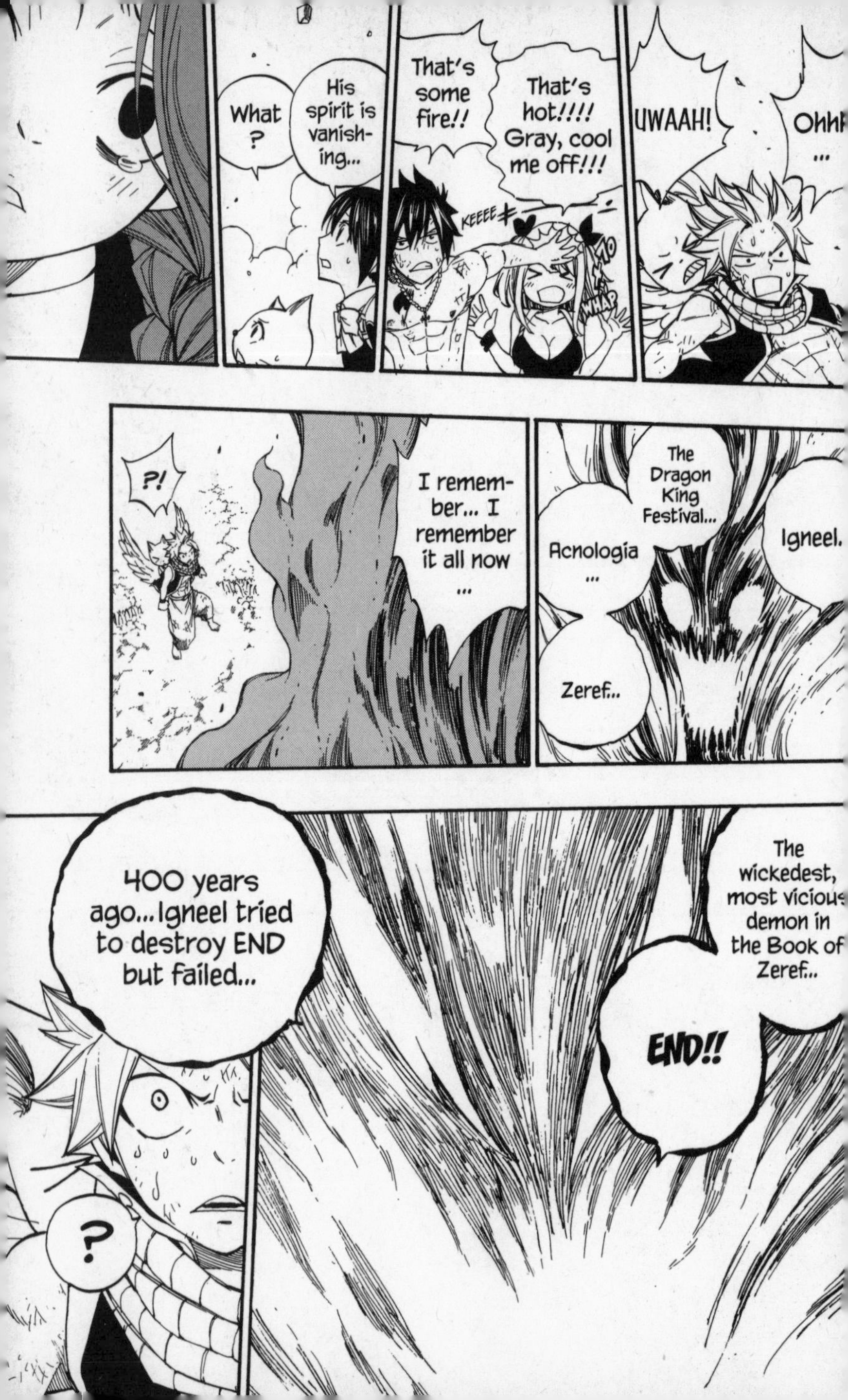
Ohh...
UWAAH!
That's hot!!!! Gray, cool me off!!!
That's some fire!!
KEEEE
WHAP
His spirit is vanishing...
What?
The Dragon King Festival...
Igneel.
Acnologia...
Zeref...
I remember... I remember it all now...
?!
The wickedest, most vicious demon in the Book of Zeref...
END!!
400 years ago...Igneel tried to destroy END but failed...
?

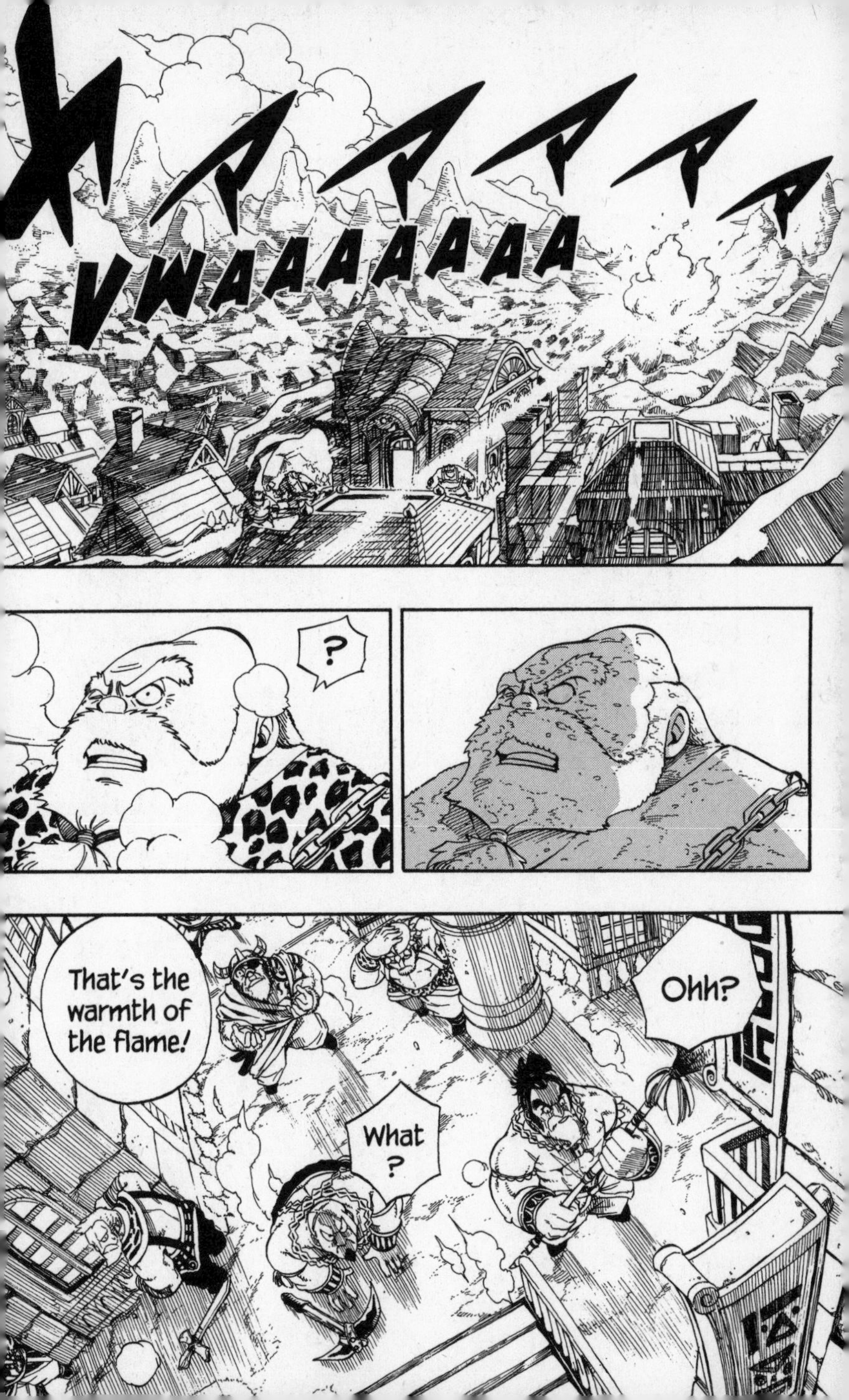
KAAAAAA
VWAAAAAAA
?
Ohh?
That's the warmth of the flame!
What?

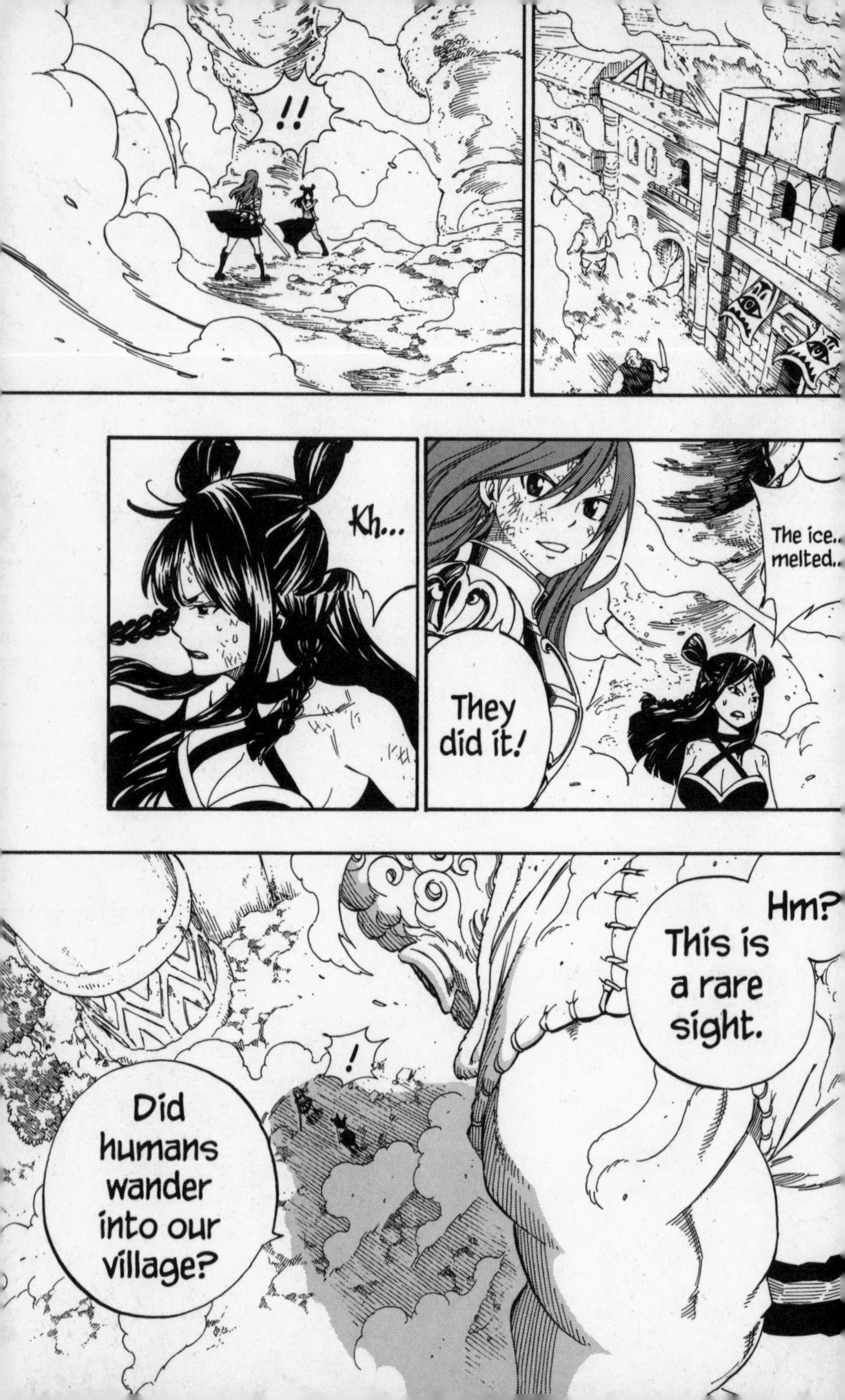
!!
The ice... melted...
They did it!
Kh...
Hm? This is a rare sight.
!
Did humans wander into our village?

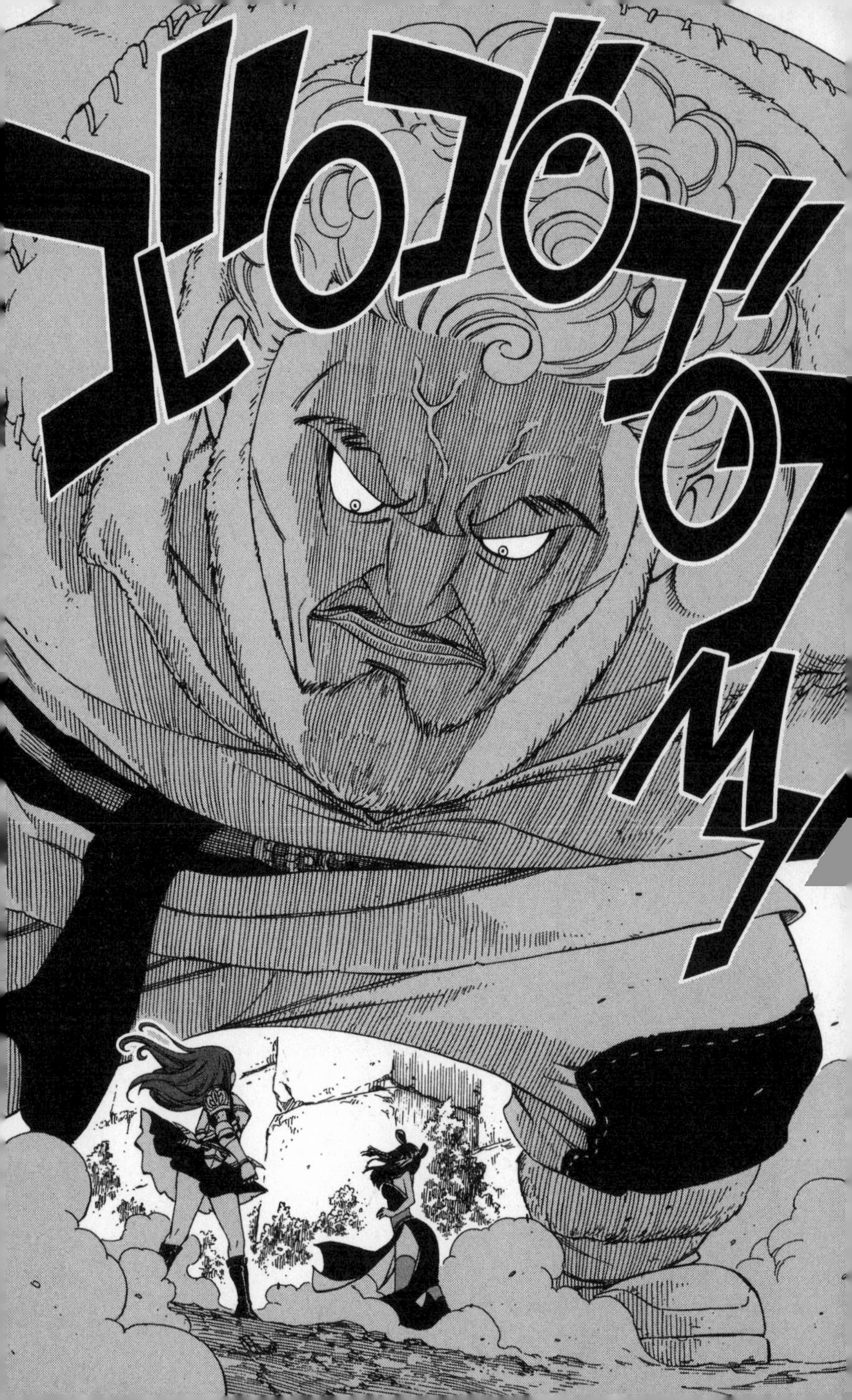

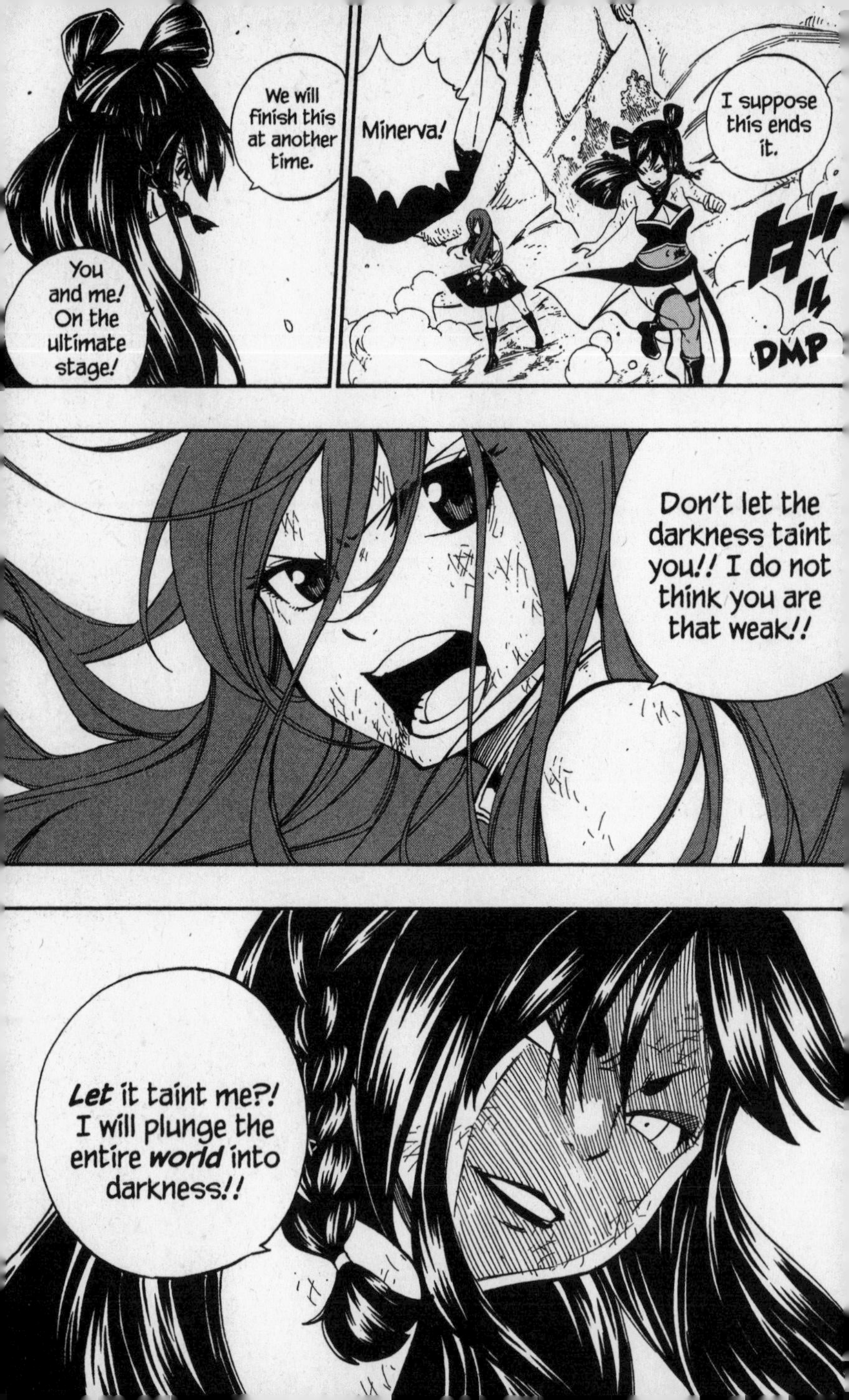

I suppose this ends it.
Minerva!
DMP
We will finish this at another time.
You and me! On the ultimate stage!
Don't let the darkness taint you!! I do not think you are that weak!!
Let it taint me?! I will plunge the entire *world* into darkness!!

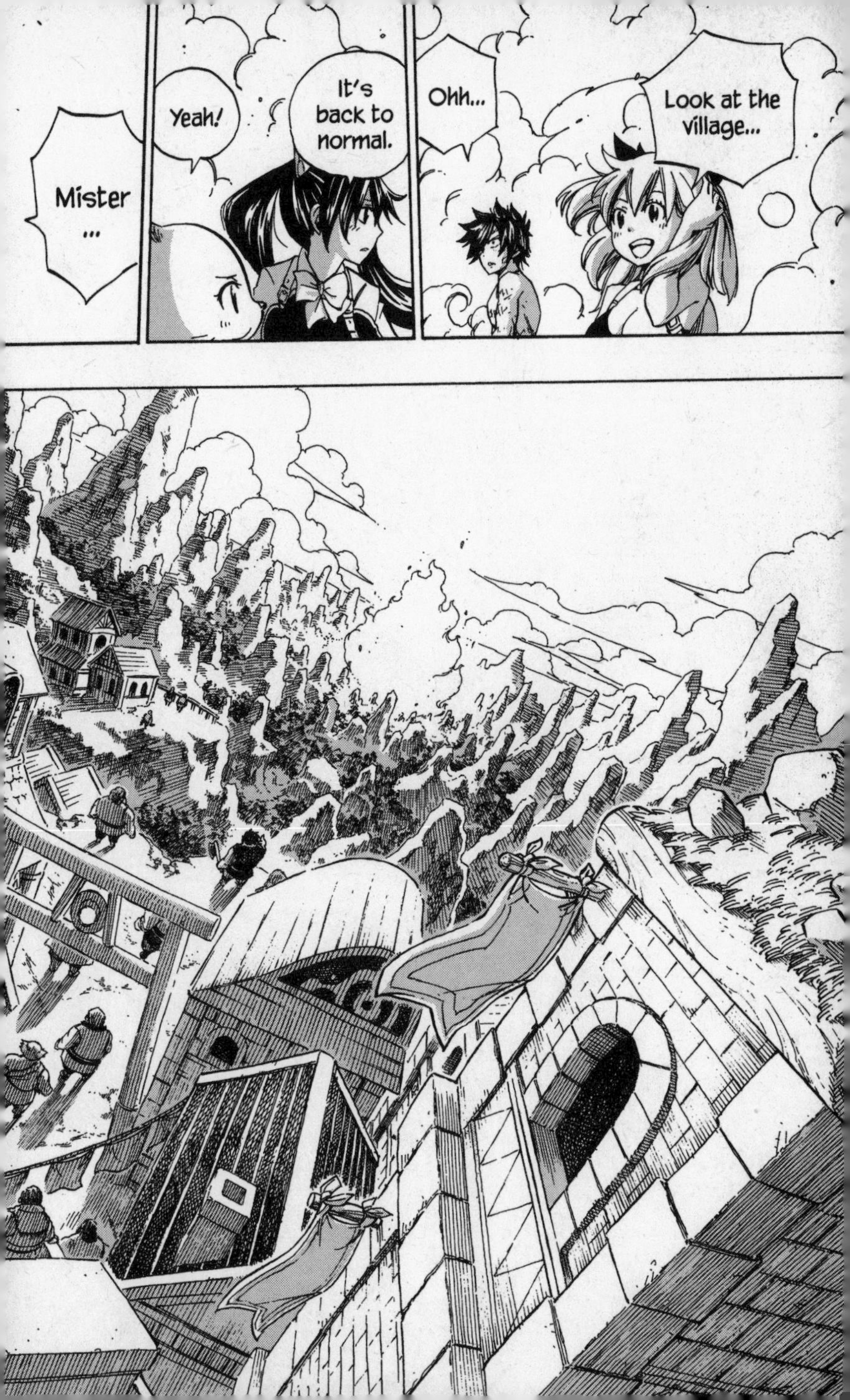
Look at the village...
Ohh...
It's back to normal.
Yeah!
Mister ...

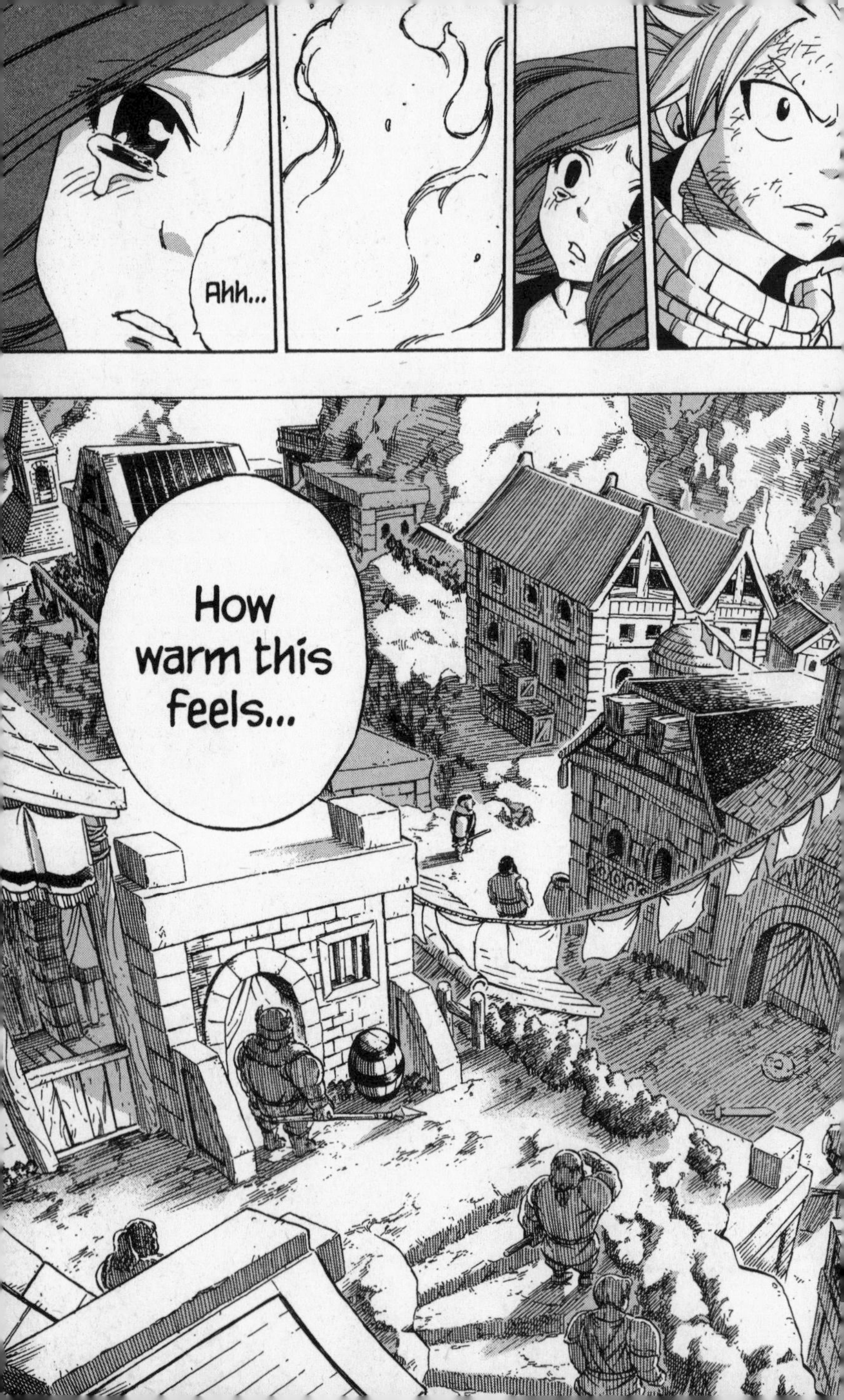
Ahh...
How warm this feels...

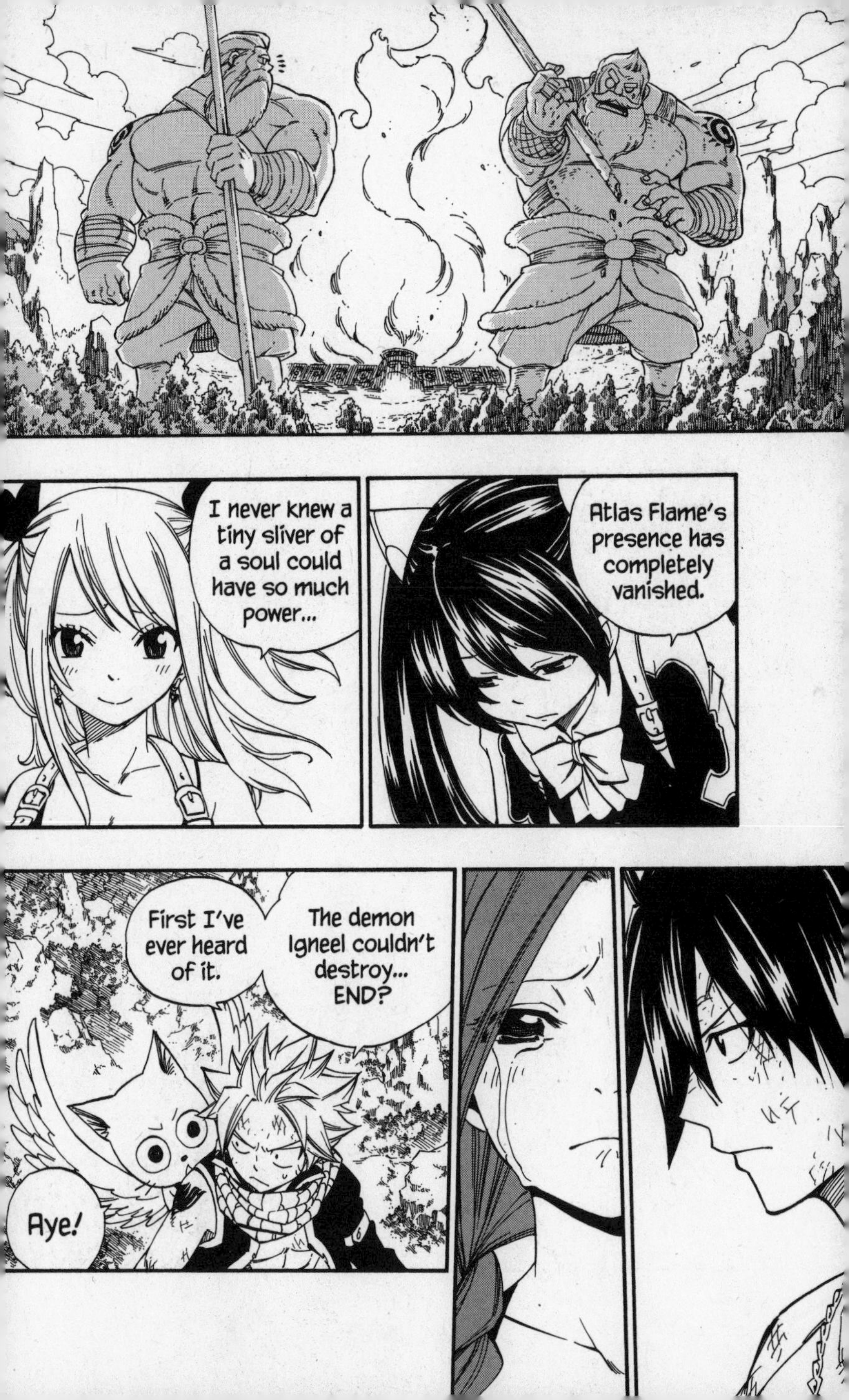
Atlas Flame's presence has completely vanished.
I never knew a tiny sliver of a soul could have so much power...
The demon Igneel couldn't destroy... END?
First I've ever heard of it.
Aye!

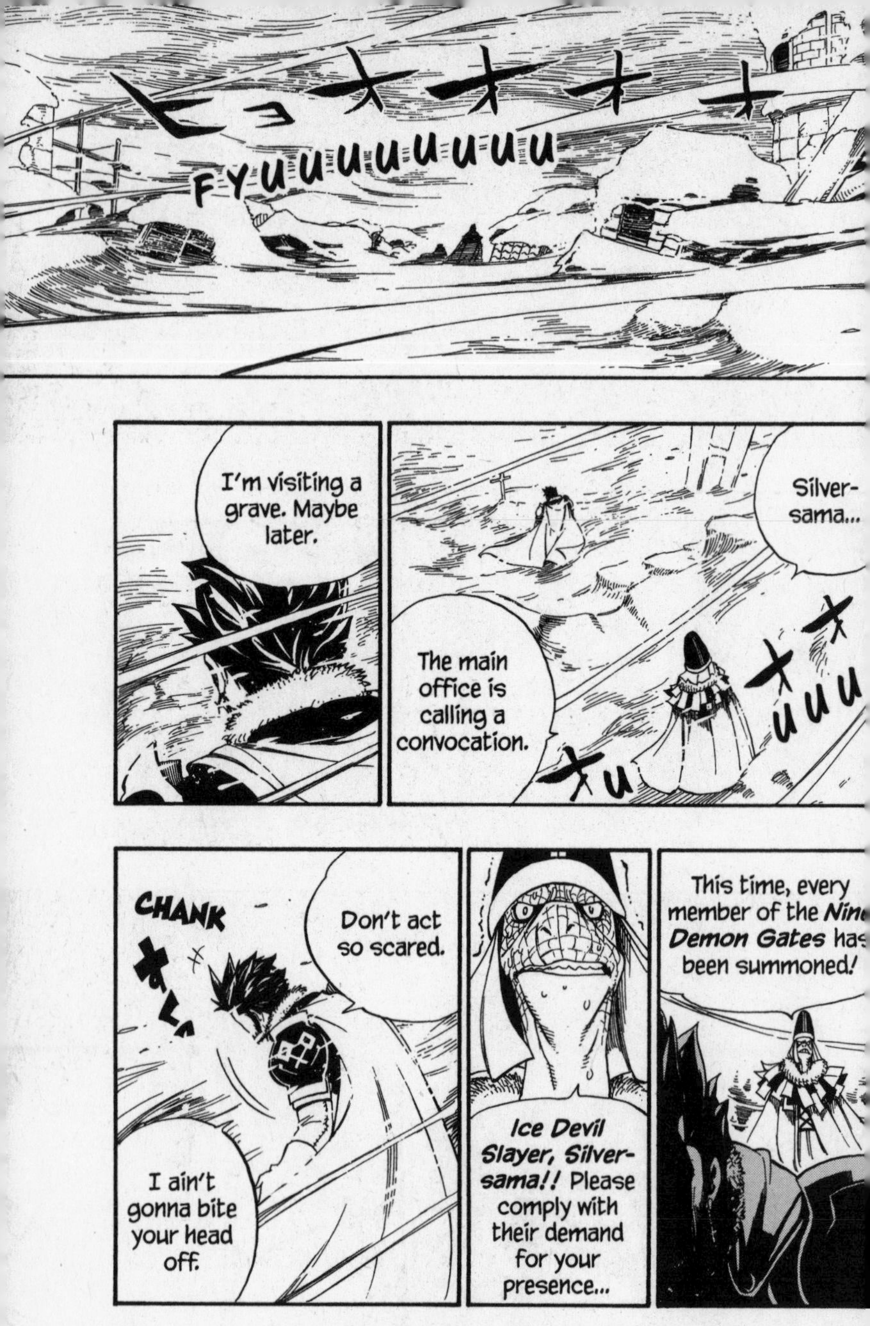
FYUUUUUUUUU
Silver-sama...
The main office is calling a convocation.
UUU
U
I'm visiting a grave. Maybe later.
This time, every member of the Nin Demon Gates has been summoned!
Ice Devil Slayer, Silver-sama!! Please comply with their demand for your presence...
CHANK
Don't act so scared.
I ain't gonna bite your head off.

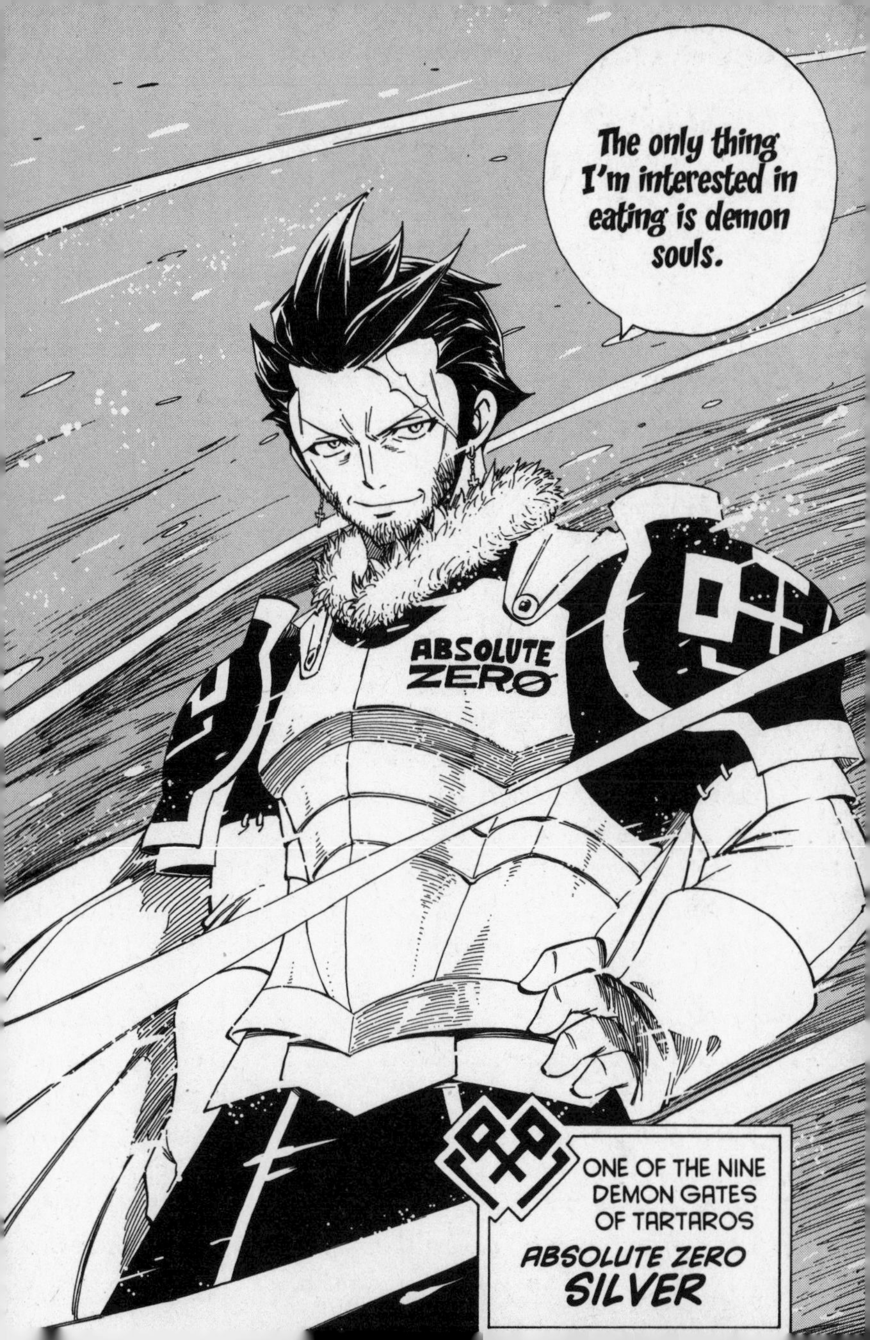
The only thing I'm interested in eating is demon souls.
ABSOLUTE ZERO
ONE OF THE NINE DEMON GATES OF TARTAROS
ABSOLUTE ZERO
SILVER

Afterword

Leaving off whether I'm good or bad, I love writing, and even dialog in a manga is, in some way, writing. And the Question Corner at the end of almost every book is nothing but writing. I'll also bet that I began this "Afterword" section out of my love of writing too, but recently with my "From the Author" comments at the beginning of the books, my margin comments in the magazine installments, and with the stupid number of tweets I do every day on my Twitter account, I've found recently a huge load of places to talk about things. And a lot of those are in pretty much real time! With all that, I've slowly begun to run out of things to put in my afterwords. This is a problem. Here in Volume 41, this whole story started with the idea that even though Erza is tiny, she's still strong! But if I did that, then people might come away with the idea that "Minerva sure has gotten weak these days," instead. So I dumped that idea and went with, "Even when tiny, Erza still keeps her eyes on the prize, and she even goes so far as to lecture people!" I also obsessed over giving Gray a featured spot considering he didn't get much to do during the Grand Magic Games, so his part in this series is a real standout.

By the way, Gray is slated to have a big part in the next arc too. That's the new series that starts in the next volume, and it's going to be another huge one. I said about the same thing before the Grand Magic Games started too, huh? (sweat) If the last series was a huge gathering of characters, this new series will be a huge gathering of different techniques. I've been building up manga-making techniques for fifteen years, and I'm going to use them to make this next series a really exciting one! Stay tuned!!

FAIRY TAIL VS. THE BALAM ALLIANCE

THE FATEFUL HISTORY

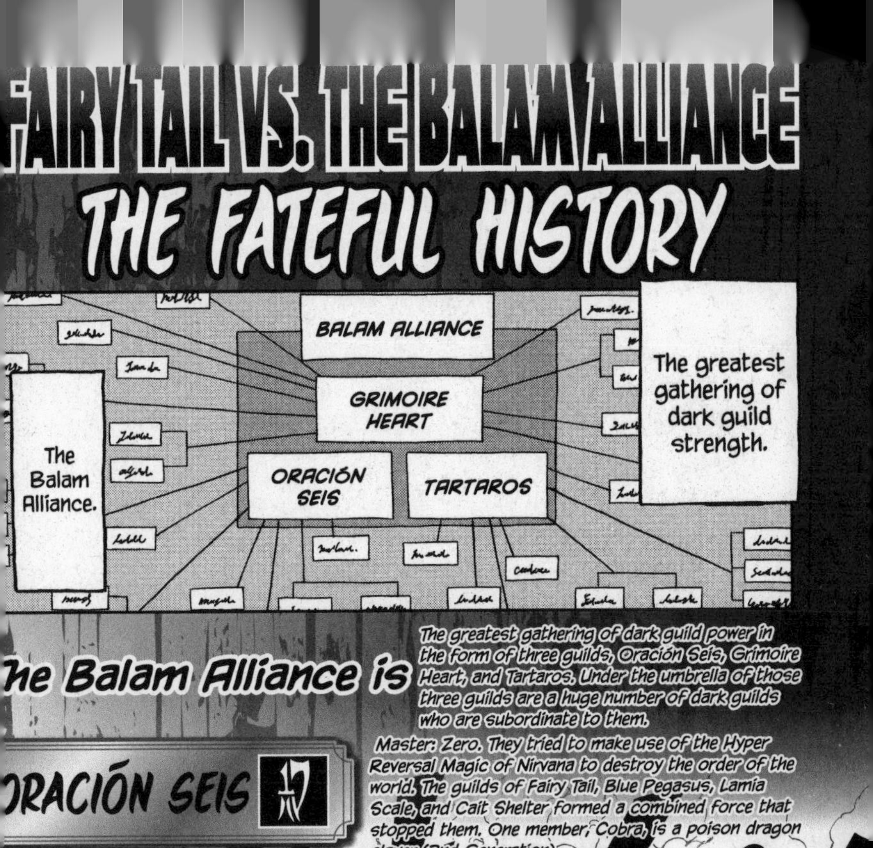
BALAM ALLIANCE
GRIMOIRE HEART
ORACIÓN SEIS
TARTAROS
The Balam Alliance.
The greatest gathering of dark guild strength.

The Balam Alliance is

The greatest gathering of dark guild power in the form of three guilds, Oración Seis, Grimoire Heart, and Tartaros. Under the umbrella of those three guilds are a huge number of dark guilds who are subordinate to them.

ORACIÓN SEIS

Master: Zero. They tried to make use of the Hyper Reversal Magic of Nirvana to destroy the order of the world. The guilds of Fairy Tail, Blue Pegasus, Lamia Scale, and Cait Shelter formed a combined force that stopped them. One member, Cobra, is a poison dragon slayer (2nd Generation).

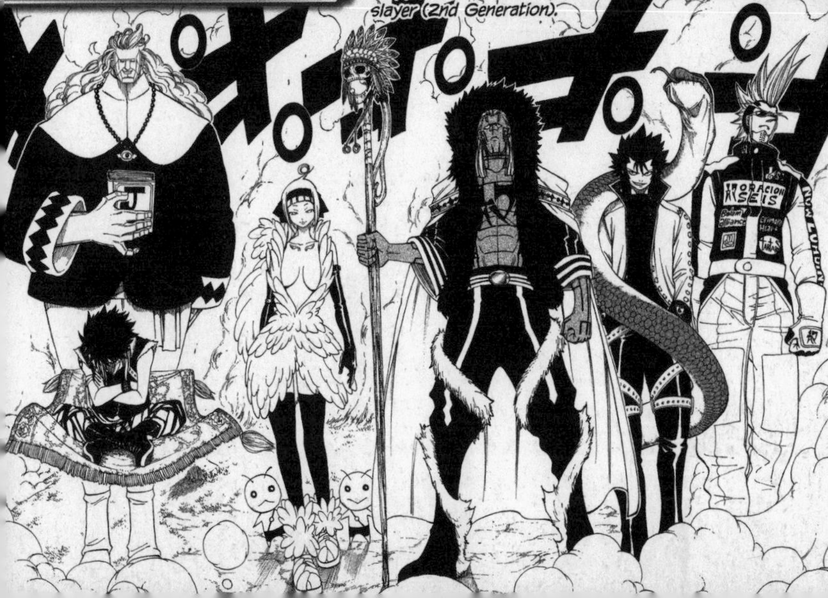
ORACIÓN SEIS

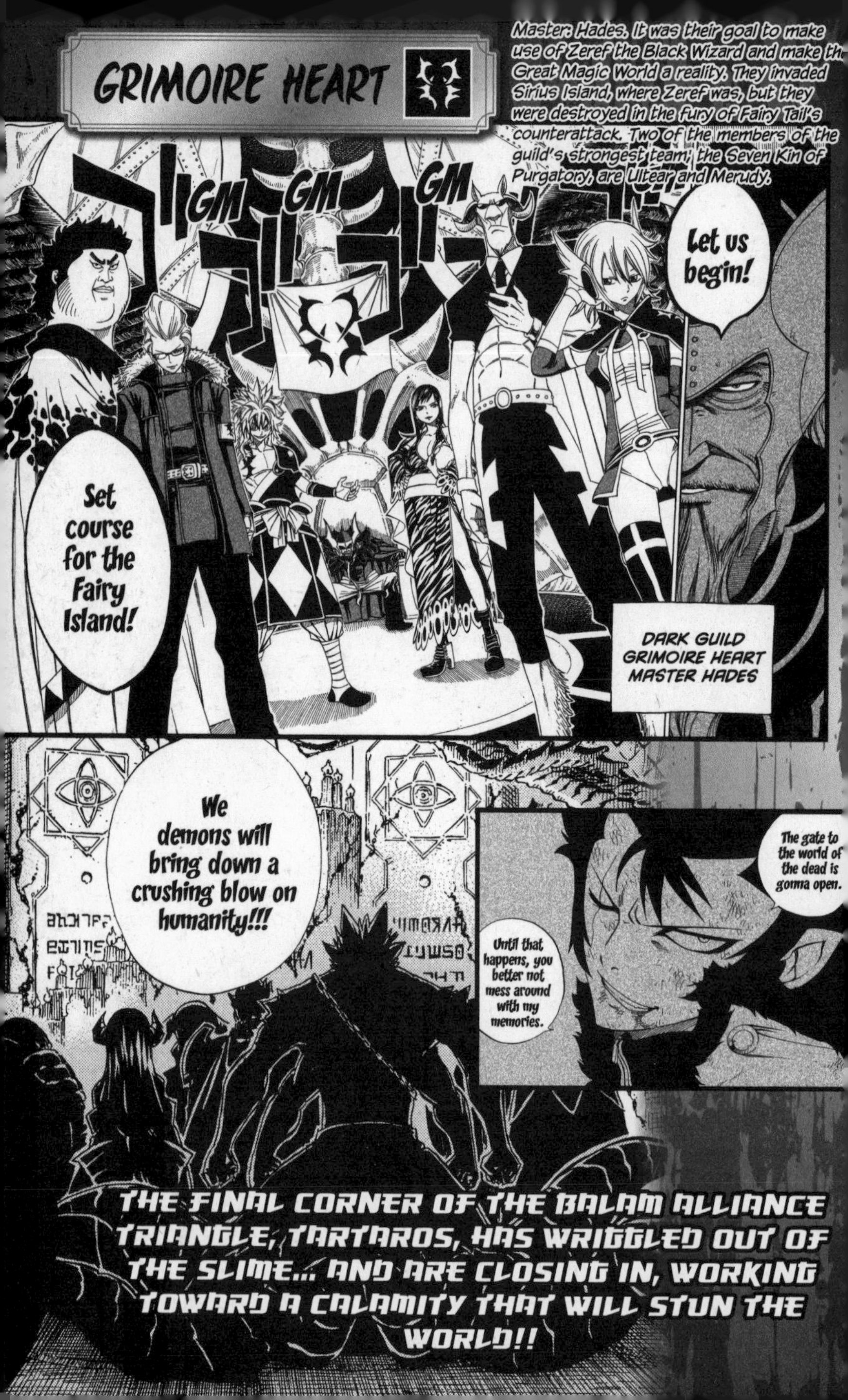
GRIMOIRE HEART
Master: Hades. It was their goal to make use of Zeref the Black Wizard and make the Great Magic World a reality. They invaded Sirius Island, where Zeref was, but they were destroyed in the fury of Fairy Tail's counterattack. Two of the members of the guild's strongest team, the Seven Kin of Purgatory, are Ultear and Merudy.
Let us begin!
DARK GUILD GRIMOIRE HEART MASTER HADES
GM GM GM
Set course for the Fairy Island!
The gate to the world of the dead is gonna open.
Until that happens, you better not mess around with my memories.
We demons will bring down a crushing blow on humanity!!!
THE FINAL CORNER OF THE BALAM ALLIANCE TRIANGLE, TARTAROS, HAS WRIGGLED OUT OF THE SLIME... AND ARE CLOSING IN, WORKING TOWARD A CALAMITY THAT WILL STUN THE WORLD!!

Continued from the left-hand page.

Lucy: Mira-san, there's that fast talk again!

Mira: Next question!

What is that mysterious language Minerva was using?

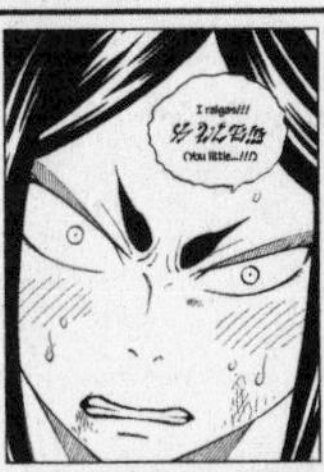
(You little...!!!)

Lucy: I wanna know the answer to that!

: I ragd!!!!

: Aah! What did you just say?

: "Be gone."

Lucy: What an awful thing to say!

Mira: I'm talking the language of Yakuma.

Lucy: Language of Yakuma?

Mira: A long time ago, there was a race called the Yakuma, and that was the language the clan used.

Lucy: The first master was really shocked and said something about the Yakuma Eighteen Battle Gods. Anything to do with that?

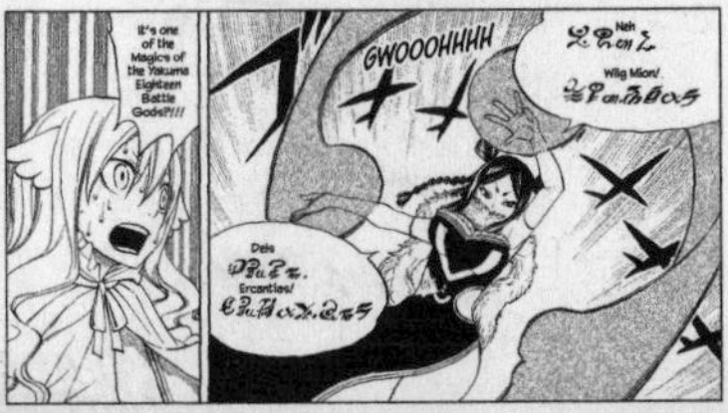
Neh
Wiig Mion!
GWOOOHHHH
It's one of the Magics of the Yakuma Eighteen Battle Gods?!!!

Mira: There were eighteen types of dangerous magics handed down through the Yakuma called the "Yakuma Eighteen Battle Gods." This was one of them.

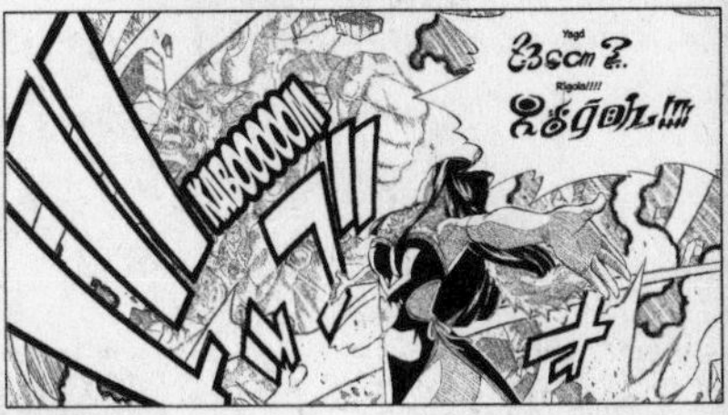
Yagd
Rigola!!!!
KABOOOOOM

: "Yagd"... "Rigola"... Those are pretty hard to pronounce!

Mira: Yagd Rigola!!!!

Lucy: Mira-san, that's amazing!!

Mira: Of course I can't use the magic. She was the first person I'd ever seen who could.

Lucy: Even the first master was shocked, huh?

Mira: Iwasshockedtoo.

: For real this time. Why the fast talk?

: Lucy, why don't you just give it a try yourself?

Lucy: Huh?

Mira: It's fun!

Lucy: O-Okay... Ahem. YoucancallmeLucy.

Mira: That's hard to read.

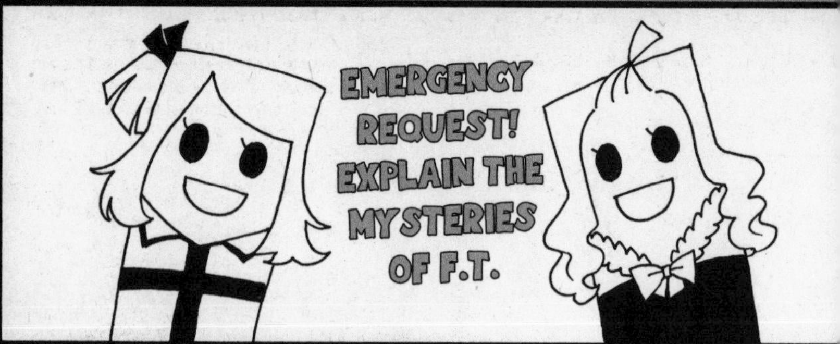

EMERGENCY REQUEST! EXPLAIN THE MYSTERIES OF F.T.

Somewhere in Magnolia...

Mira: WelcomeboysandgirlsIt'smeMira!

Lucy: ...

Mira: Herewearearquestioncorner!

Lucy: What's with the fast talk?

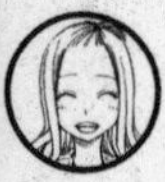

: Just a whim. I'm already tired of it, so we'll just move along.

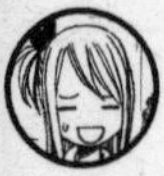

: O-Okay.

Mira: Now, our first question.

Is Warrod Human?

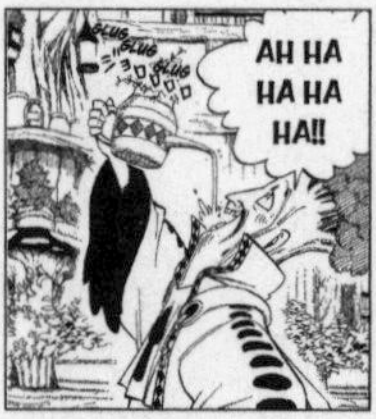
AH HA HA HA HA!!

Lucy: Heh heh!

Mira: It's rude to laugh at him... Ha ha ha!

Lucy: There are a whole lot of other suspicious people in this world aside from him, but yeah, I think he's human.

Mira: Probably human.

Lucy: Next question.

That thing that's kind of like Zeref's familiar. I'd like to know its name.

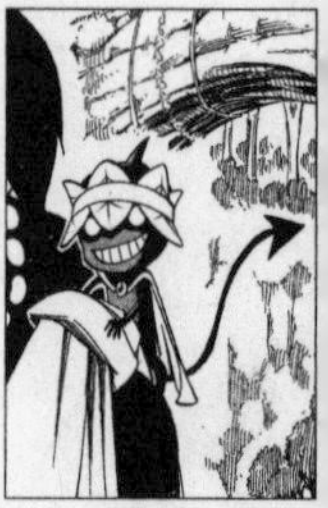

Mira: It's Obra.

Lucy: Wasn't that a member of Raven Tail?

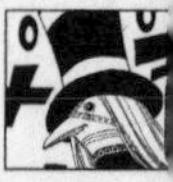

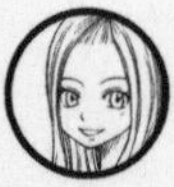

: Right. The human form was the puppet, and the little thing was the actual form of the creature.

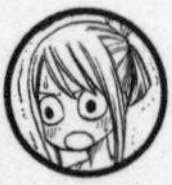

: Ehhhh...?!!

Mira: Even the master of Raven Tail, Ivan, had no idea, and that's why he allowed Obra in.

Lucy: Come to think of it, I remember a decryption of the human form (at least we thought it was human) that said he had a tendency to suddenly stop moving.

Mira: SuddenlystoppingmovingThat's scary!

Continued on the right-hand page.

The Fairy Tail Guild is looking for illustrations! Please send in your art on a postcard or at postcard size, and do it in black pen, okay? Those chosen to be published will get a signed mini poster! ♪ Make sure you write your real name and address on the back of your illustration!

d'ART

Fukuoka Prefecture, Yoshiharu

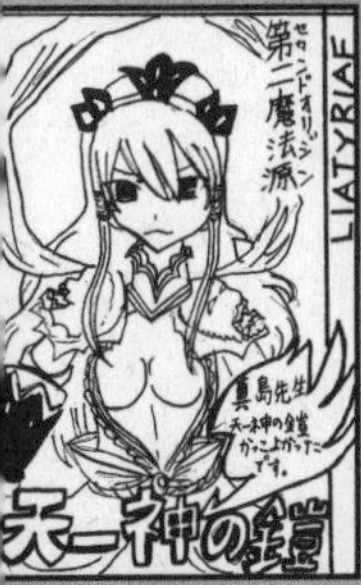
第二魔法源
天一神の鎧

▲ The strongest of Erza's resent armor. It may just ppear again!

Taiwan, Staber

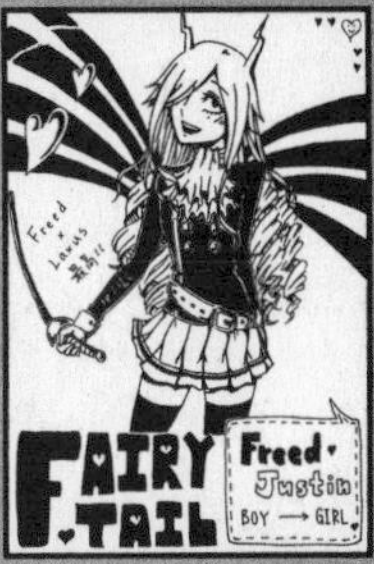
FAIRY TAIL
Freed・Justin
BOY → GIRL

▲ Cross-dressing Fried?! Huh? I-It looks good on him.

Okayama Prefecture, Yui Uzuka

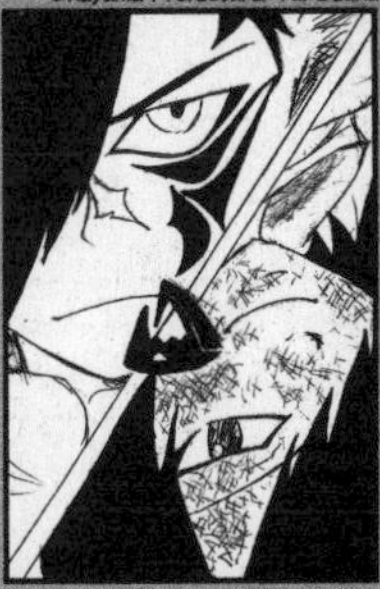

▲ So in the end, will Rogue stay with the good guys or go to the dark side?

Nagano Prefecture, Fried Pudding

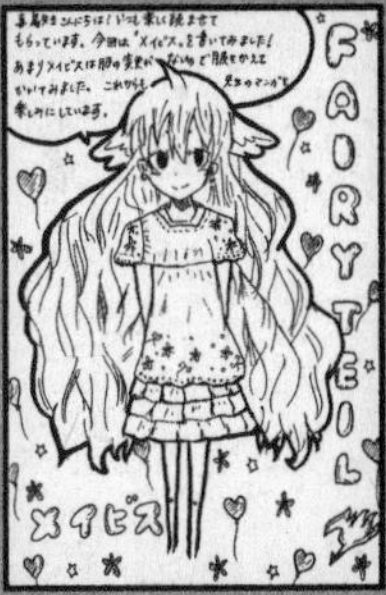
FAIRYTAIL
メイビス

▲ Mavis in uncharacteristic Western fashion. Cute!!

Shizuoka Prefecture, Piyorina

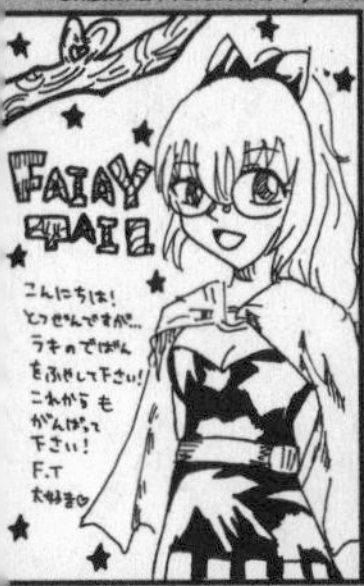

. She had a lot to do in he stories originally made or anime.

Aichi Prefecture, Shunta Suzuki

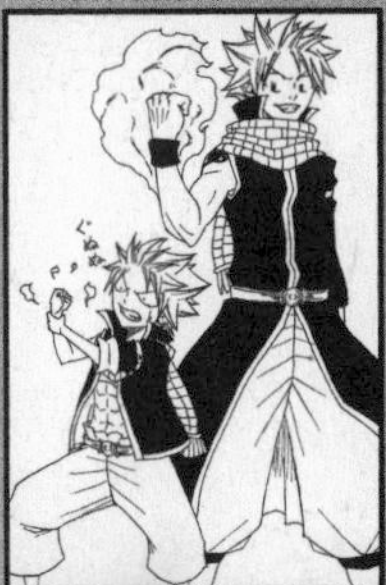

▲ Buy both big and small Natsu! They're a set!

Gunma Prefecture, Miina

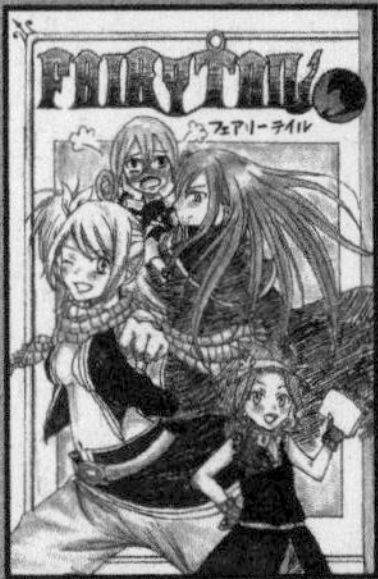
FAIRY TAIL
フェアリーテイル

▲ The Fairy Tail girls in the guys' clothes. Wait... Lucy?!

Yamagata Prefecture, Chokoron

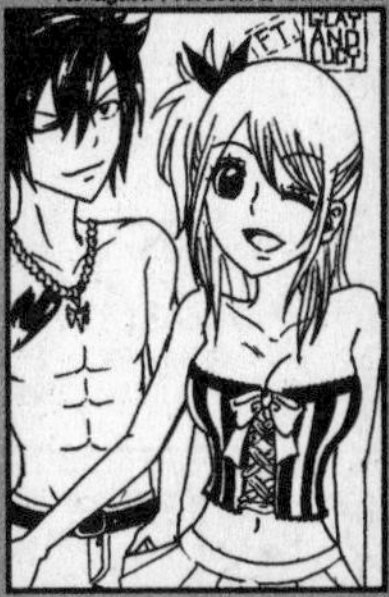

▲ A coupling we don't usually see. But they're not bad together.

Send to Hiro Mashima, Kodansha Comics
451 Park Ave. South, 7th Floor New York, NY 10016

GUILD

Kanagawa Prefecture, Akar

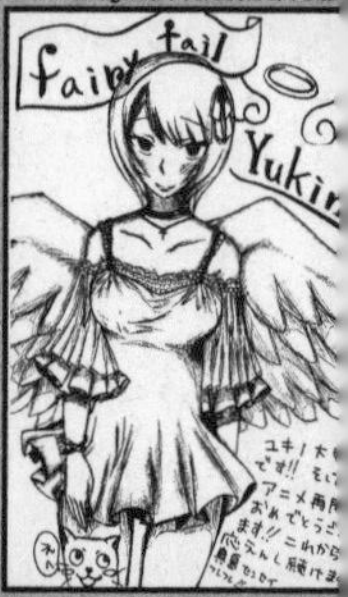

fairy tail
Yukin

▲I love the Yukino chara too. You'll see her again the future!

Fukuoka Prefecture, Mai Kawamura

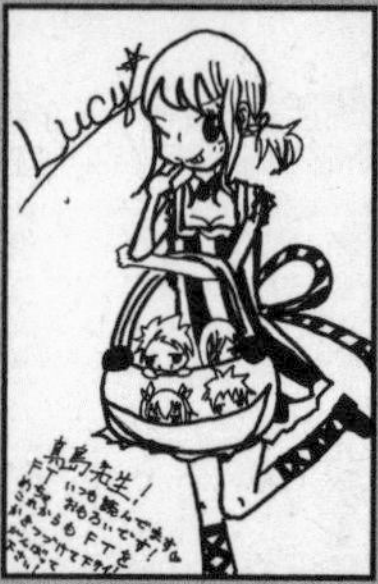

Lucy

▲I like how everyone else is in her bag.

Yamagata Prefecture, Haruka Takano

Whoa~! That's incredible!! How many characters are drawn here?! A hard job well done! ▶

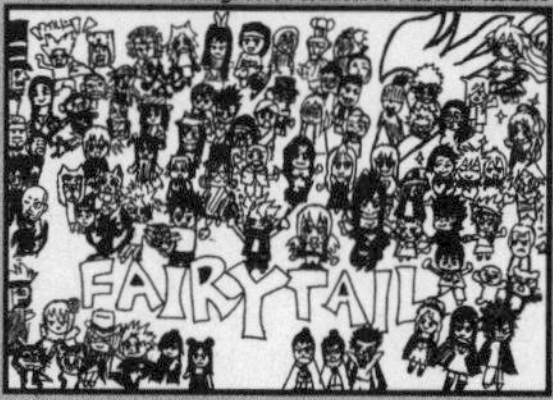

FAIRYTAIL

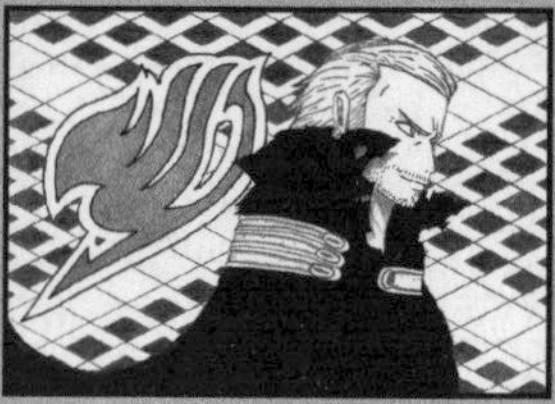

◀I wonder where he is off traveling alone right now?

Kyoto, Hand-made Croquettes

Hokkaido, Omeg

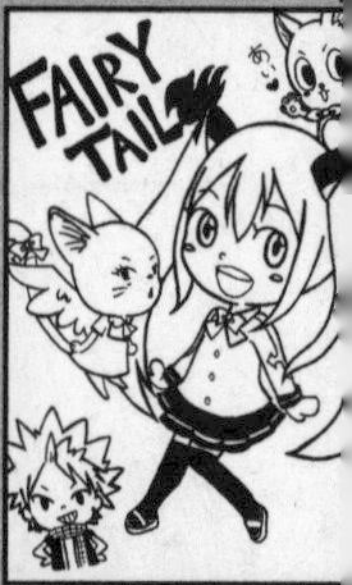

FAIRY TAIL

▲Now this is cute! I also like Happy and Carla here!

Tokyo, Kai Tôma

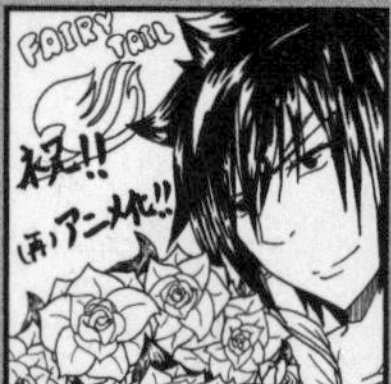

FAIRY TAIL

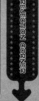

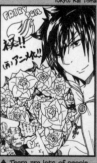

▲ There are lots of people who say they're happy about the new anime! Thank you!

By sending in letters or postcards, you give us permission to give your name, address, postal code, and any other information you include to the artist as-is. Please keep that in mind.

REJECTION CORNER

This scares even me...! It's like the manga will be overrun by sketches! ▶

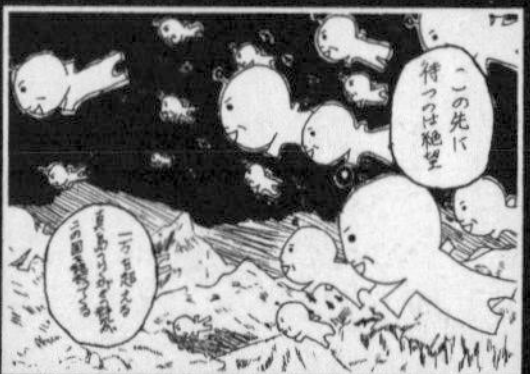

この先に
待つは絶望

Kyoto, Haruna Shibata

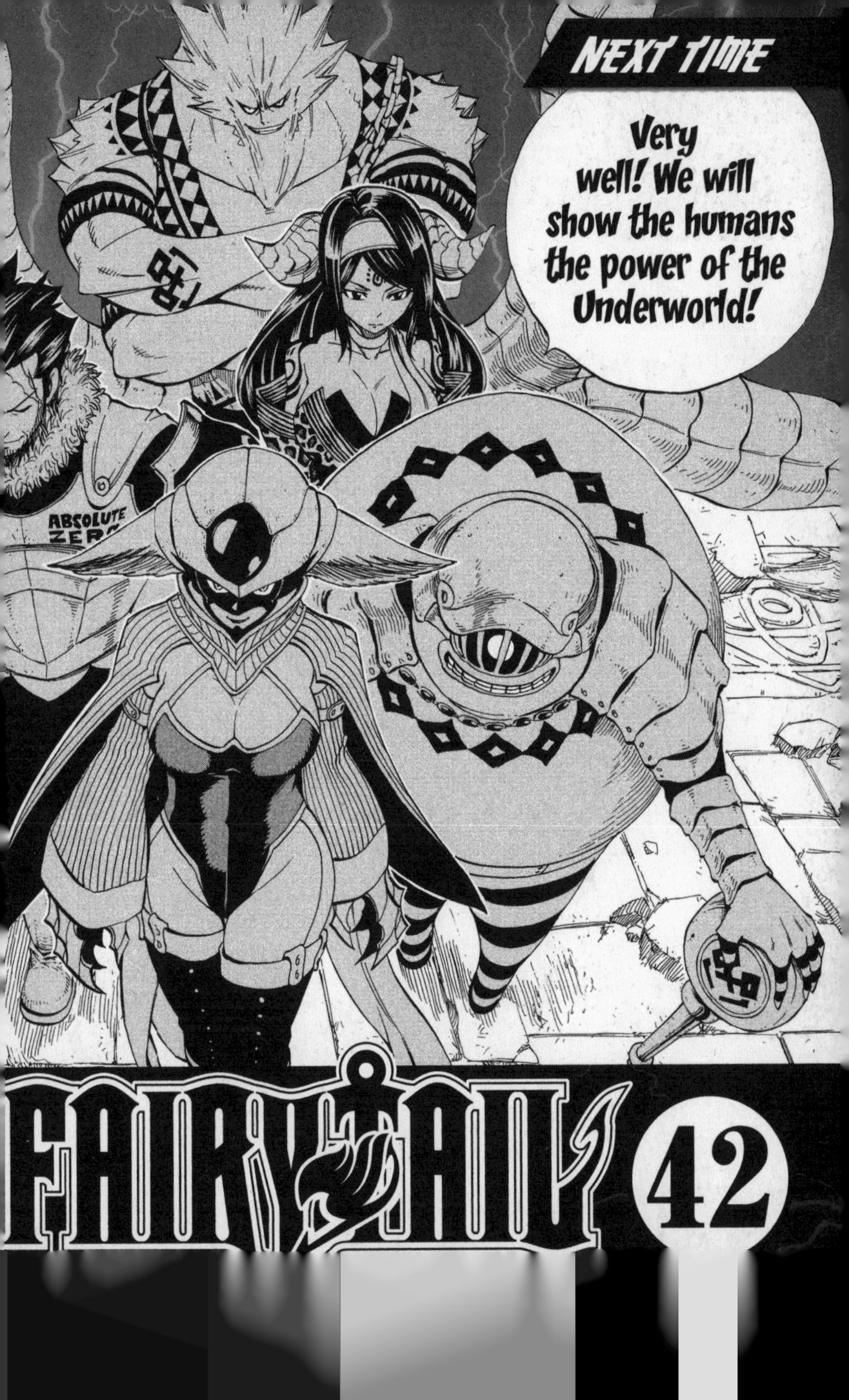
NEXT TIME
Very well! We will show the humans the power of the Underworld!
ABSOLUTE ZERO
FAIRY TAIL
42

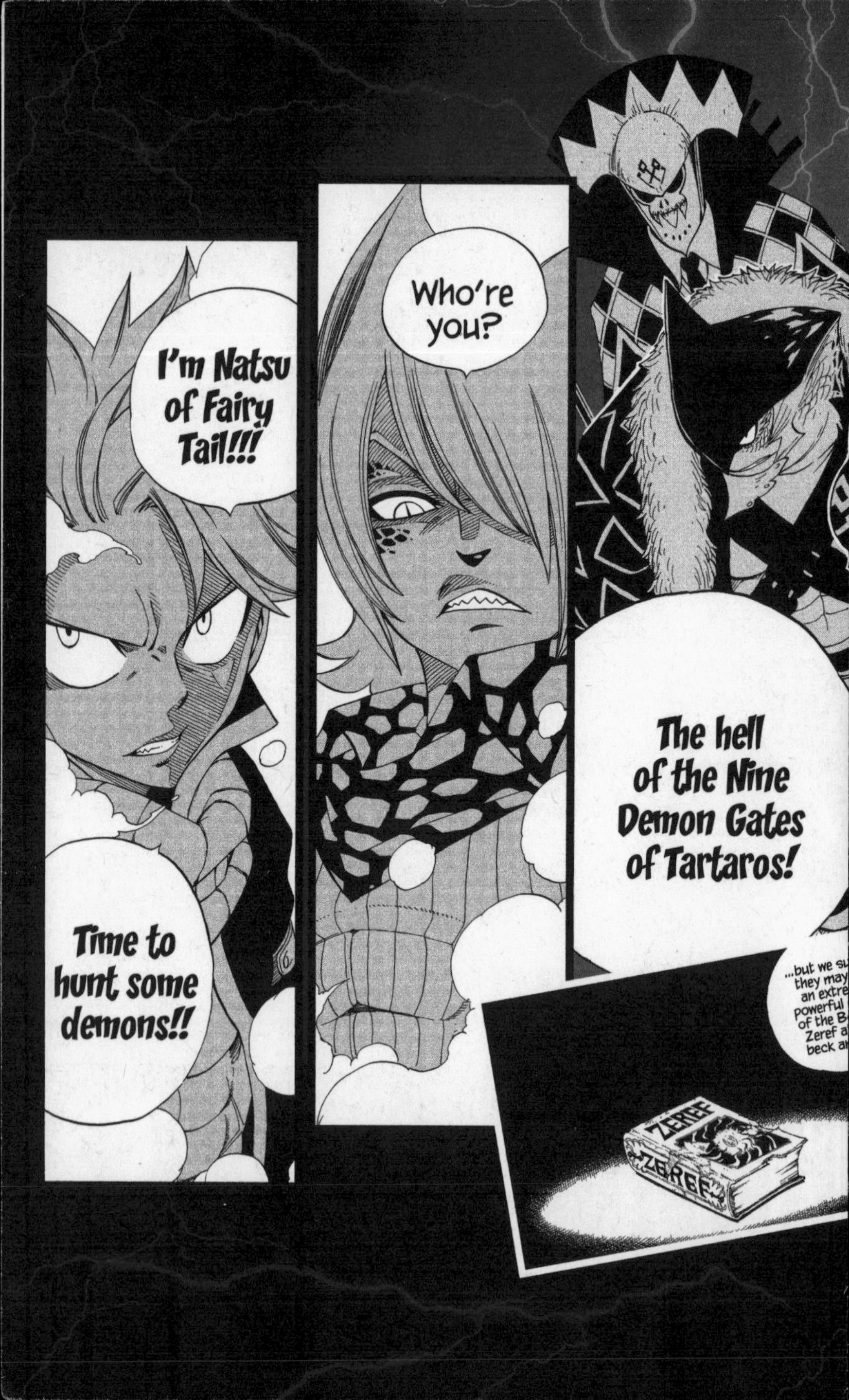
The hell of the Nine Demon Gates of Tartaros!
ZEREF
ZEREF
Who're you?
I'm Natsu of Fairy Tail!!!
Time to hunt some demons!!

FAIRY TAIL

フェアリーテイル

41

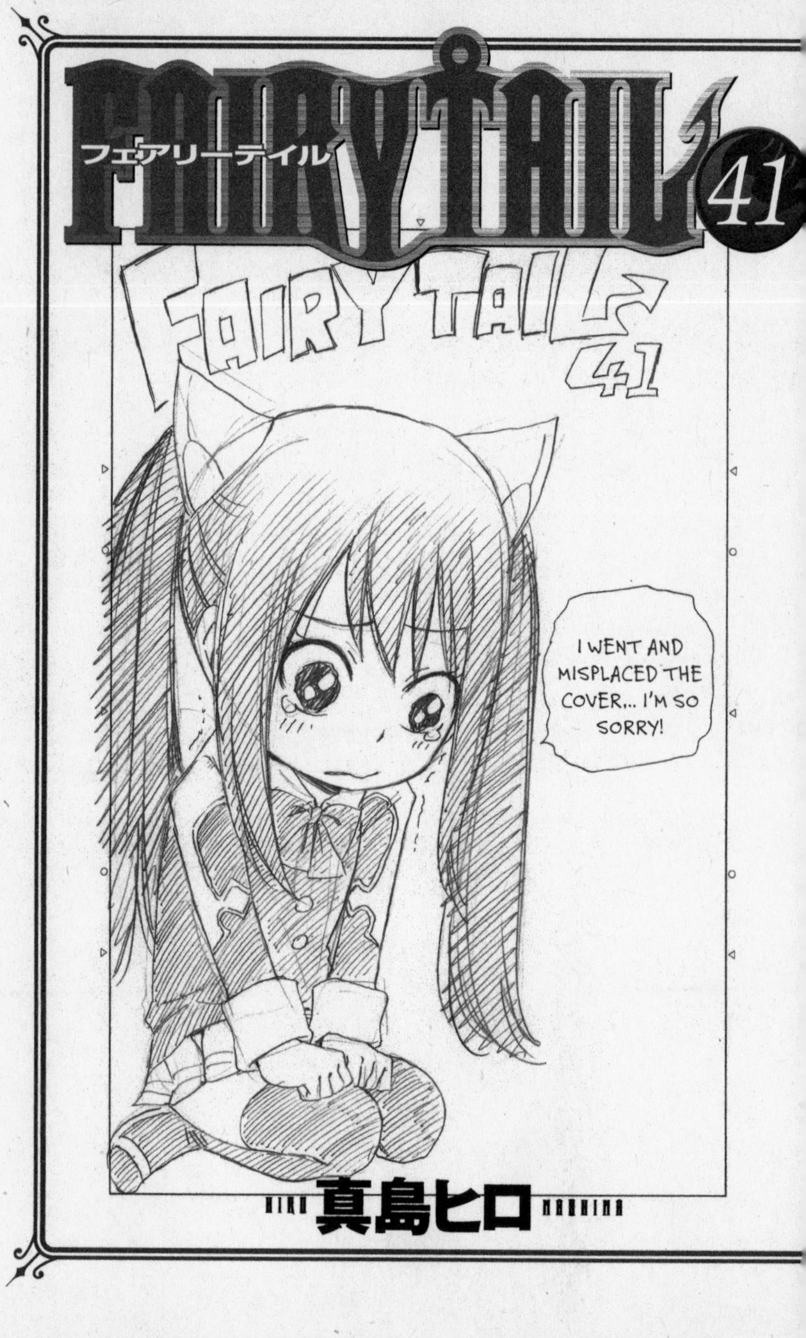
FAIRY TAIL
41
I WENT AND MISPLACED THE COVER... I'M SO SORRY!

HIRO 真島ヒロ MASHIMA

FROM HIRO MASHIMA

I'm so busy that I'm getting dizzy. But they say it's when a manga artist is busy that he or she is happiest. When one of us is **not** busy, we get so lonely we cry and wail. And I hope to always be a manga artist, so I'm going to work really hard so that I can complain, "I'm too busy," all the time!

Original Jacket Design: Hisao Ogawa

Translation Notes:

Japanese is a tricky language for most Westerners, and translation is often more art than science. For your edification and reading pleasure, here are notes on some of the places where we could have gone in a different direction with our translation of the work, or where a Japanese cultural reference is used.

Page 42, Blue-black

Jet-black hair is often called "blue-black" in the West because the highlights (reflectio of light) look almost like a very dark blue. That idea has been reflected in American comic books, where the hair is mostly blacked in, but again, the highlights are colore blue. Japanese manga artists do the same thing with hair, and Wendy's hair is a goo example of "blue-black" hair.

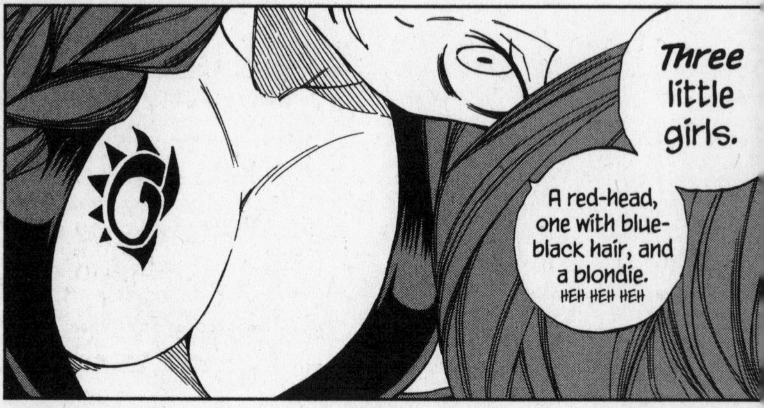

Three little girls.
A red-head, one with blue-black hair, and a blondie.
HEH HEH HEH

Page 48, Ebi

As mentioned in the notes way back in Volume 2, there is a habit of some manga characters to end their sentences with an identifiable-but-basically-meaningless word. Cats might end their sentences with "nya" (the sound of a cat's meow in Japanese). Crab characters may end their sentences with "kani" (the Japanese word for "crab"). So it was a surprise to the regular characters when Cancer the crab ended his sentences with "ebi" (the Japanese word for "shrimp").

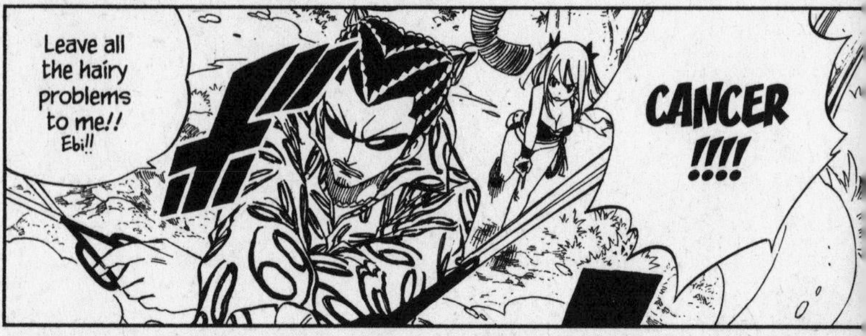

CANCER !!!!
Leave all the hairy problems to me!! Ebi!!

age 90, Shaved ice

though shaved ice (also called snowcones) is a mmertime treat in the West, it is particularly pular in Japan, with many different types topping aside from the sweet, fruit-flavored rups available in the west. Uni (sea bream), for ample, is considered a real shaved-ice luxury pping. On the other hand, shaved ice on the top a dark wizard's (or demon's) head would not be ry appetizing in either culture.

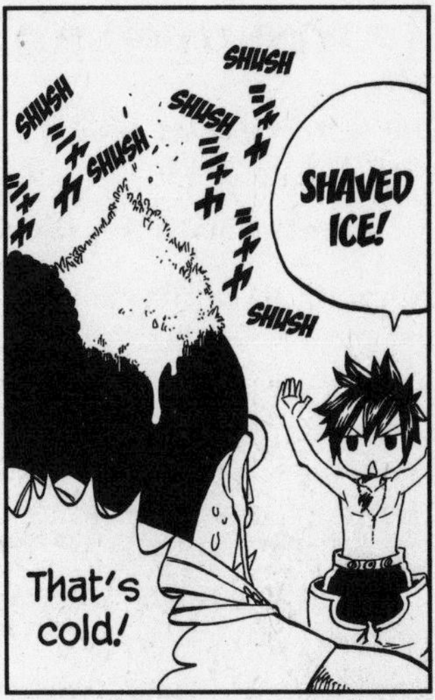
SHAVED ICE!
SHUSH
SHUSH
SHUSH
SHUSH
SHUSH
SHUSH
That's cold!

age 173, END

is isn't a Japanese word for an ending, but rather the English initials E, N, and D ritten (even in the Japanese version) in English letters. It's meant to be read out, like en dee."

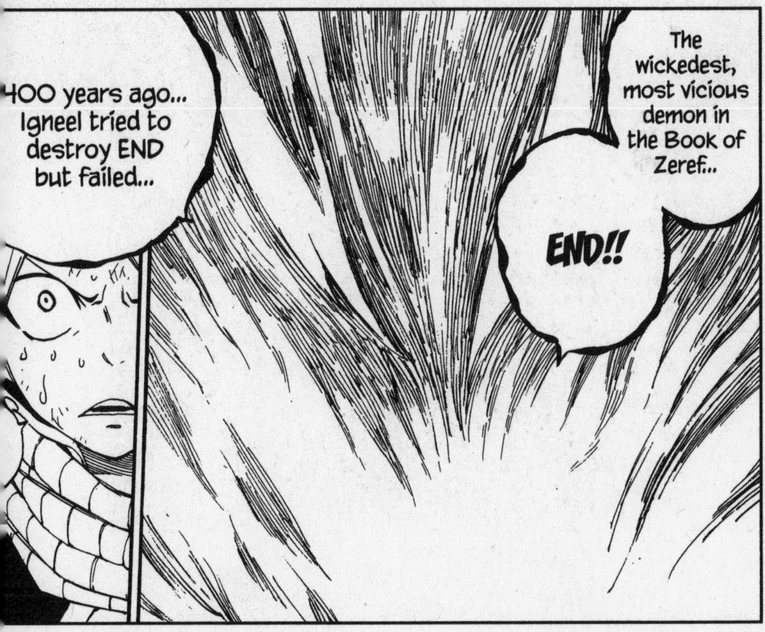
The wickedest, most vicious demon in the Book of Zeref...
END!!
400 years ago... Igneel tried to destroy END but failed...

Preview of *Fairy Tail*, volume 42

We're pleased to present you with a preview from Fairy Tail, volume 42, available now on your digital device and to print in September. See our Web site (www.kodanshacomics.com) for more details!

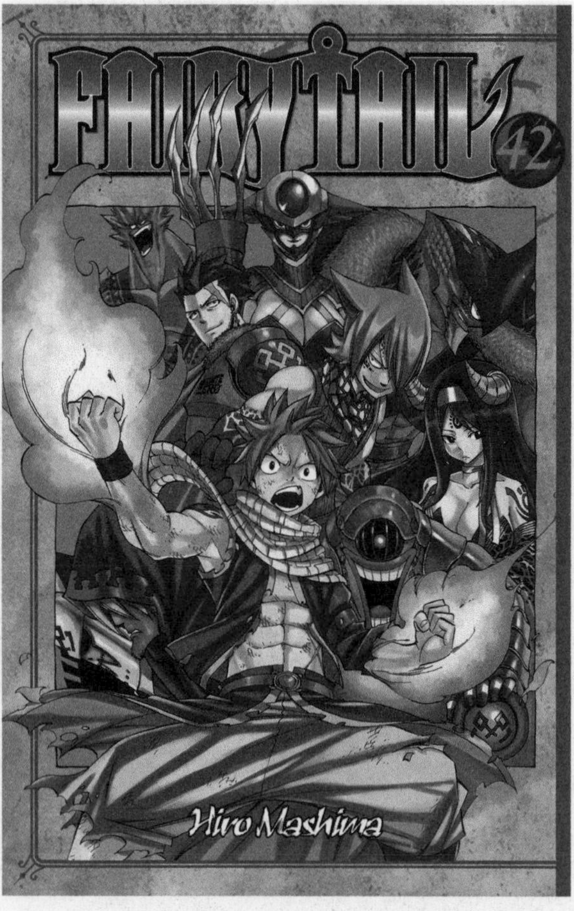
FAIRY TAIL
42
Hiro Mashima

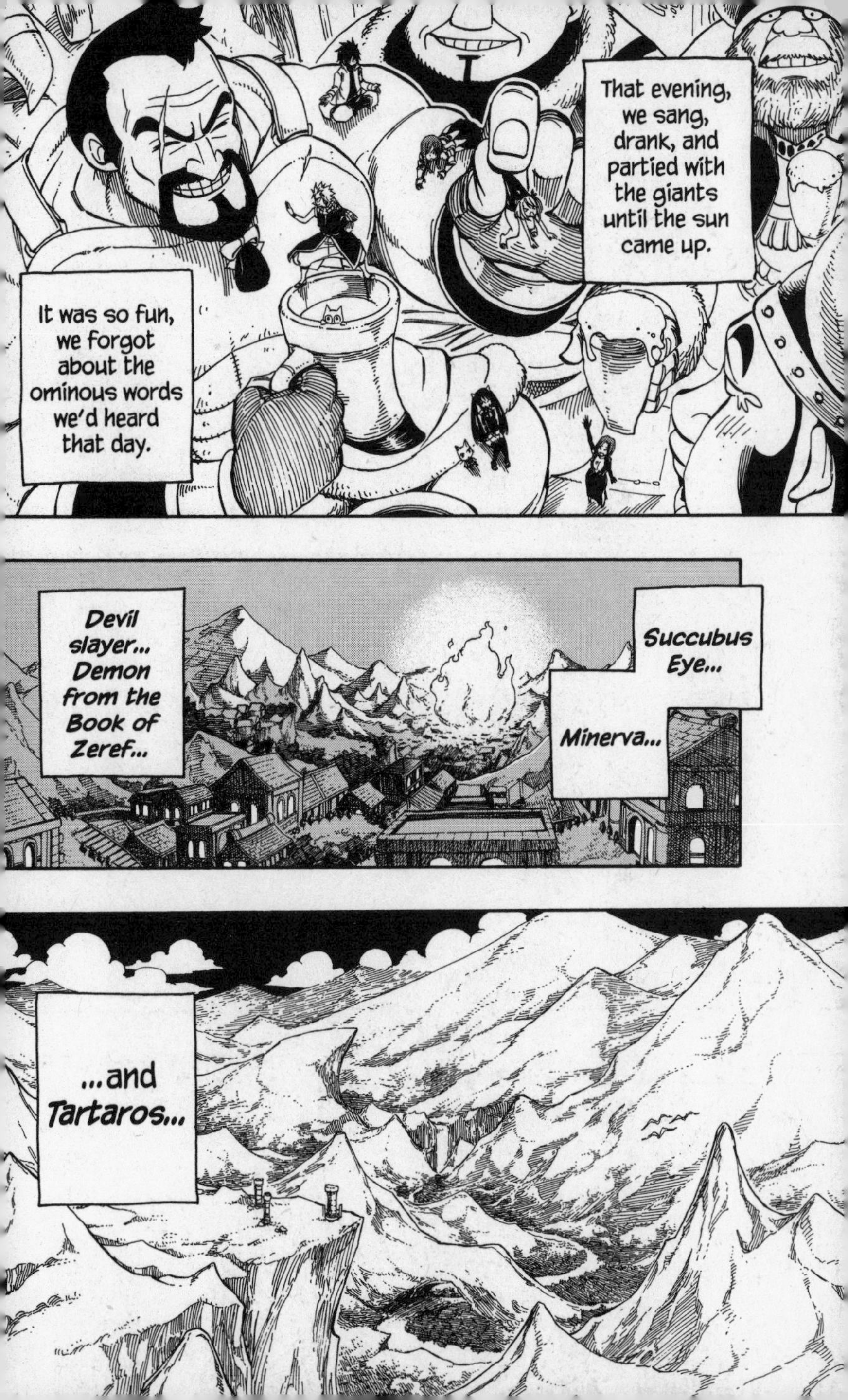
That evening, we sang, drank, and partied with the giants until the sun came up.
It was so fun, we forgot about the ominous words we'd heard that day.
Succubus Eye...
Minerva...
Devil slayer... Demon from the Book of Zeref...
...and Tartaros...

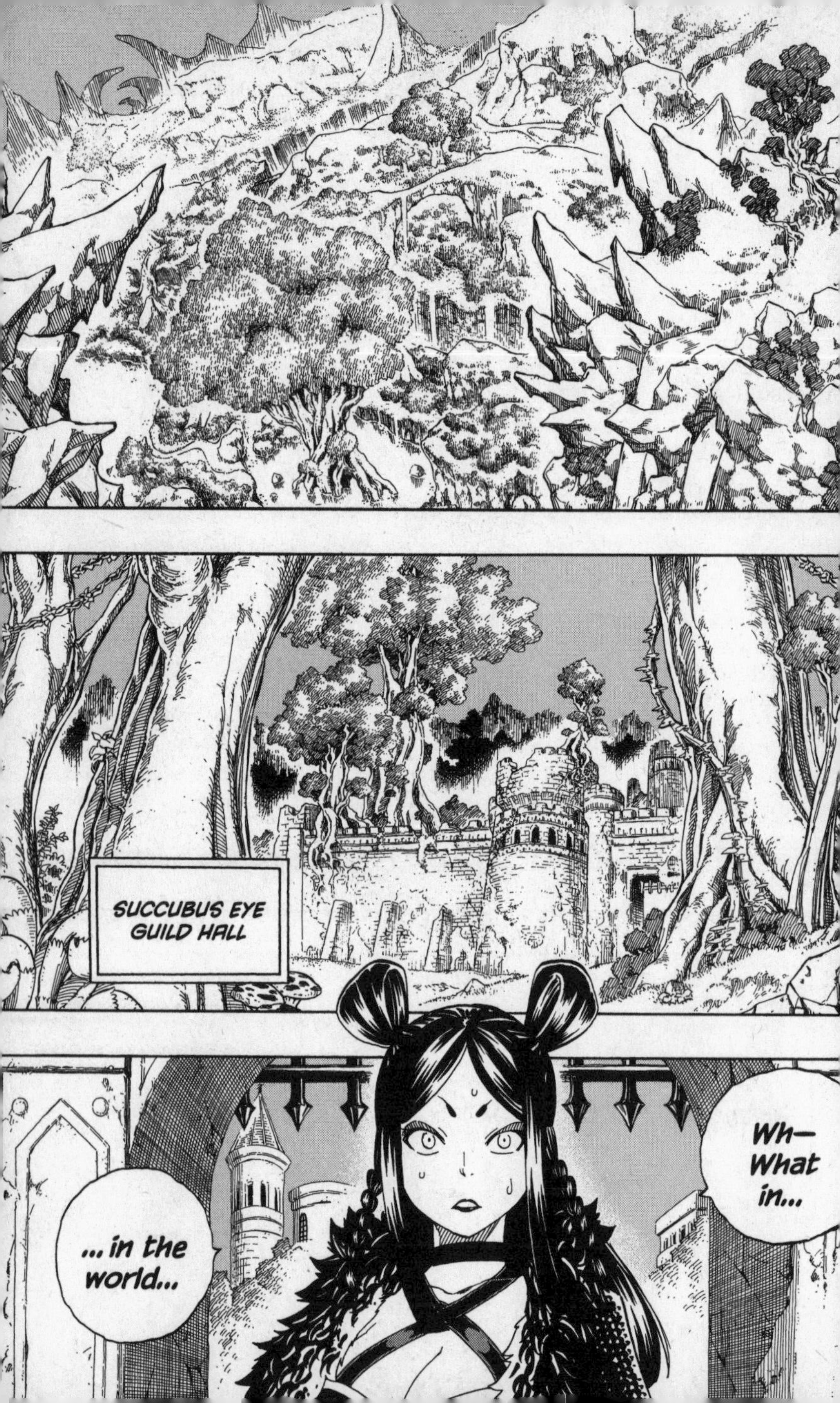
SUCCUBUS EYE GUILD HALL
Wh— What in...
...in the world...

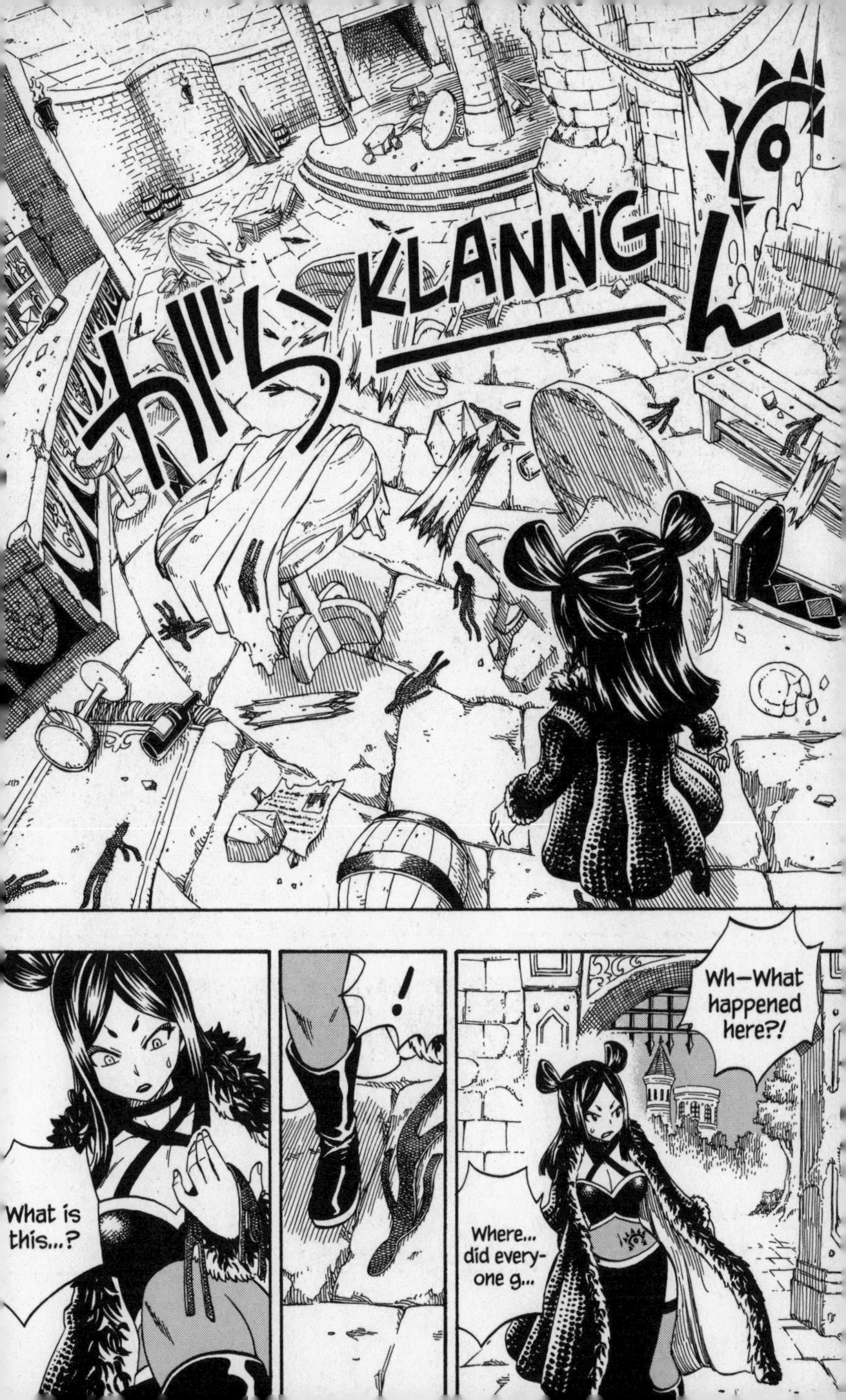
KLANNG
Wh—What happened here?!
Where... did every-one g...
!
What is this...?

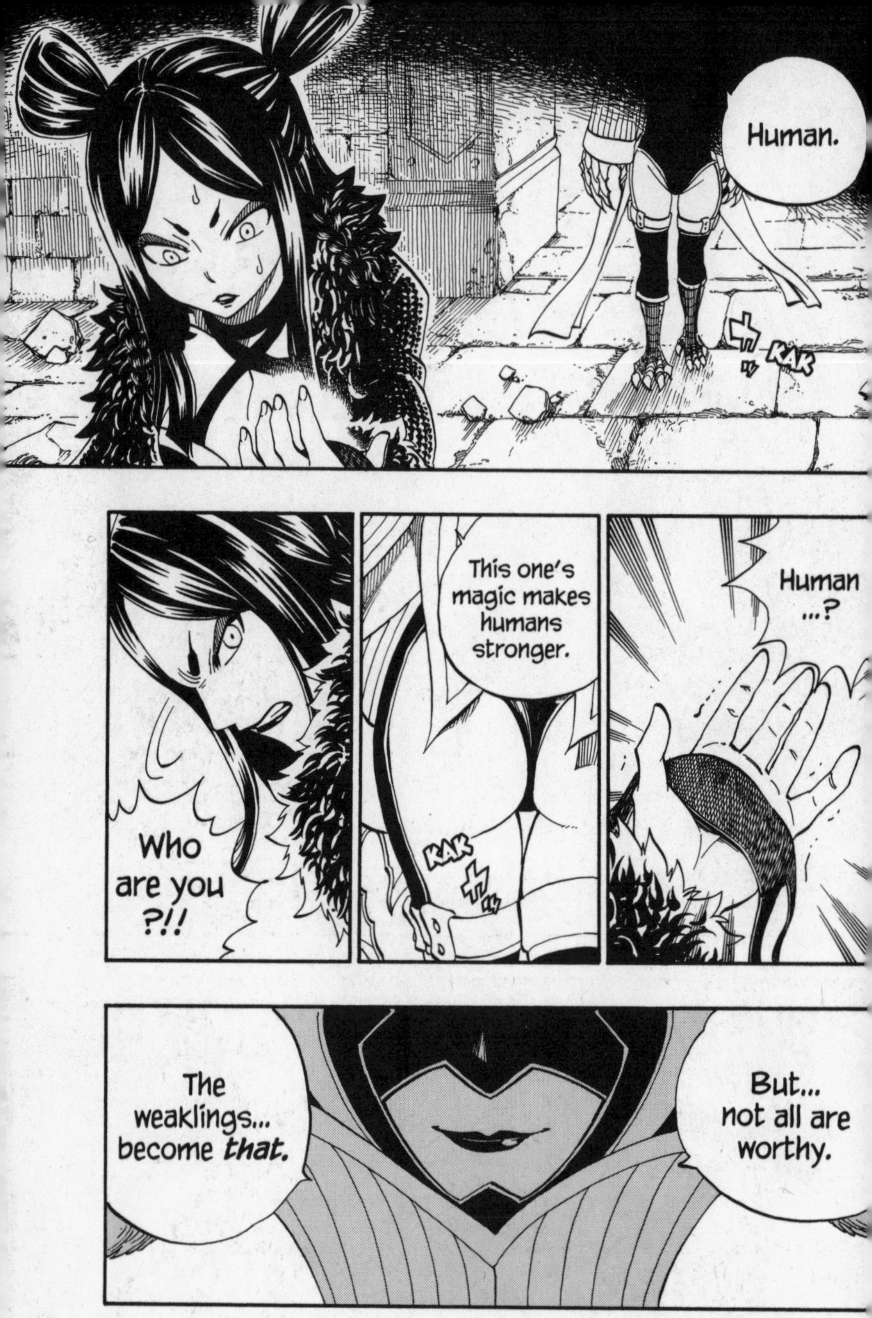
Human.
KAK
Human ...?
This one's magic makes humans stronger.
KAK
Who are you ?!!
But... not all are worthy.
The weaklings... become *that.*

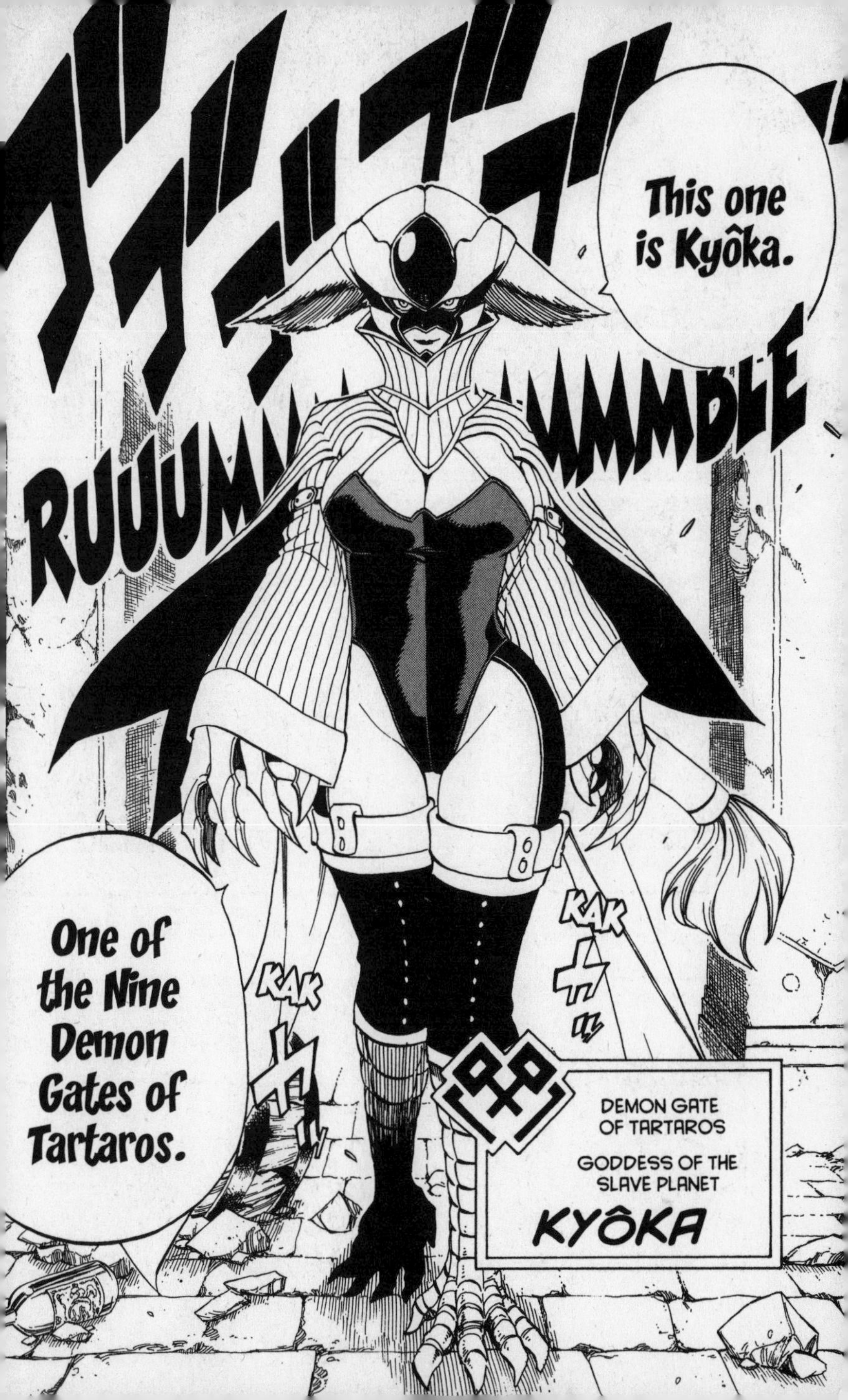
This one is Kyôka.
RUUUM MMMBLE
KAK
DEMON GATE OF TARTAROS
GODDESS OF THE SLAVE PLANET
KYÔKA
KAK
One of the Nine Demon Gates of Tartaros.

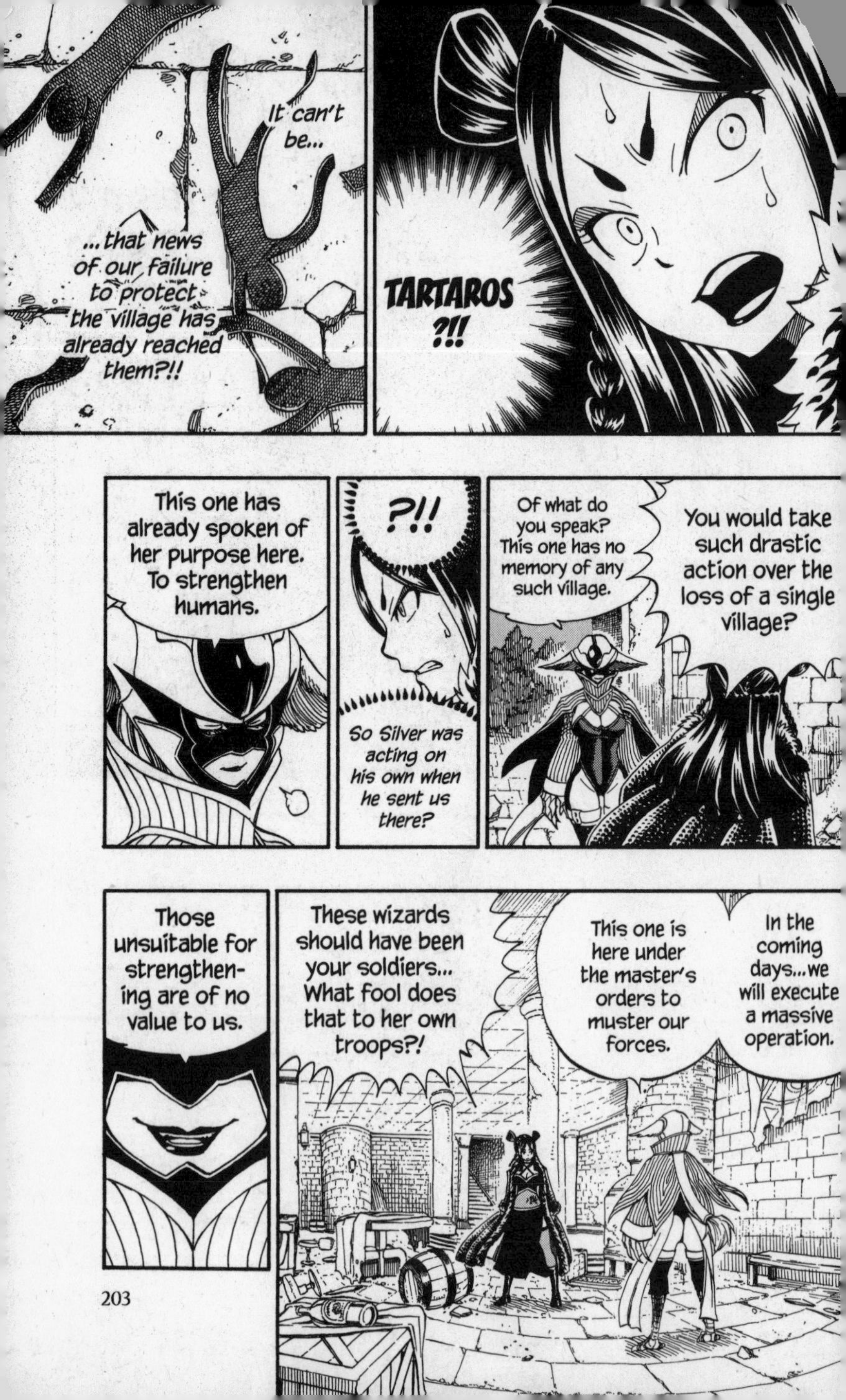
TARTAROS ?!!
It can't be...
...that news of our failure to protect the village has already reached them?!!
You would take such drastic action over the loss of a single village?
Of what do you speak? This one has no memory of any such village.
?!!
So Silver was acting on his own when he sent us there?
This one has already spoken of her purpose here. To strengthen humans.
In the coming days...we will execute a massive operation.
This one is here under the master's orders to muster our forces.
These wizards should have been your soldiers... What fool does that to her own troops?!
Those unsuitable for strengthen-ing are of no value to us.

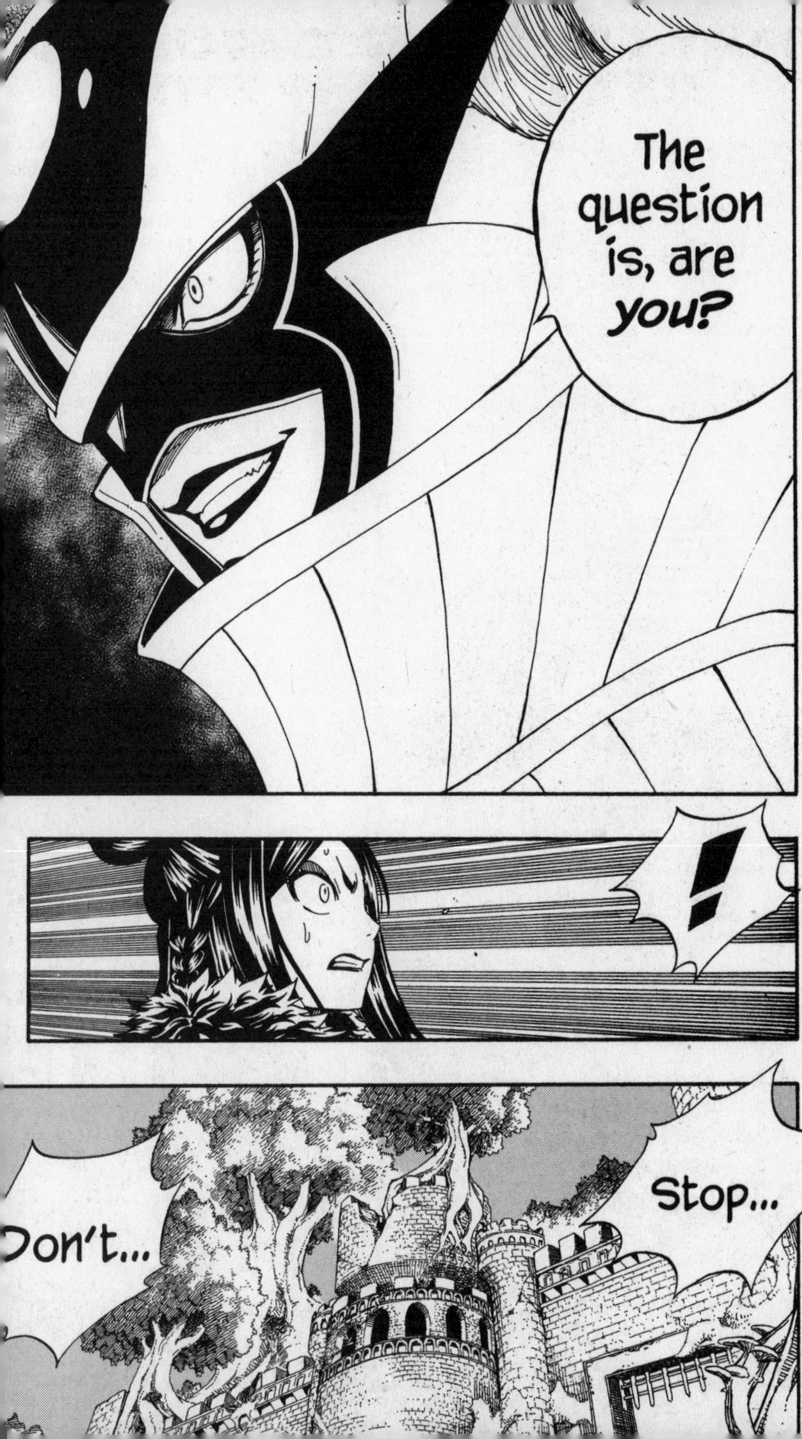
The question is, are *you*?
!
Stop...
Don't...

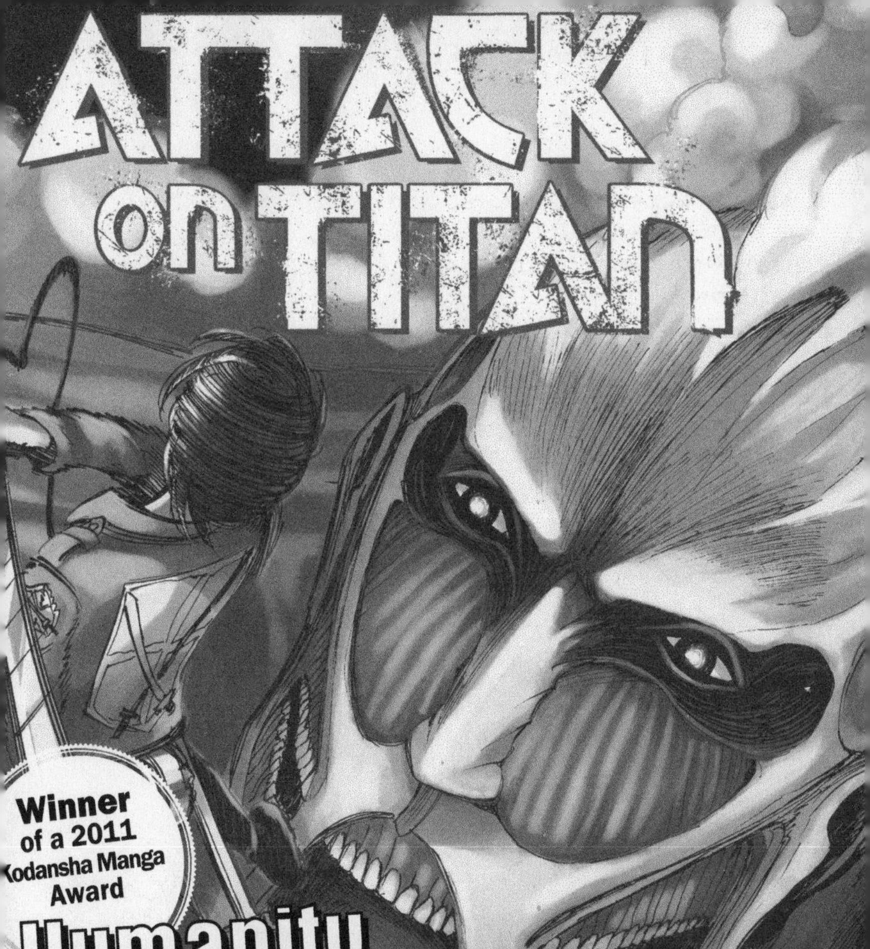

ATTACK on TITAN

Humanity has been decimated!

A century ago, the bizarre creatures known as Titans devoured most of the world's population, driving the remainder into a walled stronghold. Now, the appearance of an immense new Titan threatens the few humans left, and one restless boy decides to seize the chance to fight for his freedom, and the survival of his species!

KC KODANSHA COMICS

Fairy Tail volume 41 is a work of fiction. Names, characters, places, and incident are the products of the author's imagination or are used fictitiously. Any resemblance to actual events, locales, or persons, living or dead, is entirely coincidental.

A Kodansha Comics Trade Paperback Original.

Published in the United States by Kodansha Comics, an imprint of Kodansha USA Publishing, LLC, New York.

Publication rights for this English edition arranged through Kodansha Ltd., Tokyo.

First published in Japan in 2013 by Kodansha Ltd., Tokyo
ISBN 978-1-61262-437-2

Printed in the United States of America.

www.kodanshacomics.com

9 8 7 6 5 4 3 2 1

Translation: William Flanagan
Lettering: AndWorld Design
Editing: Ben Applegate

TOMARE!

止まれ
[STOP!]

You're going the wrong way!

Manga is a completely different type of reading experience.

To start at the *beginning,*
go to the *end!*

hat's right! Authentic manga is read the traditional Japanese way—
om right to left, exactly the *opposite* of how American books are
ead. It's easy to follow: Just go to the other end of the book and read
ch page—and each panel—from right side to left side, starting at
e top right. Now you're experiencing manga as it was meant to be!